ETS 托福考试

The People Who Make the Test!

全真试题集

Official
TOEFL iBT®
Tests with Audio *Volume 1*

群言出版社
Qunyan Press

图书在版编目(CIP)数据

托福考试全真试题集：英汉对照 / 美国教育考试服务中心编著. —北京：群言出版社，2012.12
ISBN 978-7-80256-389-6

Ⅰ. ①托… Ⅱ. ①美… Ⅲ. ①TOEFL－习题集 Ⅳ. ①H319.6

中国版本图书馆CIP数据核字（2012）第258804号

版权登记：图字01-2012-9007

出 版 人	范 芳
责任编辑	陈丹丹
封面设计	大愚设计
出版发行	群言出版社(Qunyan Press)
地 址	北京东城区东厂胡同北巷1号
邮政编码	100006
网 站	www.qypublish.com
电子信箱	bj62605588@163.com qunyancbs@126.com
总 编 办	010-65265404 65138815
编 辑 部	010-62418641 65276609 65262436
发 行 部	010-62605019 62263345 65220236
经 销	全国新华书店
读者服务	010-65220236 65265404 65263345
法律顾问	北京市国联律师事务所
印 刷	北京慧美印刷有限公司
版 次	2013 年 1 月第 1 版
印 次	2013 年 1 月第 1 次印刷
开 本	889×1194 1/16
印 张	35
字 数	492千
书 号	ISBN 978-7-80256-389-6
定 价	108.00元

Contents

TOEFL Test Prep Planner

Introduction

About the TOEFL iBT® Test

托福考试测试考生应用与理解英语的能力，等同于在大学课堂上听说读写英语的水平。目前，全球130多个国家中的8500多所大学、政府行政部门以及其他机构将托福成绩作为录取标准之一，托福也因此成为世界上应用范围最为广泛的英语考试。

托福考试由阅读、听力、口语和写作四部分测试组成。每部分测试中的题目均考查考生英语听说读写的水平。另外，还考查考生综合运用这些语言技能的能力，因此有些测试题目可能会要求考生综合使用自己的语言技能。例如，考生可能先阅读一篇文章或者听一个讲座，然后写出或者谈论刚才获取的内容。下面是每部分测试的简要介绍，包括各部分测试的内容及题型。

Reading Section

阅读部分测试考生理解英文学术文章的能力。该部分中的文章均节选自大学程度的教科书及类似的学术材料。

考生要正确回答每道题目，并不需要具备与文章所谈主题相关的背景知识。回答问题所需的全部信息都可以在文章中找到。阅读题目考查考生寻找和理解基本信息、进行推断以及通过阅读获取信息的能力。

下表是阅读部分的题型及其说明：

细节题	该题型要求考生识别出文章中明确阐述的事实信息。
排除题	该题型要求考生将真实的信息与不真实的信息或者文章中没有提到的信息区别开来。
推论题	该题型考查隐含在文章中但没有明确阐述的信息。
修辞目的题	该题型考查文章中某条特定信息的修辞功能。这种题型考查为什么作者在文章中提到或者涉及某条特定的信息。
词汇题	该题型要求考生掌握单词或短语在文章中的具体含义。
指代题	该题型考查文章中提到的观点与指代该观点的语言表述之间的关系。例如，文章中提到了一种观点，另一个句子可能将其指代为"该观点（This idea）"。问题可能会问"该观点（This idea）"指代的是什么。

简化句子题	该题型要求考生选出与文章中某个句子意思基本相同的句子。
插入句子题	该题型要求考生将题目中给出的一个新句子插入文章中最适合的位置。
文章总结题	该题型考查考生辨识文章主要观点的能力，要求考生能够将主要观点从次要观点或者文中没有提及的观点中辨别出来。要选出正确的答案，考生既要理解文中哪些信息相对重要，又要能够辨别出哪些答案综合了文中的主要观点。
填表题	该题型要求考生分别挑选出属于表格所列类别的答案选项，表格中通常包含两到三个类别。要解答该类题目，考生需要对文章中的主要观念或者要点进行组织或者分类。

Listening Section

听力部分考查考生理解英语对话和学术讲座的能力。

考生会听到两段对话。一段对话发生在教授的办公室，可能包括对学术材料或者课程要求的讨论。另一段对话发生在大学校园，包括与大学生活相关的非学术型内容的讨论。每段对话之后都有五个问题。

考生会听到四个不同话题的讲座。其中两个讲座中只有教授讲话。另外两个讲座中，学生会参与讨论；教授可能会就所讨论的话题提问并要求学生回答，或者教授回答学生的提问。每个讲座之后有六个问题。

每段对话和讲座只能听一遍。播放每段对话或讲座时，电脑屏幕上会显示相应的背景图片。有的对话和讲座还显示视图，比如写出了技术词汇或者特殊名称的黑板。

下表是听力部分的题型及其说明：

基本理解题	该类题型考查对话或者讲座的主要观点或主要目的，或者是讨论的重要细节。
整合信息题	该类题型要求考生能够确定对话或者讲座信息的组织脉络，能够将所讨论的信息要点联系起来，或者能够根据讨论的信息要点进行推论。
情景理解题	该类题型要求考生能够分辨出讲话者在说某句话或者提出某个问题时的目的，或者能够分辨出讲话者的态度、观点或确信的程度。

大部分听力问题是多选一的单选题，个别问题是有一个以上正确答案的多选题。考生可能还会遇到对流程步骤进行排序的题目，在方格中勾选合适答案的题目，或者重听某部分对话或者讲座再进行作答的题目。

Speaking Section

口语部分考查考生用英语谈论各种主题的能力。

对于每个问题，考生需要在很短的时间内准备答案。准备时间结束后，在问题给定时间内尽可能全面地回答问题。对于本书中的测试题，考生应该使用录音设备录下自己的答案。通过这样的方式，考生可以重听自己的答案并与参考答案和评分标准进行比对。

在口语部分第一题中，考生需要谈论一个熟悉的话题，比如一个自己认识的人，一个喜欢去的地方，一件重要的物品，或者一次愉快的活动。考生应该根据自己的个人经历或者自己熟悉的内容进行回答。

在口语部分第二题中，考生需要就一个熟悉的话题给出自己的观点。考生需要阐述自己的观点并解释持有此种观点的理由。

在口语部分第三题中，考生首先需要阅读一篇短文，接着听或者阅读一段相同话题的对话。然后，就这两部分被提问。考生需要结合短文和对话中的适当信息，针对问题提供完整的答案。考官会根据考生能否清晰、连贯地表达，以及能否准确地传达短文和对话中的信息，对考生的回答进行评分。

在口语部分第四题中，考生首先需要阅读一篇学术性主题的短文，接着听一个相同话题的讲座或者阅读讲座稿。然后，就这两部分被提问。考官会根据考生能否清晰、连贯地表达，以及能否整合并传达短文和讲座的关键信息，对考生的回答进行评分。

在口语部分第五题中，考生会听到或者阅读一段与校园问题相关的对话。考官会根据考生能否简要总结对话中描述的问题，能否从对话中选择自己认可的解决方案并表述清楚，以及能否就自己所做的选择给出理由，对考生的回答进行评分。

在口语部分第六题中，考生会听到讲座的部分内容或者阅读讲座稿。然后，就此内容被提问。考官会根据考生能否清晰、连贯地表达，以及能否准确地传达讲座信息，对考生的回答进行评分。

Writing Section

写作部分考查考生用英语写作进行学术交流的能力。

在写作部分第一题中，考生首先会阅读一篇文章，接着听讲座或者阅读讲座稿。然后，考生就所读文章和讲座有何关系的问题进行回答。考生应尽量使用文章和讲座中的信息全面作答。本题不要求考生表达个人观点。开始写作时，考生可能需要再次浏览阅读文章。通常，有效的回答应是一篇150-225字的作文。考官会根据考生写作的质量、内容的完整性和准确性予以评分。

在写作部分第二题中，考生需要写一篇作文，陈述、解释并支持自己对某一问题的看法。通常，一篇有效的作文至少要300字。考官会根据考生的写作质量对作文予以评分，包括考生观点的展开、作文的组织结构、表达观点时运用语言的能力与准确度。

How to Use This Book

本书有助于考生准备托福考试。书中包含五套完整的托福实考题目。全部考试题目均为全球托福考试实考题目，不过个别题目与实考题目呈现的方式略有区别。听力、口语和写作部分的音频内容在随书光盘中提供。

每套测试题的阅读和听力部分，考生都可以在试题中的答题处作答。每套测试题的写作部分，也提供了空白处供考生答题时使用。

Audio Portions

听力、口语和写作部分中，考生在需要听音频的地方，均会看到 。

每个音频文件均有编号。在光盘主菜单上点击编号就可以听到相应的音频文件。

本书附录B中有音频部分的文本内容。如果考生无法获取音频文件，但是可以接触到英语发音准确的人，则可以请这些人为自己大声地朗读出文本内容。听文本内容比自己阅读的效果更佳。别人朗读文本时，考生需要同时参看配图。

每个音频文件只能听一遍。考生可以像在实际考试中一样，边听录音边做笔记，并使用笔记帮助自己回答问题。

Answers

每套测试题之后都附有相应题目的答案。

阅读和听力部分附有答案。

口语和写作部分没有标准答案。答案部分提供了如何取得高分的策略。考生还可以使用附录A中的评分标准评估自己的答案。

对于口语部分，如果考生使用录音设备录音，可以将其与答案部分的指导说明以及评分标准进行对比。

Rubrics

评分标准用来指导评分者（即考官）评估考生口语和写作部分的答案。附录A中提供了托福考试四个测试部分的评分标准。

口语分数是对回答能否很好传达考生想法的整体性判断。对于独立口语问题（第1-2题）和综合口语问题（第3-6题），传达信息（delivery）和语言运用（language use）是评分者评分时考虑的两个关键因素。话题展开（topic development）是第三个关键因素。对于独立口语问题，话题展开要求具备的特点是，答案内容的完整性及整体的连贯性。对于综合口语问题，话题展开要求具备的特点是，答案内容的准确度和全面性，以及整体的连贯性。

写作分数同样是对作文能否很好传达考生意图的整体性判断。对于综合写作问题（第1题）和独立写作问题（第2题），写作质量（quality of the writing）是评分者评分时考虑的关键因素。高质量作文的特点是组织结构好，以及语法和词汇运用得恰当、准确。对于独立写作问题，高质量作文还要求能有效地突出主题和任务，并且能很好地展开阐述。

内容的全面性和准确性（completeness and accuracy of the content）是评分者评分时考虑的另一个关键因素。全面、准确的答案要呈现出讲座和阅读文章的相关要点，展示各个要点之间的关系，涵盖支持性细节内容，不要涉及讲座和文章中没有提及的信息。

The TOEFL® Test Prep Planner

本书最后附有托福考试备考计划（TOEFL® Test Prep Planner），这个简明的指导可以让考生了解如何有效地准备托福考试，以及要想成功通过考试如何增强必需具备的英语技能。它包含考试的基本信息、考试题型和考试前八周的备考计划建议。考生还可以从中找到技能增强活动、托福考试样题，以及有关考试当天及之后需要做什么的相关信息。

More Official Resources

为了帮助考生准备托福考试，ETS提供了多种官方学习资源，包括：

- 《托福考试官方指南》（*The Official Guide to the TOEFL® Test*）
- 托福在线练习（TOEFL® Practice Online）
- TOEFL Journey方案（The *TOEFL Journey®* Program）
- "Inside the TOEFL Test"视频（"Inside the TOEFL Test" Videos）

有关这些学习资源及更多信息，以及注册托福考试，请登录www.toeflgoanywhere.org。

TOEFL iBT Test 1

had more deer than at any other time in its history, the winter population fluctuating around approximately 320,000 deer (mule and black-tailed deer), which will yield about 65,000 of either sex and any age annually for an indefinite period."

The causes of this population rebound are consequences of other human actions. First, the major predators of deer—wolves, cougar, and lynx—have been greatly reduced in numbers. Second, conservation has been insured by limiting times for and types of hunting. But the most profound reason for the restoration of high population numbers has been the fate of the forests. Great tracts of lowland country deforested by logging, fire, or both have become ideal feeding grounds for deer. In addition to finding an increase of suitable browse, like huckleberry and vine maple, Arthur Einarsen, longtime game biologist in the Pacific Northwest, found quality of browse in the open areas to be substantially more nutritive. The protein content of shade-grown vegetation, for example, was much lower than that for plants grown in clearings.

Directions: Now answer the questions.

PARAGRAPH 1

Two species of deer have been prevalent in the Puget Sound area of Washington state in the Pacific Northwest of the United States. The black-tailed deer, a lowland, west-side cousin of the mule deer of eastern Washington, is now the most common. The other species, the Columbian white-tailed deer, in earlier times was common in the open prairie country; it is now restricted to the low, marshy islands and flood plains along the lower Columbia River.

1. According to paragraph 1, which of the following is true of the white-tailed deer of Puget Sound?

   Ⓐ It is native to lowlands and marshes.
   Ⓑ It is more closely related to the mule deer of eastern Washington than to other types of deer.
   Ⓒ It has replaced the black-tailed deer in the open prairie.
   Ⓓ It no longer lives in a particular type of habitat that it once occupied.

Nearly any kind of plant of the forest understory can be part of a deer's diet. Where the forest inhibits the growth of grass and other meadow plants, the black-tailed deer browses on huckleberry, salal, dogwood, and almost any other shrub or herb. But this is fair-weather feeding. What keeps the black-tailed deer alive in the harsher seasons of plant decay and dormancy? One compensation for not hibernating is the built-in urge to migrate. Deer may move from high-elevation browse areas in summer down to the lowland areas in late fall. Even with snow on the ground, the high bushy understory is exposed; also snow and wind bring down leafy branches of cedar, hemlock, red alder, and other arboreal fodder.

2. It can be inferred from the discussion in paragraph 2 that winter conditions

   (A) cause some deer to hibernate
   (B) make food unavailable in the highlands for deer
   (C) make it easier for deer to locate understory plants
   (D) prevent deer from migrating during the winter

3. The word "inhibits" in the passage is closest in meaning to

   (A) consists of
   (B) combines
   (C) restricts
   (D) establishes

The numbers of deer have fluctuated markedly since the entry of Europeans into Puget Sound country. The early explorers and settlers told of abundant deer in the early 1800s and yet almost in the same breath bemoaned the lack of this succulent game animal. Famous explorers of the North American frontier, Lewis and Clark arrived at the mouth of the Columbia River on November 14, 1805, in nearly starved circumstances. They had experienced great difficulty finding game west of the Rockies and not until the second of December did they kill their first elk. To keep 40 people alive that winter, they consumed approximately 150 elk and 20 deer. And when game moved out of the lowlands in early spring, the expedition decided to return east rather than face possible starvation. Later on in the early years of the nineteenth century, when Fort Vancouver became the headquarters for the Hudson's Bay Company, deer populations continued to fluctuate. David Douglas, Scottish botanical explorer of the 1830s, found a disturbing change in the animal life around the fort during the period between his first visit in 1825 and his final contact with the fort in 1832. A recent Douglas biographer states: "The deer which once picturesquely dotted the meadows around the fort were gone [in 1832], hunted to extermination in order to protect the crops."

4. The phrase "in the same breath" in the passage is closest in meaning to

   (A) impatiently
   (B) humorously
   (C) continuously
   (D) immediately

5. The author tells the story of the explorers Lewis and Clark in paragraph 3 in order to illustrate which of the following points?

   (A) The number of deer within the Puget Sound region has varied over time.
   (B) Most of the explorers who came to the Puget Sound area were primarily interested in hunting game.
   (C) There was more game for hunting in the East of the United States than in the West.
   (D) Individual explorers were not as successful at locating game as were the trading companies.

6. According to paragraph 3, how had Fort Vancouver changed by the time David Douglas returned in 1832?

   (A) The fort had become the headquarters for the Hudson's Bay Company.
   (B) Deer had begun populating the meadows around the fort.
   (C) Deer populations near the fort had been destroyed.
   (D) Crop yields in the area around the fort had decreased.

PARAGRAPH 4

Reduction in numbers of game should have boded ill for their survival in later times. A worsening of the plight of deer was to be expected as settlers encroached on the land, logging, burning, and clearing, eventually replacing a wilderness landscape with roads, cities, towns, and factories. No doubt the numbers of deer declined still further. Recall the fate of the Columbian white-tailed deer, now in a protected status. But for the black-tailed deer, human pressure has had just the opposite effect. Wildlife zoologist Helmut Buechner (1953), in reviewing the nature of biotic changes in Washington through recorded time, says that "since the early 1940s, the state has had more deer than at any other time in its history, the winter population fluctuating around approximately 320,000 deer (mule and black-tailed deer), which will yield about 65,000 of either sex and any age annually for an indefinite period."

7. Why does the author ask readers to recall "the fate of the Columbian white-tailed deer" in the discussion of changes in the wilderness landscape?

   (A) To provide support for the idea that habitat destruction would lead to population decline
   (B) To compare how two species of deer caused biotic changes in the wilderness environment
   (C) To provide an example of a species of deer that has successfully adapted to human settlement
   (D) To argue that some deer species must be given a protected status

8. The phrase "indefinite period" in the passage is closest in meaning to a period

   (A) whose end has not been determined
   (B) that does not begin when expected
   (C) that lasts only briefly
   (D) whose importance remains unknown

9. Which of the following statements about deer populations is supported by the information in paragraph 4?

   (A) Deer populations reached their highest point during the 1940s and then began to decline.

   (B) The activities of settlers contributed in unexpected ways to the growth of some deer populations in later times.

   (C) The clearing of wilderness land for construction caused biotic changes from which the black-tailed deer population has never recovered.

   (D) Since the 1940s the winter populations of deer have fluctuated more than the summer populations have.

PARAGRAPH 5

The causes of this population rebound are consequences of other human actions. First, the major predators of deer—wolves, cougar, and lynx—have been greatly reduced in numbers. Second, conservation has been insured by limiting times for and types of hunting. But the most profound reason for the restoration of high population numbers has been the fate of the forests. Great tracts of lowland country deforested by logging, fire, or both have become ideal feeding grounds for deer. In addition to finding an increase of suitable browse, like huckleberry and vine maple, Arthur Einarsen, longtime game biologist in the Pacific Northwest, found quality of browse in the open areas to be substantially more nutritive. The protein content of shade-grown vegetation, for example, was much lower than that for plants grown in clearings.

10. The word "rebound" in the passage is closest in meaning to

    (A) decline
    (B) recovery
    (C) exchange
    (D) movement

11. Which of the sentences below best expresses the essential information in the highlighted sentence in paragraph 5? Incorrect choices change the meaning in important ways or leave out essential information.

    (A) Arthur Einarsen's longtime familiarity with the Pacific Northwest helped him discover areas where deer had an increase in suitable browse.

    (B) Arthur Einarsen found that deforested feeding grounds provided deer with more and better food.

    (C) Biologists like Einarsen believe it is important to find additional open areas with suitable browse for deer to inhabit.

    (D) According to Einarsen, huckleberry and vine maple are examples of vegetation that may someday improve the nutrition of deer in the open areas of the Pacific Northwest.

12. Which of the following is NOT mentioned in paragraph 5 as a factor that has increased deer populations?

    Ⓐ A reduction in the number of predators
    Ⓑ Restrictions on hunting
    Ⓒ The effects of logging and fire
    Ⓓ Laws that protect feeding grounds of deer

PARAGRAPHS 2 & 3

What keeps the black-tailed deer alive in the harsher seasons of plant decay and dormancy? One compensation for not hibernating is the built-in urge to migrate. ■ Deer may move from high-elevation browse areas in summer down to the lowland areas in late fall. ■ Even with snow on the ground, the high bushy understory is exposed; also snow and wind bring down leafy branches of cedar, hemlock, red alder, and other arboreal fodder. ■

The numbers of deer have fluctuated markedly since the entry of Europeans into Puget Sound country. ■ The early explorers and settlers told of abundant deer in the early 1800s and yet almost in the same breath bemoaned the lack of this succulent game animal.

13. Look at the four squares [■] that indicate where the following sentence can be added to the passage.

    There food is available and accessible throughout the winter.

    Where would the sentence best fit?

    Ⓐ What keeps the black-tailed deer alive in the harsher seasons of plant decay and dormancy? One compensation for not hibernating is the built-in urge to migrate. **There food is available and accessible throughout the winter.** Deer may move from high-elevation browse areas in summer down to the lowland areas in late fall. ■ Even with snow on the ground, the high bushy understory is exposed; also snow and wind bring down leafy branches of cedar, hemlock, red alder, and other arboreal fodder. ■

    The numbers of deer have fluctuated markedly since the entry of Europeans into Puget Sound country. ■ The early explorers and settlers told of abundant deer in the early 1800s and yet almost in the same breath bemoaned the lack of this succulent game animal.

    Ⓑ What keeps the black-tailed deer alive in the harsher seasons of plant decay and dormancy? One compensation for not hibernating is the built-in urge to migrate. ■ Deer may move from high-elevation browse areas in summer down to the lowland areas in late fall. **There food is available and accessible throughout the winter.** Even with snow on the ground, the high bushy understory is exposed; also snow and wind bring down leafy branches of cedar, hemlock, red alder, and other arboreal fodder. ■

The numbers of deer have fluctuated markedly since the entry of Europeans into Puget Sound country. ■ The early explorers and settlers told of abundant deer in the early 1800s and yet almost in the same breath bemoaned the lack of this succulent game animal.

Ⓒ What keeps the black-tailed deer alive in the harsher seasons of plant decay and dormancy? One compensation for not hibernating is the built-in urge to migrate. ■ Deer may move from high-elevation browse areas in summer down to the lowland areas in late fall. ■ Even with snow on the ground, the high bushy understory is exposed; also snow and wind bring down leafy branches of cedar, hemlock, red alder, and other arboreal fodder. **There food is available and accessible throughout the winter.**

The numbers of deer have fluctuated markedly since the entry of Europeans into Puget Sound country. ■ The early explorers and settlers told of abundant deer in the early 1800s and yet almost in the same breath bemoaned the lack of this succulent game animal.

Ⓓ What keeps the black-tailed deer alive in the harsher seasons of plant decay and dormancy? One compensation for not hibernating is the built-in urge to migrate. ■ Deer may move from high-elevation browse areas in summer down to the lowland areas in late fall. ■ Even with snow on the ground, the high bushy understory is exposed; also snow and wind bring down leafy branches of cedar, hemlock, red alder, and other arboreal fodder. ■

The numbers of deer have fluctuated markedly since the entry of Europeans into Puget Sound country. **There food is available and accessible throughout the winter.** The early explorers and settlers told of abundant deer in the early 1800s and yet almost in the same breath bemoaned the lack of this succulent game animal.

14. **Directions**: An introductory sentence for a brief summary of the passage is provided below. Complete the summary by selecting the THREE answer choices that express the most important ideas in the passage. Some sentences do not belong in the summary because they express ideas that are not presented in the passage or are minor ideas in the passage.

Write your answer choices in the spaces where they belong. You can either write the letter of your answer choice or you can copy the sentence.

> **Deer in the Puget Sound area eat a wide variety of foods and migrate seasonally to find food.**
>
> ●
>
> ●
>
> ●

Answer Choices

A The balance of deer species in the Puget Sound region has changed over time, with the Columbian white-tailed deer now outnumbering other types of deer.

B Because Puget Sound deer migrate, it was and still remains difficult to determine accurately how many deer are living at any one time in the western United States.

C Deer populations naturally fluctuate, but early settlers in the Puget Sound environment caused an overall decline in the deer populations of the area at that time.

D Although it was believed that human settlement of the American West would cause the total number of deer to decrease permanently, the opposite has actually occurred for certain types of deer.

E In the long term, black-tailed deer in the Puget Sound area have benefitted from human activities through the elimination of their natural predators, and more and better food in deforested areas.

F Wildlife biologists have long been concerned that the loss of forests may create nutritional deficiencies for deer.

Directions: Read the passage. Then answer the questions. Give yourself 20 minutes to complete this practice set.

CAVE ART IN EUROPE

The earliest discovered traces of art are beads and carvings, and then paintings, from sites dating back to the Upper Paleolithic period. We might expect that early artistic efforts would be crude, but the cave paintings of Spain and southern France show a marked degree of skill. So do the naturalistic paintings on slabs of stone excavated in southern Africa. Some of those slabs appear to have been painted as much as 28,000 years ago, which suggests that painting in Africa is as old as painting in Europe. But painting may be even older than that. The early Australians may have painted on the walls of rock shelters and cliff faces at least 30,000 years ago, and maybe as much as 60,000 years ago.

The researchers Peter Ucko and Andrée Rosenfeld identified three principal locations of paintings in the caves of western Europe: (1) in obviously inhabited rock shelters and cave entrances; (2) in galleries immediately off the inhabited areas of caves; and (3) in the inner reaches of caves, whose difficulty of access has been interpreted by some as a sign that magical-religious activities were performed there.

The subjects of the paintings are mostly animals. The paintings rest on bare walls, with no backdrops or environmental trappings. Perhaps, like many contemporary peoples, Upper Paleolithic men and women believed that the drawing of a human image could cause death or injury, and if that were indeed their belief, it might explain why human figures are rarely depicted in cave art. Another explanation for the focus on animals might be that these people sought to improve their luck at hunting. This theory is suggested by evidence of chips in the painted figures, perhaps made by spears thrown at the drawings. But if improving their hunting luck was the chief motivation for the paintings, it is difficult to explain why only a few show signs of having been speared. Perhaps the paintings were inspired by the need to increase the supply of animals. Cave art seems to have reached a peak toward the end of the Upper Paleolithic period, when the herds of game were decreasing.

The particular symbolic significance of the cave paintings in southwestern France is more explicitly revealed, perhaps, by the results of a study conducted by researchers Patricia Rice and Ann Paterson. The data they present suggest that the animals portrayed in the cave paintings were mostly the ones that the painters preferred for meat and for materials such as hides. For example, wild cattle (bovines) and horses are portrayed more often than we would expect by chance, probably because they were larger and heavier (meatier) than other animals in the environment. In addition, the paintings mostly portray animals that the painters may have feared the most because of their size, speed, natural weapons such as tusks and horns, and the unpredictability of their behavior. That is, mammoths, bovines, and horses are portrayed more often than deer and reindeer. Thus, the paintings are consistent with the idea that the art is related to the importance of hunting in the economy of Upper Paleolithic people. Consistent with this idea, according to the investigators, is the fact that the art of the cultural period that followed the Upper Paleolithic also seems to reflect how people got their food. But in that period, when getting food no longer depended on hunting large game animals (because they were becoming extinct), the art ceased to focus on portrayals of animals.

Upper Paleolithic art was not confined to cave paintings. Many shafts of spears and similar objects were decorated with figures of animals. The anthropologist Alexander Marshack has an interesting interpretation of some of the engravings made during the Upper Paleolithic. He believes that as far back as 30,000 B.C., hunters may have used a system of notation, engraved on bone and stone, to mark phases of the Moon. If this is true, it would mean that Upper Paleolithic people were capable of complex thought and were consciously aware of their environment. In addition to other artworks, figurines representing the human female in exaggerated form have also been found at Upper Paleolithic sites. It has been suggested that these figurines were an ideal type or an expression of a desire for fertility.

Directions: Now answer the questions.

PARAGRAPH 1

The earliest discovered traces of art are beads and carvings, and then paintings, from sites dating back to the Upper Paleolithic period. We might expect that early artistic efforts would be crude, but the cave paintings of Spain and southern France show a marked degree of skill. So do the naturalistic paintings on slabs of stone excavated in southern Africa. Some of those slabs appear to have been painted as much as 28,000 years ago, which suggests that painting in Africa is as old as painting in Europe. But painting may be even older than that. The early Australians may have painted on the walls of rock shelters and cliff faces at least 30,000 years ago, and maybe as much as 60,000 years ago.

15. The word "marked" in the passage is closest in meaning to
    (A) considerable
    (B) surprising
    (C) limited
    (D) adequate

16. Paragraph 1 supports which of the following statements about painting in Europe?
    (A) It is much older than painting in Australia.
    (B) It is as much as 28,000 years old.
    (C) It is not as old as painting in southern Africa.
    (D) It is much more than 30,000 years old.

The researchers Peter Ucko and Andrée Rosenfeld identified three principal locations of paintings in the caves of western Europe: (1) in obviously inhabited rock shelters and cave entrances; (2) in galleries immediately off the inhabited areas of caves; and (3) in the inner reaches of caves, whose difficulty of access has been interpreted by some as a sign that magical-religious activities were performed there.

17. The word "principal" in the passage is closest in meaning to

   Ⓐ major
   Ⓑ likely
   Ⓒ well protected
   Ⓓ distinct

18. According to paragraph 2, what makes some researchers think that certain cave paintings were connected with magical-religious activities?

   Ⓐ The paintings were located where many people could easily see them, allowing groups of people to participate in the magical-religious activities.
   Ⓑ Upper Paleolithic people shared similar beliefs with contemporary peoples who use paintings of animals in their magical-religious rituals.
   Ⓒ Evidence of magical-religious activities has been found in galleries immediately off the inhabited areas of caves.
   Ⓓ The paintings were found in hard-to-reach places away from the inhabited parts of the cave.

The subjects of the paintings are mostly animals. The paintings rest on bare walls, with no backdrops or environmental trappings. Perhaps, like many contemporary peoples, Upper Paleolithic men and women believed that the drawing of a human image could cause death or injury, and if that were indeed their belief, it might explain why human figures are rarely depicted in cave art. Another explanation for the focus on animals might be that these people sought to improve their luck at hunting. This theory is suggested by evidence of chips in the painted figures, perhaps made by spears thrown at the drawings. But if improving their hunting luck was the chief motivation for the paintings, it is difficult to explain why only a few show signs of having been speared. Perhaps the paintings were inspired by the need to increase the supply of animals. Cave art seems to have reached a peak toward the end of the Upper Paleolithic period, when the herds of game were decreasing.

19. The word "trappings" in the passage is closest in meaning to

   Ⓐ conditions
   Ⓑ problems
   Ⓒ influences
   Ⓓ decorations

20. Which of the sentences below best expresses the essential information in the highlighted sentence in paragraph 3? Incorrect choices change the meaning in important ways or leave out essential information.

Ⓐ Upper Paleolithic people, like many contemporary peoples, believed that if they drew a human image in their cave art, it would cause death or injury.

Ⓑ Many contemporary peoples believe that the drawing of a human image can cause death or injury, so they, like Upper Paleolithic people, rarely depict human figures in their cave art.

Ⓒ If Upper Paleolithic people, like many contemporary peoples, believed that the drawing of a human image could cause death or injury, this belief might explain why human figures are rarely depicted in cave art.

Ⓓ Although many contemporary peoples believe that the drawing of a human image can cause death or injury, researchers cannot explain why Upper Paleolithic people rarely depicted human figures in their cave art.

21. According to paragraph 3, scholars explained chips in the painted figures of animals by proposing that

Ⓐ Upper Paleolithic artists used marks to record the animals they had seen

Ⓑ the paintings were inspired by the need to increase the supply of animals for hunting

Ⓒ the artists had removed rough spots on the cave walls

Ⓓ Upper Paleolithic people used the paintings to increase their luck at hunting

22. Why does the author mention that Upper Paleolithic cave art seemed to have "reached a peak toward the end of the Upper Paleolithic period, when the herds of game were decreasing"?

Ⓐ To argue that Upper Paleolithic art ceased to include animals when herds of game became scarce

Ⓑ To provide support for the idea that the aim of the paintings was to increase the supply of animals for hunting

Ⓒ To emphasize the continued improvement in the quality of cave art throughout the Upper Paleolithic period

Ⓓ To show the direct connection between the decrease in herds of game and the end of the Upper Paleolithic period

PARAGRAPH 4

The particular symbolic significance of the cave paintings in southwestern France is more explicitly revealed, perhaps, by the results of a study conducted by researchers Patricia Rice and Ann Paterson. The data they present suggest that the animals portrayed in the cave paintings were mostly the ones that the painters preferred for meat and for materials such as hides. For example, wild cattle (bovines) and horses are portrayed more often than we would expect by chance, probably because they were larger and heavier (meatier) than other animals in the environment. In addition, the paintings mostly portray animals that the painters may have feared the most because of their size, speed, natural weapons such as tusks and horns, and the unpredictability of their behavior. That is, mammoths, bovines, and horses are portrayed more often than deer and reindeer. Thus, the paintings are consistent with the idea that the art is related to the importance of hunting in the economy of Upper Paleolithic people. Consistent with this idea, according to the investigators, is the fact that the art of the cultural period that followed the Upper Paleolithic also seems to reflect how people got their food. But in that period, when getting food no longer depended on hunting large game animals (because they were becoming extinct), the art ceased to focus on portrayals of animals.

23. According to paragraph 4, scholars believe that wild cattle, horses, and mammoths are the animals most frequently portrayed in cave paintings for all of the following reasons EXCEPT:

  Ⓐ These animals were difficult to hunt because of their unpredictable behavior.
  Ⓑ People preferred these animals for their meat and for their skins.
  Ⓒ The painters admired the beauty of these large animals.
  Ⓓ People feared these animals because of their size and speed.

24. According to paragraph 4, which of the following may best represent the attitude of hunters toward deer and reindeer in the Upper Paleolithic period?

  Ⓐ Hunters did not fear deer and reindeer as much as they did large game animals such as horses and mammoths.
  Ⓑ Hunters were not interested in hunting deer and reindeer because of their size and speed.
  Ⓒ Hunters preferred the meat and hides of deer and reindeer to those of other animals.
  Ⓓ Hunters avoided deer and reindeer because of their natural weapons, such as horns.

25. According to paragraph 4, what change is evident in the art of the period following the Upper Paleolithic?

  Ⓐ This new art starts to depict small animals rather than large ones.
  Ⓑ This new art ceases to reflect the ways in which people obtained their food.
  Ⓒ This new art no longer consists mostly of representations of animals.
  Ⓓ This new art begins to show the importance of hunting to the economy.

PARAGRAPH 5

Upper Paleolithic art was not confined to cave paintings. Many shafts of spears and similar objects were decorated with figures of animals. The anthropologist Alexander Marshack has an interesting interpretation of some of the engravings made during the Upper Paleolithic. He believes that as far back as 30,000 B.C., hunters may have used a system of notation, engraved on bone and stone, to mark phases of the Moon. If this is true, it would mean that Upper Paleolithic people were capable of complex thought and were consciously aware of their environment. In addition to other artworks, figurines representing the human female in exaggerated form have also been found at Upper Paleolithic sites. It has been suggested that these figurines were an ideal type or an expression of a desire for fertility.

26. According to paragraph 5, which of the following has been used as evidence to suggest that Upper Paleolithic people were capable of complex thought and conscious awareness of their environment?

    (A) They engraved animal figures on the shafts of spears and other objects.
    (B) They may have used engraved signs to record the phases of the Moon.
    (C) Their figurines represented the human female in exaggerated form.
    (D) They may have used figurines to portray an ideal type or to express a desire for fertility.

PARAGRAPH 3

The subjects of the paintings are mostly animals. The paintings rest on bare walls, with no backdrops or environmental trappings. Perhaps, like many contemporary peoples, Upper Paleolithic men and women believed that the drawing of a human image could cause death or injury, and if that were indeed their belief, it might explain why human figures are rarely depicted in cave art. Another explanation for the focus on animals might be that these people sought to improve their luck at hunting. ■ This theory is suggested by evidence of chips in the painted figures, perhaps made by spears thrown at the drawings. ■ But if improving their hunting luck was the chief motivation for the paintings, it is difficult to explain why only a few show signs of having been speared. ■ Perhaps the paintings were inspired by the need to increase the supply of animals. Cave art seems to have reached a peak toward the end of the Upper Paleolithic period, when the herds of game were decreasing. ■

27. Look at the four squares [■] that indicate where the following sentence can be added to the passage.

    Therefore, if the paintings were connected with hunting, some other explanation is needed.

    Where would the sentence best fit?

    (A) The subjects of the paintings are mostly animals. The paintings rest on bare walls, with no backdrops or environmental trappings. Perhaps, like many contemporary peoples, Upper Paleolithic men and women believed that the drawing of a human image could cause death or injury, and if that were indeed their belief, it might explain why human figures are rarely depicted in cave art. Another explanation for the focus on animals might be that these people sought to improve their luck at hunting. **Therefore, if the paintings were connected with hunting, some other explanation is needed.** This theory is suggested by evidence of chips in the painted figures, perhaps made by spears thrown at the drawings. ■ But if improving their hunting luck was the chief motivation for the paintings, it is difficult to explain why only a few show signs of having been speared. ■ Perhaps the paintings were inspired by the need to increase the supply of animals. Cave art seems to have reached a peak toward the end of the Upper Paleolithic period, when the herds of game were decreasing. ■

Ⓑ The subjects of the paintings are mostly animals. The paintings rest on bare walls, with no backdrops or environmental trappings. Perhaps, like many contemporary peoples, Upper Paleolithic men and women believed that the drawing of a human image could cause death or injury, and if that were indeed their belief, it might explain why human figures are rarely depicted in cave art. Another explanation for the focus on animals might be that these people sought to improve their luck at hunting. ■ This theory is suggested by evidence of chips in the painted figures, perhaps made by spears thrown at the drawings. **Therefore, if the paintings were connected with hunting, some other explanation is needed.** But if improving their hunting luck was the chief motivation for the paintings, it is difficult to explain why only a few show signs of having been speared. ■ Perhaps the paintings were inspired by the need to increase the supply of animals. Cave art seems to have reached a peak toward the end of the Upper Paleolithic period, when the herds of game were decreasing. ■

Ⓒ The subjects of the paintings are mostly animals. The paintings rest on bare walls, with no backdrops or environmental trappings. Perhaps, like many contemporary peoples, Upper Paleolithic men and women believed that the drawing of a human image could cause death or injury, and if that were indeed their belief, it might explain why human figures are rarely depicted in cave art. Another explanation for the focus on animals might be that these people sought to improve their luck at hunting. ■ This theory is suggested by evidence of chips in the painted figures, perhaps made by spears thrown at the drawings. ■ But if improving their hunting luck was the chief motivation for the paintings, it is difficult to explain why only a few show signs of having been speared. **Therefore, if the paintings were connected with hunting, some other explanation is needed.** Perhaps the paintings were inspired by the need to increase the supply of animals. Cave art seems to have reached a peak toward the end of the Upper Paleolithic period, when the herds of game were decreasing. ■

Ⓓ The subjects of the paintings are mostly animals. The paintings rest on bare walls, with no backdrops or environmental trappings. Perhaps, like many contemporary peoples, Upper Paleolithic men and women believed that the drawing of a human image could cause death or injury, and if that were indeed their belief, it might explain why human figures are rarely depicted in cave art. Another explanation for the focus on animals might be that these people sought to improve their luck at hunting. ■ This theory is suggested by evidence of chips in the painted figures, perhaps made by spears thrown at the drawings. ■ But if improving their hunting luck was the chief motivation for the paintings, it is difficult to explain why only a few show signs of having been speared. ■ Perhaps the paintings were inspired by the need to increase the supply of animals. Cave art seems to have reached a peak toward the end of the Upper Paleolithic period, when the herds of game were decreasing. **Therefore, if the paintings were connected with hunting, some other explanation is needed.**

28. **Directions**: An introductory sentence for a brief summary of the passage is provided below. Complete the summary by selecting the THREE answer choices that express the most important ideas in the passage. Some sentences do not belong in the summary because they express ideas that are not presented in the passage or are minor ideas in the passage.

Write your answer choices in the spaces where they belong. You can either write the letter of your answer choice or you can copy the sentence.

> **Upper Paleolithic cave paintings in western Europe are among humanity's earliest artistic efforts.**
>
> -
>
> -
>
> -

Answer Choices

A Researchers have proposed several different explanations for the fact that animals were the most common subjects in the cave paintings.

B The cave paintings focus on portraying animals without also depicting the natural environments in which these animals are typically found.

C The art of the cultural period that followed the Upper Paleolithic ceased to portray large game animals and focused instead on the kinds of animals that people of that period preferred to hunt.

D Some researchers have argued that the cave paintings mostly portrayed large animals that provided Upper Paleolithic people with meat and materials.

E Some researchers believe that the paintings found in France provide more explicit evidence of their symbolic significance than those found in Spain, southern Africa, and Australia.

F Besides cave paintings, Upper Paleolithic people produced several other kinds of artwork, one of which has been thought to provide evidence of complex thought.

Directions: Read the passage. Then answer the questions. Give yourself 20 minutes to complete this practice set.

PETROLEUM RESOURCES

Petroleum, consisting of crude oil and natural gas, seems to originate from organic matter in marine sediment. Microscopic organisms settle to the seafloor and accumulate in marine mud. The organic matter may partially decompose, using up the dissolved oxygen in the sediment. As soon as the oxygen is gone, decay stops and the remaining organic matter is preserved.

Continued sedimentation—the process of deposits' settling on the sea bottom— buries the organic matter and subjects it to higher temperatures and pressures, which convert the organic matter to oil and gas. As muddy sediments are pressed together, the gas and small droplets of oil may be squeezed out of the mud and may move into sandy layers nearby. Over long periods of time (millions of years), accumulations of gas and oil can collect in the sandy layers. Both oil and gas are less dense than water, so they generally tend to rise upward through water-saturated rock and sediment.

Oil pools are valuable underground accumulations of oil, and oil fields are regions underlain by one or more oil pools. When an oil pool or field has been discovered, wells are drilled into the ground. Permanent towers, called derricks, used to be built to handle the long sections of drilling pipe. Now portable drilling machines are set up and are then dismantled and removed. When the well reaches a pool, oil usually rises up the well because of its density difference with water beneath it or because of the pressure of expanding gas trapped above it. Although this rise of oil is almost always carefully controlled today, spouts of oil, or gushers, were common in the past. Gas pressure gradually dies out, and oil is pumped from the well. Water or steam may be pumped down adjacent wells to help push the oil out. At a refinery, the crude oil from underground is separated into natural gas, gasoline, kerosene, and various oils. Petrochemicals such as dyes, fertilizer, and plastic are also manufactured from the petroleum.

As oil becomes increasingly difficult to find, the search for it is extended into more-hostile environments. The development of the oil field on the North Slope of Alaska and the construction of the Alaska pipeline are examples of the great expense and difficulty involved in new oil discoveries. Offshore drilling platforms extend the search for oil to the ocean's continental shelves—those gently sloping submarine regions at the edges of the continents. More than one-quarter of the world's oil and almost one-fifth of the world's natural gas come from offshore, even though offshore drilling is six to seven times more expensive than drilling on land. A significant part of this oil and gas comes from under the North Sea between Great Britain and Norway.

Of course, there is far more oil underground than can be recovered. It may be in a pool too small or too far from a potential market to justify the expense of drilling. Some oil lies under regions where drilling is forbidden, such as national parks or other public lands. Even given the best extraction techniques, only about 30 to 40 percent of the oil in a given pool can be brought to the surface. The rest is far too difficult to extract and has to remain underground.

Moreover, getting petroleum out of the ground and from under the sea and to the consumer can create environmental problems anywhere along the line. Pipelines carrying oil can be broken by faults or landslides, causing serious oil spills. Spillage from huge oil-carrying cargo ships, called tankers, involved in collisions or accidental groundings can create oil slicks at sea. Offshore platforms may also lose oil, creating oil slicks that drift ashore and foul the beaches, harming the environment. Sometimes, the ground at an oil field may subside as oil is removed. The Wilmington field near Long Beach, California, has subsided nine meters in 50 years; protective barriers have had to be built to prevent seawater from flooding the area. Finally, the refining and burning of petroleum and its products can cause air pollution. Advancing technology and strict laws, however, are helping control some of these adverse environmental effects.

Directions: Now answer the questions.

PARAGRAPHS 1 & 2

Petroleum, consisting of crude oil and natural gas, seems to originate from organic matter in marine sediment. Microscopic organisms settle to the seafloor and accumulate in marine mud. The organic matter may partially decompose, using up the dissolved oxygen in the sediment. As soon as the oxygen is gone, decay stops and the remaining organic matter is preserved.

Continued sedimentation—the process of deposits' settling on the sea bottom—buries the organic matter and subjects it to higher temperatures and pressures, which convert the organic matter to oil and gas. As muddy sediments are pressed together, the gas and small droplets of oil may be squeezed out of the mud and may move into sandy layers nearby. Over long periods of time (millions of years), accumulations of gas and oil can collect in the sandy layers. Both oil and gas are less dense than water, so they generally tend to rise upward through water-saturated rock and sediment.

29. The word "accumulate" in the passage is closest in meaning to
   A grow up
   B build up
   C spread out
   D break apart

30. According to paragraph 1, which of the following is true about petroleum formation?
   A Microscopic organisms that live in mud produce crude oil and natural gas.
   B Large amounts of oxygen are needed for petroleum formation to begin.
   C Petroleum is produced when organic material in sediments combines with decaying marine organisms.
   D Petroleum formation appears to begin in marine sediments where organic matter is present.

31. In paragraphs 1 and 2, the author's primary purpose is to

    (A) describe how petroleum is formed

    (B) explain why petroleum formation is a slow process

    (C) provide evidence that a marine environment is necessary for petroleum formation

    (D) show that oil commonly occurs in association with gas

32. Which of the sentences below best expresses the essential information in the highlighted sentence in paragraph 2? Incorrect choices change the meaning in important ways or leave out essential information.

    (A) Higher temperatures and pressures promote sedimentation, which is responsible for petroleum formation.

    (B) Deposits of sediments on top of organic matter increase the temperature of and pressure on the matter.

    (C) Increased pressure and heat from the weight of the sediment turn the organic remains into petroleum.

    (D) The remains of microscopic organisms transform into petroleum once they are buried under mud.

PARAGRAPH 3

    Oil pools are valuable underground accumulations of oil, and oil fields are regions underlain by one or more oil pools. When an oil pool or field has been discovered, wells are drilled into the ground. Permanent towers, called derricks, used to be built to handle the long sections of drilling pipe. Now portable drilling machines are set up and are then dismantled and removed. When the well reaches a pool, oil usually rises up the well because of its density difference with water beneath it or because of the pressure of expanding gas trapped above it. Although this rise of oil is almost always carefully controlled today, spouts of oil, or gushers, were common in the past. Gas pressure gradually dies out, and oil is pumped from the well. Water or steam may be pumped down adjacent wells to help push the oil out. At a refinery, the crude oil from underground is separated into natural gas, gasoline, kerosene, and various oils. Petrochemicals such as dyes, fertilizer, and plastic are also manufactured from the petroleum.

33. The word "adjacent" in the passage is closest in meaning to

    (A) nearby

    (B) existing

    (C) special

    (D) deep

34. Which of the following can be inferred from paragraph 3 about gushers?

    (A) They make bringing the oil to the surface easier.

    (B) They signal the presence of huge oil reserves.

    (C) They waste more oil than they collect.

    (D) They are unlikely to occur nowadays.

PARAGRAPH 4

As oil becomes increasingly difficult to find, the search for it is extended into more-hostile environments. The development of the oil field on the North Slope of Alaska and the construction of the Alaska pipeline are examples of the great expense and difficulty involved in new oil discoveries. Offshore drilling platforms extend the search for oil to the ocean's continental shelves—those gently sloping submarine regions at the edges of the continents. More than one-quarter of the world's oil and almost one-fifth of the world's natural gas come from offshore, even though offshore drilling is six to seven times more expensive than drilling on land. A significant part of this oil and gas comes from under the North Sea between Great Britain and Norway.

35. Which of the following strategies for oil exploration is described in paragraph 4?

    Ⓐ Drilling under the ocean's surface
    Ⓑ Limiting drilling to accessible locations
    Ⓒ Using highly sophisticated drilling equipment
    Ⓓ Constructing technologically advanced drilling platforms

36. What does the development of the Alaskan oil field mentioned in paragraph 4 demonstrate?

    Ⓐ More oil is extracted from the sea than from land.
    Ⓑ Drilling for oil requires major financial investments.
    Ⓒ The global demand for oil has increased over the years.
    Ⓓ The North Slope of Alaska has substantial amounts of oil.

37. The word "sloping" in the passage is closest in meaning to

    Ⓐ shifting
    Ⓑ inclining
    Ⓒ forming
    Ⓓ rolling

PARAGRAPH 5

Of course, there is far more oil underground than can be recovered. It may be in a pool too small or too far from a potential market to justify the expense of drilling. Some oil lies under regions where drilling is forbidden, such as national parks or other public lands. Even given the best extraction techniques, only about 30 to 40 percent of the oil in a given pool can be brought to the surface. The rest is far too difficult to extract and has to remain underground.

38. According to paragraph 5, the decision to drill for oil depends on all of the following factors EXCEPT

    Ⓐ permission to access the area where oil has been found
    Ⓑ the availability of sufficient quantities of oil in a pool
    Ⓒ the location of the market in relation to the drilling site
    Ⓓ the political situation in the region where drilling would occur

PARAGRAPH 6

Moreover, getting petroleum out of the ground and from under the sea and to the consumer can create environmental problems anywhere along the line. Pipelines carrying oil can be broken by faults or landslides, causing serious oil spills. Spillage from huge oil-carrying cargo ships, called tankers, involved in collisions or accidental groundings can create oil slicks at sea. Offshore platforms may also lose oil, creating oil slicks that drift ashore and foul the beaches, harming the environment. Sometimes, the ground at an oil field may subside as oil is removed. The Wilmington field near Long Beach, California, has subsided nine meters in 50 years; protective barriers have had to be built to prevent seawater from flooding the area. Finally, the refining and burning of petroleum and its products can cause air pollution. Advancing technology and strict laws, however, are helping control some of these adverse environmental effects.

39. The word "foul" in the passage is closest in meaning to

   Ⓐ reach
   Ⓑ flood
   Ⓒ pollute
   Ⓓ alter

40. In paragraph 6, the author's primary purpose is to

   Ⓐ provide examples of how oil exploration can endanger the environment
   Ⓑ describe accidents that have occurred when oil activities were in progress
   Ⓒ give an analysis of the effects of oil spills on the environment
   Ⓓ explain how technology and legislation help reduce oil spills

PARAGRAPH 2

Continued sedimentation—the process of deposits' settling on the sea bottom—buries the organic matter and subjects it to higher temperatures and pressures, which convert the organic matter to oil and gas. ■ As muddy sediments are pressed together, the gas and small droplets of oil may be squeezed out of the mud and may move into sandy layers nearby. ■ Over long periods of time (millions of years), accumulations of gas and oil can collect in the sandy layers. ■ Both oil and gas are less dense than water, so they generally tend to rise upward through water-saturated rock and sediment. ■

41. Look at the four squares [■] that indicate where the following sentence can be added to the passage.

   Unless something acts to halt this migration, these natural resources will eventually reach the surface.

   Where would the sentence best fit?

Ⓐ Continued sedimentation—the process of deposits' settling on the sea bottom—buries the organic matter and subjects it to higher temperatures and pressures, which convert the organic matter to oil and gas. **Unless something acts to halt this migration, these natural resources will eventually reach the surface.** As muddy sediments are pressed together, the gas and small droplets of oil may be squeezed out of the mud and may move into sandy layers nearby. ■ Over long periods of time (millions of years), accumulations of gas and oil can collect in the sandy layers. ■ Both oil and gas are less dense than water, so they generally tend to rise upward through water-saturated rock and sediment. ■

Ⓑ Continued sedimentation—the process of deposits' settling on the sea bottom—buries the organic matter and subjects it to higher temperatures and pressures, which convert the organic matter to oil and gas. ■ As muddy sediments are pressed together, the gas and small droplets of oil may be squeezed out of the mud and may move into sandy layers nearby. **Unless something acts to halt this migration, these natural resources will eventually reach the surface.** Over long periods of time (millions of years), accumulations of gas and oil can collect in the sandy layers. ■ Both oil and gas are less dense than water, so they generally tend to rise upward through water-saturated rock and sediment. ■

Ⓒ Continued sedimentation—the process of deposits' settling on the sea bottom—buries the organic matter and subjects it to higher temperatures and pressures, which convert the organic matter to oil and gas. ■ As muddy sediments are pressed together, the gas and small droplets of oil may be squeezed out of the mud and may move into sandy layers nearby. ■ Over long periods of time (millions of years), accumulations of gas and oil can collect in the sandy layers. **Unless something acts to halt this migration, these natural resources will eventually reach the surface.** Both oil and gas are less dense than water, so they generally tend to rise upward through water-saturated rock and sediment. ■

Ⓓ Continued sedimentation—the process of deposits' settling on the sea bottom—buries the organic matter and subjects it to higher temperatures and pressures, which convert the organic matter to oil and gas. ■ As muddy sediments are pressed together, the gas and small droplets of oil may be squeezed out of the mud and may move into sandy layers nearby. ■ Over long periods of time (millions of years), accumulations of gas and oil can collect in the sandy layers. ■ Both oil and gas are less dense than water, so they generally tend to rise upward through water-saturated rock and sediment. **Unless something acts to halt this migration, these natural resources will eventually reach the surface.**

42. **Directions**: An introductory sentence for a brief summary of the passage is provided below. Complete the summary by selecting the THREE answer choices that express the most important ideas in the passage. Some sentences do not belong in the summary because they express ideas that are not presented in the passage or are minor ideas in the passage.

Write your answer choices in the spaces where they belong. You can either write the letter of your answer choice or you can copy the sentence.

> **"Petroleum" is a broad term that includes both crude oil and natural gas.**
>
> ●
>
> ●
>
> ●

Answer Choices

A Petroleum formation is the result of biological as well as chemical activity.
B Petroleum tends to rise to the surface, since it is lower in density than water.
C The difficulty of finding adequate sources of oil on land has resulted in a greater number of offshore drilling sites.
D Current methods of petroleum extraction enable oil producers to recover about half of the world's petroleum reserves.
E Petroleum extraction can have a negative impact on the environment.
F Accidents involving oil tankers occur when tankers run into shore reefs or collide with other vessels.

LISTENING

Directions: This section measures your ability to understand conversations and lectures in English.

Listen to each conversation and lecture only one time. After each conversation and lecture, you will answer some questions about it. Answer each question based on what is stated or implied by the speakers.

You may take notes while you listen and use your notes to help you answer the questions. Your notes will **not** be scored.

In some questions you will see this icon: 🎧. This means that you will hear, but not see, the question.

Answer each question before moving on. Do not return to previous questions.

It will take about 60 minutes to listen to the conversations and lectures and answer the questions about them.

Directions: Listen to Track 1.

Directions: Now answer the questions.

1. Why does the man need the woman's assistance? *Choose 2 answers.*

   A He does not know the publication date of some reviews he needs.
   B He does not know the location of the library's video collection of plays.
   C He does not know how to find out where the play is currently being performed.
   D He does not know how to determine which newspapers he should look at.

2. What does the woman imply about critical reaction to the play *Happy Strangers*?

   A Negative critical reaction led to its content being revised after it premiered.
   B The play has always been quite popular among university students.
   C Reactions to the play are more positive nowadays than they were in the past.
   D The play is rarely performed nowadays because critics have never liked it.

3. What does the woman say about her experience seeing a performance of *Happy Strangers* when she was younger? *Choose 2 answers.*

   A It was the first play she had seen performed professionally.
   B She saw it against the wishes of her parents.
   C She was surprised at how traditional the performance was.
   D She had a variety of emotional reactions to the play.

4. What is the man's attitude toward his current assignment?

   A He is not confident that he will find the materials he needs.
   B He feels that performing in a play is less boring than reading one.
   C He thinks his review of the play will be more objective than the contemporary reviews were.
   D He is optimistic that he will learn to appreciate the play he is researching.

5. Listen to Track 2.
   - (A) To ask the man to clarify his request
   - (B) To state the man's request more precisely
   - (C) To make sure that she heard the man correctly
   - (D) To correct a mistake the man has made

Directions: Listen to Track 3.

Biology

displacement activity

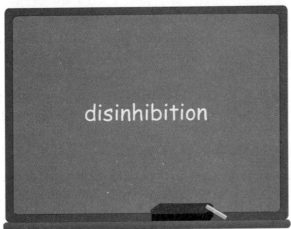

Directions: Now answer the questions.

6. What is the lecture mainly about?

    Ⓐ Methods of observing unusual animal behavior
    Ⓑ A theory about ways birds attract mates
    Ⓒ Ways animals behave when they have conflicting drives
    Ⓓ Criteria for classifying animal behaviors

7. Indicate whether each of the activities below describes a displacement activity.
    Put a check (✓) in the correct boxes.

	Yes	No
An animal attacks the ground instead of its enemy.		
An animal falls asleep in the middle of a mating ritual.		
An animal eats some food when confronted by its enemy.		
An animal takes a drink of water after grooming itself.		

8. What does the professor say about disinhibition?

    Ⓐ It can prevent displacement activities from occurring.
    Ⓑ It can cause animals to act on more than one drive at a time.
    Ⓒ It is not useful for explaining many types of displacement activities.
    Ⓓ It is responsible for the appearance of seemingly irrelevant behavior.

9. According to the lecture, what is one possible reason that displacement activities are often grooming behaviors?

    Ⓐ Grooming may cause an enemy or predator to be confused.
    Ⓑ Grooming is a convenient and accessible behavior.
    Ⓒ Grooming often occurs before eating and drinking.
    Ⓓ Grooming is a common social activity.

10. Why does the professor mention the wood thrush?

    Ⓐ To contrast its displacement activities with those of other animal species
    Ⓑ To explain that some animals display displacement activities other than grooming
    Ⓒ To point out how displacement activities are influenced by the environment
    Ⓓ To give an example of an animal that does not display displacement activities

11. Listen to Track 4.

    Ⓐ She is impressed by how much the student knows about redirecting.
    Ⓑ She thinks it is time to move on to the next part of this lecture.
    Ⓒ The student's answer is not an example of a displacement activity.
    Ⓓ The student should suggest a different animal behavior to discuss next.

Directions: Listen to Track 5.

Directions: Now answer the questions.

12. What is the main purpose of the lecture?

    Ⓐ To point out similarities in Emerson's essays and poems

    Ⓑ To prepare the students to read an essay by Emerson

    Ⓒ To compare Emerson's concept of universal truth to that of other authors

    Ⓓ To show the influence of early United States society on Emerson's writing

13. On what basis did Emerson criticize the people of his time?

    Ⓐ They refused to recognize universal truths.

    Ⓑ They did not recognize the genius of certain authors.

    Ⓒ Their convictions were not well-defined.

    Ⓓ They were too interested in conformity.

14. What does Emerson say about the past?

   Ⓐ It should guide a person's present actions.
   Ⓑ It must be examined closely.
   Ⓒ It is less important than the future.
   Ⓓ It lacks both clarity and universal truth.

15. What point does the professor make when he mentions a ship's path?

   Ⓐ It is easy for people to lose sight of their true path.
   Ⓑ Most people are not capable of deciding which path is best for them.
   Ⓒ The path a person takes can only be seen clearly after the destination has been reached.
   Ⓓ A person should establish a goal before deciding which path to take.

16. What does the professor imply about himself when he recounts some life experiences he had before becoming a literature professor? *Choose 2 answers.*

   Ⓐ He did not consider the consequences of his decisions.
   Ⓑ He did not plan to become a literature professor.
   Ⓒ He has always tried to act consistently.
   Ⓓ He has trusted in himself and his decisions.

17. Listen to Track 6. 🎧

   Ⓐ To suggest that United States citizens have not changed much over time
   Ⓑ To encourage the class to find more information about this time period
   Ⓒ To explain why Emerson's essay has lost some relevance
   Ⓓ To provide background for the concept he is explaining

Directions: Listen to Track 7.

Directions: Now answer the questions.

18. What is the conversation mainly about?
    Ⓐ Methods for finding appropriate sources for a project
    Ⓑ Reasons the woman is having difficulties with a project
    Ⓒ Criteria the professor uses to evaluate group projects
    Ⓓ Ways to develop the skills needed to work in groups

19. Why does the professor mention the "free-rider" problem?
    Ⓐ To review a concept he explained in class
    Ⓑ To give the student a plan to solve her problem
    Ⓒ To clarify the problem the student is facing
    Ⓓ To explain a benefit of working in groups

20. What is the professor's opinion of the other students in the woman's group?
    Ⓐ They try to take credit for work they did not do.
    Ⓑ They did not perform well in previous courses with him.
    Ⓒ They are more motivated when they are working in a group.
    Ⓓ They do good work when they are interested in the subject.

21. Why did the woman choose property rights as a topic?
    Ⓐ The professor recommended the topic.
    Ⓑ She already had a lot of reference materials on the subject.
    Ⓒ She wanted to learn something new.
    Ⓓ It was easy to research at the school library.

22. What mistakes does the professor imply the woman has made while working on a project? *Choose 2 answers.*

    A Finding sources for her group partners

    B Writing the weekly progress reports for her group

    C Forgetting to pay attention to the project's deadlines

    D Failing to involve the group members in the selection of a topic

Directions: Listen to Track 8.

Directions: Now answer the questions.

23. What does the professor mainly discuss?

    Ⓐ His plans for research involving moving rocks

    Ⓑ A difference between two geological forces that cause rocks to move

    Ⓒ Theories about why desert rocks move

    Ⓓ Reasons why geologists should study moving rocks

24. According to the professor, what have the researchers agreed on?

    Ⓐ The rocks cannot move after ice storms.

    Ⓑ The rocks do not move at night.

    Ⓒ The rocks never move in circles.

    Ⓓ The rocks are not moved by people.

25. The professor mentions an experiment done five to ten years ago on the wind speed necessary to move rocks. What opinion does the professor express about the experiment?

    Ⓐ The researchers reached the correct conclusion despite some miscalculations.

    Ⓑ The researchers should have chosen a different location for their experiment.

    Ⓒ The experiment should have been conducted on wetter ground.

    Ⓓ The experiment was not continued long enough to achieve clear results.

26. What important point does the professor make about the area where the rocks are found?

    Ⓐ It has been the site of Earth's highest wind speeds.

    Ⓑ It is subject to laws that restrict experimentation.

    Ⓒ It is accessible to heavy machinery.

    Ⓓ It is not subject to significant changes in temperature.

27. What is the professor's purpose in telling the students about moving rocks?

    Ⓐ To teach a lesson about the structure of solid matter

    Ⓑ To share a recent advance in geology

    Ⓒ To give an example of how ice can move rocks

    Ⓓ To show how geologists need to combine information from several fields

28. Listen to Track 9.

    Ⓐ The movement pattern of the rocks was misreported by researchers.

    Ⓑ The rocks are probably being moved by people.

    Ⓒ The movement pattern of the rocks does not support the wind theory.

    Ⓓ There must be differences in the rocks' composition.

Directions: Listen to Track 10.

United States Government

National Endowment for the Arts (NEA)

Directions: Now answer the questions.

29. What is the discussion mainly about?

Ⓐ Reasons the United States government should not support the arts

Ⓑ The history of government support for the arts in the United States

Ⓒ Strengths and weaknesses of different government-sponsored arts programs

Ⓓ Different ways in which governments can help support artists

30. According to the discussion, in what two ways was the Federal Art Project successful? *Choose 2 answers.*

Ⓐ It established standards for art schools.

Ⓑ It provided jobs for many artists.

Ⓒ It produced many excellent artists.

Ⓓ It gave many people greater access to the arts.

31. The class discusses some important events related to government support for the arts in the United States. Put the events in order from earliest to latest.

Write your answer choices in the spaces where they belong. You can either write the letter of your answer choice or you can copy the sentence. The first one is done for you.

1. The government provided no official support for the arts.
2.
3.
4.
5.

Answer Choices

Ⓐ Arts councils were established in all 50 states of the country.

Ⓑ The federal budget supporting the arts was reduced by half.

Ⓒ The Federal Art Project helped reduce unemployment.

Ⓓ The National Endowment for the Arts was established.

32. Why does the professor mention the Kennedy Center and Lincoln Center?

Ⓐ To give examples of institutions that benefit from corporate support

Ⓑ To illustrate why some artists oppose the building of cultural centers

Ⓒ To show how two centers were named after presidents who supported the arts

Ⓓ To name two art centers built by the government during the Depression

33. What does the professor say about artists' opinions of government support for the arts?

    Ⓐ Most artists believe that the government should provide more funding for the arts.

    Ⓑ Most artists approve of the ways in which the government supports the arts.

    Ⓒ Even artists do not agree on whether the government should support the arts.

    Ⓓ Even artists have a low opinion of government support for the arts.

34. Listen to Track 11.

    Ⓐ Other students should comment on the man's remark.

    Ⓑ Most people would agree with the man's opinion.

    Ⓒ Artwork funded by the government is usually of excellent quality.

    Ⓓ The government project was not a waste of money.

SPEAKING

This section measures your ability to speak in English about a variety of topics.

There are six questions in this section. For each question, you will be given a short time to prepare your response. When the preparation time is up, answer the question as completely as possible in the time indicated for that question. You should record your responses so that you can review them later and compare them with the answer key and scoring rubrics.

1. You will now be asked to speak about a familiar topic. Give yourself 15 seconds to prepare your response. Then record yourself speaking for 45 seconds.

    Listen to Track 12.

    > What do you miss most about your home when you are away? Use specific details in your explanation.
    >
    > | **Preparation Time: 15 seconds** |
    > | :---: |
    > | **Response Time: 45 seconds** |

2. You will now be asked to give your opinion about a familiar topic. Give yourself 15 seconds to prepare your response. Then record yourself speaking for 45 seconds.

    Listen to Track 13.

    > Many universities now offer academic courses over the Internet. However, some people still prefer learning in traditional classrooms. Which do you think is better? Explain why.
    >
    > | **Preparation Time: 15 seconds** |
    > | :---: |
    > | **Response Time: 45 seconds** |

3. You will now read a short passage and listen to a conversation on the same topic. You will then be asked a question about them. After you hear the question, give yourself 30 seconds to prepare your response. Then record yourself speaking for 60 seconds.

    Listen to Track 14.

Reading Time: 45 seconds

Evening Computer Classes May Be Added

The computer department is considering offering evening classes in the fall. The proposal to add the classes is a response to student complaints that daytime computer classes have become increasingly overcrowded and there are no longer enough computers available. The department has decided that despite some added expense, the most cost-effective way of addressing this problem is by adding computer classes in the evening. It is hoped that this change will decrease the number of students enrolled in day classes and thus guarantee individual access to computers for all students in computer classes.

Listen to Track 15.

The man expresses his opinion about the proposal described in the article. Briefly summarize the proposal. Then state his opinion about the proposal and explain the reasons he gives for holding that opinion.

Preparation Time: 30 seconds
Response Time: 60 seconds

4. You will now read a short passage and listen to a lecture on the same topic. You will then be asked a question about them. After you hear the question, give yourself 30 seconds to prepare your response. Then record yourself speaking for 60 seconds.

Listen to Track 16.

Reading Time: 45 seconds

Verbal and Nonverbal Communication

When we speak with other people face-to-face, the nonverbal signals we give—our facial expressions, hand gestures, body movements, and tone of voice—often communicate as much as, or more than, the words we utter. When our nonverbal signals, which we often produce unconsciously, agree with our verbal message, the verbal message is enhanced and supported, made more convincing. But when they conflict with the verbal message, we may be communicating an entirely different and more accurate message than what we intend.

Listen to Track 17.

Explain how the examples from the professor's lecture illustrate the relationship between verbal and nonverbal communication.

Preparation Time: 30 seconds
Response Time: 60 seconds

5. You will now listen to part of a conversation. You will then be asked a question about it. After you hear the question, give yourself 20 seconds to prepare your response. Then record yourself speaking for 60 seconds.

Listen to Track 18.

Briefly summarize the problem the speakers are discussing. Then state which of the two solutions from the conversation you would recommend. Explain the reasons for your recommendation.

Preparation Time: 20 seconds
Response Time: 60 seconds

6. You will now listen to part of a lecture. You will then be asked a question about it. After you hear the question, give yourself 20 seconds to prepare your response. Then record yourself speaking for 60 seconds.

Listen to Track 19.

Using points and examples from the lecture, explain the importance of visual elements in painting.

Preparation Time: 20 seconds
Response Time: 60 seconds

WRITING

This section measures your ability to write in English to communicate in an academic environment.

There are two writing questions in this section.

For question 1, you will read a passage and listen to a lecture about the same topic. You may take notes while you read and listen. Then you will write a response to a question based on what you have read and heard. You may look back at the passage when answering the question. You may use your notes to help you answer the question. You have 20 minutes to plan and write your response.

For question 2, you will write an essay based on your own knowledge and experience. You have 30 minutes to plan and complete your essay.

1. **Directions:** Give yourself 3 minutes to read the passage.

Endotherms are animals such as modern birds and mammals that keep their body temperatures constant. For instance, humans are endotherms and maintain an internal temperature of 37°C, no matter whether the environment is warm or cold. Because dinosaurs were reptiles, and modern reptiles are not endotherms, it was long assumed that dinosaurs were not endotherms. However, dinosaurs differ in many ways from modern reptiles, and there is now considerable evidence that dinosaurs were, in fact, endotherms.

Polar dinosaurs

One reason for believing that dinosaurs were endotherms is that dinosaur fossils have been discovered in polar regions. Only animals that can maintain a temperature well above that of the surrounding environment could be active in such cold climates.

Leg position and movement

There is a connection between endothermy and the position and movement of the legs. The physiology of endothermy allows sustained physical activity, such as running. But running is efficient only if an animal's legs are positioned underneath its body, not at the body's side, as they are for crocodiles and many lizards. The legs of all modern endotherms are underneath the body, and so were the legs of dinosaurs. This strongly suggests that dinosaurs were endotherms.

Haversian canals

There is also a connection between endothermy and bone structure. The bones of endotherms usually include structures called Haversian canals. These canals house nerves and blood vessels that allow the living animal to grow quickly, and rapid body growth is in fact a characteristic of endothermy. The presence of Haversian canals in bone is a strong indicator that the animal is an endotherm, and fossilized bones of dinosaurs are usually dense with Haversian canals.

Listen to Track 20.

Directions: You have 20 minutes to plan and write your response. Your response will be judged on the basis of the quality of your writing and on how well your response presents the points in the lecture and their relationship to the reading passage. Typically, an effective response will be 150 to 225 words.

Listen to Track 21.

Response Time: 20 minutes

Summarize the points made in the lecture, being sure to explain how they challenge the specific points made in the reading passage.

_____

_____

_____

_____

_____

_____

_____

_____

_____

2. **Directions**: Read the question below. You have 30 minutes to plan, write, and revise your essay. Typically, an effective response will contain a minimum of 300 words.

Response Time: 30 minutes

Do you agree or disagree with the following statement?

In twenty years there will be fewer cars in use than there are today.

Use specific reasons and examples to support your answer.

_____

_____

_____

_____

_____

_____

_____

_____

_____

_____

_____

_____

_____

_____

_____

_____

_____

_____

_____

_____

ANSWERS

Reading Section

1. D	22. B
2. B	23. C
3. C	24. A
4. D	25. C
5. A	26. B
6. C	27. C
7. A	28. A, D, F
8. A	29. B
9. B	30. D
10. B	31. A
11. B	32. C
12. D	33. A
13. B	34. D
14. C, D, E	35. A
15. A	36. B
16. B	37. B
17. A	38. D
18. D	39. C
19. D	40. A
20. C	41. D
21. D	42. A, C, E

Listening Section

1. A, D
2. C
3. A, D
4. D
5. B
6. C
7.

	Yes	No
An animal attacks the ground instead of its enemy.		✓
An animal falls asleep in the middle of a mating ritual.	✓	
An animal eats some food when confronted by its enemy.	✓	
An animal takes a drink of water after grooming itself.		✓

8. D
9. B
10. C
11. C
12. B
13. D
14. C
15. C
16. B, D
17. D
18. B
19. C
20. D
21. C
22. A, D
23. C
24. D
25. A
26. B
27. D
28. C
29. B
30. B, D
31. C, D, A, B
32. A
33. C
34. D

Speaking Section

1. There are many ways you could answer this particular question. You will need to talk about one or more things about your home that you miss when you are away and provide explanations for why you miss them.

   You should begin by providing a specific example of something that you miss about your home. For example, this could be your family, your favorite room, or your mother's cooking. You should then provide more details about why you miss this. For example, you could describe your favorite room and talk about the comfortable chair that is in it and how you have had wonderful talks with your family and friends there. Or you could say that you miss your mother's cooking because she prepares special, spicy food that you cannot get when you are away from home. It is important to develop your ideas with specific explanations. You should not merely give a list of things you miss without providing details that help the listener understand why you miss them.

Your response should be intelligible, should demonstrate effective use of grammar and vocabulary, and should be well developed and coherent. Your response is scored using the Independent Speaking Rubric (see Appendix A).

2.   To respond to this particular question, you should clearly state what your opinion is: Do you think it is better to learn in traditional classrooms or take classes over the Internet? Then you should give reasons to support your opinion. If you take the position that you believe Internet or online courses are more effective, you might give the reason that they are more effective because a student can study at anytime from anywhere. You might further support that reason by using an example from your own experience. You might say that you learn best in the evenings and so online courses allow you to learn when you are best able to concentrate, whereas in a traditional classroom, you have to concentrate at a particular time.

If you believe that online courses are not better than learning in a traditional classroom, you might give an example of something that happens in the classroom that makes learning effective. You might say that direct contact with a teacher is important. You could continue to develop your response by giving examples of how direct contact is beneficial to learning.

Keep in mind that there is no "correct" answer to this question. Whether you prefer courses over the Internet or in traditional classrooms, your answer can be supported with examples and details. It is important to make sure that you state your opinion and develop your response with good examples and relevant details.

Your response should be intelligible, should demonstrate effective use of grammar and vocabulary, and should be well developed and coherent. Your response is scored using the Independent Speaking Rubric (see Appendix A).

3.   First, as the question states, you should provide a brief summary of the proposal, which is for the computer department to add evening classes in the fall. You can also provide a brief summary of the reason that they are doing this (overcrowded conditions in the daytime computer classes). You should not spend too much time on this summary; if you attempt to provide many details from the reading, you may not have enough time to discuss both of the man's reasons for disagreeing with the proposal. For this item type, a brief summary is all that is necessary. You should make sure that your summary is clear enough for the listener to understand the proposal without having access to additional information.

After the summary, you should state the man's opinion of the university's proposal to add computer courses in the evening. In this case, the man disagrees with the university's proposal.

You should then convey the two main reasons he gives for holding that opinion. You will need to connect information from the conversation to the reading in order for your response to be complete. First, the man says that the idea to add evening classes will not solve the problem of overcrowding because most students are too busy to take classes at night. You could also provide one of the examples why students are busy, such as jobs or family.

Your response should also convey the man's second reason for not agreeing with the university's proposal. You should say that the man thinks that offering evening classes won't save money because it will be expensive to add the new classes, and it will be more expensive than buying new computers. You could add that hiring new teachers and keeping the building open late is expensive, or that the rooms are big enough for more computers and that computers are now less expensive than they used to be. You do not, however, have to describe every detail from the conversation as long as you make it clear why the man disagrees with the proposal.

Your response should be intelligible, should demonstrate effective use of grammar and vocabulary, and should be well developed and coherent. Your response is scored using the Integrated Speaking Rubric (see Appendix A).

4.   To respond to this particular question, you should discuss how verbal and nonverbal communication are related and explain how the examples that the professor gives support the reading text. You should include relevant points and examples from the lecture (and not from any other source).

To begin your response, you could give a brief summary of the reading, such as a definition of what verbal and nonverbal communication is; that is, that gestures and body movements often provide as much information to a person as spoken language does. You could also say that nonverbal signals can agree or conflict with a verbal message.

Then you should explain how the professor's examples illustrate these general ideas. In the first example, the professor's happy nonverbal behaviors on seeing his uncle, such as his big smile, and his jumping up and down, agreed with his verbal message, so the verbal message was supported. You could also say that his uncle knew he was very happy.

You should then discuss the second example. In this example, when the professor hit himself with the hammer, he did not want to upset his daughter and told her not to worry. These words, however, conflicted with his nonverbal behavior, such as his shaking his hand in pain and his trembling voice, so his daughter did not believe

the verbal message. In this case, the nonverbal message was more accurate.

You will not have time to repeat all of the details from the lecture and reading, and you should not try to do that. You should integrate points from both to answer the question completely. You need to give only sufficient details to explain how the two examples relate to the overall idea of how nonverbal communication contributes to verbal messages.

Your response should be intelligible, should demonstrate effective use of grammar and vocabulary, and should be well developed and coherent. Your response is scored using the Integrated Speaking Rubric (see Appendix A).

5.   To respond to this particular question you should *briefly* describe the problem. It is enough to say that the man has left his class schedule back at the dorm and doesn't know what room his class is in. You do not need to give many details at this point.

Next, you need to choose *one* of the two solutions and explain why you think that solution is best. The two solutions in this conversation are: 1) go to the student center and use a computer to find out where the class is, or 2) check each lecture hall until he finds his class. It does not matter which of the two proposed solutions you chose, since there is no "right" solution or "wrong" solution. You should choose the solution that you think is best and support your choice with reasons why you think it is best. The reasons you give can include information provided by the speakers as well as your own experiences.

For example, if you believe the first solution is preferable, you would probably begin by saying that you think it would be best for the man to go use the computer in the student center in order to find the room number, then you would proceed to explain why. There are any number of reasons you can give: you might say that it's best to check the computer because he can also find out where his other classes are, since he doesn't have the schedule. You could also speak about the disadvantages of the second solution; you might say that he would be embarrassed to look in the other rooms, and he wouldn't know what the professor looks like anyway. Remember, this type of question can be answered in many different ways.

Your response should be intelligible, should demonstrate effective use of grammar and vocabulary, and should be well developed and coherent. Your response is scored using the Integrated Speaking Rubric (see Appendix A).

6. To respond to this particular question, you should talk about some of the visual elements of painting and explain why they are important. You should include relevant points and examples from the lecture (and not from any other source).

To begin your response, you should briefly state the main idea, that visual elements convey meaning and express emotion in paintings. You would then talk about the different points the professor gives to support this. You would say, for example, that colors can evoke strong emotions, and give the example that red can evoke anger or blue can make somebody feel calm. Then you could talk about texture. You could say that texture can be physical or visual or that texture can also evoke emotions; for example, a smooth texture can be calming. You could then talk about how artists combine these elements to create meaning; for example, strong colors, such as reds, plus wide sweeping brushstrokes suggest chaos and stronger emotions.

As the goal of this item is to provide a summary of the professor's lecture, you do not need to repeat all of the details from the lecture. You need to only give sufficient details to explain why visual details are important in a painting.

Your response should be intelligible, should demonstrate effective use of grammar and vocabulary, and should be well developed and coherent. Your response is scored using the Integrated Speaking Rubric (see Appendix A).

Writing Section

1. What is important to understand from the lecture is that the professor disagrees with the arguments presented in the reading to support the idea that dinosaurs were endotherms, namely that dinosaurs inhabited polar regions; that their legs were positioned underneath their bodies; and that their bones included structures called Haversian canals.

In your response, you should convey the reasons presented by the professor for why the information presented in the reading does not prove that dinosaurs were endotherms. A high-scoring response will include the following points made by the professor that cast doubt on the points made in the reading:

Point made in the reading	Counterpoint made in the lecture
The presence of dinosaur fossils in the polar regions indicates that dinosaurs were able to survive in very cold climates and therefore must have been endotherms.	When dinosaurs lived, the polar regions were much warmer than they are today, so even animals that were not endotherms could have survived there for at least part of the year. Furthermore, polar dinosaurs could have migrated or hibernated during the months when the temperatures were the coldest.
Dinosaurs' legs were positioned underneath their bodies. Such leg positioning allows for running and similar physical activities typical of endotherms.	The positioning of dinosaurs' legs underneath their bodies may have served a function unrelated to running and similar activities. The positioning of legs underneath the body may have evolved to support the great body weight of many dinosaurs.
Dinosaurs' bones contained Haversian canals, structures that allow for fast bone growth and, again, are typical of endotherms.	Despite containing Haversian canals, dinosaur bones also had features one would expect to see in animals that are not endotherms. In particular, dinosaur bones contained growth rings, which indicate periods of slow growth alternating with periods of fast growth. Such an uneven pattern of growth is typical of animals that are not endotherms.

Your response is scored using the Integrated Writing Rubric (see Appendix A). A response that receives a score of 5 clearly conveys all three of the main points in the table using accurate sentence structure and vocabulary.

2. To earn a top score, you should develop a multi-paragraph essay that responds to the issue of whether you believe there will be fewer cars in use twenty years from now. Typically an effective response will contain a minimum of 300 words.

One successful way to express agreement with the statement is to develop your response around the central concept that the costs of driving cars in the future may become prohibitive for many workers; because the cost of nonrenewable fuels keeps going up, people twenty years from now would realize how much they could save by taking public transportation.

Another aspect is that people are becoming more and more unhappy with time spent waiting in traffic or finding parking places, so they might be willing to give up their cars and rely on public transportation.

A successful way to disagree with the statement is to focus on the problems that not having a car create as a reason why the number of cars will not be reduced; you could point to the lack of public transportation in some areas, or the inconvenience of having to structure life and work around public transportation schedules. You could also argue that expected advances in technology and clean energy will probably mean that in twenty years, cars will be different, but not fewer.

Keep in mind that there is no "correct" answer to this question. Either side of the issue can be supported with examples and reasons. It is important to make sure that you state your opinion and develop a response that explains your opinion. The development of your essay is judged by how effectively you support your opinion; a well-developed essay will contain clearly appropriate reasons, examples, and details that illustrate your opinion. Development is not evaluated simply in terms of how many words you write.

Your response should be well organized. A well-organized essay allows an evaluator to read from the beginning to the end of the essay without becoming confused. You should be sure not to just repeat the same information in different ways.

The quality and accuracy of the sentence structure and vocabulary you use to express your ideas is also very important.

Your response is scored using the Independent Writing Rubric (see Appendix A).

TOEFL iBT Test 2

READING

This section measures your ability to understand academic passages in English.

There are three passages in the section. Give yourself 20 minutes to read each passage and answer the questions about it. The entire section will take 60 minutes to complete.

You may look back at a passage when answering the questions. You can skip questions and go back to them later as long as there is time remaining.

Directions: Read the passage. Then answer the questions. Give yourself 20 minutes to complete this practice set.

MINERALS AND PLANTS

Research has shown that certain minerals are required by plants for normal growth and development. The soil is the source of these minerals, which are absorbed by the plant with the water from the soil. Even nitrogen, which is a gas in its elemental state, is normally absorbed from the soil as nitrate ions. Some soils are notoriously deficient in micro nutrients and are therefore unable to support most plant life. So-called serpentine soils, for example, are deficient in calcium, and only plants able to tolerate low levels of this mineral can survive. In modern agriculture, mineral depletion of soils is a major concern, since harvesting crops interrupts the recycling of nutrients back to the soil.

Mineral deficiencies can often be detected by specific symptoms such as chlorosis (loss of chlorophyll resulting in yellow or white leaf tissue), necrosis (isolated dead patches), anthocyanin formation (development of deep red pigmentation of leaves or stem), stunted growth, and development of woody tissue in an herbaceous plant. Soils are most commonly deficient in nitrogen and phosphorus. Nitrogen-deficient plants exhibit many of the symptoms just described. Leaves develop chlorosis; stems are short and slender; and anthocyanin discoloration occurs on stems, petioles, and lower leaf surfaces. Phosphorus-deficient plants are often stunted, with leaves turning a characteristic dark green, often with the accumulation of anthocyanin. Typically, older leaves are affected first as the phosphorus is mobilized to young growing tissue. Iron deficiency is characterized by chlorosis between veins in young leaves.

Much of the research on nutrient deficiencies is based on growing plants hydroponically, that is, in soilless liquid nutrient solutions. This technique allows researchers to create solutions that selectively omit certain nutrients and then observe the resulting effects on the plants. Hydroponics has applications beyond basic research, since it facilitates the growing of greenhouse vegetables during winter. Aeroponics, a technique in which plants are suspended and the roots misted with a nutrient solution, is another method for growing plants without soil.

While mineral deficiencies can limit the growth of plants, an overabundance of certain minerals can be toxic and can also limit growth. Saline soils, which have high concentrations of sodium chloride and other salts, limit plant growth, and research continues to focus on developing salt-tolerant varieties of agricultural crops. Research has focused on the toxic effects of heavy metals such as lead, cadmium, mercury, and aluminum; however, even copper and zinc, which are essential elements, can become toxic in high concentrations. Although most plants cannot survive in these soils, certain plants have the ability to tolerate high levels of these minerals.

Scientists have known for some time that certain plants, called hyperaccumulators, can concentrate minerals at levels a hundredfold or greater than normal. A survey of known hyperaccumulators identified that 75 percent of them amassed nickel; cobalt, copper, zinc, manganese, lead, and cadmium are other minerals of choice. Hyperaccumulators run the entire range of the plant world. They may be herbs, shrubs, or trees. Many members of the mustard family, spurge family, legume family, and grass family are top hyperaccumulators. Many are found in tropical and subtropical areas of the world, where accumulation of high concentrations of metals may afford some protection against plant-eating insects and microbial pathogens.

Only recently have investigators considered using these plants to clean up soil and waste sites that have been contaminated by toxic levels of heavy metals—an environmentally friendly approach known as phytoremediation. This scenario begins with the planting of hyperaccumulating species in the target area, such as an abandoned mine or an irrigation pond contaminated by runoff. Toxic minerals would first be absorbed by roots but later relocated to the stem and leaves. A harvest of the shoots would remove the toxic compounds off site to be burned or composted to recover the metal for industrial uses. After several years of cultivation and harvest, the site would be restored at a cost much lower than the price of excavation and reburial, the standard practice for remediation of contaminated soils. For example, in field trials, the plant alpine pennycress removed zinc and cadmium from soils near a zinc smelter, and Indian mustard, native to Pakistan and India, has been effective in reducing levels of selenium salts by 50 percent in contaminated soils.

Directions: Now answer the questions.

PARAGRAPH 1

Research has shown that certain minerals are required by plants for normal growth and development. The soil is the source of these minerals, which are absorbed by the plant with the water from the soil. Even nitrogen, which is a gas in its elemental state, is normally absorbed from the soil as nitrate ions. Some soils are notoriously deficient in micro nutrients and are therefore unable to support most plant life. So-called serpentine soils, for example, are deficient in calcium, and only plants able to tolerate low levels of this mineral can survive. In modern agriculture, mineral depletion of soils is a major concern, since harvesting crops interrupts the recycling of nutrients back to the soil.

1. According to paragraph 1, what is true of plants that can grow in serpentine soils?

   (A) They absorb micronutrients unusually well.
   (B) They require far less calcium than most plants do.
   (C) They are able to absorb nitrogen in its elemental state.
   (D) They are typically crops raised for food.

P A R A G R A P H 2

Mineral deficiencies can often be detected by specific symptoms such as chlorosis (loss of chlorophyll resulting in yellow or white leaf tissue), necrosis (isolated dead patches), anthocyanin formation (development of deep red pigmentation of leaves or stem), stunted growth, and development of woody tissue in an herbaceous plant. Soils are most commonly deficient in nitrogen and phosphorus. Nitrogen-deficient plants exhibit many of the symptoms just described. Leaves develop chlorosis; stems are short and slender; and anthocyanin discoloration occurs on stems, petioles, and lower leaf surfaces. Phosphorus-deficient plants are often stunted, with leaves turning a characteristic dark green, often with the accumulation of anthocyanin. Typically, older leaves are affected first as the phosphorus is mobilized to young growing tissue. Iron deficiency is characterized by chlorosis between veins in young leaves.

2. The word "exhibit" in the passage is closest in meaning to

   (A) fight off
   (B) show
   (C) cause
   (D) spread

3. According to paragraph 2, which of the following symptoms occurs in phosphorus-deficient plants but not in plants deficient in nitrogen or iron?

   (A) Chlorosis on leaves
   (B) Change in leaf pigmentation to a dark shade of green
   (C) Short, stunted appearance of stems
   (D) Reddish pigmentation on the leaves or stem

4. According to paragraph 2, a symptom of iron deficiency is the presence in young leaves of

   (A) deep red discoloration between the veins
   (B) white or yellow tissue between the veins
   (C) dead spots between the veins
   (D) characteristic dark green veins

P A R A G R A P H 3

Much of the research on nutrient deficiencies is based on growing plants hydroponically, that is, in soilless liquid nutrient solutions. This technique allows researchers to create solutions that selectively omit certain nutrients and then observe the resulting effects on the plants. Hydroponics has applications beyond basic research, since it facilitates the growing of greenhouse vegetables during winter. Aeroponics, a technique in which plants are suspended and the roots misted with a nutrient solution, is another method for growing plants without soil.

5. The word "facilitates" in the passage is closest in meaning to

   (A) slows down
   (B) affects
   (C) makes easier
   (D) focuses on

6. According to paragraph 3, what is the advantage of hydroponics for research on nutrient deficiencies in plants?

    (A) It allows researchers to control what nutrients a plant receives.

    (B) It allows researchers to observe the growth of a large number of plants simultaneously.

    (C) It is possible to directly observe the roots of plants.

    (D) It is unnecessary to keep misting plants with nutrient solutions.

7. The word "suspended" in the passage is closest in meaning to

    (A) grown

    (B) protected

    (C) spread out

    (D) hung

PARAGRAPH 5

Scientists have known for some time that certain plants, called hyperaccumulators, can concentrate minerals at levels a hundredfold or greater than normal. A survey of known hyperaccumulators identified that 75 percent of them amassed nickel; cobalt, copper, zinc, manganese, lead, and cadmium are other minerals of choice. Hyperaccumulators run the entire range of the plant world. They may be herbs, shrubs, or trees. Many members of the mustard family, spurge family, legume family, and grass family are top hyperaccumulators. Many are found in tropical and subtropical areas of the world, where accumulation of high concentrations of metals may afford some protection against plant-eating insects and microbial pathogens.

8. Why does the author mention "herbs," "shrubs," and "trees"?

    (A) To provide examples of plant types that cannot tolerate high levels of harmful minerals

    (B) To show why so many plants are hyperaccumulators

    (C) To help explain why hyperaccumulators can be found in so many different places

    (D) To emphasize that hyperaccumulators occur in a wide range of plant types

9. The word "afford" in the passage is closest in meaning to

    (A) offer

    (B) prevent

    (C) increase

    (D) remove

PARAGRAPH 6

Only recently have investigators considered using these plants to clean up soil and waste sites that have been contaminated by toxic levels of heavy metals—an environmentally friendly approach known as phytoremediation. This scenario begins with the planting of hyperaccumulating species in the target area, such as an abandoned mine or an irrigation pond contaminated by runoff. Toxic minerals would first be absorbed by roots but later relocated to the stem and leaves. A harvest of the shoots would remove the toxic compounds off site to be burned or composted to recover the metal for industrial uses. After several years of cultivation and harvest, the site would be restored at a cost much lower than the price of excavation and reburial, the standard practice for remediation of contaminated soils. For example, in field trials, the plant alpine pennycress removed zinc and cadmium from soils near a zinc smelter, and Indian mustard, native to Pakistan and India, has been effective in reducing levels of selenium salts by 50 percent in contaminated soils.

10. Which of the sentences below best expresses the essential information in the highlighted sentence in paragraph 6? Incorrect choices change the meaning in important ways or leave out essential information.

  Ⓐ Before considering phytoremediation, hyperaccumulating species of plants local to the target area must be identified.

  Ⓑ The investigation begins with an evaluation of toxic sites in the target area to determine the extent of contamination.

  Ⓒ The first step in phytoremediation is the planting of hyperaccumulating plants in the area to be cleaned up.

  Ⓓ Mines and irrigation ponds can be kept from becoming contaminated by planting hyperaccumulating species in targeted areas.

11. It can be inferred from paragraph 6 that compared with standard practices for remediation of contaminated soils, phytoremediation

  Ⓐ does not allow for the use of the removed minerals for industrial purposes

  Ⓑ can be faster to implement

  Ⓒ is equally friendly to the environment

  Ⓓ is less suitable for soils that need to be used within a short period of time

12. Why does the author mention "Indian mustard"?

  Ⓐ To warn about possible risks involved in phytoremediation

  Ⓑ To help illustrate the potential of phytoremediation

  Ⓒ To show that hyperaccumulating plants grow in many regions of the world

  Ⓓ To explain how zinc contamination can be reduced

Scientists have known for some time that certain plants, called hyperaccumulators, can concentrate minerals at levels a hundredfold or greater than normal. ■ A survey of known hyperaccumulators identified that 75 percent of them amassed nickel; cobalt, copper, zinc, manganese, lead, and cadmium are other minerals of choice. ■ Hyperaccumulators run the entire range of the plant world. ■ They may be herbs, shrubs, or trees. ■ Many members of the mustard family, spurge family, legume family, and grass family are top hyperaccumulators. Many are found in tropical and subtropical areas of the world, where accumulation of high concentrations of metals may afford some protection against plant-eating insects and microbial pathogens.

13. Look at the four squares [■] that indicate where the following sentence can be added to the passage.

Certain minerals are more likely to be accumulated in large quantities than others.

Where would the sentence best fit?

Ⓐ Scientists have known for some time that certain plants, called hyperaccumulators, can concentrate minerals at levels a hundredfold or greater than normal. **Certain minerals are more likely to be accumulated in large quantities than others.** A survey of known hyperaccumulators identified that 75 percent of them amassed nickel; cobalt, copper, zinc, manganese, lead, and cadmium are other minerals of choice. ■ Hyperaccumulators run the entire range of the plant world. ■ They may be herbs, shrubs, or trees. ■ Many members of the mustard family, spurge family, legume family, and grass family are top hyperaccumulators. Many are found in tropical and subtropical areas of the world, where accumulation of high concentrations of metals may afford some protection against plant-eating insects and microbial pathogens.

Ⓑ Scientists have known for some time that certain plants, called hyperaccumulators, can concentrate minerals at levels a hundredfold or greater than normal. ■ A survey of known hyperaccumulators identified that 75 percent of them amassed nickel; cobalt, copper, zinc, manganese, lead, and cadmium are other minerals of choice. **Certain minerals are more likely to be accumulated in large quantities than others.** Hyperaccumulators run the entire range of the plant world. ■ They may be herbs, shrubs, or trees. ■ Many members of the mustard family, spurge family, legume family, and grass family are top hyperaccumulators. Many are found in tropical and subtropical areas of the world, where accumulation of high concentrations of metals may afford some protection against plant-eating insects and microbial pathogens.

Ⓒ Scientists have known for some time that certain plants, called hyperaccumulators, can concentrate minerals at levels a hundredfold or greater than normal. ■ A survey of known hyperaccumulators identified that 75 percent of them amassed nickel; cobalt, copper, zinc, manganese, lead, and cadmium are other minerals of choice. ■ Hyperaccumulators run the entire range of the plant world. **Certain minerals are more likely to be accumulated in large quantities than others.** They may be herbs, shrubs, or trees. ■ Many members of the mustard family, spurge family, legume family, and grass family are top hyperaccumulators. Many are found in tropical and subtropical areas of the world, where accumulation of high concentrations of metals may afford some protection against plant-eating insects and microbial pathogens.

Ⓓ Scientists have known for some time that certain plants, called hyperaccumulators, can concentrate minerals at levels a hundredfold or greater than normal. ■ A survey of known hyperaccumulators identified that 75 percent of them amassed nickel; cobalt, copper, zinc, manganese, lead, and cadmium are other minerals of choice. ■ Hyperaccumulators run the entire range of the plant world. ■ They may be herbs, shrubs, or trees. **Certain minerals are more likely to be accumulated in large quantities than others.** Many members of the mustard family, spurge family, legume family, and grass family are top hyperaccumulators. Many are found in tropical and subtropical areas of the world, where accumulation of high concentrations of metals may afford some protection against plant-eating insects and microbial pathogens.

14. **Directions:** An introductory sentence for a brief summary of the passage is provided below. Complete the summary by selecting the THREE answer choices that express the most important ideas in the passage. Some sentences do not belong in the summary because they express ideas that are not presented in the passage or are minor ideas in the passage.

Write your answer choices in the spaces where they belong. You can either write the letter of your answer choice or you can copy the sentence.

Plants need to absorb certain minerals from the soil in adequate quantities for normal growth and development.

-
-
-

Answer Choices

[A] Some plants can tolerate comparatively low levels of certain minerals, but such plants are of little use for recycling nutrients back into depleted soils.

[B] When plants do not absorb sufficient amounts of essential minerals, characteristic abnormalities result.

[C] Mineral deficiencies in many plants can be cured by misting their roots with a nutrient solution or by transferring the plants to a soilless nutrient solution.

[D] Though beneficial in lower levels, high levels of salts, other minerals, and heavy metals can be harmful to plants.

[E] Because high concentrations of sodium chloride and other salts limit growth in most plants, much research has been done in an effort to develop salt-tolerant agricultural crops.

[F] Some plants are able to accumulate extremely high levels of certain minerals and thus can be used to clean up soils contaminated with toxic levels of these minerals.

Directions: Read the passage. Then answer the questions. Give yourself 20 minutes to complete this practice set.

THE ORIGIN OF THE PACIFIC ISLAND PEOPLE

The greater Pacific region, traditionally called Oceania, consists of three cultural areas: Melanesia, Micronesia, and Polynesia. Melanesia, in the southwest Pacific, contains the large islands of New Guinea, the Solomons, Vanuatu, and New Caledonia. Micronesia, the area north of Melanesia, consists primarily of small scattered islands. Polynesia is the central Pacific area in the great triangle defined by Hawaii, Easter Island, and New Zealand. Before the arrival of Europeans, the islands in the two largest cultural areas, Polynesia and Micronesia, together contained a population estimated at 700,000.

Speculation on the origin of these Pacific islanders began as soon as outsiders encountered them; in the absence of solid linguistic, archaeological, and biological data, many fanciful and mutually exclusive theories were devised. Pacific islanders were variously thought to have come from North America, South America, Egypt, Israel, and India, as well as Southeast Asia. Many older theories implicitly deprecated the navigational abilities and overall cultural creativity of the Pacific islanders. For example, British anthropologists G. Elliot Smith and W. J. Perry assumed that only Egyptians would have been skilled enough to navigate and colonize the Pacific. They inferred that the Egyptians even crossed the Pacific to found the great civilizations of the New World (North and South America). In 1947 Norwegian adventurer Thor Heyerdahl drifted on a balsa-log raft westward with the winds and currents across the Pacific from South America to prove his theory that Pacific islanders were Native Americans (also called American Indians). Later Heyerdahl suggested that the Pacific was peopled by three migrations: by Native Americans from the Pacific Northwest of North America drifting to Hawaii, by Peruvians drifting to Easter Island, and by Melanesians. In 1969 he crossed the Atlantic in an Egyptian-style reed boat to prove Egyptian influences in the Americas. Contrary to these theorists, the overwhelming evidence of physical anthropology, linguistics, and archaeology shows that the Pacific islanders came from Southeast Asia and were skilled enough as navigators to sail against the prevailing winds and currents.

The basic cultural requirements for the successful colonization of the Pacific islands include the appropriate boat-building, sailing, and navigation skills to get to the islands in the first place; domesticated plants and gardening skills suited to often marginal conditions; and a varied inventory of fishing implements and techniques. It is now generally believed that these prerequisites originated with peoples speaking Austronesian languages (a group of several hundred related languages) and began to emerge in Southeast Asia by about 5000 B.C.E. The culture of that time, based on archaeology and linguistic reconstruction, is assumed to have had a broad inventory of cultivated plants including taro, yams, banana, sugarcane, breadfruit, coconut, sago, and rice. Just as important, the culture also possessed the basic foundation for an effective maritime adaptation, including outrigger canoes and a variety of fishing techniques that could be effective for overseas voyaging.

Contrary to the arguments of some that much of the Pacific was settled by Polynesians accidentally marooned after being lost and adrift, it seems reasonable that this feat was accomplished by deliberate colonization expeditions that set out fully stocked with food and domesticated plants and animals. Detailed studies of the winds and currents using computer simulations suggest that drifting canoes would have been a most unlikely means of colonizing the Pacific. These expeditions were likely driven by population growth and political dynamics on the home islands, as well as the challenge and excitement of exploring unknown waters. Because all Polynesians, Micronesians, and many Melanesians speak Austronesian languages and grow crops derived from Southeast Asia, all these peoples most certainly derived from that region and not the New World or elsewhere. The undisputed pre-Columbian presence in Oceania of the sweet potato, which is a New World domesticate, has sometimes been used to support Heyerdahl's "American Indians in the Pacific" theories. However, this is one plant out of a long list of Southeast Asian domesticates. As Patrick Kirch, an American anthropologist, points out, rather than being brought by rafting South Americans, sweet potatoes might just have easily been brought back by returning Polynesian navigators who could have reached the west coast of South America.

Directions: Now answer the questions.

PARAGRAPH 1

The greater Pacific region, traditionally called Oceania, consists of three cultural areas: Melanesia, Micronesia, and Polynesia. Melanesia, in the southwest Pacific, contains the large islands of New Guinea, the Solomons, Vanuatu, and New Caledonia. Micronesia, the area north of Melanesia, consists primarily of small scattered islands. Polynesia is the central Pacific area in the great triangle defined by Hawaii, Easter Island, and New Zealand. Before the arrival of Europeans, the islands in the two largest cultural areas, Polynesia and Micronesia, together contained a population estimated at 700,000.

15. According to paragraph 1, all of the following are true statements about Melanesia, Micronesia, and Polynesia EXCEPT:

    Ⓐ Collectively, these regions are traditionally known as Oceania.
    Ⓑ The islands of Micronesia are small and spread out.
    Ⓒ Hawaii, Easter Island, and New Zealand mark the boundaries of Polynesia.
    Ⓓ Melanesia is situated to the north of Micronesia.

Speculation on the origin of these Pacific islanders began as soon as outsiders encountered them; in the absence of solid linguistic, archaeological, and biological data, many fanciful and mutually exclusive theories were devised. Pacific islanders were variously thought to have come from North America, South America, Egypt, Israel, and India, as well as Southeast Asia. Many older theories implicitly deprecated the navigational abilities and overall cultural creativity of the Pacific islanders. For example, British anthropologists G. Elliot Smith and W. J. Perry assumed that only Egyptians would have been skilled enough to navigate and colonize the Pacific. They inferred that the Egyptians even crossed the Pacific to found the great civilizations of the New World (North and South America). In 1947 Norwegian adventurer Thor Heyerdahl drifted on a balsa-log raft westward with the winds and currents across the Pacific from South America to prove his theory that Pacific islanders were Native Americans (also called American Indians). Later Heyerdahl suggested that the Pacific was peopled by three migrations: by Native Americans from the Pacific Northwest of North America drifting to Hawaii, by Peruvians drifting to Easter Island, and by Melanesians. In 1969 he crossed the Atlantic in an Egyptian-style reed boat to prove Egyptian influences in the Americas. Contrary to these theorists, the overwhelming evidence of physical anthropology, linguistics, and archaeology shows that the Pacific islanders came from Southeast Asia and were skilled enough as navigators to sail against the prevailing winds and currents.

16. By stating that the theories are "mutually exclusive" the author means that

Ⓐ if one of the theories is true, then all the others must be false
Ⓑ the differences between the theories are unimportant
Ⓒ taken together, the theories cover all possibilities
Ⓓ the theories support each other

17. The word "overwhelming" in the passage is closest in meaning to

Ⓐ powerful
Ⓑ favorable
Ⓒ current
Ⓓ reasonable

18. According to paragraph 2, which of the following led some early researchers to believe that the Pacific islanders originally came from Egypt?

Ⓐ Egyptians were known to have founded other great civilizations.
Ⓑ Sailors from other parts of the world were believed to lack the skills needed to travel across the ocean.
Ⓒ Linguistic, archaeological, and biological data connected the islands to Egypt.
Ⓓ Egyptian accounts claimed responsibility for colonizing the Pacific as well as the Americas.

19. Which of the following can be inferred from paragraph 2 about early theories of where the first inhabitants of the Pacific islands came from?

    Ⓐ They were generally based on solid evidence.

    Ⓑ They tried to account for the origin of the characteristic features of the languages spoken by Pacific islanders.

    Ⓒ They assumed that the peoples living in Southeast Asia did not have the skills needed to sail to the Pacific islands.

    Ⓓ They questioned the ideas of G. Elliot Smith and W. J. Perry.

PARAGRAPH 3

The basic cultural requirements for the successful colonization of the Pacific islands include the appropriate boat-building, sailing, and navigation skills to get to the islands in the first place; domesticated plants and gardening skills suited to often marginal conditions; and a varied inventory of fishing implements and techniques. It is now generally believed that these prerequisites originated with peoples speaking Austronesian languages (a group of several hundred related languages) and began to emerge in Southeast Asia by about 5000 B.C.E. The culture of that time, based on archaeology and linguistic reconstruction, is assumed to have had a broad inventory of cultivated plants including taro, yams, banana, sugarcane, breadfruit, coconut, sago, and rice. Just as important, the culture also possessed the basic foundation for an effective maritime adaptation, including outrigger canoes and a variety of fishing techniques that could be effective for overseas voyaging.

20. The word "implements" in the passage is closest in meaning to

    Ⓐ skills

    Ⓑ tools

    Ⓒ opportunities

    Ⓓ practices

21. All of the following are mentioned in paragraph 3 as required for successful colonization of the Pacific islands EXCEPT

    Ⓐ knowledge of various Austronesian languages

    Ⓑ a variety of fishing techniques

    Ⓒ navigational skills

    Ⓓ knowledge of plant cultivation

22. In paragraph 3, why does the author provide information about the types of crops grown and boats used in Southeast Asia during the period around 5000 B.C.E.?

    Ⓐ To evaluate the relative importance of agriculture and fishing to early Austronesian peoples

    Ⓑ To illustrate the effectiveness of archaeological and linguistic methods in discovering details about life in ancient times

    Ⓒ To contrast living conditions on the continent of Asia with living conditions on the Pacific islands

    Ⓓ To demonstrate that people from this region had the skills and resources necessary to travel to and survive on the Pacific islands

PARAGRAPH 4

Contrary to the arguments of some that much of the Pacific was settled by Polynesians accidentally marooned after being lost and adrift, it seems reasonable that this feat was accomplished by deliberate colonization expeditions that set out fully stocked with food and domesticated plants and animals. Detailed studies of the winds and currents using computer simulations suggest that drifting canoes would have been a most unlikely means of colonizing the Pacific. These expeditions were likely driven by population growth and political dynamics on the home islands, as well as the challenge and excitement of exploring unknown waters. Because all Polynesians, Micronesians, and many Melanesians speak Austronesian languages and grow crops derived from Southeast Asia, all these peoples most certainly derived from that region and not the New World or elsewhere. The undisputed pre-Columbian presence in Oceania of the sweet potato, which is a New World domesticate, has sometimes been used to support Heyerdahl's "American Indians in the Pacific" theories. However, this is one plant out of a long list of Southeast Asian domesticates. As Patrick Kirch, an American anthropologist, points out, rather than being brought by rafting South Americans, sweet potatoes might just have easily been brought back by returning Polynesian navigators who could have reached the west coast of South America.

23. Which of the sentences below best expresses the essential information in the highlighted sentence in paragraph 4? Incorrect choices change the meaning in important ways or leave out essential information.

   Ⓐ Some people have argued that the Pacific was settled by traders who became lost while transporting domesticated plants and animals.

   Ⓑ The original Polynesian settlers were probably marooned on the islands, but they may have been joined later by carefully prepared colonization expeditions.

   Ⓒ Although it seems reasonable to believe that colonization expeditions would set out fully stocked, this is contradicted by much of the evidence.

   Ⓓ The settlement of the Pacific islands was probably intentional and well planned rather than accidental as some people have proposed.

24. The word "undisputed" in the passage is closest in meaning to

   Ⓐ mysterious
   Ⓑ unexpected
   Ⓒ acknowledged
   Ⓓ significant

25. According to paragraph 4, which of the following is NOT an explanation for why a group of people might have wanted to colonize the Pacific islands?

   Ⓐ As their numbers increased, they needed additional territory.
   Ⓑ The winds and currents made the islands easy to reach.
   Ⓒ The political situation at home made emigration desirable.
   Ⓓ They found exploration challenging and exciting.

26. Why does the author mention the views of "Patrick Kirch"?

  Ⓐ To present evidence in favor of Heyerdahl's idea about American Indians reaching Oceania

  Ⓑ To emphasize the familiarity of Pacific islanders with crops from many different regions of the world

  Ⓒ To indicate that a supposed proof for Heyerdahl's theory has an alternative explanation

  Ⓓ To demonstrate that some of the same crops were cultivated in both South America and Oceania

PARAGRAPH 2

Speculation on the origin of these Pacific islanders began as soon as outsiders encountered them; in the absence of solid linguistic, archaeological, and biological data, many fanciful and mutually exclusive theories were devised. Pacific islanders were variously thought to have come from North America, South America, Egypt, Israel, and India, as well as Southeast Asia. ■ Many older theories implicitly deprecated the navigational abilities and overall cultural creativity of the Pacific islanders. ■ For example, British anthropologists G. Elliot Smith and W. J. Perry assumed that only Egyptians would have been skilled enough to navigate and colonize the Pacific. ■ They inferred that the Egyptians even crossed the Pacific to found the great civilizations of the New World (North and South America). ■ In 1947 Norwegian adventurer Thor Heyerdahl drifted on a balsa-log raft westward with the winds and currents across the Pacific from South America to prove his theory that Pacific islanders were Native Americans (also called American Indians). Later Heyerdahl suggested that the Pacific was peopled by three migrations: by Native Americans from the Pacific Northwest of North America drifting to Hawaii, by Peruvians drifting to Easter Island, and by Melanesians. In 1969 he crossed the Atlantic in an Egyptian-style reed boat to prove Egyptian influences in the Americas. Contrary to these theorists, the overwhelming evidence of physical anthropology, linguistics, and archaeology shows that the Pacific islanders came from Southeast Asia and were skilled enough as navigators to sail against the prevailing winds and currents.

27. Look at the four squares [■] that indicate where the following sentence can be added to the passage.

  Later theories concentrated on journeys in the other direction.

  Where would the sentence best fit?

  Ⓐ Speculation on the origin of these Pacific islanders began as soon as outsiders encountered them; in the absence of solid linguistic, archaeological, and biological data, many fanciful and mutually exclusive theories were devised. Pacific islanders were variously thought to have come from North America, South America, Egypt, Israel, and India, as well as Southeast Asia. **Later theories concentrated on journeys in the other direction.** Many older theories implicitly deprecated the navigational abilities and overall cultural creativity of the Pacific islanders. ■ For example, British anthropologists G. Elliot Smith and W. J. Perry assumed that only Egyptians would have been skilled enough to navigate and colonize the Pacific. ■ They inferred that the Egyptians even crossed the Pacific to found the great civilizations of the New World (North and South America). ■ In 1947 Norwegian adventurer Thor Heyerdahl drifted on a balsa-log raft westward with the winds and currents across the Pacific from South America to prove his theory that Pacific islanders were Native Americans (also called American Indians). Later Heyerdahl suggested that the Pacific was peopled by three migrations: by Native Americans from the Pacific Northwest of North America drifting to Hawaii, by Peruvians drifting to Easter Island, and by Melanesians. In 1969 he crossed the Atlantic in an Egyptian-style reed boat to prove Egyptian influences in the Americas. Contrary to these theorists, the overwhelming evidence of physical anthropology, linguistics, and archaeology shows that the Pacific islanders came from Southeast Asia and were skilled enough as navigators to sail against the prevailing winds and currents.

Ⓑ Speculation on the origin of these Pacific islanders began as soon as outsiders encountered them; in the absence of solid linguistic, archaeological, and biological data, many fanciful and mutually exclusive theories were devised. Pacific islanders were variously thought to have come from North America, South America, Egypt, Israel, and India, as well as Southeast Asia. ■ Many older theories implicitly deprecated the navigational abilities and overall cultural creativity of the Pacific islanders. **Later theories concentrated on journeys in the other direction.** For example, British anthropologists G. Elliot Smith and W. J. Perry assumed that only Egyptians would have been skilled enough to navigate and colonize the Pacific. ■ They inferred that the Egyptians even crossed the Pacific to found the great civilizations of the New World (North and South America). ■ In 1947 Norwegian adventurer Thor Heyerdahl drifted on a balsa-log raft westward with the winds and currents across the Pacific from South America to prove his theory that Pacific islanders were Native Americans (also called American Indians). Later Heyerdahl suggested that the Pacific was peopled by three migrations: by Native Americans from the Pacific Northwest of North America drifting to Hawaii, by Peruvians drifting to Easter Island, and by Melanesians. In 1969 he crossed the Atlantic in an Egyptian-style reed boat to prove Egyptian influences in the Americas. Contrary to these theorists, the overwhelming evidence of physical anthropology, linguistics, and archaeology shows that the Pacific islanders came from Southeast Asia and were skilled enough as navigators to sail against the prevailing winds and currents.

Ⓒ Speculation on the origin of these Pacific islanders began as soon as outsiders encountered them; in the absence of solid linguistic, archaeological, and biological data, many fanciful and mutually exclusive theories were devised. Pacific islanders were variously thought to have come from North America, South America, Egypt, Israel, and India, as well as Southeast Asia. ■ Many older theories implicitly deprecated the navigational abilities and overall cultural creativity of the Pacific islanders. ■ For example, British anthropologists G. Elliot Smith and W. J. Perry assumed that only Egyptians would have been skilled enough to navigate and colonize the Pacific. **Later theories concentrated on journeys in the other direction.** They inferred that the Egyptians even crossed the Pacific to found the great civilizations of the New World (North and South America). ■ In 1947 Norwegian adventurer Thor Heyerdahl drifted on a balsa-log raft westward with the winds and currents across the Pacific from South America to prove his theory that Pacific islanders were Native Americans (also called American Indians). Later Heyerdahl suggested that the Pacific was peopled by three migrations: by Native Americans from the Pacific Northwest of North America drifting to Hawaii, by Peruvians drifting to Easter Island, and by Melanesians. In 1969 he crossed the Atlantic in an Egyptian-style reed boat to prove Egyptian influences in the Americas. Contrary to these theorists, the overwhelming evidence of physical anthropology, linguistics, and archaeology shows that the Pacific islanders came from Southeast Asia and were skilled enough as navigators to sail against the prevailing winds and currents.

Ⓓ Speculation on the origin of these Pacific islanders began as soon as outsiders encountered them; in the absence of solid linguistic, archaeological, and biological data, many fanciful and mutually exclusive theories were devised. Pacific islanders were variously thought to have come from North America, South America, Egypt, Israel, and India, as well as Southeast Asia. ■ Many older theories implicitly deprecated the navigational abilities and overall cultural creativity of the Pacific islanders. ■ For example, British anthropologists G. Elliot Smith and W. J. Perry assumed that only Egyptians would have been skilled enough to navigate and colonize the Pacific. ■ They inferred that the Egyptians even crossed the Pacific to found the great civilizations of the New World (North and South America). **Later theories concentrated on journeys in the other direction.** In 1947 Norwegian adventurer Thor Heyerdahl drifted on a balsa-log raft westward with the winds and currents across the Pacific from South America to prove his theory that Pacific islanders were Native Americans (also called American Indians). Later Heyerdahl suggested that the Pacific was peopled by three migrations: by Native Americans from the Pacific Northwest of North America drifting to Hawaii, by Peruvians drifting to Easter Island, and by Melanesians. In 1969 he crossed the Atlantic in an Egyptian-style reed boat to prove Egyptian influences in the Americas. Contrary to these theorists, the overwhelming evidence of physical anthropology, linguistics, and archaeology shows that the Pacific islanders came from Southeast Asia and were skilled enough as navigators to sail against the prevailing winds and currents.

28. **Directions:** An introductory sentence for a brief summary of the passage is provided below. Complete the summary by selecting the THREE answer choices that express the most important ideas in the passage. Some sentences do not belong in the summary because they express ideas that are not presented in the passage or are minor ideas in the passage.

    Write your answer choices in the spaces where they belong. You can either write the letter of your answer choice or you can copy the sentence.

    > **Together, Melanesia, Micronesia, and Polynesia make up the region described as the Pacific islands, or Oceania.**
    >
    > ●
    >
    > ●
    >
    > ●

Answer Choices

[A] Many theories about how inhabitants first came to the islands have been proposed, including the idea that North and South Americans simply drifted across the ocean.

[B] Although early colonizers of the islands probably came from agriculture-based societies, they were obliged to adopt an economy based on fishing.

[C] New evidence suggests that, rather than being isolated, Pacific islanders engaged in trade and social interaction with peoples living in Southeast Asia.

[D] Computer simulations of the winds and currents in the Pacific have shown that reaching the Pacific Islands was probably much easier than previously thought.

[E] It is now believed that the process of colonization required a great deal of skill, determination, and planning and could not have happened by chance.

[F] Using linguistic and archaeological evidence, anthropologists have determined that the first Pacific islanders were Austronesian people from Southeast Asia.

Directions: Read the passage. Then answer the questions. Give yourself 20 minutes to complete this practice set.

THE CAMBRIAN EXPLOSION

The geologic timescale is marked by significant geologic and biological events, including the origin of Earth about 4.6 billion years ago, the origin of life about 3.5 billion years ago, the origin of eukaryotic life-forms (living things that have cells with true nuclei) about 1.5 billion years ago, and the origin of animals about 0.6 billion years ago. The last event marks the beginning of the Cambrian period. Animals originated relatively late in the history of Earth—in only the last 10 percent of Earth's history. During a geologically brief 100-million-year period, all modern animal groups (along with other animals that are now extinct) evolved. This rapid origin and diversification of animals is often referred to as "the Cambrian explosion."

Scientists have asked important questions about this explosion for more than a century. Why did it occur so late in the history of Earth? The origin of multicellular forms of life seems a relatively simple step compared to the origin of life itself. Why does the fossil record not document the series of evolutionary changes during the evolution of animals? Why did animal life evolve so quickly? Paleontologists continue to search the fossil record for answers to these questions.

One interpretation regarding the absence of fossils during this important 100-million-year period is that early animals were soft bodied and simply did not fossilize. Fossilization of soft-bodied animals is less likely than fossilization of hard-bodied animals, but it does occur. Conditions that promote fossilization of soft-bodied animals include very rapid covering by sediments that create an environment that discourages decomposition. In fact, fossil beds containing soft-bodied animals have been known for many years.

The Ediacara fossil formation, which contains the oldest known animal fossils, consists exclusively of soft-bodied forms. Although named after a site in Australia, the Ediacara formation is worldwide in distribution and dates to Precambrian times. This 700-million-year-old formation gives few clues to the origins of modern animals, however, because paleontologists believe it represents an evolutionary experiment that failed. It contains no ancestors of modern animal groups.

A slightly younger fossil formation containing animal remains is the Tommotian formation, named after a locale in Russia. It dates to the very early Cambrian period, and it also contains only soft-bodied forms. At one time, the animals present in these fossil beds were assigned to various modern animal groups, but most paleontologists now agree that all Tommotian fossils represent unique body forms that arose in the early Cambrian period and disappeared before the end of the period, leaving no descendants in modern animal groups.

A third fossil formation containing both soft-bodied and hard-bodied animals provides evidence of the result of the Cambrian explosion. This fossil formation, called the Burgess Shale, is in Yoho National Park in the Canadian Rocky Mountains of British Columbia. Shortly after the Cambrian explosion, mud slides rapidly buried thousands of marine animals under conditions that favored fossilization. These fossil beds provide evidence of about 32 modern animal groups, plus about 20 other animal body forms that are so different from any modern animals that they cannot be assigned to any one of the modern groups. These unassignable animals include a large swimming predator called *Anomalocaris* and a soft-bodied animal called *Wiwaxia*, which ate detritus or algae. The Burgess Shale formation also has fossils of many extinct representatives of modern animal groups. For example, a well-known Burgess Shale animal called *Sidneyia* is a representative of a previously unknown group of arthropods (a category of animals that includes insects, spiders, mites, and crabs).

Fossil formations like the Burgess Shale show that evolution cannot always be thought of as a slow progression. The Cambrian explosion involved rapid evolutionary diversification, followed by the extinction of many unique animals. Why was this evolution so rapid? No one really knows. Many zoologists believe that it was because so many ecological niches were available with virtually no competition from existing species. Will zoologists ever know the evolutionary sequences in the Cambrian explosion? Perhaps another ancient fossil bed of soft-bodied animals from 600-million-year-old seas is awaiting discovery.

Directions: Now answer the questions.

PARAGRAPH 1

The geologic timescale is marked by significant geologic and biological events, including the origin of Earth about 4.6 billion years ago, the origin of life about 3.5 billion years ago, the origin of eukaryotic life-forms (living things that have cells with true nuclei) about 1.5 billion years ago, and the origin of animals about 0.6 billion years ago. The last event marks the beginning of the Cambrian period. Animals originated relatively late in the history of Earth—in only the last 10 percent of Earth's history. During a geologically brief 100-million-year period, all modern animal groups (along with other animals that are now extinct) evolved. This rapid origin and diversification of animals is often referred to as "the Cambrian explosion."

29. The word "significant" in the passage is closest in meaning to

  Ⓐ numerous
  Ⓑ important
  Ⓒ unexplained
  Ⓓ sudden

30. The word "relatively" in the passage is closest in meaning to

  Ⓐ surprisingly
  Ⓑ collectively
  Ⓒ comparatively
  Ⓓ characteristically

31. The word "diversification" in the passage is closest in meaning to

  Ⓐ emergence of many varieties
  Ⓑ steady decline in number
  Ⓒ gradual increase in body size
  Ⓓ sudden disappearance

32. The period discussed in the passage is referred to as an "explosion" because it

Ⓐ occurred 0.6 billion years ago, late in Earth's history
Ⓑ was characterized by the unusually fast evolution of many new life-forms
Ⓒ was characterized by widespread animal extinction
Ⓓ was characterized by violent volcanic eruptions

PARAGRAPHS 2 & 3

Scientists have asked important questions about this explosion for more than a century. Why did it occur so late in the history of Earth? The origin of multicellular forms of life seems a relatively simple step compared to the origin of life itself. Why does the fossil record not document the series of evolutionary changes during the evolution of animals? Why did animal life evolve so quickly? Paleontologists continue to search the fossil record for answers to these questions.

One interpretation regarding the absence of fossils during this important 100-million-year period is that early animals were soft bodied and simply did not fossilize. Fossilization of soft-bodied animals is less likely than fossilization of hard-bodied animals, but it does occur. Conditions that promote fossilization of soft-bodied animals include very rapid covering by sediments that create an environment that discourages decomposition. In fact, fossil beds containing soft-bodied animals have been known for many years.

33. According to paragraph 2, which of the following is NOT a question that paleontologists asked about the Cambrian explosion?

Ⓐ Why was the origin of life a simple step in Earth's history?
Ⓑ Why did it take so long for multicellular organisms to develop?
Ⓒ Why did animal life evolve so rapidly?
Ⓓ Why does the fossil record lack evidence of animal evolution during that time?

34. Which of the following best describes the relationship between paragraph 2 and paragraph 3?

Ⓐ Paragraph 2 puts forward several scientific claims, one of which is rejected in paragraph 3.
Ⓑ Paragraph 2 poses several questions, and paragraph 3 offers a possible answer to one of them.
Ⓒ Paragraph 2 presents outdated traditional views, while paragraph 3 presents the current scientific conclusions.
Ⓓ Paragraph 2 introduces a generalization that is illustrated by specific examples in paragraph 3.

35. The word "promote" in the passage is closest in meaning to

Ⓐ complicate
Ⓑ prevent
Ⓒ encourage
Ⓓ affect

PARAGRAPH 4

The Ediacara fossil formation, which contains the oldest known animal fossils, consists exclusively of soft-bodied forms. Although named after a site in Australia, the Ediacara formation is worldwide in distribution and dates to Precambrian times. This 700-million-year-old formation gives few clues to the origins of modern animals, however, because paleontologists believe it represents an evolutionary experiment that failed. It contains no ancestors of modern animal groups.

36. Which of the following is NOT mentioned in paragraph 4 as being true of the Ediacara formation?

Ⓐ It contains fossils that date back to the Precambrian period.

Ⓑ It contains only soft-bodied animal fossils.

Ⓒ It is located on a single site in Australia.

Ⓓ It does not contain any fossils of the ancestors of modern animals.

PARAGRAPH 5

A slightly younger fossil formation containing animal remains is the Tommotian formation, named after a locale in Russia. It dates to the very early Cambrian period, and it also contains only soft-bodied forms. At one time, the animals present in these fossil beds were assigned to various modern animal groups, but most paleontologists now agree that all Tommotian fossils represent unique body forms that arose in the early Cambrian period and disappeared before the end of the period, leaving no descendants in modern animal groups.

37. Which of the sentences below best expresses the essential information in the highlighted sentence in paragraph 5? Incorrect choices change the meaning in important ways or leave out essential information.

Ⓐ The animals found in the Tommotian fossil bed were once thought to belong to a variety of modern animal groups, but now they are thought to have descended from a single group.

Ⓑ Animals in the Tommotian fossil beds were initially assigned to modern animal groups but are now thought to belong to groups that emerged and died out during the Cambrian period.

Ⓒ Though at first they thought otherwise, paleontologists now agree that the animals in the Tommotian formation have body forms from which modern animals have descended.

Ⓓ It is unclear whether the Tommotian fossils from the early Cambrian period represent unique body forms or whether they should be assigned to various modern animal groups.

PARAGRAPH 6

A third fossil formation containing both soft-bodied and hard-bodied animals provides evidence of the result of the Cambrian explosion. This fossil formation, called the Burgess Shale, is in Yoho National Park in the Canadian Rocky Mountains of British Columbia. Shortly after the Cambrian explosion, mud slides rapidly buried thousands of marine animals under conditions that favored fossilization. These fossil beds provide evidence of about 32 modern animal groups, plus about 20 other animal body forms that are so different from any modern animals that they cannot be assigned to any one of the modern groups. These unassignable animals include a large swimming predator called Anomalocaris and a soft-bodied animal called Wiwaxia, which ate detritus or algae. The Burgess Shale formation also has fossils of many extinct representatives of modern animal groups. For example, a well-known Burgess Shale animal called Sidneyia is a representative of a previously unknown group of arthropods (a category of animals that includes insects, spiders, mites, and crabs).

38. Why does the author mention "Anomalocaris" and "Wiwaxia"?

(A) To contrast predators with animals that eat plants such as algae

(B) To question the effects of rapid mud slides on fossilization

(C) To suggest that much is still unknown about animals found in the Burgess Shale

(D) To provide examples of fossils that cannot be assigned to a modern animal group

39. "Sidneyia" is an example of

(A) a relative of Anomalocaris and Wiwaxia

(B) a previously unknown Burgess Shale animal

(C) an extinct member of a currently existing category of animals

(D) an animal that cannot be assigned to any modern animal group

PARAGRAPH 7

Fossil formations like the Burgess Shale show that evolution cannot always be thought of as a slow progression. The Cambrian explosion involved rapid evolutionary diversification, followed by the extinction of many unique animals. Why was this evolution so rapid? No one really knows. Many zoologists believe that it was because so many ecological niches were available with virtually no competition from existing species. Will zoologists ever know the evolutionary sequences in the Cambrian explosion? Perhaps another ancient fossil bed of soft-bodied animals from 600-million-year-old seas is awaiting discovery.

40. What can be inferred from paragraph 7 about why the Cambrian explosion is so unusual?

(A) It generated new ecological niches through the extinction of many unique animals.

(B) It was a period of rapid evolution, and evolution is often thought of as a slow process.

(C) It is a period whose evolutionary sequences are clearly marked.

(D) It generated a very large number of ancient fossil beds containing soft-bodied animals.

P
A
R
A
G
R
A
P
H

3

One interpretation regarding the absence of fossils during this important 100-million-year period is that early animals were soft bodied and simply did not fossilize. ■ Fossilization of soft-bodied animals is less likely than fossilization of hard-bodied animals, but it does occur. ■ Conditions that promote fossilization of soft-bodied animals include very rapid covering by sediments that create an environment that discourages decomposition. ■ In fact, fossil beds containing soft-bodied animals have been known for many years. ■

41. Look at the four squares [■] that indicate where the following sentence can be added to the passage.

It is relatively rare because the fossilization of soft-bodied animals requires a special environment.

Where would the sentence best fit?

Ⓐ One interpretation regarding the absence of fossils during this important 100-million-year period is that early animals were soft bodied and simply did not fossilize. **It is relatively rare because the fossilization of soft-bodied animals requires a special environment.** Fossilization of soft-bodied animals is less likely than fossilization of hard-bodied animals, but it does occur. ■ Conditions that promote fossilization of soft-bodied animals include very rapid covering by sediments that create an environment that discourages decomposition. ■ In fact, fossil beds containing soft-bodied animals have been known for many years. ■

Ⓑ One interpretation regarding the absence of fossils during this important 100-million-year period is that early animals were soft bodied and simply did not fossilize. ■ Fossilization of soft-bodied animals is less likely than fossilization of hard-bodied animals, but it does occur. **It is relatively rare because the fossilization of soft-bodied animals requires a special environment.** Conditions that promote fossilization of soft-bodied animals include very rapid covering by sediments that create an environment that discourages decomposition. ■ In fact, fossil beds containing soft-bodied animals have been known for many years. ■

Ⓒ One interpretation regarding the absence of fossils during this important 100-million-year period is that early animals were soft bodied and simply did not fossilize. ■ Fossilization of soft-bodied animals is less likely than fossilization of hard-bodied animals, but it does occur. ■ Conditions that promote fossilization of soft-bodied animals include very rapid covering by sediments that create an environment that discourages decomposition. **It is relatively rare because the fossilization of soft-bodied animals requires a special environment.** In fact, fossil beds containing soft-bodied animals have been known for many years. ■

Ⓓ One interpretation regarding the absence of fossils during this important 100-million-year period is that early animals were soft bodied and simply did not fossilize. ■ Fossilization of soft-bodied animals is less likely than fossilization of hard-bodied animals, but it does occur. ■ Conditions that promote fossilization of soft-bodied animals include very rapid covering by sediments that create an environment that discourages decomposition. ■ In fact, fossil beds containing soft-bodied animals have been known for many years. **It is relatively rare because the fossilization of soft-bodied animals requires a special environment.**

42. **Directions:** An introductory sentence for a brief summary of the passage is provided below. Complete the summary by selecting the THREE answer choices that express the most important ideas in the passage. Some sentences do not belong in the summary because they express ideas that are not presented in the passage or are minor ideas in the passage.

    Write your answer choices in the spaces where they belong. You can either write the letter of your answer choice or you can copy the sentence.

    The term "Cambrian explosion" refers to the geologically brief period during which all modern animal groups evolved.

    -
    -
    -

Answer Choices

Ⓐ The Cambrian period is significant because it marks the emergence of eukaryotic life-forms—organisms that have cells with true nuclei.

Ⓑ Little is known about the stages of evolution during the Cambrian period, in part because early animals were soft bodied and could fossilize only under particular conditions.

Ⓒ The Ediacara fossil formation provides the most information about the Cambrian explosion, while the earlier Tommotian and Burgess Shale formations give clues about Precambrian evolution.

Ⓓ While animal fossils from before the Cambrian explosion have no modern descendants, many animals that evolved during the Cambrian explosion can be assigned to modern groups.

Ⓔ Zoologists are awaiting the discovery of a 600-million-year-old fossil formation in order to be able to form a theory of how animal evolution progressed.

Ⓕ Although the reasons for the rapid evolution of animals during the Cambrian period are not known, one proposed explanation is an abundance of niches with a lack of competitors.

LISTENING

This section measures your ability to understand conversations and lectures in English.

Listen to each conversation and lecture only one time. After each conversation and lecture, you will answer some questions about it. Answer each question based on what is stated or implied by the speakers.

You may take notes while you listen and use your notes to help you answer the questions. Your notes will **not** be scored.

In some questions you will see this icon: 🎧. This means that you will hear, but not see, the question.

Answer each question before moving on. Do not return to previous questions.

It will take about 60 minutes to listen to the conversations and lectures and answer the questions about them.

Directions: Listen to Track 22.

Directions: Now answer the questions.

1. What do the speakers mainly discuss?

   Ⓐ Why the woman has little in common with her roommates
   Ⓑ How the woman can keep up in her academic studies
   Ⓒ The woman's adjustment to life at the university
   Ⓓ The woman's decision to transfer to another university

2. Why does the woman mention her hometown?

   Ⓐ To draw a contrast to her current situation
   Ⓑ To acknowledge that she is accustomed to living in big cities
   Ⓒ To indicate that she has known some people on campus for a long time
   Ⓓ To emphasize her previous success in academic studies

3. What does the woman imply about the incident that occurred in her sociology class?

   Ⓐ She was embarrassed because she gave an incorrect answer.
   Ⓑ She was upset because the professor seemed to ignore her.
   Ⓒ She was confused by the organization of the professor's lecture.
   Ⓓ She was surprised by the comments of the other students.

4. According to the counselor, why should the woman visit her professor's office? *Choose 2 answers.*

   Ⓐ To offer a compliment
   Ⓑ To offer to help other students
   Ⓒ To introduce herself
   Ⓓ To suggest ways of making the class more personal

5. What does the woman imply about joining the string quartet?

    Ⓐ It would enable her to continue a hobby she gave up when she was ten.

    Ⓑ It would allow her to spend more time in her major area of study.

    Ⓒ It would help her stop worrying about her academic studies.

    Ⓓ It would be a way to meet students with similar interests.

Directions: Listen to Track 23.

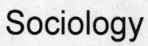

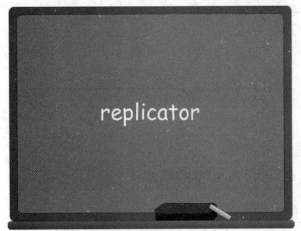

replicator

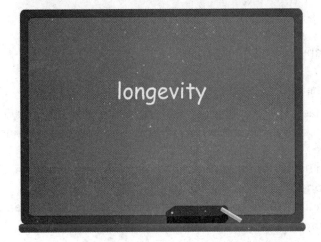

longevity

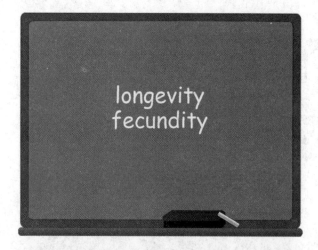

Directions: Now answer the questions.

6. What is the main purpose of the lecture?

 (A) To introduce a method that can help students remember new information

 (B) To introduce a way to study how information passes from one person to another

 (C) To explain the differences between biological information and cultural information

 (D) To explain the differences between stories, songs, and other pieces of information

7. Why does the professor tell the story about alligators?

 (A) To explain the difference between true and false stories

 (B) To draw an analogy between alligator reproduction and cultural transmission

 (C) To give an example of a piece of information that functions as a meme

 (D) To show how a story can gradually change into a song

8. According to the professor, which of the following are examples of meme transfer? *Choose 2 answers.*

    [A] Telling familiar stories
    [B] Sharing feelings
    [C] Composing original music
    [D] Learning a scientific theory

9. What example does the professor give of a meme's longevity?

    (A) A story has been changing since it first appeared in the 1930s.
    (B) A person remembers a story for many years.
    (C) A gene is passed on through many generations without changing.
    (D) A song quickly becomes popular all over the world.

10. What does the professor compare to a housefly laying many eggs?

    (A) A child learning many different ideas from his or her parents
    (B) Alligators reproducing in New York sewers
    (C) Different people remembering different versions of a story
    (D) A person singing the "Twinkle, twinkle" song many times

11. Listen to Track 24.

    (A) To explain why some memes do not change much
    (B) To ask the students for their opinion about songs as memes
    (C) To acknowledge a problem with the meme theory
    (D) To ask the students to test an idea about memes

Note: The actual lecture contains color images. The colors from one image are discussed by the professor. You do not need to see the colors to understand the lecture or to answer the questions.

Directions: Listen to Track 25.

South Pole—Aitken Basin

Directions: Now answer the questions.

12. What is the main purpose of the lecture?

   Ⓐ To explain why scientists disagree about the age of the Moon
   Ⓑ To present arguments in favor of another Moon landing
   Ⓒ To explain how scientists discovered a crater on the far side of the Moon
   Ⓓ To review some findings of a recent mission to the Moon

13. What does the professor imply about the spacecraft Clementine?

   Ⓐ It sent back the first color photographs of the Moon.
   Ⓑ It was powered by solar energy.
   Ⓒ It landed on the far side of the Moon.
   Ⓓ It flew over the Moon's polar regions.

14. Why does the professor mention the Moon's mantle?

   Ⓐ To explain how scientists are able to estimate the age of meteor impacts
   Ⓑ To indicate what part of the Moon could provide key evidence about the Moon's composition
   Ⓒ To explain how scientists know that meteors penetrate the Moon's crust
   Ⓓ To point out an obvious difference between the Moon and Earth

15. Why is the South Pole–Aitken Basin thought to be exceptionally old?

   Ⓐ The walls of the Basin are more reflective than those of most other craters.
   Ⓑ Testing of rocks from the Basin's floor proved them to be as old as the Moon itself.
   Ⓒ Many small craters have been detected at the bottom of the Basin.
   Ⓓ A large amount of dust has been detected in and around the Basin.

16. Why does the professor consider it important to find out if water ice exists on the Moon? *Choose 2 answers.*

    A Water ice could be processed to provide breathable air for astronauts.

    B One component of water ice could be used as a fuel for rockets.

    C Water ice could contain evidence of primitive life on the Moon.

    D Water ice could be tested to find out what type of meteors crashed into the Moon.

17. Listen to Track 26.

    Ⓐ It is likely that the current age estimates for the South Pole–Aitken Basin are based on incorrect assumptions.

    Ⓑ It is disappointing how little the technology to analyze Moon rocks has advanced since the days of the Moon landings.

    Ⓒ Too few of the original Moon-rock samples were dated accurately.

    Ⓓ It is important to obtain a more precise determination of the Moon's age.

Directions: Listen to Track 27.

Directions: Now answer the questions.

18. What is the conversation mainly about?

    Ⓐ An assignment about which the student would like advice

    Ⓑ Concerns as to whether the student should be in the professor's course

    Ⓒ The selection of films to be viewed by students in a film theory course

    Ⓓ The structure and sequence of courses in the Film Department

19. What is the professor's attitude toward the student's high school film course?

    Ⓐ He does not consider it satisfactory preparation for the class he teaches.

    Ⓑ He does not think that literary works should be discussed in film classes.

    Ⓒ He believes that this type of course often confuses inexperienced students.

    Ⓓ He feels that the approach taken in this course is the best way to learn about film.

20 Why was the student permitted to sign up for the professor's film theory course?

    Ⓐ Her high school course fulfilled the requirement for previous course work.

    Ⓑ The computer system that usually blocks students was not working properly.

    Ⓒ An employee in the department did not follow instructions.

    Ⓓ The professor made an exception in her case.

21. Why does the professor decide to allow the student to remain in his class?
Choose 2 answers.

    Ⓐ She needs to take the course in order to graduate.

    Ⓑ He is impressed with her eagerness to continue.

    Ⓒ She convinces him that she does have adequate preparation for the course.

    Ⓓ He learns that she is not studying film as her main course of study.

22. What does the professor advise the student to do in order to keep up with the class she is in?

(A) Take the introductory course
(B) Watch some video recordings
(C) Do extra reading
(D) Drop out of her marketing class

Directions: Listen to Track 28.

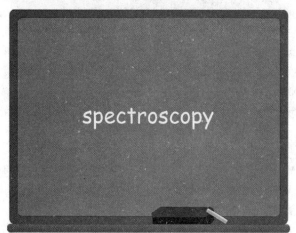

Directions: Now answer the questions.

23. What is the main purpose of the lecture?

   Ⓐ To discuss recent innovations in laboratory equipment
   Ⓑ To give an example of a practical use for a particular scientific technique
   Ⓒ To familiarize students with the chemical composition of paint pigments
   Ⓓ To show how researchers were able to restore a particular work of art

24. What does the professor imply when he mentions an art historian?

   Ⓐ Art historians have been learning how to use spectroscopes.
   Ⓑ Scientists need to learn how art historians analyze paintings.
   Ⓒ Confirming the authenticity of artworks requires collaboration.
   Ⓓ Spectroscopic analysis can help identify a painter's techniques.

25. Why does the professor discuss the presence of zinc in paint pigments?

   Ⓐ To explain why some paints may deteriorate over the course of time
   Ⓑ To stress the need for caution when attempting to restore old artworks
   Ⓒ To show how pigments differ from varnishes and binding agents
   Ⓓ To show how spectroscopy can help establish the age of a painting

26. According to the professor, what is the primary advantage of spectroscopy over other laboratory methods for analyzing artworks?

   Ⓐ It does not damage the artworks.
   Ⓑ It provides a more accurate analysis than other methods do.
   Ⓒ It uses equipment that can be transferred to other locations.
   Ⓓ It can be used by individuals with little scientific training.

27. What is one way the professor mentions that chemists can help with art restoration?

  (A) By re-creating the pigments and binding agents used by artists of earlier eras
  (B) By removing pigments and binding agents that dissolve paintings over time
  (C) By creating protective coatings of paint that do not damage original paintings
  (D) By developing ways to safely remove paint added by previous restorers

28. Listen to Track 29.

  (A) He is searching for a synonym for the term.
  (B) He is not sure how much information the students need.
  (C) He is going to briefly address a related topic.
  (D) He is giving the students a writing assignment.

Directions: Listen to Track 30.

Directions: Now answer the questions.

29. What is the lecture mainly about?

    (A) Oral traditions in folktales and fairy tales

    (B) Common characters and plots in folktales and fairy tales

    (C) Differences between folktales and fairy tales

    (D) Hidden meanings in folktales and fairy tales

30. What does the professor mean when he says that folktales are communal?

    (A) They vary little from one community to another.

    (B) They serve to strengthen ties among individuals within a community.

    (C) They relate important events in the history of a community.

    (D) They can be adapted to meet the needs of a community.

31. Why does the professor clarify the concept of a "fairy"?

  Ⓐ To explain the origins of the term "fairy tale"
  Ⓑ To eliminate a possible definition of the term "fairy tale"
  Ⓒ To support a claim about the function of fairy tales
  Ⓓ To indicate that fairies are a major element in fairy tales

32. What does the professor say about the setting of fairy tales?

  Ⓐ The tales are usually set in a nonspecific location.
  Ⓑ The location is determined by the country of origin of a tale.
  Ⓒ The tales are set in a location familiar to the author.
  Ⓓ A storyteller varies the location of a tale depending on the audience.

33. In the lecture, the professor discusses characteristics of folktales and fairy tales. Indicate the characteristics of each type of tale. *Put a check in the correct boxes.*

	Folktales	Fairy Tales
Their appeal is now mainly to children.		
The plot is the only stable element.		
The tales are transmitted orally.		
There is one accepted version.		
Characters are well developed.		
The language is relatively formal.		

34. Listen to Track 31.

  Ⓐ To support the student's statement
  Ⓑ To ask the student to clarify her statement
  Ⓒ To find out if the students know what story the line comes from
  Ⓓ To clarify the relationship between time and space in fairy tales

SPEAKING

This section measures your ability to speak in English about a variety of topics.

There are six questions in this section. For each question, you will be given a short time to prepare your response. When the preparation time is up, answer the question as completely as possible in the time indicated for that question. You should record your responses so that you can review them later and compare them with the answer key and scoring rubrics.

1. You will now be asked to speak about a familiar topic. Give yourself 15 seconds to prepare your response. Then record yourself speaking for 45 seconds.

   Listen to Track 32.

   > Talk about a place you enjoyed going to or visiting when you were a child. Describe the place. Explain why you enjoyed it.
   >
   > | **Preparation Time: 15 seconds** |
   > | **Response Time: 45 seconds** |

2. You will now be asked to give your opinion about a familiar topic. Give yourself 15 seconds to prepare your response. Then record yourself speaking for 45 seconds.

   Listen to Track 33.

   > Do you agree or disagree with the following statement? Why or why not? Use details and examples to explain your answer.
   >
   > **It is more important to study math or science than it is to study art or literature.**
   >
   > | **Preparation Time: 15 seconds** |
   > | **Response Time: 45 seconds** |

3. You will now read a short passage and listen to a conversation on the same topic. You will then be asked a question about them. After you hear the question, give yourself 30 seconds to prepare your response. Then record yourself speaking for 60 seconds.

   Listen to Track 34.

Reading Time: 50 seconds

Campus Dining Club Announced

Starting this year, the university dining hall will be transformed into The Campus Dining Club for one week at the end of each semester. During the last week of each semester, the dining hall will feature special meals prepared by the university's culinary arts students. The school feels that this will give students who are studying cooking and food preparation valuable experience that will help them later, when they pursue careers. The university has announced that it will charge a small additional fee for these dinners in order to pay for the special gourmet food ingredients that will be required.

Listen to Track 35.

The man expresses his opinion about the plan described in the article. Briefly summarize the plan. Then state his opinion about the plan and explain the reasons he gives for holding that opinion.

Preparation Time: 30 seconds
Response Time: 60 seconds

---

4. You will now read a short passage and listen to a lecture on the same topic. You will then be asked a question about them. After you hear the question, give yourself 30 seconds to prepare your response. Then record yourself speaking for 60 seconds.

Listen to Track 36.

Target Marketing

Advertisers in the past have used radio and television in an attempt to provide information about their products to large, general audiences; it was once thought that the best way to sell a product was to advertise it to as many people as possible. However, more recent trends in advertising have turned toward target marketing. Target marketing is the strategy of advertising to smaller, very specific audiences—audiences that have been determined to have the greatest need or desire for the product being marketed. Target marketing has proved to be very effective in reaching potential customers.

Listen to Track 37.

Using the professor's examples, explain the advertising technique of target marketing.

Preparation Time: 30 seconds
Response Time: 60 seconds

5. You will now listen to part of a conversation. You will then be asked a question about it. After you hear the question, give yourself 20 seconds to prepare your response. Then record yourself speaking for 60 seconds.

Listen to Track 38.

Briefly summarize the problem the speakers are discussing. Then state which of the two solutions from the conversation you would recommend. Explain the reasons for your recommendation.

Preparation Time: 20 seconds
Response Time: 60 seconds

6. You will now listen to part of a lecture. You will then be asked a question about it. After you hear the question, give yourself 20 seconds to prepare your response. Then record yourself speaking for 60 seconds.

Listen to Track 39.

Using points and examples from the talk, explain the two types of motivation.

Preparation Time: 20 seconds
Response Time: 60 seconds

WRITING

This section measures your ability to write in English to communicate in an academic environment.

There are two writing questions in this section.

For question 1, you will read a passage and listen to a lecture about the same topic. You may take notes while you read and listen. Then you will write a response to a question based on what you have read and heard. You may look back at the passage when answering the question. You may use your notes to help you answer the question. You have 20 minutes to plan and write your response.

For question 2, you will write an essay based on your own knowledge and experience. You have 30 minutes to plan and complete your essay.

1. **Directions:** Give yourself 3 minutes to read the passage.

Reading Time: 3 minutes

As early as the twelfth century A.D., the settlements of Chaco Canyon in New Mexico in the American Southwest were notable for their "great houses," massive stone buildings that contain hundreds of rooms and often stand three or four stories high. Archaeologists have been trying to determine how the buildings were used. While there is still no universally agreed upon explanation, there are three competing theories.

One theory holds that the Chaco structures were purely residential, with each housing hundreds of people. Supporters of this theory have interpreted Chaco great houses as earlier versions of the architecture seen in more recent Southwest societies. In particular, the Chaco houses appear strikingly similar to the large, well-known "apartment buildings" at Taos, New Mexico, in which many people have been living for centuries.

A second theory contends that the Chaco structures were used to store food supplies. One of the main crops of the Chaco people was grain maize, which could be stored for long periods of time without spoiling and could serve as a long-lasting supply of food. The supplies of maize had to be stored somewhere, and the size of the great houses would make them very suitable for the purpose.

A third theory proposes that houses were used as ceremonial centers. Close to one house, called Pueblo Alto, archaeologists identified an enormous mound formed by a pile of old material. Excavations of the mound revealed deposits containing a surprisingly large number of broken pots. This finding has been interpreted as evidence that people gathered at Pueblo Alto for special ceremonies. At the ceremonies, they ate festive meals and then discarded the pots in which the meals had been prepared or served. Such ceremonies have been documented for other Native American cultures.

Listen to Track 40.

Directions: You have 20 minutes to plan and write your response. Your response will be judged on the basis of the quality of your writing and on how well your response presents the points in the lecture and their relationship to the reading passage. Typically, an effective response will be 150 to 225 words.

Listen to Track 41.

Response Time: 20 minutes

Summarize the points made in the lecture, being sure to explain how they cast doubt on the specific theories discussed in the reading passage.

_____

_____

_____

_____

_____

_____

_____

_____

_____

_____

_____

_____

_____

_____

_____

_____

_____

_____

_____

2. **Directions:** Read the question below. You have 30 minutes to plan, write, and revise your essay. Typically, an effective response will contain a minimum of 300 words.

| Response Time: 30 minutes |

Do you agree or disagree with the following statement?

> **People today spend too much time on personal enjoyment—doing things they like to do—rather than doing things they should do.**

Use specific reasons and examples to support your answer.

_____

_____

_____

_____

_____

_____

_____

_____

_____

_____

_____

_____

_____

_____

_____

_____

_____

_____

ANSWERS

Reading Section

1. B	22. D
2. B	23. D
3. B	24. C
4. B	25. B
5. C	26. C
6. A	27. D
7. D	28. A, E, F
8. D	29. B
9. A	30. C
10. C	31. A
11. D	32. B
12. B	33. A
13. A	34. B
14. B, D, F	35. C
15. D	36. C
16. A	37. B
17. A	38. D
18. B	39. C
19. C	40. B
20. B	41. B
21. A	42. B, D, F

Listening Section

1. C	8. A, D
2. A	9. B
3. B	10. D
4. A, C	11. A
5. D	12. B
6. B	13. D
7. C	14. B

15. C

16. A, B

17. D

18. B

19. A

20. C

21. B, D

22. B

23. B

24. C

25. D

26. A

27. D

28. C

29. C

30. D

31. B

32. A

33.

	Folktales	Fairy Tales
Their appeal is now mainly to children.		✓
The plot is the only stable element.	✓	
The tales are transmitted orally.	✓	
There is one accepted version.		✓
Characters are well developed.		✓
The language is relatively formal.		✓

34. A

Speaking Section

1. As with many of the independent items, there are many ways you could answer this question. It is important, however, to address both parts of the prompt. You should both describe a place you enjoyed and explain why you enjoyed this place.

   You might begin by specifically naming the place you enjoyed and begin to describe it. This could be a place that you visited many times, such as an aunt's house or a nearby park, or it could be a place that you visited only once, such as a particular amusement park. Try to provide specific details in the description, such as the garden at your aunt's house. You might talk about what was growing there. Then you would need to provide reasons that explain why you enjoyed the place. In this case, you could say that you enjoyed working in your aunt's garden, or that you learned a lot about growing vegetables.

   The explanation is important because it helps listeners understand your general statements. It is better to provide one or two reasons and give full explanations than to provide a long list of reasons without explanation.

   Your response should be intelligible, should demonstrate effective use of grammar and vocabulary, and should be well developed and coherent. Your response is scored using the Independent Speaking Rubric (see Appendix A).

2. To respond to this particular question, you should clearly state what your opinion is regarding the statement. Be sure to read the statement carefully to make sure you understand it. In this case, you would either agree or disagree that studying math or science is more important than studying art or literature. You should then give reasons to support your

opinion. If you agree that math or science is more important, you might say that it is used in many important areas, such as engineering, and is necessary to make calculations when building structures, for example. You could also provide a personal example and say that you prefer math because it has helped you in certain situations, such as planning your personal finances. You may also want to make a statement about how art has not helped you as much.

If you disagree with the statement, you would also need to support this with specific information. One possibility is to say that math and science are not actually important because not many people need to know math very well. Most people need to know only a little math or science to do their jobs. Then you should provide an example of why art or literature is more important. There are many possibilities, and the specific example you choose is not important as long as it contributes to your argument. Your goal is for your listener to understand why you agree or disagree with the statement.

Your response should be intelligible, should demonstrate effective use of grammar and vocabulary, and should be well developed and coherent. Your response is scored using the Independent Speaking Rubric (see Appendix A).

3. First, as the question states, you should provide a brief summary of the university's plan from the reading, which is to offer meals prepared by culinary arts students at the dining hall. You can also provide a brief summary of the reason that they are doing this, which is to provide cooking students with some experience. You should not, however, spend too much time on this summary. Your summary should be clear enough for the listener to understand the plan without having access to additional information.

After the summary, you should state the man's opinion of the university's plan. In this case, the man agrees with the university's proposal.

You should then convey the two main reasons he gives for holding that opinion. You will need to connect information from the conversation to the reading in order for the response to be complete. The man says that he agrees that a dining club will be good experience for cooking students because cooking for many people under pressure is different from cooking for classmates. You should go beyond simply saying that the man agrees that it will be good experience. You need to give the explanation for why he believes that.

Your response should also convey the man's second reason for agreeing with the university's plan. The man agrees that the extra cost students will pay for these dinners will be worth it. He believes this because the culinary arts students will cook meals that are as good as those served in nice restaurants in the area.

You should manage your time so that you are able to discuss the summary and give a full description of both reasons that the man provides.

Your response should be intelligible, should demonstrate effective use of grammar and vocabulary, and should be well developed and coherent. Your response is scored using the Integrated Speaking Rubric (see Appendix A).

4. To respond to this particular question you should first explain the technique of target marketing as it was presented in the reading. Target marketing is designing or creating advertising so that it appeals to a specific group of people.

You should then use the example given by the professor to explain the technique. The professor discusses how a telephone company may produce two very different advertisements to be shown during different television programs, even though the phone is basically the same. A commercial shown during young people's programming, such as a music show, would appeal to their interests, and would show how the phone is fun. On the other hand, a commercial shown during a business program would emphasize factors important to businesspeople, such as efficiency. This example by the professor illustrates the concept of target marketing.

You do not need to repeat all of the details from the reading and the lecture, but instead integrate points from both to answer the question completely.

Your response should be intelligible, should demonstrate effective use of grammar and vocabulary, and should be well developed and coherent. Your response is scored using the Integrated Speaking Rubric (see Appendix A).

5.   To respond to this particular question you should *briefly* describe the problem. It is enough to say that the woman has hurt her wrist and she's supposed to play the violin in a concert next week.

Next, you need to choose *one* of the two solutions and explain why you think that solution is best. The two solutions in this conversation are: 1) perform with the group anyway, or 2) have Jim take her place. It does not matter which of the two proposed solutions you choose, since there is no "right" solution or "wrong" solution. You should choose the solution that you think is best and support your choice with reasons why you think it is best. The reasons you give can include information provided by the speakers as well as your own experiences.

For example, if you believe the first solution is preferable, you could begin by saying that you think she should have the experience of playing in the big concert and that she would be disappointed if she didn't. You could also say that she

will probably play fine. You could also speak about the disadvantages of the second solution; you might say that it is too much of a risk to ask Jim to replace her at such an important concert. Likewise, if you believe the second solution is preferable, you would state your preference for that and support it in a similar way, using specific reasons. Remember, this type of question can be answered in many different ways.

Your response should be intelligible, should demonstrate effective use of grammar and vocabulary, and should be well developed and coherent. Your response is scored using the Integrated Speaking Rubric (see Appendix A).

6.   This particular question requires you to summarize the contents of a lecture you hear. In your response, you should talk about the two different kinds of motivation (which are extrinsic—or external—motivation, and intrinsic—or internal—motivation). You should include relevant points and examples from the lecture (and not from any other source).

To begin your response, you should briefly state the main idea, that there are two types of motivation, and name the two types. You would then talk about the first type of motivation, extrinsic (or external) motivation. You would explain that when we are externally motivated, we do something for an external reward. You would then talk about the professor's example of a child doing household chores for an allowance. The money that the child receives is motivation.

You would next talk about the second type of motivation, intrinsic (or internal) motivation. You would explain that when we are internally motivated, we do something because it makes us feel good. You should then discuss the professor's example. The professor goes to the gym several times a week because it's good for his health and he enjoys it. You could then say that he has gone for several years, which shows that intrinsic motivation is long lasting. You do not, however, need to repeat all of the details from the lecture. You need to give only sufficient details to explain the types of motivation. You should plan your time so that you have enough time to cover both types of motivation and their examples.

Your response should be intelligible, should demonstrate effective use of grammar and vocabulary, and should be well developed and coherent. Your response is scored using the Integrated Speaking Rubric (see Appendix A).

Writing Section

1. What is important to understand from the lecture is that the professor disagrees with each of the theories presented in the reading about the function of the massive stone buildings, or "great houses," of Chaco Canyon, namely that the great houses served a residential purpose; that they were used to store food supplies; and that they were used to hold ceremonies.

In your response, you should convey the reasons presented by the professor for why the theories about the function of the Chaco great houses are not convincing. A high-scoring response will include the following points made by the professor that cast doubt on the points made in the reading:

Point made in the reading	Counterpoint made in the lecture
The Chaco houses may have been used for residential purposes, because they are similar to residential buildings built by other societies in the American Southwest.	It is unlikely that the Chaco houses were residential, because they contain very few fireplaces, many fewer than the families living in the houses would need for cooking.
The Chaco houses may have been used to store food. The Chaco people needed a place to store their grain maize, and the Chaco houses, thanks to their large capacity, could serve that purpose.	The theory that the function of the Chaco houses was to store grain maize is undermined by the fact that very few traces of maize or maize containers have been found during excavations of the Chaco houses.
The Chaco houses may have served as ceremonial centers. The large quantity of broken pottery in a mound located near the "Pueblo Alto" house suggests that the houses hosted ceremonial feasts after which people discarded the pots in which the food was prepared and served.	The mound near the "Pueblo Alto" house also contains construction materials and tools, which suggests that such mounds were just construction trash heaps and had nothing to do with ceremonies. The pots found in the mounds were probably used by construction workers building the houses.

Your response is scored using the Integrated Writing Rubric (see Appendix A). A response that receives a score of 5 clearly conveys all three of the main points in the table using accurate sentence structure and vocabulary.

2. To earn a top score, you should develop a multi-paragraph essay that responds to the issue of whether people today spend too much time on personal enjoyment—doing things they like to do—rather than doing things they should do. Typically an effective response will contain a minimum of 300 words.

One successful way to express agreement with the prompt is to argue that people these days are not spending their time on tasks that are meaningful, but instead are wasting their time on pleasurable but less meaningful activities. Defining what meaningful versus less meaningful activities are for you personally is important for this strategy; keep in mind that social networking, for example, might be a complete waste of time to you, but may be quite meaningful for others.

A successful way to disagree with the prompt is to explain that people nowadays work very hard at doing the things they should do—for example, in many places, people are spending more hours than ever at their jobs, because that is what the companies they work for say they should do—so whatever time they devote to personal enjoyment is not "too much," but rather is exactly what's needed to maintain their health and happiness in light of all those hours spent on the job.

Keep in mind that there is no "correct" answer to this question. Either side of the issue can be supported with examples and reasons. It is important to make sure that you state your opinion and develop a response that explains your opinion well. The development of your essay is judged by how effectively you support your opinion; a well-developed essay will contain clearly appropriate reasons, examples, and details that illustrate your opinion. Development is not evaluated simply in terms of how many words you write.

Your response should be well organized. A well-organized essay allows an evaluator to read from the beginning to the end of the essay without becoming confused. You should be sure not to just repeat the same information in different ways.

The quality and accuracy of the sentence structure and vocabulary you use to express your ideas is also very important.

Your response is scored using the Independent Writing Rubric (see Appendix A).

TOEFL iBT Test 3

READING

This section measures your ability to understand academic passages in English.

There are three passages in the section. Give yourself 20 minutes to read each passage and answer the questions about it. The entire section will take 60 minutes to complete.

You may look back at a passage when answering the questions. You can skip questions and go back to them later as long as there is time remaining.

Directions: Read the passage. Then answer the questions. Give yourself 20 minutes to complete this practice set.

POWERING THE INDUSTRIAL REVOLUTION

In Britain one of the most dramatic changes of the Industrial Revolution was the harnessing of power. Until the reign of George III (1760–1820), available sources of power for work and travel had not increased since the Middle Ages. There were three sources of power: animal or human muscles; the wind, operating on sail or windmill; and running water. Only the last of these was suited at all to the continuous operating of machines, and although waterpower abounded in Lancashire and Scotland and ran grain mills as well as textile mills, it had one great disadvantage: streams flowed where nature intended them to, and water-driven factories had to be located on their banks, whether or not the location was desirable for other reasons. Furthermore, even the most reliable waterpower varied with the seasons and disappeared in a drought. The new age of machinery, in short, could not have been born without a new source of both movable and constant power.

The source had long been known but not exploited. Early in the century, a pump had come into use in which expanding steam raised a piston in a cylinder, and atmospheric pressure brought it down again when the steam condensed inside the cylinder to form a vacuum. This "atmospheric engine," invented by Thomas Savery and vastly improved by his partner, Thomas Newcomen, embodied revolutionary principles, but it was so slow and wasteful of fuel that it could not be employed outside the coal mines for which it had been designed. In the 1760s, James Watt perfected a separate condenser for the steam, so that the cylinder did not have to be cooled at every stroke; then he devised a way to make the piston turn a wheel and thus convert reciprocating (back and forth) motion into rotary motion. He thereby transformed an inefficient pump of limited use into a steam engine of a thousand uses. The final step came when steam was introduced into the cylinder to drive the piston backward as well as forward, thereby increasing the speed of the engine and cutting its fuel consumption.

Watt's steam engine soon showed what it could do. It liberated industry from dependence on running water. The engine eliminated water in the mines by driving efficient pumps, which made possible deeper and deeper mining. The ready availability of coal inspired William Murdoch during the 1790s to develop the first new form of nighttime illumination to be discovered in a millennium and a half. Coal gas rivaled smoky oil lamps and flickering candles, and early in the new century, well-to-do Londoners grew accustomed to gaslit houses and even streets. Iron manufacturers, which had starved for fuel while depending on charcoal, also benefited from ever-increasing supplies of coal; blast furnaces with steam-powered bellows turned out more iron and steel for the new machinery. Steam became the motive force of the Industrial Revolution, as coal and iron ore were the raw materials.

By 1800 more than a thousand steam engines were in use in the British Isles, and Britain retained a virtual monopoly on steam engine production until the 1830s. Steam power did not merely spin cotton and roll iron; early in the new century, it also multiplied ten times over the amount of paper that a single worker could produce in a day. At the same time, operators of the first printing presses run by steam rather than by hand found it possible to produce a thousand pages in an hour rather than thirty. Steam also promised to eliminate a transportation problem not fully solved by either canal boats or turnpikes. Boats could carry heavy weights, but canals could not cross hilly terrain; turnpikes could cross the hills, but the roadbeds could not stand up under great weights. These problems needed still another solution, and the ingredients for it lay close at hand. In some industrial regions, heavily laden wagons, with flanged wheels, were being hauled by horses along metal rails; and the stationary steam engine was puffing in the factory and mine. Another generation passed before inventors succeeded in combining these ingredients, by putting the engine on wheels and the wheels on the rails, so as to provide a machine to take the place of the horse. Thus the railroad age sprang from what had already happened in the eighteenth century.

Directions: Now answer the questions.

PARAGRAPHS 1 & 2

In Britain one of the most dramatic changes of the Industrial Revolution was the harnessing of power. Until the reign of George III (1760–1820), available sources of power for work and travel had not increased since the Middle Ages. There were three sources of power: animal or human muscles; the wind, operating on sail or windmill; and running water. Only the last of these was suited at all to the continuous operating of machines, and although waterpower abounded in Lancashire and Scotland and ran grain mills as well as textile mills, it had one great disadvantage: streams flowed where nature intended them to, and water-driven factories had to be located on their banks, whether or not the location was desirable for other reasons. Furthermore, even the most reliable waterpower varied with the seasons and disappeared in a drought. The new age of machinery, in short, could not have been born without a new source of both movable and constant power.

The source had long been known but not exploited. Early in the century, a pump had come into use in which expanding steam raised a piston in a cylinder, and atmospheric pressure brought it down again when the steam condensed inside the cylinder to form a vacuum. This "atmospheric engine," invented by Thomas Savery and vastly improved by his partner, Thomas Newcomen, embodied revolutionary principles, but it was so slow and wasteful of fuel that it could not be employed outside the coal mines for which it had been designed. In the 1760s, James Watt perfected a separate condenser for the steam, so that the cylinder did not have to be cooled at every stroke; then he devised a way to make the piston turn a wheel and thus convert reciprocating (back and forth) motion into rotary motion. He thereby transformed an inefficient pump of limited use into a steam engine of a thousand uses. The final step came when steam was introduced into the cylinder to drive the piston backward as well as forward, thereby increasing the speed of the engine and cutting its fuel consumption.

1. Which of the sentences below best expresses the essential information in the highlighted sentence in paragraph 1? Incorrect choices change the meaning in important ways or leave out essential information.

Ⓐ Running water was the best power source for factories since it could keep machines operating continuously, but since it was abundant only in Lancashire and Scotland, most mills and factories that were located elsewhere could not be water driven.

Ⓑ The disadvantage of using waterpower is that streams do not necessarily flow in places that are the most suitable for factories, which explains why so many water-powered grain and textile mills were located in undesirable places.

Ⓒ Since machines could be operated continuously only where running water was abundant, grain and textile mills, as well as other factories, tended to be located only in Lancashire and Scotland.

Ⓓ Running water was the only source of power that was suitable for the continuous operation of machines, but to make use of it, factories had to be located where the water was, regardless of whether such locations made sense otherwise.

2. It can be inferred from paragraph 1 that before the reign of George III there were no sources of power that

Ⓐ were movable
Ⓑ were widely available
Ⓒ did not disappear during certain seasons of the year
Ⓓ could provide continuous power

3. Which of the following best describes the relation of paragraph 2 to paragraph 1?

Ⓐ Paragraph 2 shows how the problem discussed in paragraph 1 arose.
Ⓑ Paragraph 2 explains how the problem presented in paragraph 1 came to be solved.
Ⓒ Paragraph 2 provides a more technical discussion of the problem introduced in paragraph 1.
Ⓓ Paragraph 2 shows why the problem discussed in paragraph 1 was especially important to solve.

4. The word "exploited" in the passage is closest in meaning to

Ⓐ utilized
Ⓑ recognized
Ⓒ examined
Ⓓ fully understood

5. The word "vastly" in the passage is closest in meaning to

Ⓐ quickly
Ⓑ ultimately
Ⓒ greatly
Ⓓ initially

6. According to paragraph 2, the "atmospheric engine" was slow because

Ⓐ it had been designed to be used in coal mines
Ⓑ the cylinder had to cool between each stroke
Ⓒ it made use of expanding steam to raise the piston in its cylinder
Ⓓ it could be operated only when a large supply of fuel was available

7. According to paragraph 2, Watt's steam engine differed from earlier steam engines in each of the following ways EXCEPT:

Ⓐ It used steam to move a piston in a cylinder.
Ⓑ It worked with greater speed.
Ⓒ It was more efficient in its use of fuel.
Ⓓ It could be used in many different ways.

PARAGRAPH 3

Watt's steam engine soon showed what it could do. It liberated industry from dependence on running water. The engine eliminated water in the mines by driving efficient pumps, which made possible deeper and deeper mining. The ready availability of coal inspired William Murdoch during the 1790s to develop the first new form of nighttime illumination to be discovered in a millennium and a half. Coal gas rivaled smoky oil lamps and flickering candles, and early in the new century, well-to-do Londoners grew accustomed to gaslit houses and even streets. Iron manufacturers, which had starved for fuel while depending on charcoal, also benefited from ever-increasing supplies of coal; blast furnaces with steam-powered bellows turned out more iron and steel for the new machinery. Steam became the motive force of the Industrial Revolution, as coal and iron ore were the raw materials.

8. In paragraph 3, the author mentions William Murdoch's invention of a new form of nighttime illumination in order to

Ⓐ indicate one of the important developments made possible by the introduction of Watt's steam engine
Ⓑ make the point that Watt's steam engine was not the only invention of importance to the Industrial Revolution
Ⓒ illustrate how important coal was as a raw material for the Industrial Revolution
Ⓓ provide an example of another eighteenth-century invention that used steam as a power source

9. The phrase "grew accustomed to" in the passage is closest in meaning to

Ⓐ began to prefer
Ⓑ wanted to have
Ⓒ became used to
Ⓓ insisted on

By 1800 more than a thousand steam engines were in use in the British Isles, and Britain retained a virtual monopoly on steam engine production until the 1830s. Steam power did not merely spin cotton and roll iron; early in the new century, it also multiplied ten times over the amount of paper that a single worker could produce in a day. At the same time, operators of the first printing presses run by steam rather than by hand found it possible to produce a thousand pages in an hour rather than thirty. Steam also promised to eliminate a transportation problem not fully solved by either canal boats or turnpikes. Boats could carry heavy weights, but canals could not cross hilly terrain; turnpikes could cross the hills, but the roadbeds could not stand up under great weights. These problems needed still another solution, and the ingredients for it lay close at hand. In some industrial regions, heavily laden wagons, with flanged wheels, were being hauled by horses along metal rails; and the stationary steam engine was puffing in the factory and mine. Another generation passed before inventors succeeded in combining these ingredients, by putting the engine on wheels and the wheels on the rails, so as to provide a machine to take the place of the horse. Thus the railroad age sprang from what had already happened in the eighteenth century.

10. The word "retained" in the passage is closest in meaning to

Ⓐ gained
Ⓑ established
Ⓒ profited from
Ⓓ maintained

11. According to paragraph 4, which of the following statements about steam engines is true?

Ⓐ They were used for the production of paper but not for printing.
Ⓑ By 1800, significant numbers of them were produced outside of Britain.
Ⓒ They were used in factories before they were used to power trains.
Ⓓ They were used in the construction of canals and turnpikes.

12. According to paragraph 4, providing a machine to take the place of the horse involved combining which two previously separate ingredients?

Ⓐ Turnpikes and canals
Ⓑ Stationary steam engines and wagons with flanged wheels
Ⓒ Metal rails in roadbeds and wagons capable of carrying heavy loads
Ⓓ Canal boats and heavily laden wagons

**P
A
R
A
G
R
A
P
H

3**

■ Watt's steam engine soon showed what it could do. ■ It liberated industry from dependence on running water. ■ The engine eliminated water in the mines by driving efficient pumps, which made possible deeper and deeper mining. ■ The ready availability of coal inspired William Murdoch during the 1790s to develop the first new form of nighttime illumination to be discovered in a millennium and a half. Coal gas rivaled smoky oil lamps and flickering candles, and early in the new century, well-to-do Londoners grew accustomed to gaslit houses and even streets. Iron manufacturers, which had starved for fuel while depending on charcoal, also benefited from ever-increasing supplies of coal; blast furnaces with steam-powered bellows turned out more iron and steel for the new machinery. Steam became the motive force of the Industrial Revolution, as coal and iron ore were the raw materials.

13. Look at the four squares [■] that indicate where the following sentence can be added to the passage.

The factories did not have to go to the streams when power could come to the factories.

Where would the sentence best fit?

Ⓐ **The factories did not have to go to the streams when power could come to the factories.** Watt's steam engine soon showed what it could do. ■ It liberated industry from dependence on running water. ■ The engine eliminated water in the mines by driving efficient pumps, which made possible deeper and deeper mining. ■ The ready availability of coal inspired William Murdoch during the 1790s to develop the first new form of nighttime illumination to be discovered in a millennium and a half. Coal gas rivaled smoky oil lamps and flickering candles, and early in the new century, well-to-do Londoners grew accustomed to gaslit houses and even streets. Iron manufacturers, which had starved for fuel while depending on charcoal, also benefited from ever-increasing supplies of coal; blast furnaces with steam-powered bellows turned out more iron and steel for the new machinery. Steam became the motive force of the Industrial Revolution, as coal and iron ore were the raw materials.

Ⓑ ■ Watt's steam engine soon showed what it could do. **The factories did not have to go to the streams when power could come to the factories.** It liberated industry from dependence on running water. ■ The engine eliminated water in the mines by driving efficient pumps, which made possible deeper and deeper mining. ■ The ready availability of coal inspired William Murdoch during the 1790s to develop the first new form of nighttime illumination to be discovered in a millennium and a half. Coal gas rivaled smoky oil lamps and flickering candles, and early in the new century, well-to-do Londoners grew accustomed to gaslit houses and even streets. Iron manufacturers, which had starved for fuel while depending on charcoal, also benefited from ever-increasing supplies of coal; blast furnaces with steam-powered bellows turned out more iron and steel for the new machinery. Steam became the motive force of the Industrial Revolution, as coal and iron ore were the raw materials.

Ⓒ ■ Watt's steam engine soon showed what it could do. ■ It liberated industry from dependence on running water. **The factories did not have to go to the streams when power could come to the factories.** The engine eliminated water in the mines by driving efficient pumps, which made possible deeper and deeper mining. ■ The ready availability of coal inspired William Murdoch during the 1790s to develop the first new form of nighttime illumination to be discovered in a millennium and a half. Coal gas rivaled smoky oil lamps and flickering candles, and early in the new century, well-to-do Londoners grew accustomed to gaslit houses and even streets. Iron manufacturers, which had starved for fuel while depending on charcoal, also benefited from ever-increasing supplies of coal; blast furnaces with steam-powered bellows turned out more iron and steel for the new machinery. Steam became the motive force of the Industrial Revolution, as coal and iron ore were the raw materials.

Ⓓ ■ Watt's steam engine soon showed what it could do. ■ It liberated industry from dependence on running water. ■ The engine eliminated water in the mines by driving efficient pumps, which made possible deeper and deeper mining. **The factories did not have to go to the streams when power could come to the factories.** The ready availability of coal inspired William Murdoch during the 1790s to develop the first new form of nighttime illumination to be discovered in a millennium and a half. Coal gas rivaled smoky oil lamps and flickering candles, and early in the new century, well-to-do Londoners grew accustomed to gaslit houses and even streets. Iron manufacturers, which had starved for fuel while depending on charcoal, also benefited from ever-increasing supplies of coal; blast furnaces with steam-powered bellows turned out more iron and steel for the new machinery. Steam became the motive force of the Industrial Revolution, as coal and iron ore were the raw materials.

14. **Directions**: An introductory sentence for a brief summary of the passage is provided on the next page. Complete the summary by selecting the THREE answer choices that express the most important ideas in the passage. Some sentences do not belong in the summary because they express ideas that are not presented in the passage or are minor ideas in the passage.

Write your answer choices in the spaces where they belong. You can either write the letter of your answer choice or you can copy the sentence.

The Industrial Revolution would not have been possible without a new source of power that was efficient, movable, and continuously available.

- ●

- ●

- ●

Answer Choices

A In the early eighteenth century, Savery and Newcomen discovered that expanding steam could be used to raise a piston in a cylinder.

B In the mid-1700s, James Watt transformed an inefficient steam pump into a fast, flexible, fuel-efficient engine.

C Watt's steam engine played a leading role in greatly increasing industrial production of all kinds.

D In the 1790s, William Murdoch developed a new way of lighting houses and streets using coal gas.

E Until the 1830s, Britain was the world's major producer of steam engines.

F The availability of steam engines was a major factor in the development of railroads, which solved a major transportation problem.

Directions: Read the passage. Then answer the questions. Give yourself 20 minutes to complete this practice set.

WILLIAM SMITH

In 1769 in a little town in Oxfordshire, England, a child with the very ordinary name of William Smith was born into the poor family of a village blacksmith. He received rudimentary village schooling, but mostly he roamed his uncle's farm collecting the fossils that were so abundant in the rocks of the Cotswold hills. When he grew older, William Smith taught himself surveying from books he bought with his small savings, and at the age of eighteen he was apprenticed to a surveyor of the local parish. He then proceeded to teach himself geology, and when he was twenty-four, he went to work for the company that was excavating the Somerset Coal Canal in the south of England.

This was before the steam locomotive, and canal building was at its height. The companies building the canals to transport coal needed surveyors to help them find the coal deposits worth mining as well as to determine the best courses for the canals. This job gave Smith an opportunity to study the fresh rock outcrops created by the newly dug canal. He later worked on similar jobs across the length and breadth of England, all the while studying the newly revealed strata and collecting all the fossils he could find. Smith used mail coaches to travel as much as 10,000 miles per year. In 1815 he published the first modern geological map, "A Map of the Strata of England and Wales with a Part of Scotland," a map so meticulously researched that it can still be used today.

In 1831 when Smith was finally recognized by the Geological Society of London as the "father of English geology," it was not only for his maps but also for something even more important. Ever since people had begun to catalog the strata in particular outcrops, there had been the hope that these could somehow be used to calculate geological time. But as more and more accumulations of strata were cataloged in more and more places, it became clear that the sequences of rocks sometimes differed from region to region and that no rock type was ever going to become a reliable time marker throughout the world. Even without the problem of regional differences, rocks present a difficulty as unique time markers. Quartz is quartz—a silicon ion surrounded by four oxygen ions—there's no difference at all between two-million-year-old Pleistocene quartz and Cambrian quartz created over 500 million years ago.

As he collected fossils from strata throughout England, Smith began to see that the fossils told a different story from the rocks. Particularly in the younger strata, the rocks were often so similar that he had trouble distinguishing the strata, but he never had trouble telling the fossils apart. While rock between two consistent strata might in one place be shale and in another sandstone, the fossils in that shale or sandstone were always the same. Some fossils endured through so many millions of years that they appear in many strata, but others occur only in a few strata, and a few species had their births and extinctions within one particular stratum. Fossils are thus identifying markers for particular periods in Earth's history.

Not only could Smith identify rock strata by the fossils they contained, he could also see a pattern emerging: certain fossils always appear in more ancient sediments, while others begin to be seen as the strata become more recent. By following the fossils, Smith was able to put all the strata of England's earth into relative temporal sequence. About the same time, Georges Cuvier made the same discovery while studying the rocks around Paris. Soon it was realized that this principal of faunal (animal) succession was valid not only in England or France but virtually everywhere. It was actually a principle of floral succession as well, because plants showed the same transformation through time as did fauna. Limestone may be found in the Cambrian or—300 million years later—in the Jurassic strata, but a trilobite—the ubiquitous marine arthropod that had its birth in the Cambrian—will never be found in Jurassic strata, nor a dinosaur in the Cambrian.

Directions: Now answer the questions.

PARAGRAPH 1

In 1769 in a little town in Oxfordshire, England, a child with the very ordinary name of William Smith was born into the poor family of a village blacksmith. He received rudimentary village schooling, but mostly he roamed his uncle's farm collecting the fossils that were so abundant in the rocks of the Cotswold hills. When he grew older, William Smith taught himself surveying from books he bought with his small savings, and at the age of eighteen he was apprenticed to a surveyor of the local parish. He then proceeded to teach himself geology, and when he was twenty-four, he went to work for the company that was excavating the Somerset Coal Canal in the south of England.

15. The word "rudimentary" in the passage is closest in meaning to

Ⓐ thorough
Ⓑ strict
Ⓒ basic
Ⓓ occasional

16. According to paragraph 1, which of the following statements about William Smith is NOT true?

Ⓐ Smith learned surveying by reading and by apprenticing for a local surveyor.
Ⓑ Smith's family lived in a small English town and possessed little wealth.
Ⓒ Smith learned about fossils from books he borrowed from his uncle.
Ⓓ Smith eventually left his village to work on the excavation of an English canal.

This was before the steam locomotive, and canal building was at its height. The companies building the canals to transport coal needed surveyors to help them find the coal deposits worth mining as well as to determine the best courses for the canals. This job gave Smith an opportunity to study the fresh rock outcrops created by the newly dug canal. He later worked on similar jobs across the length and breadth of England, all the while studying the newly revealed strata and collecting all the fossils he could find. Smith used mail coaches to travel as much as 10,000 miles per year. In 1815 he published the first modern geological map, "A Map of the Strata of England and Wales with a Part of Scotland," a map so meticulously researched that it can still be used today.

17. Which of the following can be inferred from paragraph 2 about canal building?

    Ⓐ Canals were built primarily in the south of England rather than in other regions.

    Ⓑ Canal building decreased after the steam locomotive was invented.

    Ⓒ Canal building made it difficult to study rock strata which often became damaged in the process.

    Ⓓ Canal builders hired surveyors like Smith to examine exposed rock strata.

18. According to paragraph 2, which of the following is true of the map published by William Smith?

    Ⓐ It indicates the locations of England's major canals.

    Ⓑ It became most valuable when the steam locomotive made rail travel possible.

    Ⓒ The data for the map were collected during Smith's work on canals.

    Ⓓ It is no longer regarded as a geological masterpiece.

19. The word "meticulously" in the passage is closest in meaning to

    Ⓐ carefully

    Ⓑ quickly

    Ⓒ frequently

    Ⓓ obviously

In 1831 when Smith was finally recognized by the Geological Society of London as the "father of English geology," it was not only for his maps but also for something even more important. Ever since people had begun to catalog the strata in particular outcrops, there had been the hope that these could somehow be used to calculate geological time. But as more and more accumulations of strata were cataloged in more and more places, it became clear that the sequences of rocks sometimes differed from region to region and that no rock type was ever going to become a reliable time marker throughout the world. Even without the problem of regional differences, rocks present a difficulty as unique time markers. Quartz is quartz—a silicon ion surrounded by four oxygen ions—there's no difference at all between two-million-year-old Pleistocene quartz and Cambrian quartz created over 500 million years ago.

20. Which of the sentences below best expresses the essential information in the highlighted sentence in paragraph 3? Incorrect choices change the meaning in important ways or leave out essential information.

   (A) The discovery of regional differences in the sequences of rocks led geologists to believe that rock types could some day become reliable time markers.
   (B) Careful analysis of strata revealed that rocks cannot establish geological time because the pattern of rock layers varies from place to place.
   (C) Smith's catalogs of rock strata indicated that the sequences of rocks are different from place to place and from region to region.
   (D) Because people did not catalog regional differences in sequences of rocks, it was believed that rocks could never be reliable time markers.

21. Why does the author use the phrase "Quartz is quartz"?

   (A) To describe how the differences between Pleistocene and Cambrian quartz reveal information about dating rocks
   (B) To point out that the chemical composition of quartz makes it more difficult to date than other rocks
   (C) To provide an example of how regional differences in rock sequences can make a particular rock difficult to date
   (D) To explain that rocks are difficult to use for dating because their chemical compositions always remain the same over time

PARAGRAPH 4

As he collected fossils from strata throughout England, Smith began to see that the fossils told a different story from the rocks. Particularly in the younger strata, the rocks were often so similar that he had trouble distinguishing the strata, but he never had trouble telling the fossils apart. While rock between two consistent strata might in one place be shale and in another sandstone, the fossils in that shale or sandstone were always the same. Some fossils endured through so many millions of years that they appear in many strata, but others occur only in a few strata, and a few species had their births and extinctions within one particular stratum. Fossils are thus identifying markers for particular periods in Earth's history.

22. According to paragraph 4, it was difficult for Smith to distinguish rock strata because

  Ⓐ the rocks from different strata closely resembled each other
  Ⓑ he was often unable to find fossils in the younger rock strata
  Ⓒ their similarity to each other made it difficult for him to distinguish one rock type from another
  Ⓓ the type of rock between two consistent strata was always the same

23. The word "endured" in the passage is closest in meaning to

  Ⓐ vanished
  Ⓑ developed
  Ⓒ varied
  Ⓓ survived

PARAGRAPH 5

Not only could Smith identify rock strata by the fossils they contained, he could also see a pattern emerging: certain fossils always appear in more ancient sediments, while others begin to be seen as the strata become more recent. By following the fossils, Smith was able to put all the strata of England's earth into relative temporal sequence. About the same time, Georges Cuvier made the same discovery while studying the rocks around Paris. Soon it was realized that this principal of faunal (animal) succession was valid not only in England or France but virtually everywhere. It was actually a principle of floral succession as well, because plants showed the same transformation through time as did fauna. Limestone may be found in the Cambrian or—300 million years later—in the Jurassic strata, but a trilobite—the ubiquitous marine arthropod that had its birth in the Cambrian—will never be found in Jurassic strata, nor a dinosaur in the Cambrian.

24. The word "virtually" in the passage is closest in meaning to

  Ⓐ possibly
  Ⓑ absolutely
  Ⓒ surprisingly
  Ⓓ nearly

25. Select the TWO answer choices that are true statements based upon the discussion of the principle of faunal succession in paragraph 5. To receive credit, you must select TWO answers.

    A It was a principle that applied to fauna but not to flora.
    B It was discovered independently by two different geologists.
    C It describes how fossils are distributed in rock strata.
    D It explains why plants and animals undergo transformations through time.

26. In mentioning "trilobite," the author is making which of the following points?

    A Fossils cannot be found in more than one rock stratum.
    B Faunal succession can help put rock layers in relative temporal sequence.
    C Faunal succession cannot be applied to different strata composed of the same kind of rock.
    D The presence of trilobite fossils makes it difficult to date a rock.

PARAGRAPH 5

Not only could Smith identify rock strata by the fossils they contained, he could also see a pattern emerging: certain fossils always appear in more ancient sediments, while others begin to be seen as the strata become more recent. ■ By following the fossils, Smith was able to put all the strata of England's earth into relative temporal sequence. ■ About the same time, Georges Cuvier made the same discovery while studying the rocks around Paris. ■ Soon it was realized that this principal of faunal (animal) succession was valid not only in England or France but virtually everywhere. ■ It was actually a principle of floral succession as well, because plants showed the same transformation through time as did fauna. Limestone may be found in the Cambrian or—300 million years later—in the Jurassic strata, but a trilobite—the ubiquitous marine arthropod that had its birth in the Cambrian—will never be found in Jurassic strata, nor a dinosaur in the Cambrian.

27. Look at the four squares [■] that indicate where the following sentence can be added to the passage.

    The findings of these geologists inspired others to examine the rock and fossil records in different parts of the world.

    Where would the sentence best fit?

    A Not only could Smith identify rock strata by the fossils they contained, he could also see a pattern emerging: certain fossils always appear in more ancient sediments, while others begin to be seen as the strata become more recent. **The findings of these geologists inspired others to examine the rock and fossil records in different parts of the world.** By following the fossils, Smith was able to put all the strata of England's earth into relative temporal sequence. ■ About the same time, Georges Cuvier made the same discovery while studying the rocks around Paris. ■ Soon it was realized that this principal of faunal (animal) succession was valid not only in England or France but virtually everywhere. ■ It was actually a principle of floral succession as well, because plants showed the same transformation through time as did fauna. Limestone may be found in the Cambrian or—300 million years later—in the Jurassic strata, but a trilobite—the ubiquitous marine arthropod that had its birth in the Cambrian—will never be found in Jurassic strata, nor a dinosaur in the Cambrian.

Ⓑ Not only could Smith identify rock strata by the fossils they contained, he could also see a pattern emerging: certain fossils always appear in more ancient sediments, while others begin to be seen as the strata become more recent. ■ By following the fossils, Smith was able to put all the strata of England's earth into relative temporal sequence. **The findings of these geologists inspired others to examine the rock and fossil records in different parts of the world.** About the same time, Georges Cuvier made the same discovery while studying the rocks around Paris. ■ Soon it was realized that this principal of faunal (animal) succession was valid not only in England or France but virtually everywhere. ■ It was actually a principle of floral succession as well, because plants showed the same transformation through time as did fauna. Limestone may be found in the Cambrian or—300 million years later—in the Jurassic strata, but a trilobite—the ubiquitous marine arthropod that had its birth in the Cambrian—will never be found in Jurassic strata, nor a dinosaur in the Cambrian.

Ⓒ Not only could Smith identify rock strata by the fossils they contained, he could also see a pattern emerging: certain fossils always appear in more ancient sediments, while others begin to be seen as the strata become more recent. ■ By following the fossils, Smith was able to put all the strata of England's earth into relative temporal sequence. ■ About the same time, Georges Cuvier made the same discovery while studying the rocks around Paris. **The findings of these geologists inspired others to examine the rock and fossil records in different parts of the world.** Soon it was realized that this principal of faunal (animal) succession was valid not only in England or France but virtually everywhere. ■ It was actually a principle of floral succession as well, because plants showed the same transformation through time as did fauna. Limestone may be found in the Cambrian or—300 million years later—in the Jurassic strata, but a trilobite—the ubiquitous marine arthropod that had its birth in the Cambrian—will never be found in Jurassic strata, nor a dinosaur in the Cambrian.

Ⓓ Not only could Smith identify rock strata by the fossils they contained, he could also see a pattern emerging: certain fossils always appear in more ancient sediments, while others begin to be seen as the strata become more recent. ■ By following the fossils, Smith was able to put all the strata of England's earth into relative temporal sequence. ■ About the same time, Georges Cuvier made the same discovery while studying the rocks around Paris. ■ Soon it was realized that this principal of faunal (animal) succession was valid not only in England or France but virtually everywhere. **The findings of these geologists inspired others to examine the rock and fossil**

records in different parts of the world. It was actually a principle of floral succession as well, because plants showed the same transformation through time as did fauna. Limestone may be found in the Cambrian or—300 million years later—in the Jurassic strata, but a trilobite—the ubiquitous marine arthropod that had its birth in the Cambrian—will never be found in Jurassic strata, nor a dinosaur in the Cambrian.

28. **Directions**: An introductory sentence for a brief summary of the passage is provided below. Complete the summary by selecting the THREE answer choices that express the most important ideas in the passage. Some sentences do not belong in the summary because they express ideas that are not presented in the passage or are minor ideas in the passage.

    Write your answer choices in the spaces where they belong. You can either write the letter of your answer choice or you can copy the sentence.

> **William Smith's contributions to geology have increased our knowledge of the Earth's history.**
>
> ●
>
> ●
>
> ●

Answer Choices

A Smith found success easily in his profession because he came from a family of geologists and surveyors.

B Smith's work on canals allowed him to collect fossils and study rock layers all over England.

C Smith found that fossils are much more reliable indicators of geological time than rock strata are.

D Smith was named "the father of English geology" for his maps rather than for his other contributions to the field.

E Smith and Cuvier discovered that fossil patterns are easier to observe in ancient rock strata than in younger rock strata.

F The discovery of the principle of faunal succession allowed geologists to establish the relative age of Earth's rock layers.

Directions: Read the passage. Then answer the questions. Give yourself 20 minutes to complete this practice set.

INFANTILE AMNESIA

What do you remember about your life before you were three? Few people can remember anything that happened to them in their early years. Adults' memories of the next few years also tend to be scanty. Most people remember only a few events—usually ones that were meaningful and distinctive, such as being hospitalized or a sibling's birth.

How might this inability to recall early experiences be explained? The sheer passage of time does not account for it; adults have excellent recognition of pictures of people who attended high school with them 35 years earlier. Another seemingly plausible explanation—that infants do not form enduring memories at this point in development—also is incorrect. Children two and a half to three years old remember experiences that occurred in their first year, and eleven month olds remember some events a year later. Nor does the hypothesis that infantile amnesia reflects repression—or holding back—of sexually charged episodes explain the phenomenon. While such repression may occur, people cannot remember ordinary events from the infant and toddler periods, either.

Three other explanations seem more promising. One involves physiological changes relevant to memory. Maturation of the frontal lobes of the brain continues throughout early childhood, and this part of the brain may be critical for remembering particular episodes in ways that can be retrieved later. Demonstrations of infants' and toddlers' long-term memory have involved their repeating motor activities that they had seen or done earlier, such as reaching in the dark for objects, putting a bottle in a doll's mouth, or pulling apart two pieces of a toy. The brain's level of physiological maturation may support these types of memories, but not ones requiring explicit verbal descriptions.

A second explanation involves the influence of the social world on children's language use. Hearing and telling stories about events may help children store information in ways that will endure into later childhood and adulthood. Through hearing stories with a clear beginning, middle, and ending, children may learn to extract the gist of events in ways that they will be able to describe many years later. Consistent with this view, parents and children increasingly engage in discussions of past events when children are about three years old. However, hearing such stories is not sufficient for younger children to form enduring memories. Telling such stories to two year olds does not seem to produce long-lasting verbalizable memories.

A third likely explanation for infantile amnesia involves incompatibilities between the ways in which infants encode[1] information and the ways in which older children and adults retrieve it. Whether people can remember an event depends critically on the fit between the way in which they earlier encoded the information and the way in which they later attempt to retrieve it. The better able the person is to reconstruct the perspective from which the material was encoded, the more likely that recall will be successful.

This view is supported by a variety of factors that can create mismatches between very young children's encoding and older children's and adults' retrieval efforts. The world looks very different to a person whose head is only two or three feet above the ground than to one whose head is five or six feet above it. Older children and adults often try to retrieve the names of things they saw, but infants would not have encoded the information verbally. General knowledge of categories of events such as a birthday party or a visit to the doctor's office helps older individuals encode their experiences, but again, infants and toddlers are unlikely to encode many experiences within such knowledge structures.

These three explanations of infantile amnesia are not mutually exclusive; indeed, they support each other. Physiological immaturity may be part of why infants and toddlers do not form extremely enduring memories, even when they hear stories that promote such remembering in preschoolers. Hearing the stories may lead preschoolers to encode aspects of events that allow them to form memories they can access as adults. Conversely, improved encoding of what they hear may help them better understand and remember stories and thus make the stories more useful for remembering future events. Thus, all three explanations—physiological maturation, hearing and producing stories about past events, and improved encoding of key aspects of events—seem likely to be involved in overcoming infantile amnesia.

---

1. **encode:** transfer information from one system of communication into another

Directions: Now answer the questions.

PARAGRAPH 2

How might this inability to recall early experiences be explained? The sheer passage of time does not account for it; adults have excellent recognition of pictures of people who attended high school with them 35 years earlier. Another seemingly plausible explanation—that infants do not form enduring memories at this point in development—also is incorrect. Children two and a half to three years old remember experiences that occurred in their first year, and eleven month olds remember some events a year later. Nor does the hypothesis that infantile amnesia reflects repression—or holding back—of sexually charged episodes explain the phenomenon. While such repression may occur, people cannot remember ordinary events from the infant and toddler periods, either.

29. What purpose does paragraph 2 serve in the larger discussion of children's inability to recall early experiences?

   Ⓐ To argue that theories that are not substantiated by evidence should generally be considered unreliable

   Ⓑ To argue that the hypotheses mentioned in paragraph 2 have been more thoroughly researched than have the theories mentioned later in the passage

   Ⓒ To explain why some theories about infantile amnesia are wrong before presenting ones more likely to be true

   Ⓓ To explain why infantile amnesia is of great interest to researchers

30. The "plausible" in the passage is closest in meaning to

    Ⓐ flexible
    Ⓑ believable
    Ⓒ debatable
    Ⓓ predictable

31. The word "phenomenon" in the passage is closest in meaning to

    Ⓐ exception
    Ⓑ repetition
    Ⓒ occurrence
    Ⓓ idea

32. All of the following theories about the inability to recall early experiences are rejected in paragraph 2 EXCEPT:

    Ⓐ The ability to recall an event decreases as the time after the event increases.
    Ⓑ Young children are not capable of forming memories that last for more than a short time.
    Ⓒ People may hold back sexually meaningful memories.
    Ⓓ Most events in childhood are too ordinary to be worth remembering.

PARAGRAPH 3

Three other explanations seem more promising. One involves physiological changes relevant to memory. Maturation of the frontal lobes of the brain continues throughout early childhood, and this part of the brain may be critical for remembering particular episodes in ways that can be retrieved later. Demonstrations of infants' and toddlers' long-term memory have involved their repeating motor activities that they had seen or done earlier, such as reaching in the dark for objects, putting a bottle in a doll's mouth, or pulling apart two pieces of a toy. The brain's level of physiological maturation may support these types of memories, but not ones requiring explicit verbal descriptions.

33. What does paragraph 3 suggest about long-term memory in children?

    Ⓐ Maturation of the frontal lobes of the brain is important for the long-term memory of motor activities but not verbal descriptions.
    Ⓑ Young children may form long-term memories of actions they see earlier than of things they hear or are told.
    Ⓒ Young children have better long-term recall of short verbal exchanges than of long ones.
    Ⓓ Children's long-term recall of motor activities increases when such activities are accompanied by explicit verbal descriptions.

PARAGRAPH 4

A second explanation involves the influence of the social world on children's language use. Hearing and telling stories about events may help children store information in ways that will endure into later childhood and adulthood. Through hearing stories with a clear beginning, middle, and ending, children may learn to extract the gist of events in ways that they will be able to describe many years later. Consistent with this view, parents and children increasingly engage in discussions of past events when children are about three years old. However, hearing such stories is not sufficient for younger children to form enduring memories. Telling such stories to two year olds does not seem to produce long-lasting verbalizable memories.

34. According to paragraph 4, what role may storytelling play in forming childhood memories?

    Ⓐ It may encourage the physiological maturing of the brain.
    Ⓑ It may help preschool children tell the difference between ordinary and unusual memories.
    Ⓒ It may help preschool children retrieve memories quickly.
    Ⓓ It may provide an ordered structure that facilitates memory retrieval.

PARAGRAPHS 5 & 6

A third likely explanation for infantile amnesia involves incompatibilities between the ways in which infants encode[1] information and the ways in which older children and adults retrieve it. Whether people can remember an event depends critically on the fit between the way in which they earlier encoded the information and the way in which they later attempt to retrieve it. The better able the person is to reconstruct the perspective from which the material was encoded, the more likely that recall will be successful.

This view is supported by a variety of factors that can create mismatches between very young children's encoding and older children's and adults' retrieval efforts. The world looks very different to a person whose head is only two or three feet above the ground than to one whose head is five or six feet above it. Older children and adults often try to retrieve the names of things they saw, but infants would not have encoded the information verbally. General knowledge of categories of events such as a birthday party or a visit to the doctor's office helps older individuals encode their experiences, but again, infants and toddlers are unlikely to encode many experiences within such knowledge structures.

35. The word "critically" in the passage is closest in meaning to

    Ⓐ fundamentally
    Ⓑ partially
    Ⓒ consistently
    Ⓓ subsequently

36. The word "perspective" in the passage is closest in meaning to

    Ⓐ system
    Ⓑ theory
    Ⓒ source
    Ⓓ viewpoint

37. The phrase "This view" in the passage refers to the belief that

   Ⓐ the ability to retrieve a memory partly depends on the similarity between the encoding and retrieving process
   Ⓑ the process of encoding information is less complex for adults than it is for young adults and infants
   Ⓒ infants and older children are equally dependent on discussion of past events for the retrieval of information
   Ⓓ infants encode information in the same way older children and adults do

38. According to paragraphs 5 and 6, one disadvantage very young children face in processing information is that they cannot

   Ⓐ process a lot of information at one time
   Ⓑ organize experiences according to type
   Ⓒ block out interruptions
   Ⓓ interpret the tone of adult language

PARAGRAPH 7

These three explanations of infantile amnesia are not mutually exclusive; indeed, they support each other. Physiological immaturity may be part of why infants and toddlers do not form extremely enduring memories, even when they hear stories that promote such remembering in preschoolers. Hearing the stories may lead preschoolers to encode aspects of events that allow them to form memories they can access as adults. Conversely, improved encoding of what they hear may help them better understand and remember stories and thus make the stories more useful for remembering future events. Thus, all three explanations—physiological maturation, hearing and producing stories about past events, and improved encoding of key aspects of events—seem likely to be involved in overcoming infantile amnesia.

39. Which of the sentences below best expresses the essential information in the highlighted sentence in paragraph 7? Incorrect choices change the meaning in important ways or leave out essential information.

   Ⓐ Incomplete physiological development may partly explain why hearing stories does not improve long-term memory in infants and toddlers.
   Ⓑ One reason why preschoolers fail to comprehend the stories they hear is that they are physiologically immature.
   Ⓒ Given the chance to hear stories, infants and toddlers may form enduring memories despite physiological immaturity.
   Ⓓ Physiologically mature children seem to have no difficulty remembering stories they heard as preschoolers.

40. How does paragraph 7 relate to the earlier discussion of infantile amnesia?

   Ⓐ It introduces a new theory about the causes of infantile amnesia.
   Ⓑ It argues that particular theories discussed earlier in the passage require further research.
   Ⓒ It explains how particular theories discussed earlier in the passage may work in combination.
   Ⓓ It evaluates which of the theories discussed earlier is most likely to be true.

PARAGRAPH 1

What do you remember about your life before you were three? ■ Few people can remember anything that happened to them in their early years. ■ Adults' memories of the next few years also tend to be scanty. ■ Most people remember only a few events—usually ones that were meaningful and distinctive, such as being hospitalized or a sibling's birth. ■

41. Look at the four squares [■] that indicate where the following sentence can be added to the passage.

Other important occasions are school graduations and weddings.

Where would the sentence best fit?

Ⓐ What do you remember about your life before you were three? **Other important occasions are school graduations and weddings.** Few people can remember anything that happened to them in their early years. ■ Adults' memories of the next few years also tend to be scanty. ■ Most people remember only a few events—usually ones that were meaningful and distinctive, such as being hospitalized or a sibling's birth. ■

Ⓑ What do you remember about your life before you were three? ■ Few people can remember anything that happened to them in their early years. **Other important occasions are school graduations and weddings.** Adults' memories of the next few years also tend to be scanty. ■ Most people remember only a few events—usually ones that were meaningful and distinctive, such as being hospitalized or a sibling's birth. ■

Ⓒ What do you remember about your life before you were three? ■ Few people can remember anything that happened to them in their early years. ■ Adults' memories of the next few years also tend to be scanty. **Other important occasions are school graduations and weddings.** Most people remember only a few events—usually ones that were meaningful and distinctive, such as being hospitalized or a sibling's birth. ■

Ⓓ What do you remember about your life before you were three? ■ Few people can remember anything that happened to them in their early years. ■ Adults' memories of the next few years also tend to be scanty. ■ Most people remember only a few events—usually ones that were meaningful and distinctive, such as being hospitalized or a sibling's birth. **Other important occasions are school graduations and weddings.**

42. **Directions:** An introductory sentence for a brief summary of the passage is provided below. Complete the summary by selecting the THREE answer choices that express the most important ideas in the passage. Some sentences do not belong in the summary because they express ideas that are not presented in the passage or are minor ideas in the passage.

Write your answer choices in the spaces where they belong. You can either write the letter of your answer choice or you can copy the sentence.

> **There are several possible explanations why people cannot easily remember their early childhoods.**
>
> ●
>
> ●
>
> ●

Answer Choices

A Preschoolers typically do not recall events from their first year.

B Frontal lobe function of the brain may need to develop before memory retrieval can occur.

C Children recall physical activities more easily if they are verbalized.

D The opportunity to hear chronologically narrated stories may help three-year-old children produce long-lasting memories.

E The content of a memory determines the way in which it is encoded.

F The contrasting ways in which young children and adults process information may determine their relative success in remembering.

LISTENING

This section measures your ability to understand conversations and lectures in English.

Listen to each conversation and lecture only one time. After each conversation and lecture, you will answer some questions about it. Answer each question based on what is stated or implied by the speakers.

You may take notes while you listen and use your notes to help you answer the questions. Your notes will **not** be scored.

In some questions, you will see this icon: ( ). This means that you will hear, but not see, the question.

Answer each question before moving on. Do not return to previous questions.

It will take about 60 minutes to listen to the conversations and lectures and answer the questions about them.

Directions: Listen to Track 42.

Directions: Now answer the questions.

1. Why does the student go to the career services office?

   (A) To confirm the date and time of the career fair
   (B) To learn the location of the career fair
   (C) To find out if he is allowed to attend the career fair
   (D) To get advice about interviewing at the career fair

2. Why does the student think that companies' representatives would not be interested in talking to him?

   (A) He will not be graduating this year.
   (B) He is not currently taking business classes.
   (C) He has not declared a major yet.
   (D) He does not have a current résumé.

3. What does the woman imply about the small print on the career fair posters and flyers?

   (A) The information in the small print was incomplete.
   (B) The print was smaller than she expected it to be.
   (C) The information the small print contains will be updated.
   (D) The information in the small print will be presented in a more noticeable way.

4. What does the woman say is a good way for the student to prepare for speaking to companies' representatives? *Choose 2 answers.*

   [A] Take some business classes
   [B] Familiarize himself with certain businesses beforehand
   [C] Have questions ready to ask the representatives
   [D] Talk to people who work for accounting firms

5. Listen to Track 43.

   Ⓐ To acknowledge that he cannot go to this year's career fair

   Ⓑ To acknowledge the amount of preparation he will have

   Ⓒ To indicate that he has school work he must complete before the career fair

   Ⓓ To indicate that he needs to go to his job now

Directions: Listen to Track 44.

Economics

Directions: Now answer the questions.

6. What is the main purpose of the talk?

    Ⓐ To show what happens after an economy has experienced a boom-and-bust cycle
    Ⓑ To illustrate the conditions needed to produce a boom-and-bust cycle
    Ⓒ To demonstrate how boom-and-bust cycles have changed over time
    Ⓓ To explain why the boom-and-bust cycle is not a frequent historical occurrence

7. What is the professor's opinion about the dot-com crash?

    Ⓐ She thinks that people should have realized it would happen.
    Ⓑ She does not believe that anything like it will happen again.
    Ⓒ She is surprised that it did not have more serious consequences.
    Ⓓ She is confident that people learned a valuable lesson from it.

8. According to the professor, where did tulips originate?

    Ⓐ In the mountains of central Asia
    Ⓑ In the region around Istanbul in Turkey
    Ⓒ In the sandy soils of the Netherlands
    Ⓓ In the forests of northern Europe

9. Why does the professor mention a merchant who ate tulip bulbs?

    Ⓐ To explain how the Turks introduced the flower to European visitors
    Ⓑ To explain what happened to tulip bulbs that did not produce desirable colors
    Ⓒ To give an example of one way that the rich in the Netherlands showed off their wealth
    Ⓓ To illustrate her point that Europeans were unfamiliar with the flower

10. What were some of the factors that contributed to the tulip craze in the Netherlands in the seventeenth century? *Choose 3 answers.*

    Ⓐ Wealthy gardeners liked to compete for rare plants.
    Ⓑ The number of people with disposable income was growing.
    Ⓒ Tulip bulbs were initially cheap and easy to obtain.
    Ⓓ Tulips in the wild bloomed in unusual color combinations.
    Ⓔ The tulip market was not regulated by the government.
    Ⓕ The professor mentions the practice of trading promissory notes in the Netherlands in the 1630s.

11. What does this practice explain? *Choose 2 answers.*

    Ⓐ Why tulips replaced gold as a form of currency
    Ⓑ Why buyers were no longer interested in owning actual tulips
    Ⓒ Why borrowing in the Netherlands increased on a significant scale
    Ⓓ Why the middle class in the Netherlands expanded in size

Directions: Listen to Track 45.

Biology

Nightcap Oak

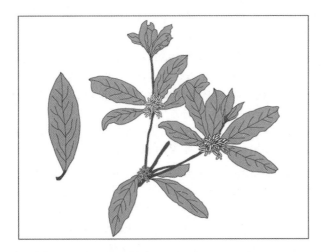

Directions: Now answer the questions.

12. What topics related to the Nightcap Oak does the professor mainly discuss?
    Choose 2 answers.

    - A Factors that relate to the size of the area in which it grows
    - B The size of its population over the last few centuries
    - C Whether anything can be done to ensure its survival
    - D Why it did not change much over the last one hundred million years

13. According to the professor, what led scientists to characterize the Nightcap Oak as primitive?

    - Ⓐ It has no evolutionary connection to other trees growing in Australia today.
    - Ⓑ It has an inefficient reproductive system.
    - Ⓒ Its flowers are located at the bases of the leaves.
    - Ⓓ It is similar to some ancient fossils.

14. What point does the professor make about the Nightcap Oak's habitat?

    Ⓐ It is stable despite its limited size.
    Ⓑ Unlike the habitats of many plants, it is expanding.
    Ⓒ Its recent changes have left the Nightcap Oak struggling to adapt.
    Ⓓ Its size is much larger than the area where the Nightcap Oak grows.

15. According to the professor, what are two factors that prevent the Nightcap Oak population from spreading? *Choose 2 answers.*

    Ⓐ The complex conditions required for the trees to produce fruit
    Ⓑ The fact that the seed cannot germinate while locked inside the shell
    Ⓒ The limited time the seed retains the ability to germinate
    Ⓓ Competition with tree species that evolved more recently

16. Why does the professor mention the size of the Nightcap Oak population over the last few hundred years?

    Ⓐ To explain why it is likely that the Nightcap Oak population will increase in the future
    Ⓑ To point out that the Nightcap Oak's limited reproductive success has not led to a decrease in its population
    Ⓒ To present evidence that the Nightcap Oak is able to tolerate major changes in its environment
    Ⓓ To point out that the Nightcap Oak is able to resist diseases that have destroyed other tree species

17. Listen to Track 46.

    Ⓐ She wants the students to think about a possible connection.
    Ⓑ She wants to know if the students have any questions.
    Ⓒ She is implying that researchers have been asking the wrong questions.
    Ⓓ She is implying that there may be no connection between the questions.

Directions: Listen to Track 47.

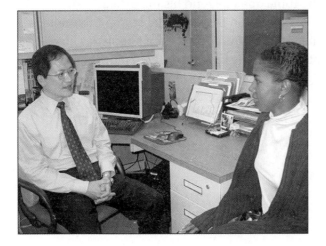

Directions: Now answer the questions.

18. Why does the student go to see the professor?

   Ⓐ She is having trouble finding a topic for her term paper.
   Ⓑ She needs his help to find resource materials.
   Ⓒ She wants to ask him for an extension on a term paper.
   Ⓓ She wants him to approve her plans for a term paper.

19. Why is the student interested in learning more about dialects?

   Ⓐ She often has trouble understanding what other students are saying.
   Ⓑ She is trying to change the way she speaks.
   Ⓒ She is aware that her own dialect differs from those of her roommates.
   Ⓓ She spent her childhood in various places where different dialects are spoken.

20. Based on the conversation, what can be concluded about "dialect accommodation"? *Choose 2 answers.*

   Ⓐ It is a largely subconscious process.
   Ⓑ It is a process that applies only to some dialects.
   Ⓒ It is a very common phenomenon.
   Ⓓ It is a topic that has not been explored extensively.

21. What does the professor want the student to do next?

   Ⓐ Read some articles he has recommended
   Ⓑ Present her proposal before the entire class
   Ⓒ Submit a design plan for the project
   Ⓓ Listen to recordings of different dialects

22. Listen to Track 48.

    (A) He thinks the topic goes beyond his expertise.

    (B) He thinks the topic is too broad for the student to manage.

    (C) He thinks the topic is not relevant for a linguistics class.

    (D) He thinks other students may have chosen the same topic.

Directions: Listen to Track 49.

Directions: Now answer the questions.

23. What aspect of creative writing does the professor mainly discuss?

 Ⓐ How to keep a reader's interest
 Ⓑ How to create believable characters
 Ⓒ Key differences between major and minor characters
 Ⓓ Techniques for developing short-story plots

24. Why does the professor recommend that students pay attention to the people they see every day?

 Ⓐ The behavior and characteristics of these people can be used in character sketches.
 Ⓑ Observing people in real-life situations can provide ideas for story plots.
 Ⓒ It is easier to observe the behavior of familiar people than of new people.
 Ⓓ Students can gather accurate physical descriptions for their characters.

25. The professor discusses an example of three friends who run out of gas. What point does he use the example to illustrate?

   Ⓐ Writers should know their characters as well as they know their friends.
   Ⓑ Writers should create characters that interact in complex ways.
   Ⓒ Friends do not always behave the way we expect them to behave.
   Ⓓ Friends' behavior is often more predictable than fictional characters' behavior.

26. What warning does the professor give when he talks about the man who lives on the mountain?

   Ⓐ Avoid placing characters in remote settings
   Ⓑ Avoid having more than one major character
   Ⓒ Avoid using people as models whose lives are unusual
   Ⓓ Avoid making characters into stereotypes

27. What does the professor imply is the importance of flat characters?

   Ⓐ They act more predictably than other characters.
   Ⓑ They are difficult for readers to understand.
   Ⓒ They help reveal the main character's personality.
   Ⓓ They are the only characters able to experience defeat.

28. Listen to Track 50.

   Ⓐ To indicate that he is about to explain what type of drawing he wants
   Ⓑ To help students understand a term that may be confusing
   Ⓒ To indicate that he used the wrong word earlier
   Ⓓ To motivate the students to do better work

Directions: Listen to Track 51.

Earth Science

Sahara Desert

Directions: Now answer the questions.

29. What is the lecture mainly about?

    Ⓐ An example of rapid climate change

    Ⓑ A comparison of two mechanisms of climate change

    Ⓒ The weather conditions in the present-day Sahara

    Ⓓ Recent geological findings made in the Sahara

30. Not long ago, the Sahara had a different climate. What evidence does the professor mention to support this? *Choose 3 answers.*

    A Ancient pollen

    B Bones from large animals

    C Rock paintings

    D Agriculture in ancient Egypt

    E Underground water

31. In the lecture, what do the Ice Age and the creation of the Sahara Desert both illustrate about past climate changes? *Choose 2 answers.*

    A That some climate changes benefitted the development of civilization

    B That some climate changes were not caused by human activity

    C That some climate changes were caused by a decrease of moisture in the atmosphere

    D That some climate changes were caused by changes in Earth's motion and position

32. What started the runaway effect that led to the Sahara area of North Africa becoming a desert?

    Ⓐ The prevailing winds became stronger.

    Ⓑ The seasonal rains moved to a different area.

    Ⓒ The vegetation started to die off in large areas.

    Ⓓ The soil lost its ability to retain rainwater.

33. The professor mentions a theory that people migrating from the Sahara were important to the development of the Egyptian civilization. Which sentence best describes the professor's attitude toward this theory?

   Ⓐ It is exciting because it perfectly explains recent archaeological discoveries.
   Ⓑ It is problematic because it goes too far beyond the generally available data.
   Ⓒ It raises an interesting possibility and he hopes to see more evidence for it.
   Ⓓ It cannot be taken seriously until it explains how the migrants got to Egypt.

34. Listen to Track 52.

   Ⓐ To correct a misstatement he made about the Sahara's climate
   Ⓑ To suggest that the current dryness of the Sahara is exaggerated
   Ⓒ To indicate that scientists are not in agreement about the Sahara's past climate
   Ⓓ To emphasize the difference between the current and past climates of the Sahara

SPEAKING

This section measures your ability to speak in English about a variety of topics.

There are six questions in this section. For each question, you will be given a short time to prepare your response. When the preparation time is up, answer the question as completely as possible in the time indicated for that question. You should record your responses so that you can review them later and compare them with the answer key and scoring rubrics.

1. You will now be asked to speak about a familiar topic. Give yourself 15 seconds to prepare your response. Then record yourself speaking for 45 seconds.

   Listen to Track 53.

   > Talk about a photograph or painting you have seen that was memorable. Explain what you liked or disliked about it.
   >
   > | Preparation Time: 15 seconds |
   > | --- |
   > | Response Time: 45 seconds |

2. You will now be asked to give your opinion about a familiar topic. Give yourself 15 seconds to prepare your response. Then record yourself speaking for 45 seconds.

   Listen to Track 54.

   > Some people have one career throughout their lives. Other people do different kinds of work at different points in their lives. Which do you think is better? Explain why.
   >
   > | Preparation Time: 15 seconds |
   > | --- |
   > | Response Time: 45 seconds |

3. You will now read a short passage and listen to a conversation on the same topic. You will then be asked a question about them. After you hear the question, give yourself 30 seconds to prepare your response. Then record yourself speaking for 60 seconds.

   Listen to Track 55.

History Seminars Should Be Shorter

Currently, all of the seminar classes in the history department are three hours long. I would like to propose that history seminars be shortened to two hours. I make this proposal for two reasons. First, most students just cannot concentrate for three hours straight. I myself have taken these three-hour seminars and found them tiring and sometimes boring. Also, when a seminar lasts that long, people stop concentrating and stop learning, so the third hour of a three-hour seminar is a waste of everyone's time. Two-hour seminars would be much more efficient.

Sincerely,

Tim Lawson

Listen to Track 56.

The woman expresses her opinion about the proposal described in the letter. Briefly summarize the proposal. Then state her opinion about the proposal and explain the reasons she gives for holding that opinion.

4. You will now read a short passage and listen to a lecture on the same topic. You will then be asked a question about them. After you hear the question, give yourself 30 seconds to prepare your response. Then record yourself speaking for 60 seconds.

Listen to Track 57.

Reading Time: 45 seconds

Explicit Memories and Implicit Memories

In everyday life, when people speak of memory, they are almost always speaking about what psychologists would call explicit memories. An explicit memory is a conscious or intentional recollection, usually of facts, names, events, or other things that a person can state or declare. There is another kind of memory that is not conscious. Memories of this kind are called implicit memories. An individual can have an experience that he or she cannot consciously recall yet still display reactions that indicate the experience has been somehow recorded in his or her brain.

Listen to Track 58.

Using the example of the car advertisement, explain what is meant by implicit memory.

Preparation Time: 30 seconds
Response Time: 60 seconds

---

5. You will now listen to part of a conversation. You will then be asked a question about it. After you hear the question, give yourself 20 seconds to prepare your response. Then record yourself speaking for 60 seconds.

Listen to Track 59.

> Briefly summarize the problem the speakers are discussing. Then state which of the two solutions from the conversation you would recommend. Explain the reasons for your recommendation.
>
> **Preparation Time: 20 seconds**
> **Response Time: 60 seconds**

6. You will now listen to part of a lecture. You will then be asked a question about it. After you hear the question, give yourself 20 seconds to prepare your response. Then record yourself speaking for 60 seconds.

Listen to Track 60.

Using points and examples from the talk, explain the difference between active and passive attention.

Preparation Time: 20 seconds
Response Time: 60 seconds

WRITING

This section measures your ability to write in English to communicate in an academic environment.

There are two writing questions in this section.

For question 1, you will read a passage and listen to a lecture about the same topic. You may take notes while you read and listen. Then you will write a response to a question based on what you have read and heard. You may look back at the passage when answering the question. You may use your notes to help you answer the question. You have 20 minutes to plan and write your response.

For question 2, you will write an essay based on your own knowledge and experience. You have 30 minutes to plan and complete your essay.

1. **Directions:** Give yourself 3 minutes to read the passage.

Reading Time: 3 minutes

Communal online encyclopedias represent one of the latest resources to be found on the Internet. They are in many respects like traditional printed encyclopedias: collections of articles on various subjects. What is specific to these online encyclopedias, however, is that any Internet user can contribute a new article or make an editorial change in an existing one. As a result, the encyclopedia is authored by the whole community of Internet users. The idea might sound attractive, but the communal online encyclopedias have several important problems that make them much less valuable than traditional, printed encyclopedias.

First, contributors to a communal online encyclopedia often lack academic credentials, thereby making their contributions partially informed at best and downright inaccurate in many cases. Traditional encyclopedias are written by trained experts who adhere to standards of academic rigor that nonspecialists cannot really achieve.

Second, even if the original entry in the online encyclopedia is correct, the communal nature of these online encyclopedias gives unscrupulous users and vandals or hackers the opportunity to fabricate, delete, and corrupt information in the encyclopedia. Once changes have been made to the original text, an unsuspecting user cannot tell the entry has been tampered with. None of this is possible with a traditional encyclopedia.

Third, the communal encyclopedias focus too frequently, and in too great a depth, on trivial and popular topics, which creates a false impression of what is important and what is not. A child doing research for a school project may discover that a major historical event receives as much attention in an online encyclopedia as, say, a single long-running television program. The traditional encyclopedia provides a considered view of what topics to include or exclude and contains a sense of proportion that online "democratic" communal encyclopedias do not.

Listen to Track 61.

Directions: You have 20 minutes to plan and write your response. Your response will be judged on the basis of the quality of your writing and on how well your response presents the points in the lecture and their relationship to the reading passage. Typically, an effective response will be 150 to 225 words.

Listen to Track 62.

Summarize the points made in the lecture, being sure to explain how they oppose the specific points made in the reading passage.

_____

_____

_____

_____

_____

_____

_____

_____

_____

_____

_____

_____

_____

_____

_____

_____

_____

_____

_____

2. **Directions:** Read the question below. You have 30 minutes to plan, write, and revise your essay. Typically, an effective response will contain a minimum of 300 words.

Response Time: 30 minutes·

Do you agree or disagree with the following statement?

Life today is easier and more comfortable than it was when your grandparents were children.

Use specific reasons and examples to support your answer.

_____

_____

_____

_____

_____

_____

_____

_____

_____

_____

_____

_____

_____

_____

_____

_____

ANSWERS

Reading Section

1. D	22. A
2. D	23. D
3. B	24. D
4. A	25. B, C
5. C	26. B
6. B	27. C
7. A	28. B, C, F
8. A	29. C
9. C	30. B
10. D	31. C
11. C	32. D
12. B	33. B
13. C	34. D
14. B, C, F	35. A
15. C	36. D
16. C	37. A
17. B	38. B
18. C	39. A
19. A	40. C
20. B	41. D
21. D	42. B, D, F

Listening Section

1. C	8. A
2. A	9. D
3. D	10. A, B, E
4. B, C	11. B, C
5. B	12. A, B
6. B	13. D
7. A	14. D

15. B, C
16. B
17. A
18. D
19. C
20. A, C
21. C
22. B
23. B
24. A

25. A
26. D
27. C
28. B
29. A
30. A, C, E
31. B, D
32. B
33. C
34. D

Speaking Section

1.   There are many ways you could answer this particular question. You could talk about a particular artist's painting or photograph, a family photograph, or even a friend's painting. You might start by giving a brief description of the photograph or painting and talk briefly about its subject matter or important features. You then will need to give at least one well-developed reason why you like or dislike the photograph or painting. You do not want to spend too much time describing the photograph and run out of time to explain why you like it.

   Your response should be intelligible, should demonstrate effective use of grammar and vocabulary, and should be well developed and coherent. Your response is scored using the Independent Speaking Rubric (see Appendix A).

2.   To respond to this particular question, you should clearly state what your opinion is: do you think it is better to have one career or do different kinds of work? You should then give reasons to support your opinion. If you think that it is better to have one career, you could say that if you have a career that you love, there is no reason to change. Many people enjoy doing one thing that they are very good

at. You may then talk about other advantages, such as money or the possibility to advance over time. You may give a more specific example to help you explain. For example, you could say that a doctor has gone to school for a long time and it takes a long time to learn to be a good doctor, so in this case changing careers would not make sense.

   If you think it is better to do different kinds of work, you would develop your opinion in a similar way. You could say that doing one job for your whole life would not be interesting, and that as technology progresses, many new fields to work in become available. You might then provide specific information about new fields, such as those connected to new computer technology.

   It is important to understand that there is no "correct" answer to this question. Whichever option you prefer, your answer should be supported with examples. It is important to make sure that you state your opinion and develop your response with good examples and relevant details.

   Your response should be intelligible, should demonstrate effective use of grammar and vocabulary, and should be well developed and coherent. Your response is scored using the Independent Speaking Rubric (see Appendix A).

3.   To respond to this particular question, you should state the woman's opinion of the letter writer's proposal to shorten history seminars to two hours. In this case, the woman disagrees with the letter writer's proposal.

After stating that the woman disagrees with the proposal, you should convey the two main reasons she gives for holding that opinion. You will need to connect information from the conversation to the reading in order for the response to be complete. The woman says that the first reason given for shortening history seminars—that students cannot concentrate for three hours—isn't valid. She says that Tim, the letter writer, is not a typical student and that he stays up late at night, and sometimes even sleeps in class.

Your response should also convey the woman's second reason for not agreeing with the letter writer's proposal. The letter writer thinks that the third hour of the seminar is a waste of time because people don't learn anything. The woman thinks, however, that the last hour is when the discussions are the most interesting and that it is the most important part of the seminar.

Your response should be intelligible, should demonstrate effective use of grammar and vocabulary, and should be well developed and coherent. Your response is scored using the Integrated Speaking Rubric (see Appendix A).

4.   To respond to this particular question you should first explain the idea of implicit memory as it was presented in the reading. An implicit memory is not conscious and cannot be recalled, but it is recorded in our brains. You may choose to contrast this with explicit memory, which is consciously recalled, but do not spend too

much time at this stage. You must give yourself enough time to discuss the professor's example.

You should then use the example given by the professor to explain implicit memory. In the example, implicit memory is demonstrated when a person drives by a billboard and sees an advertisement for a car called "Panther" but has no recollection of the billboard. Then later, the same person recalls the word "Panther" when asked to name an animal that starts with the letter "P," even though "pig" is a more common animal that begins with "p." This shows that the billboard has had an effect on the person's memory; this is an illustration of implicit memory.

You do not need to repeat all of the details from the reading and the lecture, but instead integrate points from both to answer the question completely.

Your response should be intelligible, should demonstrate effective use of grammar and vocabulary, and should be well developed and coherent. Your response is scored using the Integrated Speaking Rubric (see Appendix A).

5.   To respond to this particular question you should *briefly* describe the problem. It is enough to say that the study group hasn't been studying much because they have become friends and joke around a lot.

Next, you need to choose *one* of the two solutions and explain why you think that solution is best. The two solutions in this conversation are: (1) meet on a day other than Fridays, or (2) have somebody be the leader, who would set an agenda and make sure work gets done. It does not matter which of the two proposed solutions you choose, since there is no "right" solution or "wrong" solution. You should choose the solution that you think is best and support your choice with reasons why you think it is best. The reasons you give can include information provided by the speakers as well as your own experiences.

For example, if you believe the first solution is preferable, you could speak about the disadvantages of the second solution; you might say that having a leader would change the way the group works, and that some people might not agree with this idea. Adding a leader could create more problems than it solves, and it might be too much responsibility for the student. Therefore, changing the day of the meetings is the better solution. If you believe the second solution is preferable, you might say that organization is what the group needs, and that the woman would get good experience from being the leader of the group. These are just examples of possible responses; remember, this type of question can be answered in many different ways.

Your response should be intelligible, should demonstrate effective use of grammar and vocabulary, and should be well developed and coherent. Your response is scored using the Integrated Speaking Rubric (see Appendix A).

6.   This particular question requires you to summarize the contents of a lecture you hear. In your response, you should talk about the two different kinds of attention that the professor describes.

The order in which you discuss the two types of attention is not important as long as you discuss both types fully and make clear what is different about them. The professor says that active attention is voluntary; it occurs when people force themselves to pay attention to something. A boring lecture about frogs will require students to pay active attention, but they will not be able to maintain their attention for long.

You would then talk about passive attention. Passive attention is involuntary and requires no effort to maintain,

unlike active attention, which does require effort; it occurs when people are naturally interested in the material. If a teacher pulls out a live frog, the students become more interested and passive attention is maintained.

You should budget your time so that you are able to include a good summary of both types of attention and talk about both examples of the frog lecture.

Your response should be intelligible, should demonstrate effective use of grammar and vocabulary, and should be well developed and coherent. Your response is scored using the Integrated Speaking Rubric (see Appendix A).

Writing Section

1.   What is important to understand from the lecture is that the professor disagrees with the criticisms of communal online encyclopedias presented in the reading, namely that the encyclopedias contain inaccurate information; that unscrupulous users can tamper with the information in the encyclopedias; and that the encyclopedias do not distinguish important topics from unimportant ones.

In your response, you should convey the reasons presented by the professor for why the criticisms of communal online encyclopedias are not convincing. A high-scoring response will include the following points made by the professor that cast doubt on the points made in the reading:

Point made in the reading	Counterpoint made in the lecture
Since entries in communal online encyclopedias are not always written by experts, they can be inaccurate and unreliable.	No encyclopedia is perfectly accurate. What really matters is how easily and quickly the mistakes can be corrected. In this regard, online encyclopedias are better than the traditional ones, because inaccurate content in online encyclopedias can be revised much faster.
Because anyone can make revisions to the content of online encyclopedias, unscrupulous users, vandals, and hackers can intentionally corrupt the content of articles in the encyclopedias.	Online encyclopedias have taken steps to protect their content from unscrupulous users, vandals, and hackers. Some important content is presented in a "read-only" format that cannot be revised. Also, special editors now monitor changes made to articles and eliminate revisions that are malicious.
Communal online encyclopedias often give equal space to articles on trivial topics and articles on serious topics. This creates a false impression about which information is important and which is not.	The fact that online encyclopedias contain information on all kinds of subjects is not a weakness but a strength. Diversity of topics covered by online encyclopedias is a true reflection of the diversity of people's interests. In contrast, traditional encyclopedias have limited space, and editors who choose which entries to include do not always take diverse interests into account.

Your response is scored using the Integrated Writing Rubric (see Appendix A). A response that receives a score of 5 clearly conveys all three of the main points in the table using accurate sentence structure and vocabulary.

2. To earn a top score, you should develop a multi-paragraph essay that responds to the issue of whether life is easier and more comfortable now than when your grandparents were children. Typically an effective response will contain a minimum of 300 words.

One successful way to express agreement with the prompt is to describe how developments in a particular field have helped to make life easier. Describing how work in the household has become so much easier as a result of the availability of electronic appliances could be one way to develop such a response; you could explain how these machines save time on doing household tasks that years ago took many hours or even days to complete, and conclude that life is much easier now because we have more free time.

On the other hand, you could disagree with the prompt by explaining that life was more comfortable when your grandparents were children. For example, it may be the case that when your grandparents were children, the air and water were cleaner, food was fresher, and some types of jobs were less stressful; you could discuss the importance of any of those in support of your opinion.

Keep in mind that there is no "correct" answer to this question. Either side of the issue can be supported with examples and reasons. It is important to make sure that you state your opinion and develop a response that explains your opinion well. The development of your essay is judged by how effectively you support your opinion; a well-developed essay will contain clearly appropriate reasons, examples, and details that illustrate your opinion. Development is not evaluated simply in terms of how many words you write.

Your response should be well organized. A well-organized essay allows an evaluator to read from the beginning to the end of the essay without becoming confused. You should be sure not to just repeat the same information in different ways.

The quality and accuracy of the sentence structure and vocabulary you use to express your ideas is also very important.

Your response is scored using the Independent Writing Rubric (see Appendix A).

TOEFL iBT Test 4

READING

This section measures your ability to understand academic passages in English.

There are three passages in the section. Give yourself 20 minutes to read each passage and answer the questions about it. The entire section will take 60 minutes to complete.

You may look back at a passage when answering the questions. You can skip questions and go back to them later as long as there is time remaining.

Directions: Read the passage. Then answer the questions. Give yourself 20 minutes to complete this practice set.

POPULATION AND CLIMATE

The human population on Earth has grown to the point that it is having an effect on Earth's atmosphere and ecosystems. Burning of fossil fuels, deforestation, urbanization, cultivation of rice and cattle, and the manufacture of chlorofluorocarbons (CFCs) for propellants and refrigerants are increasing the concentration of carbon dioxide, methane, nitrogen oxides, sulphur oxides, dust, and CFCs in the atmosphere. About 70 percent of the Sun's energy passes through the atmosphere and strikes Earth's surface. This radiation heats the surface of the land and ocean, and these surfaces then reradiate infrared radiation back into space. This allows Earth to avoid heating up too much. However, not all of the infrared radiation makes it into space; some is absorbed by gases in the atmosphere and is reradiated back to Earth's surface. A greenhouse gas is one that absorbs infrared radiation and then reradiates some of this radiation back to Earth. Carbon dioxide, CFCs, methane, and nitrogen oxides are greenhouse gases. The natural greenhouse effect of our atmosphere is well established. In fact, without greenhouse gases in the atmosphere, scientists calculate that Earth would be about 33°C cooler than it currently is.

The current concentration of carbon dioxide in the atmosphere is about 360 parts per million. Human activities are having a major influence on atmospheric carbon dioxide concentrations, which are rising so fast that current predictions are that atmospheric concentrations of carbon dioxide will double in the next 50 to 100 years. The Intergovernmental Panel on Climate Change (IPCC) report in 1992, which represents a consensus of most atmospheric scientists, predicts that a doubling of carbon dioxide concentration would raise global temperatures anywhere between 1.4°C and 4.5°C. The IPCC report issued in 2001 raised the temperature prediction almost twofold. The suggested rise in temperature is greater than the changes that occurred in the past between ice ages. The increase in temperatures would not be uniform, with the smallest changes at the equator and changes two or three times as great at the poles. The local effects of these global changes are difficult to predict, but it is generally agreed that they may include alterations in ocean currents, increased winter flooding in some areas of the Northern Hemisphere, a higher incidence of summer drought in some areas, and rising sea levels, which may flood low-lying countries.

Scientists are actively investigating the feedback mechanism within the physical, chemical, and biological components of Earth's climate system in order to make accurate predictions of the effects the rise in greenhouse gases will have on future global climates. Global circulation models are important tools in this process. These models incorporate current knowledge on atmospheric circulation patterns, ocean currents, the effect of landmasses, and the like to predict climate under changed conditions. There are several models, and all show agreement on a global scale. For example, all models show substantial changes in climate when carbon dioxide concentration is doubled. However, there are significant differences in the regional climates predicted by different models. Most models project greater temperature increases in mid-latitude regions and in mid-continental regions relative to the global average. Additionally, changes in precipitation patterns are predicted, with decreases in mid-latitude regions and increased rainfall in some tropical areas. Finally, most models predict that there will be increased occurrences of extreme events, such as extended periods without rain (drought), extreme heat waves, greater seasonal variation in temperatures, and increases in the frequency and magnitude of severe storms. Plants and animals have strong responses to virtually every aspect of these projected global changes.

The challenge of predicting organismal responses to global climate change is difficult. Partly, this is due to the fact that there are more studies of short-term, individual organism responses than there are of long-term, systemwide studies. It is extremely difficult, both monetarily and physically, for scientists to conduct field studies at spatial and temporal scales that are large enough to include all the components of real-world systems, especially ecosystems with large, freely ranging organisms. One way paleobiologists try to get around this limitation is to attempt to reconstruct past climates by examining fossil life.

The relative roles that abiotic and biotic factors play in the distribution of organisms is especially important now, when the world is confronted with the consequences of a growing human population. Changes in climate, land use, and habitat destruction are currently causing dramatic decreases in biodiversity throughout the world. An understanding of climate-organism relationships is essential to efforts to preserve and manage Earth's biodiversity.

Directions: Now answer the questions.

PARAGRAPH 1

The human population on Earth has grown to the point that it is having an effect on Earth's atmosphere and ecosystems. Burning of fossil fuels, deforestation, urbanization, cultivation of rice and cattle, and the manufacture of chlorofluorocarbons (CFCs) for propellants and refrigerants are increasing the concentration of carbon dioxide, methane, nitrogen oxides, sulphur oxides, dust, and CFCs in the atmosphere. About 70 percent of the Sun's energy passes through the atmosphere and strikes Earth's surface. This radiation heats the surface of the land and ocean, and these surfaces then reradiate infrared radiation back into space. This allows Earth to avoid heating up too much. However, not all of the infrared radiation makes it into space; some is absorbed by gases in the atmosphere and is reradiated back to Earth's surface. A greenhouse gas is one that absorbs infrared radiation and then reradiates some of this radiation back to Earth. Carbon dioxide, CFCs, methane, and nitrogen oxides are greenhouse gases. The natural greenhouse effect of our atmosphere is well established. In fact, without greenhouse gases in the atmosphere, scientists calculate that Earth would be about 33°C cooler than it currently is.

1. The phrase "makes it" in the passage is closest in meaning to
   Ⓐ is reflected
   Ⓑ collects
   Ⓒ arrives
   Ⓓ blends

2. It can be inferred from paragraph 1 that one positive aspect of greenhouse gases is that they

ⓐ absorb 70 percent of the Sun's energy
ⓑ can be rapidly replenished in the atmosphere
ⓒ remove pollutants from ecosystems
ⓓ help keep Earth warm

PARAGRAPH 2

The current concentration of carbon dioxide in the atmosphere is about 360 parts per million. Human activities are having a major influence on atmospheric carbon dioxide concentrations, which are rising so fast that current predictions are that atmospheric concentrations of carbon dioxide will double in the next 50 to 100 years. The Intergovernmental Panel on Climate Change (IPCC) report in 1992, which represents a consensus of most atmospheric scientists, predicts that a doubling of carbon dioxide concentration would raise global temperatures anywhere between 1.4°C and 4.5°C. The IPCC report issued in 2001 raised the temperature prediction almost twofold. The suggested rise in temperature is greater than the changes that occurred in the past between ice ages. The increase in temperatures would not be uniform, with the smallest changes at the equator and changes two or three times as great at the poles. The local effects of these global changes are difficult to predict, but it is generally agreed that they may include alterations in ocean currents, increased winter flooding in some areas of the Northern Hemisphere, a higher incidence of summer drought in some areas, and rising sea levels, which may flood low-lying countries.

3. According to paragraph 2, what can be said about the effects of global changes?

ⓐ The local plants and animals will be permanently damaged.
ⓑ It is hard to know exactly what form the local effects will take.
ⓒ Seawater levels will fall around the world.
ⓓ The effects will not occur in some regions of the world.

4. Which of the sentences below best expresses the essential information in the highlighted sentence in paragraph 2? Incorrect choices change the meaning in important ways or leave out essential information.

ⓐ The rapid rise of carbon dioxide concentrations can be attributed largely to the actions of humans.
ⓑ Predictions about atmospheric concentrations of carbon dioxide indicate that the influence of human activities will double soon.
ⓒ In the next 50 to 100 years, human activities will no longer have an influence on atmospheric carbon dioxide concentrations.
ⓓ Human activities can influence current predictions about atmospheric conditions.

5. The word "consensus" in the passage is closest in meaning to

ⓐ publication
ⓑ debate
ⓒ collection
ⓓ agreement

**P
A
R
A
G
R
A
P
H

3**

Scientists are actively investigating the feedback mechanism within the physical, chemical, and biological components of Earth's climate system in order to make accurate predictions of the effects the rise in greenhouse gases will have on future global climates. Global circulation models are important tools in this process. These models incorporate current knowledge on atmospheric circulation patterns, ocean currents, the effect of landmasses, and the like to predict climate under changed conditions. There are several models, and all show agreement on a global scale. For example, all models show substantial changes in climate when carbon dioxide concentration is doubled. However, there are significant differences in the regional climates predicted by different models. Most models project greater temperature increases in mid-latitude regions and in mid-continental regions relative to the global average. Additionally, changes in precipitation patterns are predicted, with decreases in mid-latitude regions and increased rainfall in some tropical areas. Finally, most models predict that there will be increased occurrences of extreme events, such as extended periods without rain (drought), extreme heat waves, greater seasonal variation in temperatures, and increases in the frequency and magnitude of severe storms. Plants and animals have strong responses to virtually every aspect of these projected global changes.

6. The phrase "this process" refers to

   Ⓐ the interaction between physical and biological components of Earth's climate system
   Ⓑ the increase of greenhouse gases in the atmosphere
   Ⓒ predicting future global climate
   Ⓓ global circulation models

7. According to paragraph 3, rainfall amounts are predicted to decrease in what parts of the world?

   Ⓐ In mid-latitude regions
   Ⓑ In tropical areas
   Ⓒ In mid-continental regions
   Ⓓ At the poles

8. The word "incorporate" in the passage is closest in meaning to

   Ⓐ describe
   Ⓑ include
   Ⓒ expand
   Ⓓ present

9. The word "virtually" in the passage is closest in meaning to

   Ⓐ nearly
   Ⓑ presumably
   Ⓒ usually
   Ⓓ visually

10. According to paragraph 3, climate models predict that all of the following events will occur with the increase in greenhouse gases EXCEPT

Ⓐ greater seasonal temperature changes
Ⓑ prolonged heat waves
Ⓒ increased diversity of plants and animals
Ⓓ longer dry periods

The relative roles that abiotic and biotic factors play in the distribution of organisms is especially important now, when the world is confronted with the consequences of a growing human population. Changes in climate, land use, and habitat destruction are currently causing dramatic decreases in biodiversity throughout the world. An understanding of climate-organism relationships is essential to efforts to preserve and manage Earth's biodiversity.

11. The author's main purpose in paragraph 5 is to

Ⓐ explain the process of studying organism responses to climate change
Ⓑ stress the importance of learning how climate affects plants and animals
Ⓒ illustrate an important point about factors affecting biodiversity
Ⓓ examine current research practices on the distribution of organisms on Earth

The human population on Earth has grown to the point that it is having an effect on Earth's atmosphere and ecosystems. Burning of fossil fuels, deforestation, urbanization, cultivation of rice and cattle, and the manufacture of chlorofluorocarbons (CFCs) for propellants and refrigerants are increasing the concentration of carbon dioxide, methane, nitrogen oxides, sulphur oxides, dust, and CFCs in the atmosphere. About 70 percent of the Sun's energy passes through the atmosphere and strikes Earth's surface. This radiation heats the surface of the land and ocean, and these surfaces then reradiate infrared radiation back into space. This allows Earth to avoid heating up too much. However, not all of the infrared radiation makes it into space; some is absorbed by gases in the atmosphere and is reradiated back to Earth's surface. A greenhouse gas is one that absorbs infrared radiation and then reradiates some of this radiation back to Earth. Carbon dioxide, CFCs, methane, and nitrogen oxides are greenhouse gases. The natural greenhouse effect of our atmosphere is well established. In fact, without greenhouse gases in the atmosphere, scientists calculate that Earth would be about 33°C cooler than it currently is.

The current concentration of carbon dioxide in the atmosphere is about 360 parts per million. Human activities are having a major influence on atmospheric carbon dioxide concentrations, which are rising so fast that current predictions are that atmospheric concentrations of carbon dioxide will double in the next 50 to 100 years. The Intergovernmental Panel on Climate Change (IPCC) report in 1992, which represents a consensus of most atmospheric scientists, predicts that a doubling of carbon dioxide concentration would raise global temperatures anywhere between 1.4°C and 4.5°C. The IPCC report issued in 2001 raised the temperature prediction almost twofold. The suggested rise in temperature is greater than the changes that occurred in the past between ice ages. The increase in temperatures would not be uniform, with the smallest changes at the equator and changes two or three times as great at the poles. The local effects of these global changes are difficult to predict, but it is generally agreed that they may include alterations in ocean currents, increased winter flooding in some areas of the Northern Hemisphere, a higher incidence of summer drought in some areas, and rising sea levels, which may flood low-lying countries.

Scientists are actively investigating the feedback mechanism within the physical, chemical, and biological components of Earth's climate system in order to make accurate predictions of the effects the rise in greenhouse gases will have on future global climates. Global circulation models are important tools in this process. These models incorporate current knowledge on atmospheric circulation patterns, ocean currents, the effect of landmasses, and the like to predict climate under changed conditions. There are several models, and all show agreement on a global scale. For example, all models show substantial changes in climate when carbon dioxide concentration is doubled. However, there are significant differences in the regional climates predicted by different models. Most models project greater temperature increases in mid-latitude regions and in mid-continental regions relative to the global average. Additionally, changes in precipitation patterns are predicted, with decreases in mid-latitude regions and increased rainfall in some tropical areas. Finally, most models predict that there will be increased occurrences of extreme events, such as extended periods without rain (drought), extreme heat waves, greater seasonal variation in temperatures, and increases in the frequency and magnitude of severe storms. Plants and animals have strong responses to virtually every aspect of these projected global changes.

The challenge of predicting organismal responses to global climate change is difficult. Partly, this is due to the fact that there are more studies of short-term, individual organism responses than there are of long-term, systemwide studies. It is extremely difficult, both monetarily and physically, for scientists to conduct field studies at spatial and temporal scales that are large enough to include all the components of real-world systems, especially ecosystems with large, freely ranging organisms. One way paleobiologists try to get around this limitation is to attempt to reconstruct past climates by examining fossil life.

The relative roles that abiotic and biotic factors play in the distribution of organisms is especially important now, when the world is confronted with the consequences of a growing human population. Changes in climate, land use, and habitat destruction are currently causing dramatic decreases in biodiversity throughout the world. An understanding of climate-organism relationships is essential to efforts to preserve and manage Earth's biodiversity.

12. Look at the terms "greenhouse gas," "atmospheric circulation patterns," "global scale," and "biotic factors." Which of these terms is defined in the passage?

   Ⓐ Greenhouse gas
   Ⓑ Atmospheric circulation patterns
   Ⓒ Global scale
   Ⓓ Biotic factors

The challenge of predicting organismal responses to global climate change is difficult. ■ Partly, this is due to the fact that there are more studies of short-term, individual organism responses than there are of long-term, systemwide studies. ■ It is extremely difficult, both monetarily and physically, for scientists to conduct field studies at spatial and temporal scales that are large enough to include all the components of real-world systems, especially ecosystems with large, freely ranging organisms. ■ One way paleobiologists try to get around this limitation is to attempt to reconstruct past climates by examining fossil life. ■

13. Look at the four squares [■] that indicate where the following sentence can be added to the passage.

Much of this work depends on the assumption that life forms adapted to a particular climate in the present were adapted to the same type of climate in the past.

Where would the sentence best fit?

Ⓐ The challenge of predicting organismal responses to global climate change is difficult. **Much of this work depends on the assumption that life forms adapted to a particular climate in the present were adapted to the same type of climate in the past.** Partly, this is due to the fact that there are more studies of short-term, individual organism responses than there are of long-term, systemwide studies. ■ It is extremely difficult, both monetarily and physically, for scientists to conduct field studies at spatial and temporal scales that are large enough to include all the components of real-world systems, especially ecosystems with large, freely ranging organisms. ■ One way paleobiologists try to get around this limitation is to attempt to reconstruct past climates by examining fossil life. ■

Ⓑ The challenge of predicting organismal responses to global climate change is difficult. ■ Partly, this is due to the fact that there are more studies of short-term, individual organism responses than there are of long-term, systemwide studies. **Much of this work depends on the assumption that life forms adapted to a particular climate in the present were adapted to the same type of climate in the past.** It is extremely difficult, both monetarily and physically, for scientists to conduct field studies at spatial and temporal scales that are large enough to include all the components of real-world systems, especially ecosystems with large, freely ranging organisms. ■ One way paleobiologists try to get around this limitation is to attempt to reconstruct past climates by examining fossil life. ■

Ⓒ The challenge of predicting organismal responses to global climate change is difficult. ■ Partly, this is due to the fact that there are more studies of short-term, individual organism responses than there are of long-term, systemwide studies. ■ It is extremely difficult, both monetarily and physically, for scientists to conduct field studies at spatial and temporal scales that are large enough to include all the components of real-world systems, especially ecosystems with large, freely ranging organisms. **Much of this work depends on the assumption that life forms adapted to a particular climate in the present were adapted to the same type of climate in the past.** One way paleobiologists try to get around this limitation is to attempt to reconstruct past climates by examining fossil life. ■

Ⓓ The challenge of predicting organismal responses to global climate change is difficult. ■ Partly, this is due to the fact that there are more studies of short-term, individual organism responses than there are of long-term, systemwide studies. ■ It is extremely difficult, both monetarily and physically, for scientists to conduct field studies at spatial and temporal scales that are large enough to include all the components of real-world systems, especially ecosystems with large, freely ranging organisms. ■ One way paleobiologists try to get around this limitation is to attempt to reconstruct past climates by examining fossil life. **Much of this work depends on the assumption that life forms adapted to a particular climate in the present were adapted to the same type of climate in the past.**

14. **Directions:** An introductory sentence for a brief summary of the passage is provided below. Complete the summary by selecting the THREE answer choices that express the most important ideas in the passage. Some sentences do not belong in the summary because they express ideas that are not presented in the passage or are minor ideas in the passage.

Write your answer choices in the spaces where they belong. You can either write the letter of your answer choice or you can copy the sentence.

> **Human population on Earth is affecting both the atmosphere and the ecosystems.**
>
> ●
>
> ●
>
> ●

Answer Choices

A The survival of organisms on Earth is directly related to the amount of fossil fuels that are consumed.

B Atmospheric carbon dioxide concentrations are rising quickly.

C Scientists are working on ways to make precise forecasts of how the increase of greenhouse gases will affect Earth.

D Scientists predict that temperature changes would be greater at the poles than at the equator.

E Global circulation models can be used to measure the concentrations of chlorofluorocarbons in the atmosphere.

F The ability to make accurate predictions about global climate presents several difficulties.

Directions: Read the passage. Then answer the questions. Give yourself 20 minutes to complete this practice set.

EUROPE IN THE TWELFTH CENTURY

Europe in the eleventh century underwent enormous social, technological, and economic changes, but this did not create a new Europe—it created two new ones. The north was developed as a rigidly hierarchical society in which status was determined, or was at least indicated, by the extent to which one owned, controlled, or labored on land; whereas the Mediterranean south developed a more fluid, and therefore more chaotic, world in which industry and commerce predominated and social status both reflected and resulted from the role that one played in the public life of the community. In other words, individual identity and social community in the north were established on a personal basis, whereas in the south they were established on a civic basis. By the start of the twelfth century, northern and southern Europe were very different places indeed, and the Europeans themselves noticed it and commented on it.

Political dominance belonged to the north. Germany, France, and England had large populations and large armies that made them, in the political and military senses, the masters of western Europe. Organized by the practices known collectively as feudalism[1], these kingdoms emerged as powerful states with sophisticated machineries of government. Their kings and queens were the leading figures of the age; their castles and cathedrals stood majestically on the landscape as symbols of their might; their armies both energized and defined the age. Moreover, feudal society showed a remarkable ability to adapt to new needs by encouraging the parallel development of domestic urban life and commercial networks; in some regions of the north, in fact, feudal society may even have developed in response to the start of the trends toward bigger cities. But southern Europe took the lead in economic and cultural life. Though the leading Mediterranean states were small in size, they were considerably wealthier than their northern counterparts. The Italian city of Palermo in the twelfth century, for example, alone generated four times the commercial tax revenue of the entire kingdom of England. Southern communities also possessed urbane, multilingual cultures that made them the intellectual and artistic leaders of the age. Levels of general literacy in the south far surpassed those of the north, and the people of the south put that learning to use on a large scale. Science, mathematics, poetry, law, historical writing, religious speculation, translation, and classical studies all began to flourish; throughout most of the twelfth century, most of the continent's best brains flocked to southern Europe.

So too did a lot of the north's soldiers. One of the central themes of the political history of the twelfth century was the continual effort by the northern kingdoms to extend their control southward in the hope of tapping into the Mediterranean bonanza. The German emperors starting with Otto I (936–973), for example, struggled ceaselessly to establish their control over the cities of northern Italy, since those cities generated more revenue than all of rural Germany combined. The kings of France used every means at their disposal to push the lower border of their kingdom to the

Mediterranean shoreline. And the Normans who conquered and ruled England estab-lished outposts of Norman power in Sicily and the adjacent lands of southern Italy; the English kings also hoped or claimed at various times to be, either through money or marriage diplomacy, the rulers of several Mediterranean states. But as the northern world pressed southward, so too did some of the cultural norms and social mecha-nisms of the south expand northward. Over the course of the twelfth century, the feudal kingdoms witnessed a proliferation of cities modeled in large degree on those of the south. Contact with the merchants and financiers of the Mediterranean led to the development of northern industry and international trade (which helped to pay for many of the castles and cathedrals mentioned earlier). And education spread as well, culminating in the foundation of what is arguably medieval Europe's greatest invention: the university. The relationship of north and south was symbiotic, in other words, and the contrast between them was more one of differences in degree than of polar opposition.

---

1. feudalism: a political and economic system based on the relationship of a lord to people of lower status, who owed service and/or goods to the lord in exchange for the use of land.

Directions: Now answer the questions.

Europe in the eleventh century underwent enormous social, technological, and economic changes, but this did not create a new Europe—it created two new ones. The north was developed as a rigidly hierarchical society in which status was deter-mined, or was at least indicated, by the extent to which one owned, controlled, or labored on land; whereas the Mediterranean south developed a more fluid, and there-fore more chaotic, world in which industry and commerce predominated and social status both reflected and resulted from the role that one played in the public life of the community. In other words, individual identity and social community in the north were established on a personal basis, whereas in the south they were established on a civic basis. By the start of the twelfth century, northern and southern Europe were very different places indeed, and the Europeans themselves noticed it and com-mented on it.

15. The word "rigidly" in the passage is closest in meaning to

    Ⓐ extremely
    Ⓑ normally
    Ⓒ obviously
    Ⓓ strictly

16. According to paragraph 1, which of the following was a deciding factor in a person's place in society in northern Europe at the end of the eleventh century?

    Ⓐ Ownership of a commercial enterprise
    Ⓑ Participation in social and technological changes
    Ⓒ Role in public life in the community
    Ⓓ Relationship to land through ownership or labor

17. According to paragraph 1, which of the following best characterizes the societies in European lands close to the Mediterranean Sea at the beginning of the twelfth century?

  Ⓐ They were civic societies dominated by industry and commerce.
  Ⓑ They were based on individual social status.
  Ⓒ They had a fixed and hierarchical form of government.
  Ⓓ They were established on the idea of individual responsibility.

PARAGRAPH 2

Political dominance belonged to the north. Germany, France, and England had large populations and large armies that made them, in the political and military senses, the masters of western Europe. Organized by the practices known collectively as feudalism[1], these kingdoms emerged as powerful states with sophisticated machineries of government. Their kings and queens were the leading figures of the age; their castles and cathedrals stood majestically on the landscape as symbols of their might; their armies both energized and defined the age. Moreover, feudal society showed a remarkable ability to adapt to new needs by encouraging the parallel development of domestic urban life and commercial networks; in some regions of the north, in fact, feudal society may even have developed in response to the start of the trends toward bigger cities. But southern Europe took the lead in economic and cultural life. Though the leading Mediterranean states were small in size, they were considerably wealthier than their northern counterparts. The Italian city of Palermo in the twelfth century, for example, alone generated four times the commercial tax revenue of the entire kingdom of England. Southern communities also possessed urbane, multilingual cultures that made them the intellectual and artistic leaders of the age. Levels of general literacy in the south far surpassed those of the north, and the people of the south put that learning to use on a large scale. Science, mathematics, poetry, law, historical writing, religious speculation, translation, and classical studies all began to flourish; throughout most of the twelfth century, most of the continent's best brains flocked to southern Europe.

18. The word "counterparts" in the passage is closest in meaning to

  Ⓐ associates
  Ⓑ equivalents
  Ⓒ opponents
  Ⓓ admirers

19. Why does the author mention the "Italian city of Palermo" in the passage?

  Ⓐ It had a population that spoke several different languages.
  Ⓑ Its artists and intellectuals were famous both in the north and south.
  Ⓒ Its commerce made it richer than a large northern country.
  Ⓓ It was a relatively small and unimportant Mediterranean state.

20. The word "urbane" in the passage is closest in meaning to

  (A) cultivated
  (B) famous
  (C) popular
  (D) exceptional

21. According to paragraph 2, European intellectuals moved to southern Europe during the twelfth century because southern cities

  (A) needed learned people for commerce
  (B) paid educated people better than northern cities did
  (C) were flourishing centers of science, literature, and other studies
  (D) needed teachers to improve the levels of general learning

22. Which of the following best describes the organization of paragraph 2?

  (A) A statement of fact followed by examples
  (B) A description followed by a contrasting description
  (C) A series of detailed comparisons
  (D) A logical argument

PARAGRAPH 3

So too did a lot of the north's soldiers. One of the central themes of the political history of the twelfth century was the continual effort by the northern kingdoms to extend their control southward in the hope of tapping into the Mediterranean bonanza. The German emperors starting with Otto I (936–973), for example, struggled ceaselessly to establish their control over the cities of northern Italy, since those cities generated more revenue than all of rural Germany combined. The kings of France used every means at their disposal to push the lower border of their kingdom to the Mediterranean shoreline. And the Normans who conquered and ruled England established outposts of Norman power in Sicily and the adjacent lands of southern Italy; the English kings also hoped or claimed at various times to be, either through money or marriage diplomacy, the rulers of several Mediterranean states. But as the northern world pressed southward, so too did some of the cultural norms and social mechanisms of the south expand northward. Over the course of the twelfth century, the feudal kingdoms witnessed a proliferation of cities modeled in large degree on those of the south. Contact with the merchants and financiers of the Mediterranean led to the development of northern industry and international trade (which helped to pay for many of the castles and cathedrals mentioned earlier). And education spread as well, culminating in the foundation of what is arguably medieval Europe's greatest invention: the university. The relationship of north and south was symbiotic, in other words, and the contrast between them was more one of differences in degree than of polar opposition.

23. Which of the sentences below best expresses the essential information in the highlighted sentence in paragraph 3? Incorrect choices change the meaning in important ways or leave out essential information.

    Ⓐ In political history, northern kingdoms tried to extend their control during the twelfth century, but the south tapped into the rich treasures it had around the Mediterranean.
    Ⓑ Political history demonstrates that during the twelfth century, while southern states enjoyed the Mediterranean bonanza, northern countries increased the power of their kings.
    Ⓒ The political history of twelfth-century Europe shows particularly that northern countries continually tried to expand their rule into the south to profit from the riches there.
    Ⓓ Political history shows that northern kingdoms were so influenced by the example of Mediterranean wealth that they advanced into other areas.

24. The word "proliferation" in the passage is closest in meaning to

    Ⓐ beginning
    Ⓑ increase
    Ⓒ occupation
    Ⓓ construction

25. According to paragraph 3, northern Europe was influenced by the Mediterranean states in all of the following ways EXCEPT

    Ⓐ the design of castles and cathedrals
    Ⓑ the spread of education
    Ⓒ the construction of cities
    Ⓓ the development of industry and trade

PARAGRAPH 1

Europe in the eleventh century underwent enormous social, technological, and economic changes, but this did not create a new Europe—it created two new ones. ■ The north was developed as a rigidly hierarchical society in which status was determined, or was at least indicated, by the extent to which one owned, controlled, or labored on land; whereas the Mediterranean south developed a more fluid, and therefore more chaotic, world in which industry and commerce predominated and social status both reflected and resulted from the role that one played in the public life of the community. ■ In other words, individual identity and social community in the north were established on a personal basis, whereas in the south they were established on a civic basis. ■ By the start of the twelfth century, northern and southern Europe were very different places indeed, and the Europeans themselves noticed it and commented on it. ■

26. Look at the four squares [■] that indicate where the following sentence can be added to the passage.

There was northern Europe on the one hand and southern Europe on the other.

Where would the sentence best fit?

(A) Europe in the eleventh century underwent enormous social, technological, and economic changes, but this did not create a new Europe—it created two new ones. **There was northern Europe on the one hand and southern Europe on the other.** The north was developed as a rigidly hierarchical society in which status was determined, or was at least indicated, by the extent to which one owned, controlled, or labored on land; whereas the Mediterranean south developed a more fluid, and therefore more chaotic, world in which industry and commerce predominated and social status both reflected and resulted from the role that one played in the public life of the community. ■ In other words, individual identity and social community in the north were established on a personal basis, whereas in the south they were established on a civic basis. ■ By the start of the twelfth century, northern and southern Europe were very different places indeed, and the Europeans themselves noticed it and commented on it. ■

(B) Europe in the eleventh century underwent enormous social, technological, and economic changes, but this did not create a new Europe—it created two new ones. ■ The north was developed as a rigidly hierarchical society in which status was determined, or was at least indicated, by the extent to which one owned, controlled, or labored on land; whereas the Mediterranean south developed a more fluid, and therefore more chaotic, world in which industry and commerce predominated and social status both reflected and resulted from the role that one played in the public life of the community. **There was northern Europe on the one hand and southern Europe on the other.** In other words, individual identity and social community in the north were established on a personal basis, whereas in the south they were established on a civic basis. ■ By the start of the twelfth century, northern and southern Europe were very different places indeed, and the Europeans themselves noticed it and commented on it. ■

(C) Europe in the eleventh century underwent enormous social, technological, and economic changes, but this did not create a new Europe—it created two new ones. ■ The north was developed as a rigidly hierarchical society in which status was determined, or was at least indicated, by the extent to which one owned, controlled, or labored on land; whereas the Mediterranean south developed a more fluid, and therefore more chaotic, world in which industry and commerce predominated and social status both reflected and resulted from the role that one played in the public life of the community. ■ In other words, individual identity and social community in the north were established on a personal basis, whereas in the south they were established on a civic basis. **There was northern Europe on the one hand and southern Europe on the other.** By the start of the twelfth century, northern and southern Europe were very different places indeed, and the Europeans themselves noticed it and commented on it. ■

Ⓓ Europe in the eleventh century underwent enormous social, technological, and economic changes, but this did not create a new Europe—it created two new ones. ■ The north was developed as a rigidly hierarchical society in which status was determined, or was at least indicated, by the extent to which one owned, controlled, or labored on land; whereas the Mediterranean south developed a more fluid, and therefore more chaotic, world in which industry and commerce predominated and social status both reflected and resulted from the role that one played in the public life of the community. ■ In other words, individual identity and social community in the north were established on a personal basis, whereas in the south they were established on a civic basis. ■ By the start of the twelfth century, northern and southern Europe were very different places indeed, and the Europeans themselves noticed it and commented on it. **There was northern Europe on the one hand and southern Europe on the other.**

27. **Directions**: Select from the seven phrases below the two phrases that correctly characterize northern Europe during the twelfth century and the three phrases that correctly characterize southern Europe. Two of the phrases will NOT be used.

Write your answer choices in the spaces where they belong. You can either write the letter of your answer choice or you can copy the sentence.

Northern Europe
●
●

Southern Europe
●
●
●

Answer Choices

A Democratic social structure

B Sophisticated culture

C Small wealthy states

D Famous kings and queens

E Extensive communication systems

F Highly literate population

G Large military forces

Directions: Read the passage. Then answer the questions. Give yourself 20 minutes to complete this practice set.

WHAT IS A COMMUNITY?

The Black Hills forest, the prairie riparian forest, and other forests of the western United States can be separated by the distinctly different combinations of species they comprise. It is easy to distinguish between prairie riparian forest and Black Hills forest—one is a broad-leaved forest of ash and cottonwood trees, the other is a coniferous forest of ponderosa pine and white spruce trees. One has kingbirds; the other, juncos (birds with white outer tail feathers). The fact that ecological communities are, indeed, recognizable clusters of species led some early ecologists, particularly those living in the beginning of the twentieth century, to claim that communities are highly integrated, precisely balanced assemblages. This claim harkens back to even earlier arguments about the existence of a balance of nature, where every species is there for a specific purpose, like a vital part in a complex machine. Such a belief would suggest that to remove any species, whether it be plant, bird, or insect, would somehow disrupt the balance, and the habitat would begin to deteriorate. Likewise, to add a species may be equally disruptive.

One of these pioneer ecologists was Frederick Clements, who studied ecology extensively throughout the Midwest and other areas in North America. He held that within any given region of climate, ecological communities tended to slowly converge toward a single endpoint, which he called the "climatic climax." This "climax" community was, in Clements's mind, the most well-balanced, integrated grouping of species that could occur within that particular region. Clements even thought that the process of ecological succession—the replacement of some species by others over time—was somewhat akin to the development of an organism, from embryo to adult. Clements thought that succession represented discrete stages in the development of the community (rather like infancy, childhood, and adolescence), terminating in the climatic "adult" stage, when the community became self-reproducing and succession ceased. Clements's view of the ecological community reflected the notion of a precise balance of nature.

Clements was challenged by another pioneer ecologist, Henry Gleason, who took the opposite view. Gleason viewed the community as largely a group of species with similar tolerances to the stresses imposed by climate and other factors typical of the region. Gleason saw the element of chance as important in influencing where species occurred. His concept of the community suggests that nature is not highly integrated. Gleason thought succession could take numerous directions, depending upon local circumstances.

Who was right? Many ecologists have made precise measurements, designed to test the assumptions of both the Clements and Gleason models. For instance, along mountain slopes, does one life zone, or habitat type, grade sharply or gradually into another? If the divisions are sharp, perhaps the reason is that the community is so well integrated, so holistic, so like Clements viewed it, that whole clusters of species must remain together. If the divisions are gradual, perhaps, as Gleason suggested, each species is responding individually to its environment, and clusters of species are not so integrated that they must always occur together.

It now appears that Gleason was far closer to the truth than Clements. The ecological community is largely an accidental assemblage of species with similar responses to a particular climate. Green ash trees are found in association with plains cottonwood trees because both can survive well on floodplains and the competition between them is not so strong that only one can persevere. One ecological community often flows into another so gradually that it is next to impossible to say where one leaves off and the other begins. Communities are individualistic.

This is not to say that precise harmonies are not present within communities. Most flowering plants could not exist were it not for their pollinators—and vice versa. Predators, disease organisms, and competitors all influence the abundance and distribution of everything from oak trees to field mice. But if we see a precise balance of nature, it is largely an artifact of our perception, due to the illusion that nature, especially a complex system like a forest, seems so unchanging from one day to the next.

Directions: Now answer the questions.

PARAGRAPH 1

The Black Hills forest, the prairie riparian forest, and other forests of the western United States can be separated by the distinctly different combinations of species they comprise. It is easy to distinguish between prairie riparian forest and Black Hills forest—one is a broad-leaved forest of ash and cottonwood trees, the other is a coniferous forest of ponderosa pine and white spruce trees. One has kingbirds; the other, juncos (birds with white outer tail feathers). The fact that ecological communities are, indeed, recognizable clusters of species led some early ecologists, particularly those living in the beginning of the twentieth century, to claim that communities are highly integrated, precisely balanced assemblages. This claim harkens back to even earlier arguments about the existence of a balance of nature, where every species is there for a specific purpose, like a vital part in a complex machine. Such a belief would suggest that to remove any species, whether it be plant, bird, or insect, would somehow disrupt the balance, and the habitat would begin to deteriorate. Likewise, to add a species may be equally disruptive.

28. In paragraph 1, why does the author distinguish between prairie riparian forest and Black Hills forest?

    Ⓐ To highlight the difference between the views of various ecologists about the nature of ecological communities
    Ⓑ To illustrate why some ecologists tended to view ecological communities as highly integrated
    Ⓒ To demonstrate that one forest has a greater variety of species than the other
    Ⓓ To show how these two forests differ from others in the United States

29. According to paragraph 1, what was a common claim about ecological communities before the early twentieth century?

   (A) Every species in a community has a specific role in that community.
   (B) It is important to protect communities by removing certain species.
   (C) A precise balance is difficult to maintain in an ecological community.
   (D) It is necessary for new species to be added quickly as ecological communities develop.

30. The word "clusters" in the passage is closest in meaning to

   (A) models
   (B) categories
   (C) examples
   (D) groups

31. According to paragraph 1, the belief in a balance of nature suggests that removing a species from an ecological community would have which of the following effects?

   (A) It would reduce competition between the remaining species of the community.
   (B) It would produce a different, but equally balanced, community.
   (C) It would lead to a decline in the community.
   (D) It would cause more harm than adding a species to the community.

PARAGRAPH 2

One of these pioneer ecologists was Frederick Clements, who studied ecology extensively throughout the Midwest and other areas in North America. He held that within any given region of climate, ecological communities tended to slowly converge toward a single endpoint, which he called the "climatic climax." This "climax" community was, in Clements's mind, the most well-balanced, integrated grouping of species that could occur within that particular region. Clements even thought that the process of ecological succession—the replacement of some species by others over time—was somewhat akin to the development of an organism, from embryo to adult. Clements thought that succession represented discrete stages in the development of the community (rather like infancy, childhood, and adolescence), terminating in the climatic "adult" stage, when the community became self-reproducing and succession ceased. Clements's view of the ecological community reflected the notion of a precise balance of nature.

32. The word "ceased" in the passage is closest in meaning to

   (A) succeeded
   (B) balanced
   (C) ended
   (D) advanced

33. Which of the following best represents the view of ecological communities associated with Frederick Clements in paragraph 2?

    (A) Only when all species in a community are at the reproductive stage of development is an ecological community precisely balanced.

    (B) When an ecological community achieves "climatic climax," it begins to decline.

    (C) All climates have similar climax communities.

    (D) Ecological communities eventually reach the maximum level of balance that is possible for their region.

34. According to paragraph 2, Clements compared the process of ecological succession to

    (A) the replacement of animal habitats over time

    (B) the development of an organism

    (C) self-reproduction

    (D) changes in climate

PARAGRAPH 3

Clements was challenged by another pioneer ecologist, Henry Gleason, who took the opposite view. Gleason viewed the community as largely a group of species with similar tolerances to the stresses imposed by climate and other factors typical of the region. Gleason saw the element of chance as important in influencing where species occurred. His concept of the community suggests that nature is not highly integrated. Gleason thought succession could take numerous directions, depending upon local circumstances.

35. According to Gleason in paragraph 3, the occurrence of a species in a particular community is influenced by

    (A) unpredictable events

    (B) how individualistic the species is

    (C) the number of other species present

    (D) the tolerance of other species to stresses

Who was right? Many ecologists have made precise measurements, designed to test the assumptions of both the Clements and Gleason models. For instance, along mountain slopes, does one life zone, or habitat type, grade sharply or gradually into another? If the divisions are sharp, perhaps the reason is that the community is so well integrated, so holistic, so like Clements viewed it, that whole clusters of species must remain together. If the divisions are gradual, perhaps, as Gleason suggested, each species is responding individually to its environment, and clusters of species are not so integrated that they must always occur together.

36. What did the ecologists in paragraph 4 hope to determine with their measurements?

    Ⓐ Whether different species compete for the same environments
    Ⓑ Whether habitats are sharply separated or gradually flow into each other
    Ⓒ Whether succession differs in different types of habitats
    Ⓓ Whether integrated communities survive better than independent communities

It now appears that Gleason was far closer to the truth than Clements. The ecological community is largely an accidental assemblage of species with similar responses to a particular climate. Green ash trees are found in association with plains cottonwood trees because both can survive well on floodplains and the competition between them is not so strong that only one can persevere. One ecological community often flows into another so gradually that it is next to impossible to say where one leaves off and the other begins. Communities are individualistic.

37. In paragraph 5, why does the author mention green ash trees and plains cottonwood trees?

    Ⓐ To support the current view about how ecological communities develop
    Ⓑ To provide an example of species that prefer to live on floodplains
    Ⓒ To provide evidence that supports the theory of Clements
    Ⓓ To show where one ecological community stops and the other begins

38. The word "persevere" in the passage is closest in meaning to
    Ⓐ reproduce
    Ⓑ fail
    Ⓒ expand
    Ⓓ continue

PARAGRAPH 6

This is not to say that precise harmonies are not present within communities. Most flowering plants could not exist were it not for their pollinators—and vice versa. Predators, disease organisms, and competitors all influence the abundance and distribution of everything from oak trees to field mice. But if we see a precise balance of nature, it is largely an artifact of our perception, due to the illusion that nature, especially a complex system like a forest, seems so unchanging from one day to the next.

39. Which of the sentences below best expresses the essential information in the highlighted sentence in paragraph 6? Incorrect choices change the meaning in important ways or leave out essential information.

Ⓐ We see nature as precisely balanced because nature is unchanging.

Ⓑ A precise balance of nature is not possible because of the complexity of natural systems.

Ⓒ Our sense that nature is precisely balanced results from the illusion that it is unchanging.

Ⓓ Because nature is precisely balanced, complex systems do not seem to change.

PARAGRAPH 4

■ Who was right? ■ Many ecologists have made precise measurements, designed to test the assumptions of both the Clements and Gleason models. ■ For instance, along mountain slopes, does one life zone, or habitat type, grade sharply or gradually into another? ■ If the divisions are sharp, perhaps the reason is that the community is so well integrated, so holistic, so like Clements viewed it, that whole clusters of species must remain together. If the divisions are gradual, perhaps, as Gleason suggested, each species is responding individually to its environment, and clusters of species are not so integrated that they must always occur together.

40. Look at the four squares [■] that indicate where the following sentence can be added to the passage.

Their research has helped to decide between the two views because it has focused on questions to which Clements and Gleason would give opposing answers.

Where would the sentence best fit?

Ⓐ **Their research has helped to decide between the two views because it has focused on questions to which Clements and Gleason would give opposing answers.** Who was right? ■ Many ecologists have made precise measurements, designed to test the assumptions of both the Clements and Gleason models. ■ For instance, along mountain slopes, does one life zone, or habitat type, grade sharply or gradually into another? ■ If the divisions are sharp, perhaps the reason is that the community is so well integrated, so holistic, so like Clements viewed it, that whole clusters of species must remain together. If the divisions are gradual, perhaps, as Gleason suggested, each species is responding individually to its environment, and clusters of species are not so integrated that they must always occur together.

Ⓑ ■ Who was right? **Their research has helped to decide between the two views because it has focused on questions to which Clements and Gleason would give opposing answers.** Many ecologists have made precise measurements, designed to test the assumptions of both the Clements and Gleason models. ■ For instance, along mountain slopes, does one life zone, or habitat type, grade sharply or gradually into another? ■ If the divisions are sharp, perhaps the reason is that the community is so well integrated, so holistic, so like Clements viewed it, that whole clusters of species must remain together. If the divisions are gradual, perhaps, as Gleason suggested, each species is responding individually to its environment, and clusters of species are not so integrated that they must always occur together.

Ⓒ ■ Who was right? ■ Many ecologists have made precise measurements, designed to test the assumptions of both the Clements and Gleason models. **Their research has helped to decide between the two views because it has focused on questions to which Clements and Gleason would give opposing answers.** For instance, along mountain slopes, does one life zone, or habitat type, grade sharply or gradually into another? ■ If the divisions are sharp, perhaps the reason is that the community is so well integrated, so holistic, so like Clements viewed it, that whole clusters of species must remain together. If the divisions are gradual, perhaps, as Gleason suggested, each species is responding individually to its environment, and clusters of species are not so integrated that they must always occur together.

Ⓓ ■ Who was right? ■ Many ecologists have made precise measurements, designed to test the assumptions of both the Clements and Gleason models. ■ For instance, along mountain slopes, does one life zone, or habitat type, grade sharply or gradually into another? **Their research has helped to decide between the two views because it has focused on questions to which Clements and Gleason would give opposing answers.** If the divisions are sharp, perhaps the reason is that the community is so well integrated, so holistic, so like Clements viewed it, that whole clusters of species must remain together. If the divisions are gradual, perhaps, as Gleason suggested, each species is responding individually to its environment, and clusters of species are not so integrated that they must always occur together.

41. **Directions:** An introductory sentence for a brief summary of the passage is provided below. Complete the summary by selecting the THREE answer choices that express the most important ideas in the passage. Some sentences do not belong in the summary because they express ideas that are not presented in the passage or are minor ideas in the passage.

Write your answer choices in the spaces where they belong. You can either write the letter of your answer choice or you can copy the sentence.

Over time, a variety of views have been formed on the structure of ecological communities.

- ●
- ●
- ●

Answer Choices

A Clements held that ecological communities were like organisms that compete with each other for dominance in a particular climatic region.

B Clements saw the community as a collection of thoroughly interdependent species progressing toward a single climax community.

C Gleason held that within a single climatic region, differing local factors would cause ecological communities to develop in different ways.

D Gleason believed that sharp divisions would exist between species in different habitats.

E Today's ecologists recognize that ecological communities must be precisely and permanently balanced.

F The current thinking is that communities are individualistic and largely accidental collections of species with similar needs and tolerances.

LISTENING

This section measures your ability to understand conversations and lectures in English.

Listen to each conversation and lecture only one time. After each conversation and lecture, you will answer some questions about it. Answer each question based on what is stated or implied by the speakers.

You may take notes while you listen and use your notes to help you answer the questions. Your notes will **not** be scored.

In some questions you will see this icon: ( ). This means that you will hear, but not see, the question.

Answer each question before moving on. Do not return to previous questions.

It will take about 60 minutes to listen to the conversations and lectures and answer the questions about them.

Directions: Listen to Track 63.

Directions: Now answer the questions.

1. Why does the man go to the computer center?

   Ⓐ To learn how to use the Internet
   Ⓑ To ask the woman where he can buy a computer
   Ⓒ To ask if he can get instruction on using computers
   Ⓓ To find out where the computer labs are located

2. How did the man probably feel when he first arrived at the computer center?

   Ⓐ Embarrassed about his lack of computer skills
   Ⓑ Excited to learn about computers
   Ⓒ Upset that he needs to take an expensive computer course
   Ⓓ Nervous about an assignment to write a paper on a computer

3. What does the woman imply about the book she bought for her father?

   Ⓐ It does not include instruction on word processing.
   Ⓑ It is not available at the campus bookstore.
   Ⓒ It is intended only for people with a lot of computer experience.
   Ⓓ It might be helpful for the man.

4. What does the woman imply about the student assistants?

   Ⓐ The man will not be able to work with them for long.
   Ⓑ They may not be good instructors for beginners.
   Ⓒ They are required to teach students to use the computers.
   Ⓓ Not all of them know about computers.

5. What will the woman do to help the man?

Ⓐ Lend him a book on computers
Ⓑ Give him a list of computer courses
Ⓒ Give him a list of student assistants
Ⓓ Recommend a computer instructor

Directions: Listen to Track 64.

Directions: Now answer the questions.

6. What is the lecture mainly about?

   Ⓐ Ways to limit the expansion of international trade

   Ⓑ How restrictions on international trade can cause economic harm

   Ⓒ Factors that influence the distribution of exports

   Ⓓ Why international trade has expanded in recent years

7. According to the professor, why do many people want imports to be regulated?

   Ⓐ To allow for price increases in domestic products

   Ⓑ To make the prices of exports more competitive

   Ⓒ To protect against domestic unemployment

   Ⓓ To encourage the economic growth of certain industries

8. According to the professor, what is a negative result of limiting imports?

    Ⓐ The pace of technological innovation slows down.

    Ⓑ The number of domestic low-paying jobs decreases.

    Ⓒ People move to areas where income is lower.

    Ⓓ The potential income from exports is reduced.

9. What does the professor imply about the sugar industry in Florida?

    Ⓐ It is a good source of high-paying jobs.

    Ⓑ It should not be protected from competition from imports.

    Ⓒ It is a good example of the effect of international specialization.

    Ⓓ It is managed cost effectively.

10. What does the professor imply about the effect of increasing imports?

    Ⓐ It will eventually result in a decrease in exports.

    Ⓑ It is not necessarily bad for the economy.

    Ⓒ It creates domestic economic problems that are easily solved.

    Ⓓ Its impact on the economy is immediately apparent.

11. What is the professor's opinion of retraining and relocating unemployed people?

    Ⓐ It is more expensive over time than blocking imports.

    Ⓑ It can sometimes have unintended consequences.

    Ⓒ It is one possible way to adapt to an increase in imports.

    Ⓓ It maintains the production levels of inefficient industries.

Directions: Now answer the questions.

12. What does the professor mainly discuss?

    Ⓐ Why some whales do not migrate

    Ⓑ How and why baleen whales migrate

    Ⓒ How baleen whales communicate with other whales

    Ⓓ How different whales hunt for their food

13. According to the professor, what is a common reason for migration that does NOT apply to baleen whales?

    Ⓐ The need to avoid lower water temperatures

    Ⓑ The need to raise young in a suitable environment

    Ⓒ The need to find better feeding grounds

    Ⓓ The need to find a mating partner

14. In order to prove or disprove the balancing-act theory of whale migration, what question needs to be answered?

    Ⓐ Whether or not whales have good eyesight

    Ⓑ How long baleen whales are able to survive without food

    Ⓒ How fast baleen whales can swim compared with other kinds of whales

    Ⓓ Whether moving south saves whales more energy than staying north

15. According to the professor, what are the possible means used by migrating whales to find the right direction? *Choose 3 answers.*

    Ⓐ Using magnetic fields as a guide

    Ⓑ Recognizing coastal landmarks

    Ⓒ Following the heat of the tropical water

    Ⓓ Listening to sounds that bounce off of the land

    Ⓔ Following the migrating plankton

16. Listen to Track 66.

    Ⓐ She is not an expert on what she is about to discuss.

    Ⓑ She will discuss only what is relevant to her main point.

    Ⓒ She thinks her students already understand her point.

    Ⓓ She will not repeat what was discussed in previous classes.

17. Listen to Track 67.

    Ⓐ It is not obvious how whales find their way.

    Ⓑ Different whales have different ways of locating food.

    Ⓒ Whales have a poor sense of orientation.

    Ⓓ Scientists have not been able to track the whales.

Directions: Listen to Track 68.

Directions: Now answer the questions.

18. Why does the student go to see her advisor, Professor Anderson?

    Ⓐ She wants Professor Anderson's help with her research.
    Ⓑ She is responding to Professor Anderson's invitation.
    Ⓒ She has a complaint about another professor.
    Ⓓ She wants to get a letter of recommendation to law school.

19. Why does the student mention Professor Connelly's class?

    Ⓐ She was not happy with the grade she received in the class.
    Ⓑ She might be able to expand the research she did in the class.
    Ⓒ It was the most difficult class she ever took.
    Ⓓ Professor Connelly took the class on a trip to Venezuela.

20. What does the student tell Professor Anderson she will do before their next meeting?

    Ⓐ Register for Professor Connelly's class
    Ⓑ Begin to write her honors thesis
    Ⓒ Turn in her honors project to Professor Connelly
    Ⓓ Talk to Professor Connelly about doing an honors project

21. Listen to Track 69.

    Ⓐ Very few students are asked to consider writing an honors thesis.
    Ⓑ The woman has shown poor research skills in the past.
    Ⓒ An honors thesis could help the woman get into law school.
    Ⓓ The woman should write a proposal outlining her research skills.

22. Listen to Track 70.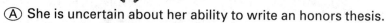

  (A) She is uncertain about her ability to write an honors thesis.
  (B) She does not think an honors thesis would be useful to her.
  (C) She considers herself to be a good writer.
  (D) She has only written one research paper before.

Directions: Listen to Track 71.

Directions: Now answer the questions.

23. What is the lecture mainly about?

Ⓐ Why some newspapers do not improve their services
Ⓑ What newspapers can do to increase their readership
Ⓒ Why local newspapers cannot compete with major newspapers
Ⓓ How the topics that interest readers have changed over the years

24. According to the professor, what topics are newspaper readers most interested in? *Choose 2 answers.*

Ⓐ Political issues
Ⓑ Entertainment and weather
Ⓒ Natural disasters and accidents
Ⓓ Ordinary people

25. According to the professor, how can newspapers attract readers to serious stories?

Ⓐ By including photos that provide background information
Ⓑ By making minor revisions to the content of the story
Ⓒ By making the format more appealing to readers
Ⓓ By gradually increasing the number of serious stories

26. What does the professor imply about the use of colors in newspapers?

Ⓐ It has been greatly influenced by reader preferences.
Ⓑ It is more effective than early research indicated.
Ⓒ It has not resulted in significant increases in the number of readers.
Ⓓ It has been neglected in the study of journalism.

27. Listen to Track 72.

    (A) He agrees with the professor completely.

    (B) He is surprised by the professor's point of view.

    (C) He is not familiar with the topic the professor is discussing.

    (D) He can offer a solution to the problem being discussed.

28. Listen to Track 73.

    (A) He fully supports the student's statement.

    (B) His experience this morning was unexpected.

    (C) He was not affected by what happened this morning.

    (D) The student should not complain.

Directions: Listen to Track 74.

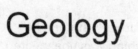

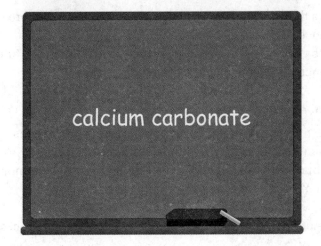

Directions: Now answer the questions.

29. What aspect of the Earth 750 million years ago is the lecture mainly about?

    (A) The changes in locations of the continents
    (B) The effect of greenhouse gases on the atmosphere
    (C) Factors that influenced the ocean currents
    (D) Factors that contributed to a global freeze

30. According to the professor, how do geologists interpret the presence of erratics in the tropics?

    (A) It indicates that carbon-dioxide levels were once higher there.
    (B) It is evidence of global glaciation.
    (C) It indicates that the Earth may cool off at some point in the future.
    (D) It is evidence that some glaciers originated there.

31. What is the ice-albedo effect?

    (A) Global warming is balanced by carbon dioxide in the oceans.
    (B) Solar radiation retained in the atmosphere melts ice.
    (C) Large amounts of carbon dioxide are removed from the atmosphere.
    (D) Reflection of heat by glaciers contributes to their growth.

32. What is the relationship between carbon dioxide and silicate rocks?

    (A) Silicate rocks are largely composed of carbon dioxide.
    (B) Silicate rocks contribute to the creation of carbon dioxide.
    (C) The erosion of silicate rocks reduces carbon-dioxide levels in the atmosphere.
    (D) The formation of silicate rocks removes carbon dioxide from the oceans.

33. What was one feature of the Earth that contributed to the runaway freeze 750 million years ago?

   (A) Carbon-dioxide levels in the oceans were low.
   (B) The continents were located close to the equator.
   (C) The movement of glaciers carried away large quantities of rock.
   (D) The level of greenhouse gases in the atmosphere was high.

34. Listen to Track 75.

   (A) To compare an unfamiliar object to a familiar one
   (B) To reveal evidence that contradicts his point
   (C) To indicate uncertainty as to what deposits from glaciers look like
   (D) To encourage students to examine rocks in streams

SPEAKING

This section measures your ability to speak in English about a variety of topics.

There are six questions in this section. For each question, you will be given a short time to prepare your response. When the preparation time is up, answer the question as completely as possible in the time indicated for that question. You should record your responses so that you can review them later and compare them with the answer key and scoring rubrics.

1. You will now be asked to speak about a familiar topic. Give yourself 15 seconds to prepare your response. Then record yourself speaking for 45 seconds.

   Listen to Track 76.

   > Sometimes one individual can have a great impact on a group or community. Select one person and explain how you think this person has affected others in the group or community. Give specific details and examples to explain your answer.
   >
   > **Preparation Time: 15 seconds**
   > **Response Time: 45 seconds**

2. You will now be asked to give your opinion about a familiar topic. Give yourself 15 seconds to prepare your response. Then record yourself speaking for 45 seconds.

   Listen to Track 77.

   > When some people visit a city or country for the first time, they prefer to take an organized tour. Other people prefer to explore new places on their own. Which do you prefer and why?
   >
   > **Preparation Time: 15 seconds**
   > **Response Time: 45 seconds**

3. You will now read a short passage and listen to a conversation on the same topic. You will then be asked a question about them. After you hear the question, give yourself 30 seconds to prepare your response. Then record yourself speaking for 60 seconds.

   Listen to Track 78.

Professor Fox Accepts New Position

We are happy to announce that Professor Fox will be filling the vacant Dean of Students position. Strong organizational skills are important for this position. Professor Fox has demonstrated such skills in her role as Head of the Philosophy Department, where she has coordinated department affairs for five years. Additionally, the Dean of Students must be someone who is able to work well with students, since responsibilities include counseling and advising students who are dealing with personal problems. As our head women's soccer coach, Professor Fox has proven to be a supportive role model for team members, always offering assistance when they ask for personal guidance.

Listen to Track 79.

The woman expresses her opinion about the change described in the article. Briefly summarize the change. Then state her opinion about the change and explain the reasons she gives for holding that opinion.

Preparation Time: 30 seconds
Response Time: 60 seconds

4. You will now read a short passage and listen to a lecture on the same topic. You will then be asked a question about them. After you hear the question, give yourself 30 seconds to prepare your response. Then record yourself speaking for 60 seconds.

Listen to Track 80.

Reading Time: 45 seconds

Critical Period

It is generally believed that for many organisms, there is a specific time period, a so-called "window of opportunity," during which the organism must receive crucial input from its environment in order for normal development to occur. This period is called the *critical period*. If the needed environmental input is not received during this period, the normal development of certain physical attributes or behaviors may never occur. In other words, if the organism is not provided with the needed stimulus or influence during the critical period, it may permanently lose the capacity to ever obtain a particular physical attribute or behavior.

Listen to Track 81.

Using the examples of kittens and geese, explain the idea of a critical period.

Preparation Time: 30 seconds
Response Time: 60 seconds

5. You will now listen to part of a conversation. You will then be asked a question about it. After you hear the question, give yourself 20 seconds to prepare your response. Then record yourself speaking for 60 seconds.

Listen to Track 82.

Briefly summarize the problem the speakers are discussing. Then state which of the two solutions from the conversation you would recommend. Explain the reasons for your recommendation.

Preparation Time: 20 seconds
Response Time: 60 seconds

6. You will now listen to part of a lecture. You will then be asked a question about it. After you hear the question, give yourself 20 seconds to prepare your response. Then record yourself speaking for 60 seconds.

Listen to Track 83.

Using the example of the vacuum cleaner, explain when it is legally acceptable to use exaggeration in advertising and when it is not.

| Preparation Time: 20 seconds |
| Response Time: 60 seconds |

WRITING

This section measures your ability to write in English to communicate in an academic environment.

There are two writing questions in this section.

For question 1, you will read a passage and listen to a lecture about the same topic. You may take notes while you read and listen. Then you will write a response to a question based on what you have read and heard. You may look back at the passage when answering the question. You may use your notes to help you answer the question. You have 20 minutes to plan and write your response.

For question 2, you will write an essay based on your own knowledge and experience. You have 30 minutes to plan and complete your essay.

1. **Directions:** Give yourself 3 minutes to read the passage.

Reading Time: 3 minutes

Many people dream of owning their own business but are afraid of the risks. Instead of starting a new business, however, one can buy a franchise. A franchise is a license issued by a large, usually well-known, company to a small business owner. Under the license, the owner acquires the right to use the company's brand name and agrees to sell its products. In return, the franchising company receives a percent of the sales.

A major problem for first-time business owners is finding reliable suppliers of the goods and services they need: equipment, raw materials, maintenance, etc. It is easy to choose the wrong supplier, and doing so can be costly. Buying a franchise eliminates much of this problem. Most franchising companies have already found reliable suppliers, and franchise contracts typically specify which suppliers are to be used. This protects franchise owners from the risk of serious losses.

Another advantage of a franchise is that it can save a new business a lot of money on advertising. Advertising one's product to potential customers is a crucial factor in a business's success. A franchise owner, however, sells an already popular and recognized brand and also gets the benefit of sophisticated and expensive advertising paid by the parent company.

Finally, a franchise offers more security than starting an independent (nonfranchise) business. The failure rate for starting independent businesses is very high during the first few years; the failure rate for starting franchises is much lower. Finding one's own way in today's competitive business environment is difficult, and buying a franchise allows an inexperienced business owner to use a proven business model.

Listen to Track 84.

Directions: You have 20 minutes to plan and write your response. Your response will be judged on the basis of the quality of your writing and on how well your response presents the points in the lecture and their relationship to the reading passage. Typically, an effective response will be 150 to 225 words.

Listen to Track 85.

Response Time: 20 minutes

Summarize the points made in the lecture, being sure to explain how they challenge specific points made in the reading passage.

2. **Directions:** Read the question below. You have 30 minutes to plan, write, and revise your essay. Typically, an effective response will contain a minimum of 300 words.

Response Time: 30 minutes

Do you agree or disagree with the following statement?

> **People learn things better from those at their own level—such as fellow students or co-workers—than from those at a higher level, such as teachers or supervisors.**

Use specific reasons and examples to support your answer.

_____

_____

_____

_____

_____

_____

_____

_____

_____

_____

_____

_____

_____

_____

_____

_____

_____

_____

_____

ANSWERS

Reading Section

1. C
2. D
3. B
4. A
5. D
6. C
7. A
8. B
9. A
10. C
11. B
12. A
13. D
14. B, C, F
15. D
16. D
17. A
18. B
19. C
20. A
21. C
22. B
23. C
24. B
25. A
26. A
27. D, G, B, C, F
28. B
29. A
30. D
31. C
32. C
33. D
34. B
35. A
36. B
37. A
38. D
39. C
40. C
41. B, C, F

Listening Section

1. C
2. A
3. D
4. B
5. C
6. B
7. C
8. D
9. B
10. B
11. C
12. B
13. C
14. D

15. A, B, D

16. B

17. A

18. B

19. B

20. D

21. C

22. A

23. B

24. B, D

25. C

26. C

27. B

28. A

29. D

30. B

31. D

32. C

33. B

34. A

Speaking Section

1. There are many ways you could answer this particular question. You first need to choose one person and explain how that person has had a great impact on a group. It is important to provide an explanation for your choice beyond simply stating that the person is important or great. You should provide clear support so that your listeners understand why this person was important or great.

As an example, you may choose to talk about a person that you work with. You could say that this person is a very good leader, and this person's leadership has enabled your company to achieve many great things, such as obtain many new clients. Also, you could say that this person has had an effect on the other members of the group because the other members have followed this person's example to be better employees.

Your response should be intelligible, should demonstrate effective use of grammar and vocabulary, and should be well developed and coherent. Your response is scored using the Independent Speaking Rubric (see Appendix A).

2. To respond to this particular question, you should clearly state what your opinion is: do you prefer to take an organized tour when visiting a place for the first time, or do you prefer to explore the new place on your own? There is no "correct" answer to this question. Whichever option you prefer, your answer should be supported with examples.

If you think that it is better to take an organized tour, you could say that a tour is better, especially if you do not know much about the new place. You might not know where to go or what to see. Plus, the guide will have more knowledge than you do. You might give a specific example of a tour that you have been on yourself.

If you prefer to explore a place on your own, you might say that a tour would limit you, because you would be told where to go. There might be a situation where you want to stay in one place for a longer time, but the tour would not allow this. In this case, you could also give a specific example of a time when you explored a place on your own and why this was good.

It is important to make sure that you state your opinion and develop your response with good examples and relevant details.

Your response should be intelligible, should demonstrate effective use of grammar and vocabulary, and should be well developed and coherent. Your response is scored using the Independent Speaking Rubric (see Appendix A).

3. To respond to this particular question, you should state the woman's opinion of the university's decision to give the position of Dean of Students to Professor Fox. In this case, the woman disagrees with the decision.

After stating that the woman disagrees with the decision, you should convey the two main reasons she gives for holding that opinion. You will need to connect information from the conversation to the reading in order for the response to be complete. The woman says that the first reason given for appointing Professor Fox—that she has strong organizational skills—is not valid. You should provide as her explanation either that some classes were cancelled because Professor Fox did not organize enough teaching assistants or that she missed a philosophy course in Europe because Professor Fox did not sign her paperwork in time.

Your response should also convey the woman's second reason for not agreeing with the university's decision to make Professor Fox Dean of Students. The woman disagrees that Professor Fox works well with students. As support, she says that Professor Fox has an aggressive coaching style. She also gives an example of her friend who was criticized by Professor Fox when she was looking for emotional support. This shows that, in the woman's opinion, Professor Fox would not be a good Dean of Students.

As you need to discuss *both* of the woman's reasons for disagreeing with the university's decision, you should not include too much detail from the reading or concentrate too much on one of the reasons. Give yourself enough time to discuss both reasons.

Your response should be intelligible, should demonstrate effective use of grammar and vocabulary, and should be well developed and coherent. Your response is scored using the Integrated Speaking Rubric (see Appendix A).

4. To respond to this particular question you should first explain the idea of a critical period as it was presented in the reading. The critical period is a specific time period for many organisms. Organisms must receive external or environmental input during this critical period in order to develop normally. Do not spend too much time summarizing all of the content of the reading.

You should then use the examples given by the professor to explain critical periods. In the first example, the professor discusses a critical period that affects a physical attribute. Vision in kittens will not develop normally if they are not exposed to light within the first four months of life. In the second example, the professor discusses a critical period affecting a behavior. Baby geese will adopt whatever large moving object they first see within the first two days of their lives as their parent. They will follow this "parent" even if it's a different species. That behavior cannot be changed even if a real goose reappears.

You do not need to repeat all of the details from the reading and the lecture, but instead integrate points from both to answer the question completely. For this question, you need to give yourself enough time to talk about both examples.

Your response should be intelligible, should demonstrate effective use of grammar and vocabulary, and should be well developed and coherent. Your response is scored using the Integrated Speaking Rubric (see Appendix A).

5. To respond to this particular question you should *briefly* describe the problem. In this case the problem is that the woman does not want to cook her own meals because the kitchen in the dorm is always a mess.

Next, you need to choose *one* of the two solutions and explain why you think that solution is best. Note that you are not required to talk about both solutions. The two solutions in this conversation are: 1) put up a schedule so people can sign up to use the kitchen. Anyone who uses the kitchen must clean up, or 2) hire someone to clean the kitchen once a week. It does not matter which of the two proposed solutions you choose, since there is no "right" solution or "wrong" solution. You should choose the solution that you think is best and support your choice with reasons why you think it is best. The reasons you give can include information provided by the speakers as well as your own experiences.

For example, if you believe the first solution is preferable, you could say that it should be the students' responsibility to clean the kitchen. Cleaning the kitchen is important because it could lead to good habits, and eventually these students will be responsible for their own kitchens. Another way to discuss this is to talk about the disadvantage of the other solution. In this case you might say that hiring somebody else is not a good idea because it costs money, and students do not usually have a lot of money. They would be better off using this money to buy food for themselves.

If you believe the second solution is preferable, you might say that students don't really have enough time to clean. They are already very busy with their schoolwork, so cleaning is something that they should get somebody else to do. Also, somebody else might do a better job since many students don't have a lot of experience cleaning.

These are just examples of possible responses; remember, this type of question can be answered in many different ways.

Your response should be intelligible, should demonstrate effective use of grammar and vocabulary, and should be well developed and coherent. Your response is scored using the Integrated Speaking Rubric (see Appendix A).

6.   This particular question requires you to summarize the contents of a lecture you hear. In your response, you should talk about exaggeration in advertising, including the examples of when it is legal to use exaggeration and when it is not legal to use exaggeration.

You should begin with a general statement about the lecture, such as that exaggeration in advertising has to be so extreme that nobody will believe it. If it isn't, this advertising may be illegal. You would then talk about the first example that the professor gives. An advertiser that wanted to make the point that its vacuum cleaner is very light showed it in a television ad floating in the air. This kind of advertisement was legal because no one would really believe that a vacuum cleaner floated in the air.

You should then talk about the professor's second example. The professor says that if the company showed the vacuum cleaner cleaning a big dirty carpet in just a few seconds that is an exaggeration and would be unacceptable because someone might actually believe it. We can imagine someone buying the vacuum cleaner and being disappointed that it didn't work that well.

You should read the question carefully and respond with the appropriate information. This question clearly directs you to talk about a time when it is acceptable to use exaggeration and a time when it is not acceptable. You should budget your time so that you are able to talk about both examples.

Your response should be intelligible, should demonstrate effective use of grammar and vocabulary, and should be well developed and coherent. Your response is scored using the Integrated Speaking Rubric (see Appendix A).

Writing Section

1. What is important to understand from the lecture is that the professor disagrees with the advantages of buying franchises presented in the reading, namely that a franchise owner does not have to look for suppliers; that a franchise owner gets the benefit of advertising done by the parent company; and that franchises provide more security than other types of business.

In your response, you should convey the reasons presented by the professor for why buying a franchise is not the best way of becoming a business owner. A high-scoring response will include the following points made by the professor that cast doubt on the points made in the reading:

Point made in the reading	Counterpoint made in the lecture
Since franchising companies have already selected reliable suppliers for franchise owners to use, a new franchise owner does not run the risk of working with unreliable suppliers.	A franchise owner is forced to use the suppliers identified by the parent company. Such suppliers often charge too much for their goods and services. A franchise owner cannot use cheaper suppliers that may be available.
Franchise owners save money on advertising because they sell well-known brands and because they get the benefit of advertising paid for by the parent companies.	In fact, franchise owners have to pay a portion of their income to the parent company in return for advertising services. However, advertising by the parent company focuses on the brand and not on the owner's individual business. Owners would get greater benefit for less money if they did their own advertising.
Buying a franchise offers very good security. The failure rate of starting franchises is much lower than the failure rate of starting independent businesses.	There is in fact an option for starting business owners that is more secure than buying a franchise: buying an already-existing independent business. Independent businesses bought from previous owners have twice as much chance of success as new franchises.

Your response is scored using the Integrated Writing Rubric (see Appendix A). A response that receives a score of 5 clearly conveys all three of the main points in the table using accurate sentence structure and vocabulary.

2. To earn a top score, you should develop a multi-paragraph essay that responds to the issue of whether people learn things better from those at their own level—such as fellow students or coworkers—than from those at a higher level, such as teachers or supervisors. Typically an effective response will contain a minimum of 300 words.

One successful way to express agreement with the prompt is to explain that you can learn better from your fellow students or coworkers—at least those whom you enjoy being around—because when these people try to teach you something, it will be in a relaxed, friendly atmosphere with no pressure. You might go on to argue that if you're relaxed, you'll learn better.

A successful way to disagree with the prompt is to describe the advantage of learning from someone with expert knowledge and teaching ability; you may have had a teacher who is not only great at math, for example, but is also much more skilled and experienced at transmitting this knowledge to others than a classmate of yours might be, even if the classmate also has tremendous knowledge of the subject matter.

Keep in mind that there is no "correct" answer to this question. Either side of the issue can be supported with examples and reasons. It is important to make sure that you state your opinion and develop a response that explains your opinion well. The development of your essay is judged by how effectively you support your opinion; a well-developed essay will contain clearly appropriate reasons, examples, and details that illustrate your opinion. Development is not evaluated simply in terms of how many words you write.

Your response should be well organized. A well-organized essay allows an evaluator to read from the beginning to the end of the essay without becoming confused. You should be sure not to just repeat the same information in different ways.

The quality and accuracy of the sentence structure and vocabulary you use to express your ideas is also very important.

Your response is scored using the Independent Writing Rubric (see Appendix A).

TOEFL iBT Test 5

READING

This section measures your ability to understand academic passages in English.

There are three passages in the section. Give yourself 20 minutes to read each passage and answer the questions about it. The entire section will take 60 minutes to complete.

You may look back at a passage when answering the questions. You can skip questions and go back to them later as long as there is time remaining.

Directions: Read the passage. Then answer the questions. Give yourself 20 minutes to complete this practice set.

HABITATS AND CHIPMUNK SPECIES

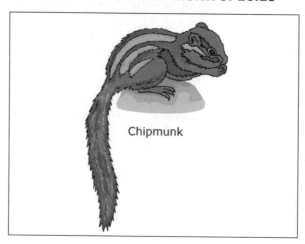

Chipmunk

There are eight chipmunk species in the Sierra Nevada mountain range, and most of them look pretty much alike. But eight different species of chipmunks scurrying around a picnic area will not be found. Nowhere in the Sierra do all eight species occur together. Each species tends strongly to occupy a specific habitat type, within an elevational range, and the overlap among them is minimal.

The eight chipmunk species of the Sierra Nevada represent but a few of the 15 species found in western North America, yet the whole of eastern North America makes do with but one species: the Eastern chipmunk. Why are there so many very similar chipmunks in the West? The presence of tall mountains interspersed with vast areas of arid desert and grassland makes the West ecologically far different from the East. The West affords much more opportunity for chipmunk populations to become geographically isolated from one another, a condition of species formation. Also, there are more extremes in western habitats. In the Sierra Nevada, high elevations are close to low elevations, at least in terms of mileage, but ecologically they are very different.

Most ecologists believe that ancient populations of chipmunks diverged genetically when isolated from one another by mountains and unfavorable ecological habitat. These scattered populations first evolved into races—adapted to the local ecological conditions—and then into species, reproductively isolated from one another. This period of evolution was relatively recent, as evidenced by the similar appearance of all the western chipmunk species.

Ecologists have studied the four chipmunk species that occur on the eastern slope of the Sierra and have learned just how these species interact while remaining separate, each occupying its own elevational zone. The sagebrush chipmunk is found at the lowest elevation, among the sagebrush. The yellow pine chipmunk is common in low to mid-elevations and open conifer forests, including piñon and ponderosa and Jeffrey pine forests. The lodgepole chipmunk is found at higher elevations, among the lodgepoles, firs, and high-elevation pines. The alpine chipmunk is higher still, venturing among the talus slopes, alpine meadows, and high-elevation pines and junipers. Obviously, the ranges of each species overlap. Why don't sagebrush chipmunks move into the pine zones? Why don't alpine chipmunks move to lower elevations and share the conifer forests with lodgepole chipmunks?

The answer, in one word, is aggression. Chipmunk species actively defend their ecological zones from encroachment by neighboring species. The yellow pine chipmunk is more aggressive than the sagebrush chipmunk, possibly because it is a bit larger. It successfully bullies its smaller evolutionary cousin, excluding it from the pine forests. Experiments have shown that the sagebrush chipmunk is physiologically able to live anywhere in the Sierra Nevada, from high alpine zones to the desert. The little creature is apparently restricted to the desert not because it is specialized to live only there but because that is the only habitat where none of the other chipmunk species can live. The fact that sagebrush chipmunks tolerate very warm temperatures makes them, and only them, able to live where they do. The sagebrush chipmunk essentially occupies its habitat by default. In one study, ecologists established that yellow pine chipmunks actively exclude sagebrush chipmunks from pine forests; the ecologists simply trapped all the yellow pine chipmunks in a section of forest and moved them out. Sagebrush chipmunks immediately moved in, but yellow pine chipmunks did not enter sagebrush desert when sagebrush chipmunks were removed.

The most aggressive of the four eastern-slope species is the lodgepole chipmunk, a feisty rodent indeed. It actively prevents alpine chipmunks from moving downslope, and yellow pine chipmunks from moving upslope. There is logic behind the lodgepole's aggressive demeanor. It lives in the cool, shaded conifer forests, and of the four species, it is the least able to tolerate heat stress. It is, in other words, the species of the strictest habitat needs: it simply must be in those shaded forests. However, if it shared its habitat with alpine and yellow pine chipmunks, either or both of these species might outcompete it, taking most of the available food. Such a competition could effectively eliminate lodgepole chipmunks from the habitat. Lodgepoles survive only by virtue of their aggression.

Directions: Now answer the questions.

PARAGRAPH 1

There are eight chipmunk species in the Sierra Nevada mountain range, and most of them look pretty much alike. But eight different species of chipmunks scurrying around a picnic area will not be found. Nowhere in the Sierra do all eight species occur together. Each species tends strongly to occupy a specific habitat type, within an elevational range, and the overlap among them is minimal.

1. Why does the author mention a "picnic area" in paragraph 1?

   (A) To identify a site where a variety of different species of chipmunks can be seen

   (B) To support the point that each species of chipmunk inhabits a distinct location

   (C) To emphasize the idea that all species of chipmunks have a similar appearance

   (D) To provide an example of a location to which chipmunks are likely to scurry for food

PARAGRAPH 2

The eight chipmunk species of the Sierra Nevada represent but a few of the 15 species found in western North America, yet the whole of eastern North America makes do with but one species: the Eastern chipmunk. Why are there so many very similar chipmunks in the West? The presence of tall mountains interspersed with vast areas of arid desert and grassland makes the West ecologically far different from the East. The West affords much more opportunity for chipmunk populations to become geographically isolated from one another, a condition of species formation. Also, there are more extremes in western habitats. In the Sierra Nevada, high elevations are close to low elevations, at least in terms of mileage, but ecologically they are very different.

2. The phrase "interspersed with" in the passage is closest in meaning to
   Ⓐ distributed among
   Ⓑ covered by
   Ⓒ positioned above
   Ⓓ evolved from

3. In paragraph 2, the author indicates that a large variety of chipmunk species exist in western North America because of
   Ⓐ a large migration of chipmunks from eastern North America in an earlier period
   Ⓑ the inability of chipmunks to adapt to the high mountainous regions of eastern North America
   Ⓒ the ecological variety and extremes of the West that caused chipmunks to become geographically isolated
   Ⓓ the absence of large human populations that discouraged species formation among chipmunks in the East

PARAGRAPH 3

Most ecologists believe that ancient populations of chipmunks diverged genetically when isolated from one another by mountains and unfavorable ecological habitat. These scattered populations first evolved into races—adapted to the local ecological conditions—and then into species, reproductively isolated from one another. This period of evolution was relatively recent, as evidenced by the similar appearance of all the western chipmunk species.

4. The word "diverged" in the passage is closest in meaning to
   Ⓐ declined
   Ⓑ competed
   Ⓒ progressed
   Ⓓ separated

5. The phrase "one another" in the passage refers to
   Ⓐ populations
   Ⓑ races
   Ⓒ ecological conditions
   Ⓓ species

Ecologists have studied the four chipmunk species that occur on the eastern slope of the Sierra and have learned just how these species interact while remaining separate, each occupying its own elevational zone. The sagebrush chipmunk is found at the lowest elevation, among the sagebrush. The yellow pine chipmunk is common in low to mid-elevations and open conifer forests, including piñon and ponderosa and Jeffrey pine forests. The lodgepole chipmunk is found at higher elevations, among the lodgepoles, firs, and high-elevation pines. The alpine chipmunk is higher still, venturing among the talus slopes, alpine meadows, and high-elevation pines and junipers. Obviously, the ranges of each species overlap. Why don't sagebrush chipmunks move into the pine zones? Why don't alpine chipmunks move to lower elevations and share the conifer forests with lodgepole chipmunks?

6. Which of the sentences below best expresses the essential information in the highlighted sentence in paragraph 4? Incorrect choices change the meaning in important ways or leave out essential information.

Ⓐ Ecologists studied how the geographic characteristics of the eastern slope of the Sierra influenced the social development of chipmunks.

Ⓑ Ecologists learned exactly how chipmunk species separated from each other on the eastern slope of the Sierra relate to one another.

Ⓒ Ecologists discovered that chipmunks of the eastern slope of the Sierra invade and occupy higher elevational zones when threatened by another species.

Ⓓ Ecologists studied how individual chipmunks of the eastern slope of the Sierra avoid interacting with others of their species.

7. Where does paragraph 4 indicate that the yellow pine chipmunk can be found in relationship to the other species of the eastern slope of the Sierra?

Ⓐ Below the sagebrush chipmunk
Ⓑ Above the alpine chipmunk
Ⓒ At the same elevation as the sagebrush chipmunk
Ⓓ Below the lodgepole chipmunk

The answer, in one word, is aggression. Chipmunk species actively defend their ecological zones from encroachment by neighboring species. The yellow pine chipmunk is more aggressive than the sagebrush chipmunk, possibly because it is a bit larger. It successfully bullies its smaller evolutionary cousin, excluding it from the pine forests. Experiments have shown that the sagebrush chipmunk is physiologically able to live anywhere in the Sierra Nevada, from high alpine zones to the desert. The little creature is apparently restricted to the desert not because it is specialized to live only there but because that is the only habitat where none of the other chipmunk species can live. The fact that sagebrush chipmunks tolerate very warm temperatures makes them, and only them, able to live where they do. The sagebrush chipmunk essentially occupies its habitat by default. In one study, ecologists established that yellow pine chipmunks actively exclude sagebrush chipmunks from pine forests; the ecologists simply trapped all the yellow pine chipmunks in a section of forest and moved them out. Sagebrush chipmunks immediately moved in, but yellow pine chipmunks did not enter sagebrush desert when sagebrush chipmunks were removed.

P A R A G R A P H 5

8. The word "encroachment" in the passage is closest in meaning to

   (A) complete destruction
   (B) gradual invasion
   (C) excessive development
   (D) substitution

9. Paragraph 5 mentions all of the following as true of the relationship of sagebrush chipmunks to their habitats EXCEPT:

   (A) Sagebrush chipmunks are able to survive in any habitat of the Sierra Nevada.
   (B) Sagebrush chipmunks occupy their habitat because of the absence of competition from other chipmunks.
   (C) Sagebrush chipmunks are better able to survive in hot temperatures than other species of chipmunks.
   (D) Sagebrush chipmunks spend the warm season at the higher elevations of the alpine zone.

10. Which of the following statements is supported by the results of the experiment described at the end of paragraph 5?

    (A) The habitat of the yellow pine chipmunk is a desirable one to other species, but the habitat of the sagebrush chipmunk is not.
    (B) It was more difficult to remove sagebrush chipmunks from their habitat than it was to remove yellow pine chipmunks from theirs.
    (C) Yellow pine chipmunks and sagebrush chipmunks require the same environmental conditions in their habitats.
    (D) The temperature of the habitat is not an important factor to either the yellow pine chipmunk or the sagebrush chipmunk.

The most aggressive of the four eastern-slope species is the lodgepole chipmunk, a feisty rodent indeed. It actively prevents alpine chipmunks from moving downslope, and yellow pine chipmunks from moving upslope. There is logic behind the lodgepole's aggressive demeanor. It lives in the cool, shaded conifer forests, and of the four species, it is the least able to tolerate heat stress. It is, in other words, the species of the strictest habitat needs: it simply must be in those shaded forests. However, if it shared its habitat with alpine and yellow pine chipmunks, either or both of these species might outcompete it, taking most of the available food. Such a competition could effectively eliminate lodgepole chipmunks from the habitat. Lodgepoles survive only by virtue of their aggression.

11. According to paragraph 6, why is the lodgepole chipmunk so protective of its habitat from competing chipmunks?

Ⓐ It has specialized food requirements.
Ⓑ It cannot tolerate cold temperatures well.
Ⓒ It requires the shade provided by forest trees.
Ⓓ It prefers to be able to move between areas that are downslope and upslope.

12. The phrase "by virtue of" in the passage is closest in meaning to

Ⓐ in spite of
Ⓑ because of
Ⓒ unconcerned about
Ⓓ with attention to

Ecologists have studied the four chipmunk species that occur on the eastern slope of the Sierra and have learned just how these species interact while remaining separate, each occupying its own elevational zone. The sagebrush chipmunk is found at the lowest elevation, among the sagebrush. The yellow pine chipmunk is common in low to mid-elevations and open conifer forests, including piñon and ponderosa and Jeffrey pine forests. The lodgepole chipmunk is found at higher elevations, among the lodgepoles, firs, and high-elevation pines. The alpine chipmunk is higher still, venturing among the talus slopes, alpine meadows, and high-elevation pines and junipers. ■ Obviously, the ranges of each species overlap. ■ Why don't sagebrush chipmunks move into the pine zones? ■ Why don't alpine chipmunks move to lower elevations and share the conifer forests with lodgepole chipmunks? ■

13. Look at the four squares [■] that indicate where the following sentence can be added to the passage.

Yet each species remains within a fairly well-defined elevational zone.

Where would the sentence best fit?

Ⓐ Ecologists have studied the four chipmunk species that occur on the eastern slope of the Sierra and have learned just how these species interact while remaining separate, each occupying its own elevational zone. The sagebrush chipmunk is found at the lowest elevation, among the sagebrush. The yellow pine chipmunk is common in low to mid-elevations and open conifer forests, including piñon and ponderosa and Jeffrey pine forests. The lodgepole chipmunk is found at higher elevations, among the lodgepoles, firs, and high-elevation pines. The alpine chipmunk is higher still, venturing among the talus slopes, alpine meadows, and high-elevation pines and junipers. **Yet each species remains within a fairly well-defined elevational zone.** Obviously, the ranges of each species overlap. ■ Why don't sagebrush chipmunks move into the pine zones? ■ Why don't alpine chipmunks move to lower elevations and share the conifer forests with lodgepole chipmunks? ■

Ⓑ Ecologists have studied the four chipmunk species that occur on the eastern slope of the Sierra and have learned just how these species interact while remaining separate, each occupying its own elevational zone. The sagebrush chipmunk is found at the lowest elevation, among the sagebrush. The yellow pine chipmunk is common in low to mid-elevations and open conifer forests, including piñon and ponderosa and Jeffrey pine forests. The lodgepole chipmunk is found at higher elevations, among the lodgepoles, firs, and high-elevation pines. The alpine chipmunk is higher still, venturing among the talus slopes, alpine meadows, and high-elevation pines and junipers. ■ Obviously, the ranges of each species overlap. **Yet each species remains within a fairly well-defined elevational zone.** Why don't sagebrush chipmunks move into the pine zones? ■ Why don't alpine chipmunks move to lower elevations and share the conifer forests with lodgepole chipmunks? ■

Ⓒ Ecologists have studied the four chipmunk species that occur on the eastern slope of the Sierra and have learned just how these species interact while remaining separate, each occupying its own elevational zone. The sagebrush chipmunk is found at the lowest elevation, among the sagebrush. The yellow pine chipmunk is common in low to mid-elevations and open conifer forests, including piñon and ponderosa and Jeffrey pine forests. The lodgepole chipmunk is found at higher elevations, among the lodgepoles, firs, and high-elevation pines. The alpine chipmunk is higher still, venturing among the talus slopes, alpine meadows, and high-elevation pines and junipers. ■ Obviously, the ranges of each species overlap. ■ Why don't sagebrush chipmunks move into the pine zones? **Yet each species remains within a fairly well-defined elevational zone.** Why don't alpine chipmunks move to lower elevations and share the conifer forests with lodgepole chipmunks? ■

Ⓓ Ecologists have studied the four chipmunk species that occur on the eastern slope of the Sierra and have learned just how these species interact while remaining separate, each occupying its own elevational zone. The sagebrush chipmunk is found at the lowest elevation, among the sagebrush. The yellow pine chipmunk is common in low to mid-elevations and open conifer forests, including piñon and ponderosa and Jeffrey pine forests. The lodgepole chipmunk is found at higher elevations, among the lodgepoles, firs, and high-elevation pines. The alpine chipmunk is higher still, venturing among the talus slopes, alpine meadows, and high-elevation pines and junipers. ■ Obviously, the ranges of each species overlap. ■ Why don't sagebrush chipmunks move into the pine zones? ■ Why don't alpine chipmunks move to lower elevations and share the conifer forests with lodgepole chipmunks? **Yet each species remains within a fairly well-defined elevational zone.**

14. **Directions**: An introductory sentence for a brief summary of the passage is provided below. Complete the summary by selecting the THREE answer choices that express the most important ideas in the passage. Some sentences do not belong in the summary because they express ideas that are not presented in the passage or are minor ideas in the passage.

    Write your answer choices in the spaces where they belong. You can either write the letter of your answer choice or you can copy the sentence.

    A variety of chipmunk species inhabit western North America.

    -
    -
    -

    Answer Choices

    A Ecological variation of the Sierra Nevada resulted in the differentiation of chipmunk species.
    B Only one species of chipmunk inhabits eastern North America.
    C Although chipmunk species of the Sierra Nevada have the ability to live at various elevations, each species inhabits a specifically restricted one.
    D Chipmunks aggressively defend their habitats from invasion by other species of chipmunks.
    E Experimental studies indicate that sagebrush chipmunks live in the desert because of their physiological requirements.
    F The most aggressive of the chipmunk species is the lodgepole chipmunk.

Directions: Read the passage. Then answer the questions. Give yourself 20 minutes to complete this practice set.

CETACEAN INTELLIGENCE

We often hear that whales, dolphins, and porpoises are as intelligent as humans, maybe even more so. Are they really that smart? There is no question that cetaceans are among the most intelligent of animals. Dolphins, killer whales, and pilot whales in captivity quickly learn tricks. The military has trained bottlenose dolphins to find bombs and missile heads and to work as underwater spies.

This type of learning, however, is called conditioning. The animal simply learns that when it performs a particular behavior, it gets a reward, usually a fish. Many animals, including rats, birds, and even invertebrates, can be conditioned to perform tricks. We certainly don't think of these animals as our mental rivals. Unlike most other animals, however, dolphins quickly learn by observations and may spontaneously imitate human activities. One tame dolphin watched a diver cleaning an underwater viewing window, seized a feather in its beak, and began imitating the diver—complete with sound effects! Dolphins have also been seen imitating seals, turtles, and even water-skiers.

Given the seeming intelligence of cetaceans, people are always tempted to compare them with humans and other animals. Studies on discrimination and problem-solving skills in the bottlenose dolphin, for instance, have concluded that its intelligence lies "somewhere between that of a dog and a chimpanzee." Such comparisons are unfair. It is important to realize that intelligence is a very human concept and that we evaluate it in human terms. After all, not many people would consider themselves stupid because they couldn't locate and identify a fish by its echo. Why should we judge cetaceans by their ability to solve human problems?

Both humans and cetaceans have large brains with an expanded and distinctively folded surface, the cortex. The cortex is the dominant association center of the brain, where abilities such as memory and sensory perception are centered. Cetaceans have larger brains than ours, but the ratio of brain to body weight is higher in humans. Again, direct comparisons are misleading. In cetaceans it is mainly the portions of the brain associated with hearing and the processing of sound information that are expanded. The enlarged portions of our brain deal largely with vision and hand-eye coordination. Cetaceans and humans almost certainly perceive the world in very different ways. Their world is largely one of sounds, ours one of sights.

Contrary to what is depicted in movies and on television, the notion of "talking" to dolphins is also misleading. Although they produce a rich repertoire of complex sounds, they lack vocal cords and their brains probably process sound differently from ours. Bottlenose dolphins have been trained to make sounds through the blowhole that sound something like human sounds, but this is a far cry from human speech. By the same token, humans cannot make whale sounds. We will probably never be able to carry on an unaided conversation with cetaceans.

As in chimpanzees, captive bottlenose dolphins have been taught American Sign Language. These dolphins have learned to communicate with trainers who use sign language to ask simple questions. Dolphins answer back by pushing a "yes" or "no" paddle. They have even been known to give spontaneous responses not taught by the trainers. Evidence also indicates that these dolphins can distinguish between commands that differ from each other only by their word order, a truly remarkable achievement. Nevertheless, dolphins do not seem to have a real language like ours. Unlike humans, dolphins probably cannot convey very complex messages.

Observations of cetaceans in the wild have provided some insights on their learning abilities. Several bottlenose dolphins off western Australia, for instance, have been observed carrying large cone-shaped sponges over their beaks. They supposedly use the sponges for protection against stingrays and other hazards on the bottom as they search for fish to eat. This is the first record of the use of tools among wild cetaceans.

Instead of "intelligence," some people prefer to speak of "awareness." In any case, cetaceans probably have a very different awareness and perception of their environment than do humans. Maybe one day we will come to understand cetaceans on their terms instead of ours, and perhaps we will discover a mental sophistication rivaling our own.

Directions: Now answer the questions.

PARAGRAPH 1

We often hear that whales, dolphins, and porpoises are as intelligent as humans, maybe even more so. Are they really that smart? There is no question that cetaceans are among the most intelligent of animals. Dolphins, killer whales, and pilot whales in captivity quickly learn tricks. The military has trained bottlenose dolphins to find bombs and missile heads and to work as underwater spies.

15. The author asks the question "Are they really that smart?" for which of the following reasons?

Ⓐ To question the notion that humans are the most intelligent of animals
Ⓑ To introduce the discussion of intelligence that follows
Ⓒ To explain why dolphins, killer whales, and pilot whales can learn tricks
Ⓓ To emphasize the ways that dolphins can help the military

This type of learning, however, is called conditioning. The animal simply learns that when it performs a particular behavior, it gets a reward, usually a fish. Many animals, including rats, birds, and even invertebrates, can be conditioned to perform tricks. We certainly don't think of these animals as our mental rivals. Unlike most other animals, however, dolphins quickly learn by observations and may spontaneously imitate human activities. One tame dolphin watched a diver cleaning an underwater viewing window, seized a feather in its beak, and began imitating the diver—complete with sound effects! Dolphins have also been seen imitating seals, turtles, and even water-skiers.

16. According to the passage, which of the following animals is most likely to learn by watching another animal perform an activity?

   Ⓐ Rats
   Ⓑ Birds
   Ⓒ Invertebrates
   Ⓓ Dolphins

Given the seeming intelligence of cetaceans, people are always tempted to compare them with humans and other animals. Studies on discrimination and problem-solving skills in the bottlenose dolphin, for instance, have concluded that its intelligence lies "somewhere between that of a dog and a chimpanzee." Such comparisons are unfair. It is important to realize that intelligence is a very human concept and that we evaluate it in human terms. After all, not many people would consider themselves stupid because they couldn't locate and identify a fish by its echo. Why should we judge cetaceans by their ability to solve human problems?

17. The word "tempted" in the passage is closest in meaning to

   Ⓐ conditioned
   Ⓑ reluctant
   Ⓒ inclined
   Ⓓ invited

18. According to the passage, why are the studies that conclude that dolphin intelligence is " 'somewhere between that of a dog and a chimpanzee' " not correct?

   Ⓐ The human method of drawing comparisons is not relevant to animal intelligence.
   Ⓑ Dolphins have actually been shown to be much more intelligent than chimpanzees.
   Ⓒ The studies were not conducted according to standard research methods.
   Ⓓ Dolphins do not typically demonstrate conditioned responses for humans to observe.

Both humans and cetaceans have large brains with an expanded and distinctively folded surface, the cortex. The cortex is the dominant association center of the brain, where abilities such as memory and sensory perception are centered. Cetaceans have larger brains than ours, but the ratio of brain to body weight is higher in humans. Again, direct comparisons are misleading. In cetaceans it is mainly the portions of the brain associated with hearing and the processing of sound information that are expanded. The enlarged portions of our brain deal largely with vision and hand-eye coordination. Cetaceans and humans almost certainly perceive the world in very different ways. Their world is largely one of sounds, ours one of sights.

19. The word "dominant" in the passage is closest in meaning to

(A) local

(B) natural

(C) chief

(D) specific

As in chimpanzees, captive bottlenose dolphins have been taught American Sign Language. These dolphins have learned to communicate with trainers who use sign language to ask simple questions. Dolphins answer back by pushing a "yes" or "no" paddle. They have even been known to give spontaneous responses not taught by the trainers. Evidence also indicates that these dolphins can distinguish between commands that differ from each other only by their word order, a truly remarkable achievement. Nevertheless, dolphins do not seem to have a real language like ours. Unlike humans, dolphins probably cannot convey very complex messages.

20. The word "spontaneous" in the passage is closest in meaning to

(A) sophisticated

(B) sensible

(C) appropriate

(D) unprompted

Observations of cetaceans in the wild have provided some insights on their learning abilities. Several bottlenose dolphins off western Australia, for instance, have been observed carrying large cone-shaped sponges over their beaks. They supposedly use the sponges for protection against stingrays and other hazards on the bottom as they search for fish to eat. This is the first record of the use of tools among wild cetaceans.

21. The word "insights" in the passage is closest in meaning to

(A) examples

(B) understanding

(C) directions

(D) discussion

22. Scientific observations show that cetaceans are able to do all of the following EXCEPT

   (A) use natural objects as tools for self-protection
   (B) produce complex sounds through their blowholes
   (C) answer spoken questions
   (D) distinguish between very similar spoken sentences

23. The word "hazards" in the passage is closest in meaning to

   (A) objects
   (B) dangers
   (C) species
   (D) debris

PARAGRAPH 8

Instead of "intelligence," some people prefer to speak of "awareness." In any case, cetaceans probably have a very different awareness and perception of their environment than do humans. Maybe one day we will come to understand cetaceans on their terms instead of ours, and perhaps we will discover a mental sophistication rivaling our own.

24. What does the author conclude about the intelligence of cetaceans?

   (A) It is not appropriate to judge cetacean intelligence in human terms.
   (B) Cetaceans probably possess a mental sophistication that is as complex as that of humans.
   (C) Although cetaceans may appear to be intelligent, they have fewer problem-solving skills than most animals.
   (D) Their ability to learn American Sign Language indicates that cetaceans have a high level of intelligence.

PARAGRAPH 2

This type of learning, however, is called conditioning. ■ The animal simply learns that when it performs a particular behavior, it gets a reward, usually a fish. ■ Many animals, including rats, birds, and even invertebrates, can be conditioned to perform tricks. ■ We certainly don't think of these animals as our mental rivals. ■ Unlike most other animals, however, dolphins quickly learn by observations and may spontaneously imitate human activities. One tame dolphin watched a diver cleaning an underwater viewing window, seized a feather in its beak, and began imitating the diver—complete with sound effects! Dolphins have also been seen imitating seals, turtles, and even water-skiers.

25. Look at the four squares [■] that indicate where the following sentence can be added to the passage.

This reward is merely one possible type of positive reinforcement that leads to more frequent repetition of the behavior in the future.

Where would the sentence best fit?

(A) This type of learning, however, is called conditioning. **This reward is merely one possible type of positive reinforcement that leads to more frequent repetition of the behavior in the future.** The animal simply learns that when it performs a particular behavior, it gets a reward, usually a fish. ■ Many animals, including rats, birds, and even invertebrates, can be conditioned to perform tricks. ■ We certainly don't think of these animals as our mental rivals. ■ Unlike most other animals, however, dolphins quickly learn by observations and may spontaneously imitate human activities. One tame dolphin watched a diver cleaning an underwater viewing window, seized a feather in its beak, and began imitating the diver—complete with sound effects! Dolphins have also been seen imitating seals, turtles, and even water-skiers.

(B) This type of learning, however, is called conditioning. ■ The animal simply learns that when it performs a particular behavior, it gets a reward, usually a fish. **This reward is merely one possible type of positive reinforcement that leads to more frequent repetition of the behavior in the future.** Many animals, including rats, birds, and even invertebrates, can be conditioned to perform tricks. ■ We certainly don't think of these animals as our mental rivals. ■ Unlike most other animals, however, dolphins quickly learn by observations and may spontaneously imitate human activities. One tame dolphin watched a diver cleaning an underwater viewing window, seized a feather in its beak, and began imitating the diver—complete with sound effects! Dolphins have also been seen imitating seals, turtles, and even water-skiers.

(C) This type of learning, however, is called conditioning. ■ The animal simply learns that when it performs a particular behavior, it gets a reward, usually a fish. ■ Many animals, including rats, birds, and even invertebrates, can be conditioned to perform tricks. **This reward is merely one possible type of positive reinforcement that leads to more frequent repetition of the behavior in the future.** We certainly don't think of these animals as our mental rivals. ■ Unlike most other animals, however, dolphins quickly learn by observations and may spontaneously imitate human activities. One tame dolphin watched a diver cleaning an underwater viewing window, seized a feather in its beak, and began imitating the diver—complete with sound effects! Dolphins have also been seen imitating seals, turtles, and even water-skiers.

(D) This type of learning, however, is called conditioning. ■ The animal simply learns that when it performs a particular behavior, it gets a reward, usually a fish. ■ Many animals, including rats, birds, and even invertebrates, can be conditioned to perform tricks. ■ We certainly don't think of these animals as our mental rivals. **This reward is merely one possible type of positive reinforcement that leads to more frequent repetition of the behavior in**

the future. Unlike most other animals, however, dolphins quickly learn by observations and may spontaneously imitate human activities. One tame dolphin watched a diver cleaning an underwater viewing window, seized a feather in its beak, and began imitating the diver—complete with sound effects! Dolphins have also been seen imitating seals, turtles, and even water-skiers.

26. **Directions**: Select the appropriate phrases from the answer choices below and match them to the type of animal to which they relate. ONE of the answer choices will NOT be used.

   Write your answer choices in the spaces where they belong. You can either write the letter of your answer choice or you can copy the sentence.

Humans

-
-

Cetaceans

-
-

BOTH Humans and Cetaceans

-
-
-

Answer Choices

A The ability to converse unaided with other species
B A brain with a cortex
C A set of vocal cords
D The ability to use tools
E The ability to locate objects by using echo
F An enlarged portion of the brain for processing sound
G An enlarged portion of the brain for processing vision
H The ability to learn by observation

Directions: Read the passage. Then answer the questions. Give yourself 20 minutes to complete this practice set.

A MODEL OF URBAN EXPANSION

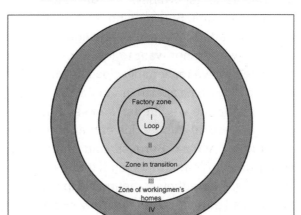

In the early twentieth century, the science of sociology found supporters in the United States and Canada partly because the cities there were growing so rapidly. It often appeared that North American cities would be unable to absorb all the new-comers arriving in such large numbers. Presociological thinkers like Frederick Law Olmsted, the founder of the movement to build parks and recreation areas in cities, and Jacob Riis, an advocate of slum reform, urged the nation's leaders to invest in improving the urban environment, building parks and beaches, and making better housing available to all. These reform efforts were greatly aided by sociologists who conducted empirical research on the social conditions in cities. In the early twentieth century, many sociologists lived in cities like Chicago that were characterized by rapid population growth and serious social problems. It seemed logical to use empirical research to construct theories about how cities grow and change in response to major social forces as well as more controlled urban planning.

The founders of the Chicago school of sociology, Robert Park and Ernest Burgess, attempted to develop a dynamic model of the city, one that would account not only for the expansion of cities in terms of population and territory but also for the patterns of settlement and land use within cities. They identified several factors that influence the physical form of cities. As Park stated, among them are "transportation and communication, tramways and telephones, newspapers and advertising, steel construction and elevators—all things, in fact, which tend to bring about at once a greater mobility and a greater concentration of the urban populations."

Park and Burgess based their model of urban growth on the concept of "natural areas"—that is, areas such as occupational suburbs or residential enclaves in which the population is relatively homogeneous and land is used in similar ways without deliberate planning. Park and Burgess saw urban expansion as occurring through a series of "invasions" of successive zones or areas surrounding the center of the city. For example, people from rural areas and other societies "invaded" areas where housing was inexpensive. Those areas tended to be close to the places where they worked. In turn, people who could afford better housing and the cost of commuting "invaded" areas farther from the business district.

Park and Burgess's model has come to be known as the "concentric-zone model" (represented by the figure). Because the model was originally based on studies of Chicago, its center is labeled "Loop," the term commonly applied to that city's central commercial zone. Surrounding the central zone is a "zone in transition," an area that is being invaded by business and light manufacturing. The third zone is inhabited by workers who do not want to live in the factory or business district but at the same time need to live reasonably close to where they work. The fourth or residential zone consists of upscale apartment buildings and single-family homes. And the outermost ring, outside the city limits, is the suburban or commuters' zone; its residents live within a 30- to 60-minute ride of the central business district.

Studies by Park, Burgess, and other Chicago-school sociologists showed how new groups of immigrants tended to be concentrated in separate areas within inner-city zones, where they sometimes experienced tension with other ethnic groups that had arrived earlier. Over time, however, each group was able to adjust to life in the city and to find a place for itself in the urban economy. Eventually many of the immigrants moved to unsegregated areas in outer zones; the areas they left behind were promptly occupied by new waves of immigrants.

The Park and Burgess model of growth in zones and natural areas of the city can still be used to describe patterns of growth in cities that were built around a central business district and that continue to attract large numbers of immigrants. But this model is biased toward the commercial and industrial cities of North America, which have tended to form around business centers rather than around palaces or cathedrals, as is often the case in some other parts of the world. Moreover, it fails to account for other patterns of urbanization, such as the rapid urbanization that occurs along commercial transportation corridors and the rise of nearby satellite cities.

Directions: Now answer the questions.

PARAGRAPH 1

In the early twentieth century, the science of sociology found supporters in the United States and Canada partly because the cities there were growing so rapidly. It often appeared that North American cities would be unable to absorb all the newcomers arriving in such large numbers. Presociological thinkers like Frederick Law Olmsted, the founder of the movement to build parks and recreation areas in cities, and Jacob Riis, an advocate of slum reform, urged the nation's leaders to invest in improving the urban environment, building parks and beaches, and making better housing available to all. These reform efforts were greatly aided by sociologists who conducted empirical research on the social conditions in cities. In the early twentieth century, many sociologists lived in cities like Chicago that were characterized by rapid population growth and serious social problems. It seemed logical to use empirical research to construct theories about how cities grow and change in response to major social forces as well as more controlled urban planning.

27. Which of the following can be inferred from paragraph 1 about what Olmsted and Riis had in common?

    Ⓐ Both constructed theories based on empirical research on cities.
    Ⓑ Both were among a large number of newcomers to North American cities.
    Ⓒ Both wanted to improve the conditions of life in cities.
    Ⓓ Both hoped to reduce the rapid growth of large cities.

28. Which of the following best states the relationship that Olmsted and Riis had to the study of sociology?

    Ⓐ Their goals were supported by the research conducted later by sociologists.
    Ⓑ Their approach led them to oppose empirical sociological studies.
    Ⓒ They had difficulty establishing that their work was as important as sociological research.
    Ⓓ They used evidence from sociological research to urge national leaders to invest in urban development.

PARAGRAPH 2

The founders of the Chicago school of sociology, Robert Park and Ernest Burgess, attempted to develop a dynamic model of the city, one that would account not only for the expansion of cities in terms of population and territory but also for the patterns of settlement and land use within cities. They identified several factors that influence the physical form of cities. As Park stated, among them are "transportation and communication, tramways and telephones, newspapers and advertising, steel construction and elevators—all things, in fact, which tend to bring about at once a greater mobility and a greater concentration of the urban populations."

29. Which of the sentences below best expresses the essential information in the highlighted sentence in paragraph 2? Incorrect choices change the meaning in important ways or leave out essential information.

    Ⓐ The Chicago school of sociology founded by Park and Burgess attempted to help the population of growing cities protect the land around them.
    Ⓑ The model that Park and Burgess created was intended to explain both why the population and area of a city like Chicago grew and in what way urban land was used or settled.
    Ⓒ The founders of the Chicago school of sociology wanted to make Chicago a dynamic model for how other cities should use and settle their land.
    Ⓓ Park and Burgess were concerned that cities like Chicago should follow a model of good land use as the population grew and settled new areas.

30. The author includes the statement by Robert Park in paragraph 2 in order to

    Ⓐ establish the specific topics about which Park and Burgess may have disagreed
    Ⓑ identify the aspects of Chicago's development that required careful planning
    Ⓒ specify some of the factors that contributed to the pattern of development of cities
    Ⓓ compare the definitions given by Park and Burgess for the physical form of cities

Park and Burgess based their model of urban growth on the concept of "natural areas"—that is, areas such as occupational suburbs or residential enclaves in which the population is relatively homogeneous and land is used in similar ways without deliberate planning. Park and Burgess saw urban expansion as occurring through a series of "invasions" of successive zones or areas surrounding the center of the city. For example, people from rural areas and other societies "invaded" areas where housing was inexpensive. Those areas tended to be close to the places where they worked. In turn, people who could afford better housing and the cost of commuting "invaded" areas farther from the business district.

31. Paragraph 3 indicates that all of the following are true of "natural areas" as conceived by Park and Burgess EXCEPT:

Ⓐ Use of the land in natural areas follows a consistent pattern but is generally unplanned.

Ⓑ People living in natural areas tend to have much in common.

Ⓒ Natural areas are usually protected from "invasion" by people in other areas.

Ⓓ Natural areas are an important basic component of the model Park and Burgess developed.

Park and Burgess's model has come to be known as the "concentric-zone model" (represented by the figure). Because the model was originally based on studies of Chicago, its center is labeled "Loop," the term commonly applied to that city's central commercial zone. Surrounding the central zone is a "zone in transition," an area that is being invaded by business and light manufacturing. The third zone is inhabited by workers who do not want to live in the factory or business district but at the same time need to live reasonably close to where they work. The fourth or residential zone consists of upscale apartment buildings and single-family homes. And the outermost ring, outside the city limits, is the suburban or commuters' zone; its residents live within a 30- to 60-minute ride of the central business district.

32. According to paragraph 4, why is the term "Loop" used in the concentric-zone model?

Ⓐ It indicates the many connections between each of the zones in the model.

Ⓑ It indicates that zones are often in transition and frequently changing.

Ⓒ It reflects the fact that the model was created with the city of Chicago in mind.

Ⓓ It emphasizes the fact that populations often returned to zones in which they used to live.

33. Which of the following can be inferred from paragraph 4 about the third zone?

Ⓐ It is the most expensive area in which to live.

Ⓑ It does not have factories and businesses.

Ⓒ People who live there travel long distances to work.

Ⓓ Most of the residents there work and live in the same zone.

34. The word "outermost" in the passage is closest in meaning to
    (A) most visible
    (B) best protected
    (C) farthest away
    (D) wealthiest

Studies by Park, Burgess, and other Chicago-school sociologists showed how new groups of immigrants tended to be concentrated in separate areas within inner-city zones, where they sometimes experienced tension with other ethnic groups that had arrived earlier. Over time, however, each group was able to adjust to life in the city and to find a place for itself in the urban economy. Eventually many of the immigrants moved to unsegregated areas in outer zones; the areas they left behind were promptly occupied by new waves of immigrants.

35. The word "they" in the passage refers
    (A) Chicago-school sociologists
    (B) new groups of immigrants
    (C) separate areas
    (D) inner-city zones

36. The word "concentrated" in the passage is closest in meaning to
    (A) divided
    (B) reduced
    (C) interested
    (D) gathered

37. The word "promptly" in the passage is closest in meaning to
    (A) quickly
    (B) usually
    (C) eventually
    (D) easily

The Park and Burgess model of growth in zones and natural areas of the city can still be used to describe patterns of growth in cities that were built around a central business district and that continue to attract large numbers of immigrants. But this model is biased toward the commercial and industrial cities of North America, which have tended to form around business centers rather than around palaces or cathedrals, as is often the case in some other parts of the world. Moreover, it fails to account for other patterns of urbanization, such as the rapid urbanization that occurs along commercial transportation corridors and the rise of nearby satellite cities.

PARAGRAPH 6

38. Paragraph 6 indicates which of the following about the application of the Park and Burgess model to modern North American cities?

Ⓐ It is especially useful for those cities that have been used as models for international development.

Ⓑ It remains useful in explaining the development of some urban areas but not all cities.

Ⓒ It can be applied equally well to cities with commercial centers and those with palaces and cathedrals at their center.

Ⓓ It is less applicable to modern cities because of changes in patterns of immigration.

PARAGRAPHS 5 & 6

Studies by Park, Burgess, and other Chicago-school sociologists showed how new groups of immigrants tended to be concentrated in separate areas within inner-city zones, where they sometimes experienced tension with other ethnic groups that had arrived earlier. Over time, however, each group was able to adjust to life in the city and to find a place for itself in the urban economy. ■ Eventually many of the immigrants moved to unsegregated areas in outer zones; the areas they left behind were promptly occupied by new waves of immigrants.

The Park and Burgess model of growth in zones and natural areas of the city can still be used to describe patterns of growth in cities that were built around a central business district and that continue to attract large numbers of immigrants. ■ But this model is biased toward the commercial and industrial cities of North America, which have tended to form around business centers rather than around palaces or cathedrals, as is often the case in some other parts of the world. ■ Moreover, it fails to account for other patterns of urbanization, such as the rapid urbanization that occurs along commercial transportation corridors and the rise of nearby satellite cities. ■

39. Look at the four squares [■] that indicate where the following sentence can be added to the passage.

Typical of this kind of urban growth is the steel-producing center of Gary, Indiana, outside of Chicago, which developed because massive heavy industry could not be located within the major urban center itself.

Where would the sentence best fit?

Ⓐ Studies by Park, Burgess, and other Chicago-school sociologists showed how new groups of immigrants tended to be concentrated in separate areas within inner-city zones, where they sometimes experienced tension with other ethnic groups that had arrived earlier. Over time, however, each group was able to adjust to life in the city and to find a place for itself in the urban economy. **Typical of this kind of urban growth is the steel-producing center of Gary, Indiana, outside of Chicago, which developed because massive heavy industry could not be located within the major urban center itself.** Eventually many of the immigrants moved to unsegregated areas in outer zones; the areas they left behind were promptly occupied by new waves of immigrants.

The Park and Burgess model of growth in zones and natural areas of the city can still be used to describe patterns of growth in cities that were built around a central business district and that continue to attract large numbers of immigrants. ■ But this model is biased toward the commercial and industrial cities of North America, which have tended to form around business centers rather than around palaces or cathedrals, as is often the case in some other parts of the world. ■ Moreover, it fails to account for other patterns of urbanization, such as the rapid urbanization that occurs along commercial transportation corridors and the rise of nearby satellite cities. ■

Ⓑ Studies by Park, Burgess, and other Chicago-school sociologists showed how new groups of immigrants tended to be concentrated in separate areas within inner-city zones, where they sometimes experienced tension with other ethnic groups that had arrived earlier. Over time, however, each group was able to adjust to life in the city and to find a place for itself in the urban economy. ■ Eventually many of the immigrants moved to unsegregated areas in outer zones; the areas they left behind were promptly occupied by new waves of immigrants.

The Park and Burgess model of growth in zones and natural areas of the city can still be used to describe patterns of growth in cities that were built around a central business district and that continue to attract large numbers of immigrants. **Typical of this kind of urban growth is the steel-producing center of Gary, Indiana, outside of Chicago, which developed because massive heavy industry could not be located within the major urban center itself.** But this model is biased toward the commercial and industrial cities of North America, which have tended to form around business centers rather than around palaces or cathedrals, as is often the case in some other parts of the world. ■ Moreover, it fails to account for other patterns of urbanization, such as the rapid urbanization that occurs along commercial transportation corridors and the rise of nearby satellite cities. ■

Ⓒ Studies by Park, Burgess, and other Chicago-school sociologists showed how new groups of immigrants tended to be concentrated in separate areas within inner-city zones, where they sometimes experienced tension with other ethnic groups that had arrived earlier. Over time, however, each group was able to adjust to life in the city and to find a place for itself in the urban economy. ■ Eventually many of the immigrants moved to unsegregated areas in outer zones; the areas they left behind were promptly occupied by new waves of immigrants.

The Park and Burgess model of growth in zones and natural areas of the city can still be used to describe patterns of growth in cities that were built around a central business district and that continue to attract large numbers of immigrants. ■ But this model is biased toward the commercial and industrial cities of North America, which have tended to form around business centers rather than around palaces or cathedrals, as is often the case in some other parts of the world. **Typical of this kind of urban growth is the steel-producing center of Gary, Indiana, outside of Chicago, which developed because massive heavy industry could not be located within the major urban center itself.** Moreover, it fails to account for other patterns of urbanization, such as the rapid urbanization that occurs along commercial transportation corridors and the rise of nearby satellite cities. ■

Ⓓ Studies by Park, Burgess, and other Chicago-school sociologists showed how new groups of immigrants tended to be concentrated in separate areas within inner-city zones, where they sometimes experienced tension with other ethnic groups that had arrived earlier. Over time, however, each group was able to adjust to life in the city and to find a place for itself in the urban economy. ■ Eventually many of the immigrants moved to unsegregated areas in outer zones; the areas they left behind were promptly occupied by new waves of immigrants.

The Park and Burgess model of growth in zones and natural areas of the city can still be used to describe patterns of growth in cities that were built around a central business district and that continue to attract large numbers of immigrants. ■ But this model is biased toward the commercial and industrial cities of North America, which have tended to form around business centers rather than around palaces or cathedrals, as is often the case in some other parts of the world. ■ Moreover, it fails to account for other patterns of urbanization, such as the rapid urbanization that occurs along commercial transportation corridors and the rise of nearby satellite cities. **Typical of this kind of urban growth is the steel-producing center of Gary, Indiana, outside of Chicago, which developed because massive heavy industry could not be located within the major urban center itself.**

40. **Directions:** An introductory sentence for a brief summary of the passage is provided here. Complete the summary by selecting the THREE answer choices that express the most important ideas in the passage. Some sentences do not belong in the summary because they express ideas that are not presented in the passage or are minor ideas in the passage.

Write your answer choices in the spaces where they belong. You can either write the letter of your answer choice or you can copy the sentence.

Two sociologists, Robert Park and Ernest Burgess, developed the "concentric-zone model" of how cities use land and grow.

- ●

- ●

- ●

Answer Choices

A The model was developed to explain how the city of Chicago was developing around centrally located transportation and communication systems.

B The model arose out of concern for the quality of life in the rapidly growing cities of early twentieth-century America.

C The founders of the model did not believe in formal city planning and instead advocated growth through the expansion of so-called "natural areas."

D According to the model, a group new to the city tends to live together near the center and over time moves to outer areas that are more diverse ethnically and occupationally.

E The model is applicable to cities that grow by attracting large numbers of workers to centrally located businesses.

F The model predicts that eventually the inner city becomes so crowded that its residents move to new satellite cities outside the city limits.

LISTENING

This section measures your ability to understand conversations and lectures in English.

Listen to each conversation and lecture only one time. After each conversation and lecture, you will answer some questions about it. Answer each question based on what is stated or implied by the speakers.

You may take notes while you listen and use your notes to help you answer the questions. Your notes will **not** be scored.

In some questions you will see this icon: ( ). This means that you will hear, but not see, the question.

Answer each question before moving on. Do not return to previous questions.

It will take about 60 minutes to listen to the conversations and lectures and answer the questions about them.

Directions: Listen to Track 86.

Directions: Now answer the questions.

1. What are the speakers mainly discussing?

   (A) Getting financial aid for college
   (B) Planning a student's course schedule for the next four years
   (C) Taking courses during the summer session
   (D) Differences in admissions requirements between Hooper University and two other schools

2. Why does the student want to take classes at City College?

   (A) Because Hooper University does not offer the classes he wants
   (B) Because City College classes cost less money than ones at Hooper University
   (C) So that he can take classes on the weekend
   (D) So that he can graduate from Hooper University early

3. Why will the man probably take only two courses?

   (A) Students are limited to two summer courses.
   (B) He can attend classes only on Saturday and Sunday.
   (C) His financial aid will pay for only two courses.
   (D) His summer job will keep him from taking more than two courses.

4. What will Ms. Brinker probably do for the man? *Choose 2 answers.*

   [A] Give the man a student ID number
   [B] Give the man a financial aid form
   [C] Help the man figure out which classes to take
   [D] Help the man apply to Hooper University
   [E] Put the man's information into the City College admission system

5. Listen to Track 87.
   - Ⓐ The man waited too long to apply to City College.
   - Ⓑ The man should not attend Hooper University.
   - Ⓒ The man will be able to do what he wants to do.
   - Ⓓ The man is very unlucky.

Directions: Listen to Track 88.

Directions: Now answer the questions.

6. What is the main purpose of the lecture?

   Ⓐ To compare the study of world history to the study of United States history

   Ⓑ To explain to the students their next assignment

   Ⓒ To explain different approaches to the study of world history

   Ⓓ To explain the origins of history as an academic discipline

7. Why does the professor mention the Western-Heritage Model used in her high school?

   Ⓐ To explain why she prefers using the model

   Ⓑ To emphasize that the model was widely used in the past

   Ⓒ To correct an error in a student's description of the model

   Ⓓ To compare high school history courses to college history courses

8. According to the professor, what is an advantage of the Different-Cultures Model?

   Ⓐ It focuses on the history of the United States.

   Ⓑ It is based upon the most widely researched theories.

   Ⓒ It includes the history of a variety of cultural groups.

   Ⓓ It makes thematic connections across different cultural groups.

9. What aspect of Islamic civilization will the professor likely discuss in the course?

   Ⓐ A succession of Islamic rulers

   Ⓑ The ancient origins of Islamic architecture

   Ⓒ The isolation of European cultures from Islamic influence

   Ⓓ Islamic elements in African cultures

10. Match each of the topics below with the type of world history course in which it would most likely be discussed.

Write your answer choices in the spaces where they belong.

The Western-Heritage Model	The Different-Cultures Model	The Patterns-of-Change Model

Answer Choices

A The contributions of Native American art to United States culture
B The independent discovery of printing techniques in Asia and Europe
C Ancient Roman foundations of the United States legal system

11. Listen to Track 89.

Ⓐ She doubts that the course will fulfill the students' expectations.
Ⓑ She hopes that the students selected the course because of their interest.
Ⓒ She is pleased that the course will fulfill the requirements.
Ⓓ She is worried that the students might not be familiar with the course requirements.

Directions: Listen to Track 90.

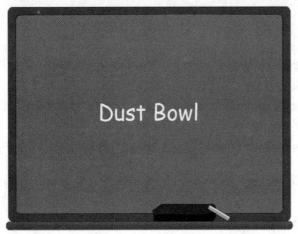

Directions: Now answer the questions.

12. What does the professor mainly discuss?

    Ⓐ A common weather pattern in the southern Great Plains region

    Ⓑ Factors that created an ecological and human disaster

    Ⓒ Farming techniques introduced during the Dust Bowl era

    Ⓓ The erosion of grasslands by excessive rainfall

13. What happened during the agricultural expansion in the southern Great Plains?

    Ⓐ People improved the soil by planting wheat.

    Ⓑ Raising cattle and other livestock became less common.

    Ⓒ Most of the landowners became farmers.

    Ⓓ Much of the grassland was destroyed.

14. What point does the professor make when he mentions that good topsoil takes thousands of years to form?

    Ⓐ It takes a long time to ruin good topsoil.

    Ⓑ It was wrong to believe that land could not be damaged.

    Ⓒ Farmers should not have moved on to other places.

    Ⓓ Plowing the land creates good topsoil faster than natural processes do.

15. Why does the professor mention that drought is often blamed as the cause of the Dust Bowl?

    Ⓐ To explain that many tenant farmers had to leave their land before the Dust Bowl era

    Ⓑ To emphasize that the Dust Bowl resulted mainly from soil erosion

    Ⓒ To show why the local population increased when rainfall returned to normal

    Ⓓ To prove that the drought was the worst on record at that time

16. According to the professor, what did the Soil Erosion Act do to improve soil conservation? *Choose 2 answers.*

    A It provided special equipment for farmers.
    B It encouraged farmers to use better farming techniques.
    C It turned damaged farmland into permanent grassland.
    D It increased the variety of crops grown on each farm.

17. Listen to Track 91.

    Ⓐ To ask the students for their opinions
    Ⓑ To express uncertainty about a historical situation
    Ⓒ To emphasize a point he has just made
    Ⓓ To correct an earlier statement

Directions: Listen to Track 92.

Directions: Now answer the questions.

18. Why does the man go to see the woman?

　　Ⓐ To ask her to talk to his professor about an exam
　　Ⓑ To get help completing an assignment
　　Ⓒ To get help understanding why he is having trouble in his classes
　　Ⓓ To ask her opinion about which class he should take

19. What does the man imply about his Spanish class?

　　Ⓐ He helps other students in the class.
　　Ⓑ He is doing well in the class.
　　Ⓒ He cannot complete all the assignments.
　　Ⓓ He needs to study more for the class.

20. What problem does the man have with his reading assignments?

    (A) He is not interested in what he reads.
    (B) He cannot memorize definitions of terms.
    (C) He is overwhelmed by the amount he has to read.
    (D) He has difficulty identifying what is important information.

21. Why does the woman tell the man about her own experience as a student?

    (A) To make him aware that other students have similar problems
    (B) To encourage him to spend more time studying at the library
    (C) To explain the importance of remembering details
    (D) To convince him to take a study-skills course

22. What recommendations does the woman make about what the man should do?
    Choose 2 answers.

    A Underline definitions in the text as he reads
    B Write a summary of what he reads
    C Read the text twice
    D Find additional texts on his own

Directions: Listen to Track 93.

Directions: Now answer the questions.

23. What is the lecture mainly about?
    - Ⓐ How astronomers found the correct interpretation for a certain observation
    - Ⓑ How astronomers distinguish between two kinds of nebulae
    - Ⓒ Various improvements to the telescope over the last 300 years
    - Ⓓ An old problem in astronomy that remains unsolved

24. According to the lecture, how did distant galaxies appear to eighteenth-century astronomers?
    - Ⓐ Like the moons of planets
    - Ⓑ Like small clouds
    - Ⓒ Like variable stars
    - Ⓓ Like bright points of light

25. What could astronomers better estimate once they knew what nebulae really were?
    - Ⓐ The diameter of variable stars
    - Ⓑ The density of cosmic dust
    - Ⓒ The size of the universe
    - Ⓓ The average number of planets in a galaxy

26. According to the professor, what did a 1920s telescope allow astronomers to do for the first time?
    - Ⓐ Study the moons of Jupiter
    - Ⓑ Observe gamma-ray bursters
    - Ⓒ Reject the dust theory of nebulae
    - Ⓓ Prove that galaxies are surprisingly small

27. What did eighteenth-century astronomers have in common with astronomers today?
    - Ⓐ They could not explain everything they detected with their instruments.
    - Ⓑ They knew the correct distances of objects they could not identify.
    - Ⓒ Their instruments were not powerful enough to detect spiral nebulae.
    - Ⓓ They argued over the natural brightness of variable stars.

28. Listen to Track 94.
    - Ⓐ She is certain about the correct answer.
    - Ⓑ She is now aware that her original idea had a weakness.
    - Ⓒ She is not convinced that the professor is right.
    - Ⓓ She thinks that the professor misunderstood what she said earlier.

Directions: Listen to Track 95.

Directions: Now answer the questions.

29. What is the lecture mainly about?

   (A) Various painting techniques
   (B) Ways to determine the purpose of a piece of art
   (C) How moral values are reflected in art
   (D) How to evaluate a piece of art

30. According to the professor, what did ancient Greek philosophers value in a work of art?

   (A) An accurate imitation of life
   (B) An unusual perspective on life
   (C) The expression of complex emotions
   (D) The use of symbolism

31. Why does the professor talk about personal taste?

   (A) To point out its importance in the evaluation of art
   (B) To help students understand the meaning of aesthetics
   (C) To show that personal taste and aesthetics are the same
   (D) To help explain art from different cultures

32. Why does the professor mention wheels and spheres?

   (A) To illustrate how movement can be expressed in a piece of art
   (B) To demonstrate that objects are more important than colors in a piece of art
   (C) To give an example of objects that have symbolic significance
   (D) To explain why some objects rarely appear in works of art

33. The professor mentions four formal steps used in examining a piece of art. Place the steps in order from first to last.

Write your answer choices in the spaces where they belong. You can either write the letter of your answer choice or you can copy the sentence.

1	
2	
3	
4	

Answer Choices

A̲ Give an opinion about the piece of art.
B̲ Identify possible symbols.
C̲ Describe the piece of art.
D̲ Determine the artist's meaning.

34. Listen to Track 96.

Ⓐ He will assign 12 pieces of art to evaluate.
Ⓑ He is organizing a class trip to the art museum.
Ⓒ It takes a lot of time to evaluate a piece of art.
Ⓓ Students will now be able to evaluate art quickly.

SPEAKING

This section measures your ability to speak in English about a variety of topics.

There are six questions in this section. For each question, you will be given a short time to prepare your response. When the preparation time is up, answer the question as completely as possible in the time indicated for that question. You should record your responses so that you can review them later and compare them with the answer key and scoring rubrics.

1. You will now be asked to speak about a familiar topic. Give yourself 15 seconds to prepare your response. Then record yourself speaking for 45 seconds.

   Listen to Track 97.

   > Talk about a city or town you have visited in the past. Explain what you liked most about the city and why. Include specific reasons and examples in your response.
   >
   > **Preparation Time: 15 seconds**
   > **Response Time: 45 seconds**

2. You will now be asked to give your opinion about a familiar topic. Give yourself 15 seconds to prepare your response. Then record yourself speaking for 45 seconds.

   Listen to Track 98.

   > Some people enjoy watching movies or television in their spare time. Others prefer reading books or magazines. State which you prefer and explain why.
   >
   > **Preparation Time: 15 seconds**
   > **Response Time: 45 seconds**

3. You will now read a short passage and listen to a conversation on the same topic. You will then be asked a question about them. After you hear the question, give yourself 30 seconds to prepare your response. Then record yourself speaking for 60 seconds.

   Listen to Track 99.

Plans for Campus Gym

The recreational services department will receive special funding from this year's budget to increase the number of exercise machines in the campus gym. The increase is in response to numerous student complaints regarding the insufficient number of machines available. Recreational services department agrees that, due to an increase in university enrollment, more students are using the gym. They, therefore, welcomed the proposal, adding that it would encourage even more students to exercise and would help to promote a healthier lifestyle among students.

Listen to Track 100.

The woman expresses her opinion about the plan described in the announcement. Briefly summarize the plan. Then state her opinion about the plan and explain the reasons she gives for holding that opinion.

Preparation Time: 30 seconds
Response Time: 60 seconds

4. You will now read a short passage and listen to a lecture on the same topic. You will then be asked a question about them. After you hear the question, give yourself 30 seconds to prepare your response. Then record yourself speaking for 60 seconds.

Listen to Track 101.

Reading Time: 50 seconds

Keystone Species

Within a habitat, each species depends on other species, and contributes to the overall stability of that ecosystem. However, some species do more than others by providing essential services. Without the influence of these key species, the habitat changes significantly. Scientists refer to these important players in an ecosystem as *keystone species*. When a keystone species disappears from its habitat, the habitat changes dramatically. Their disappearance can then trigger the loss of other species. As some species vanish, others move in or become more abundant. The new mix of species changes the habitat's appearance and character.

Listen to Track 102.

The professor gives examples of the effects of elephants on the African grasslands habitat. Using the examples from the talk, explain why elephants are considered a keystone species.

Preparation Time: 30 seconds
Response Time: 60 seconds

5. You will now listen to part of a conversation. You will then be asked a question about it. After you hear the question, give yourself 20 seconds to prepare your response. Then record yourself speaking for 60 seconds.

Listen to Track 103.

Briefly summarize the problem the speakers are discussing. Then state which of the two solutions from the conversation you would recommend. Explain the reasons for your recommendation.

> **Preparation Time: 20 seconds**
> **Response Time: 60 seconds**

6. You will now listen to part of a lecture. You will then be asked a question about it. After you hear the question, give yourself 20 seconds to prepare your response. Then record yourself speaking for 60 seconds.

Listen to Track 104.

Using the examples mentioned by the professor, describe two ways that writers create emphasis when writing dialogue.

| Preparation Time: 20 seconds |
| Response Time: 60 seconds |

WRITING

This section measures your ability to write in English to communicate in an academic environment.

There are two writing questions in this section.

For question 1, you will read a passage and listen to a lecture about the same topic. You may take notes while you read and listen. Then you will write a response to a question based on what you have read and heard. You may look back at the passage when answering the question. You may use your notes to help you answer the question. You have 20 minutes to plan and write your response.

For question 2, you will write an essay based on your own knowledge and experience. You have 30 minutes to plan and complete your essay.

1.   **Directions:** Give yourself 3 minutes to read the passage.

Reading Time: 3 minutes

Soon technology will provide smart cars: cars that virtually drive themselves. A computer in the car determines the speed and route to the desired destination. The computer is in continuous contact with a global positioning system and other technologies that will provide extremely accurate information about the location of the car, other cars on the road, congestion, accidents, and so forth. The human driver will be little more than a passenger. Smart cars promise to make driving safer, quicker, and less expensive.

First of all, smart cars will prevent many accidents, thereby saving lives. The cars will be equipped with a variety of sensors that very accurately detect cars and other obstacles in their path, and they will have automatic programs that control braking and turning to avoid collisions. Given the hundreds of accidents that occur on highways daily, it is clear that humans do a poor job of avoiding accidents and that computer control would be a great improvement.

Second, with the wide use of smart cars, traffic problems will practically disappear. These computer-controlled cars can follow each other closely, even at high speeds. This ability will result in increased highway speeds. Today commuting by car can take hours a day. So the increased speed of smart cars will be a great benefit, welcomed by the many people who commute by car.

Finally, smart cars will bring a reduction in the costs of driving. Because smart cars are programmed to drive the most direct routes, car owners will have to spend less money on repairs and replacement parts. Expensive items such as brakes, tires, and transmissions will last much longer in smart cars than in other cars.

Listen to Track 105.

Directions: You have 20 minutes to plan and write your response. Your response will be judged on the basis of the quality of your writing and on how well your response presents the points in the lecture and their relationship to the reading passage. Typically, an effective response will be 150 to 225 words.

Listen to Track 106.

Response Time: 20 minutes

Summarize the points made in the lecture, being sure to explain how they challenge specific points made in the reading passage.

_____

_____

_____

_____

_____

_____

_____

_____

_____

_____

_____

_____

_____

_____

_____

_____

_____

_____

2. **Directions:** Read the question below. You have 30 minutes to plan, write, and revise your essay. Typically, an effective response will contain a minimum of 300 words.

Response Time: 30 minutes

Do you agree or disagree with the following statement?

   A person should never make an important decision alone.

Use specific reasons and examples to support your answer.

_____

_____

_____

_____

_____

_____

_____

_____

_____

_____

_____

_____

_____

_____

_____

_____

_____

_____

_____

ANSWERS

Reading Section

1. B	21. B
2. A	22. C
3. C	23. B
4. D	24. A
5. D	25. B
6. B	26. C, G, E, F, B, D, H
7. D	27. C
8. B	28. A
9. D	29. B
10. A	30. C
11. C	31. C
12. B	32. C
13. B	33. B
14. A, C, D	34. C
15. B	35. B
16. D	36. D
17. C	37. A
18. A	38. B
19. C	39. D
20. D	40. B, D, E

Listening Section

1. C	9. D
2. D	10. C, A, B
3. A	11. B
4. A, E	12. B
5. C	13. D
6. C	14. B
7. B	15. B
8. C	16. B, C

17. C

18. C

19. B

20. D

21. A

22. B, C

23. A

24. B

25. C

26. C

27. A

28. B

29. D

30. A

31. B

32. C

33. C, B, D, A

34. C

Speaking Section

1. There are many ways you could answer this particular question. You will need to talk about what you liked most about a city or town you have visited and explain why.

    You may begin by providing a specific example of what you liked most about the city that you choose. There are many possibilities to choose from, and there is no answer that is better than another. You could say you liked the people, a museum or other attraction, the weather, the town's shops, and so on. You should then provide more details about why you liked this most. For example, if you say that you visited New York City and you liked the stores and shopping the most, you could say that it has the biggest, oldest department stores that you have ever seen. The buildings are beautiful, and they are full of goods that you cannot find anywhere else. You might give an example of something that you bought there, such as a sweater, and explain how you would not have been able to find this sweater in another city. The important thing is to develop your ideas. You should not merely give a long list of reasons without providing details that help the listener understand why you liked that part of the city. You should also not simply give a general description of a city, but respond to the specific focus that the question asks for: the thing you liked most about the city and why.

    Your response should be intelligible, should demonstrate effective use of grammar and vocabulary, and should be well developed and coherent. Your response is scored using the Independent Speaking Rubric (see Appendix A).

2. To respond to this particular question, you should clearly state what your opinion is: Do you prefer to watch movies or television in your spare time or do you prefer to read books or magazines? Then you should give reasons to support your opinion. If you prefer to watch movies or television, you might give the reason that you enjoy the visual nature of films, and that you particularly enjoy seeing other places shown in films. You might then describe a particular film that you have enjoyed, such as a travel film, and say that these films inspire you to do your own traveling.

    If you say that you prefer reading books or magazines, you might say that you prefer to imagine something that you read yourself, rather than seeing a movie of it. You could say that you are often disappointed when you see a movie that was based on a book because you had imagined the scenes and characters differently and this is why you prefer to read. You may develop this further by describing a particular film and book.

Keep in mind that there is no "correct" answer to this question. Whatever your preference is, your answer should be supported with examples. It is important to make sure that you state your opinion and develop your response with good examples and relevant details.

Your response should be intelligible, should demonstrate effective use of grammar and vocabulary, and should be well developed and coherent. Your response is scored using the Independent Speaking Rubric (see Appendix A).

3. First, as the question states, you should provide a brief summary of the university's plan, which is to increase the number of exercise machines in the gym. You can also provide a brief summary of the reasons that they're doing this: 1) fewer machines are available because of increased student enrollment, and 2) it will encourage more students to exercise. You should not spend too much time on this summary; if you attempt to provide many details from the reading, you may not have enough time to discuss both of the woman's reasons for disagreeing with the proposal. For this item type, a brief summary is all that is necessary. You should make sure that your summary is clear enough for the listener to understand the proposal without having access to additional information.

After the summary, you should state the woman's opinion of the university's plan to add exercise machines. In this case, the woman disagrees with the university's plan.

You should then convey the two main reasons she gives for holding that opinion. You will need to connect information from the conversation to the reading in order for the response to be complete. The woman disagrees with the first point about fewer machines being available. She says even though she does see more people in the gym, she does not have to wait to use the equipment.

Your response should also convey the woman's second reason for not agreeing with the university's plan. She thinks that adding new machines would not encourage more people to exercise. She says that the university already provides enough opportunities for students to exercise and have a healthy lifestyle. For example, there's a swimming pool, running paths, and sport teams.

Your response should be intelligible, should demonstrate effective use of grammar and vocabulary, and should be well developed and coherent. Your response is scored using the Integrated Speaking Rubric (see Appendix A).

4. To respond to this particular question you should first explain the concept of keystone species as it was presented in the reading. You can talk about this as it relates to the elephant. Keystone species are important because the habitat they live in would change dramatically without them. Elephants living in grassland habitats in Africa are an example of a keystone species.

You should then discuss the professor's examples. Note that you do not need to repeat all of the details from the reading and the lecture, but instead integrate points from both to answer the question completely.

As one example of how the grasslands habitat would change without elephants, the professor says that elephants eat or destroy tree and shrub seeds and small plants, preventing many trees from growing in the grasslands. If they did not remove these trees, many trees would block sunshine, so grasses would die. The trees would eventually replace grasses, and the forest would replace the grasslands.

The professor discusses another way that the lack of elephants would impact the habitat. He says that other animals in this habitat depend on grasses for food and survival. When grasses die, these animals leave the habitat and new species move into the habitat. Both of these examples show why the elephant is a keystone species.

This is an example of a possible response. There are other effective ways to organize your answer. The most important thing is to discuss the specific information that is asked for in the question. Listeners should understand that elephants are considered a keystone species because they have an important effect on their environment and it would change greatly without them. The details you choose to discuss from the reading and the lecture should lead to this understanding.

Your response should be intelligible, should demonstrate effective use of grammar and vocabulary, and should be well developed and coherent. Your response is scored using the Integrated Speaking Rubric (see Appendix A).

5. To respond to this particular question you should *briefly* describe the problem. It is enough to say that too many students have enrolled in a biology class. Some students who need to take the class this semester were unable to register for the class and are complaining. You do not need to give many details at this point.

Next, you need to choose *one* of the two solutions and explain why you think that solution is best. The two solutions in this conversation are: 1) open another biology section (or class) and hire a teaching assistant to teach it, or 2) ask some of the students that don't need the class this semester to drop the class. It does not matter which of the two proposed solutions you choose, since there is no "right" solution or "wrong" solution. You should choose the solution that you think is best

and support your choice with reasons why you think it is best. The reasons you give can include information provided by the speakers as well as your own experiences.

You may describe both solutions before choosing one of them, but you are not required to. You want to have enough time to summarize the problem, state which solution you prefer, and then provide an explanation for why you prefer that solution. Without any of these three parts, the response would be incomplete.

In discussing your preferences, if you believe the first solution is preferable, you might say that this is the best solution because it is fair to all the students. You might discuss why the second solution would not work. You could say that it is not fair to force first-year students out of the class because they might have the same problem with registering for it next year.

If you prefer the second solution, you might say that it would be too difficult to find another teaching assistant now, and if they did, the person might not be prepared to teach the class. It might be a waste of time for the students that are in that new class.

These are only examples of possible responses. This type of question can be answered in many different ways.

Your response should be intelligible, should demonstrate effective use of grammar and vocabulary, and should be well developed and coherent. Your response is scored using the Integrated Speaking Rubric (see Appendix A).

6. This particular question requires you to summarize the contents of a lecture you hear. In your response, you should talk about the two ways that writers create emphasis when writing dialogue. The professor says that exaggeration and understatement are two ways to create emphasis or impact.

After your general introduction, you should then talk about the first way that writers can create emphasis. The professor says that exaggeration can create impact or emphasis by describing something as bigger or more than it is. For example, a character in a story who is tired from a long walk might say, "I can't take another step" instead of saying "I'm tired." This exaggeration is more forceful and interesting.

You should then talk about the second way to create emphasis. The professor says that with understatement you can create emphasis by saying less than you mean.

For example, the professor complimented her friend on a great meal by saying that it was "not bad." Using understatement makes for a stronger statement.

You should make sure that you leave yourself enough time to talk about the second example. You will be expected to cover both examples.

Your response should be intelligible, should demonstrate effective use of grammar and vocabulary, and should be well developed and coherent. Your response is scored using the Integrated Speaking Rubric (see Appendix A).

Writing Section

1.   What is important to understand from the lecture is that the professor disagrees with the advantages of smart cars presented in the reading, namely that smart cars will reduce the number of accidents; that smart cars will reduce commuting time; and that smart cars will save their owners money.

In your response, you should convey the reasons presented by the professor for why smart cars will not produce the benefits predicted in the reading. A high-scoring response will include the following points made by the professor that cast doubt on the points made in the reading:

Point made in the reading	Counterpoint made in the lecture
Since smart cars will be equipped with sophisticated technology to detect obstacles and control braking and turning, many accidents that human drivers cause today will be prevented.	Technologies used in smart cars will fail occasionally, as all technologies do. Since smart cars will travel at greater speeds and closer together, such technology failures will result in accidents that will be more serious than accidents caused nowadays by human drivers.
Commuting time for many people will be reduced because smart cars will be able to travel at greater speeds and closer together.	Every improvement in driving convenience usually results in more people taking to the road. The introduction of smart cars will likely result in more cars on the road, which will cause additional traffic congestion. Commuting time is therefore not likely to decrease.
Smart cars will be able to choose the most direct routes. With less distance traveled, smart car owners will save money on repair and part replacement costs.	Sophisticated technologies used by smart cars will make the cars more expensive to buy and also more expensive to repair. These added costs will offset the savings identified in the reading.

Your response is scored using the Integrated Writing Rubric (see Appendix A). A response that receives a score of 5 clearly conveys all three of the main points in the table using accurate sentence structure and vocabulary.

2.   To earn a top score, you should develop a multi-paragraph essay that responds to the issue of whether you believe a person should never make an important decision alone. Typically an effective response will contain a minimum of 300 words.

There are a number of ways to approach this topic. One way would be to describe a number of important decisions that have already been made or will likely have to be made by you or by an unspecified person who represents a group (for example, college students). You could then go on to discuss reasons why these decisions are better made alone. Alternatively, you could discuss why input from others is helpful in decision-making; one reason for this could be that the experiences that others have had can help guide you. Or you could describe different kinds of decisions and explain why some of them should involve getting help from others, and why other kinds are best made by you alone.

Keep in mind that there is no "correct" answer to this question. Either or both sides of the issue can be supported with examples and reasons. It is important to make sure that you state your opinion and develop a response that explains your opinion. The development of your essay is judged by how effectively you support your opinion; a well-developed essay will contain clearly appropriate reasons, examples, and details that illustrate your opinion. Development is not evaluated simply in terms of how many words you write.

Your response should be well organized. A well-organized essay allows an evaluator to read from the beginning to the end of the essay without becoming confused. You should be sure not to just repeat the same information in different ways.

The quality and accuracy of the sentence structure and vocabulary you use to express your ideas is also very important.

Your response is scored using the Independent Writing Rubric (see Appendix A).

Appendix A

Speaking and Writing Scoring Rubrics

This section contains all the rubrics used by raters to score Speaking and Writing section responses. There are two different rubrics used to score the Speaking section, and two used to score the Writing section.

Speaking questions 1 and 2 are scored using the Independent Speaking Rubric, while questions 3–6 are scored using the Integrated Speaking Rubric. Writing question 1 is scored using the Integrated Writing Rubric, while question 2 is scored using the Independent Writing Rubric.

The chart below shows the main features of responses that must be considered when assigning a score.

Section	Question	Rubric	Main features considered when scoring
Speaking	1–2	Independent Speaking	**Delivery** • How clear is your speech? Good responses are fluid and clear, have good pronunciation, a natural pace, and natural-sounding intonation patterns. • Even at the highest level, there may be some minor problems; however, they do not cause difficulty for the listener. **Language use** • How effectively do you use grammar and vocabulary to convey ideas? In a good response, there is control of both basic and more complex language structures, and appropriate vocabulary is used. • Even at the highest level, some minor or systematic errors may be noticeable; however, they do not obscure meaning. **Topic development** • How fully do you answer the question, and how coherently do you present your ideas? In a good response, the relationship between ideas is clear and easy to follow, as is the progression from one idea to the next. Good responses generally use all or most of the time allotted.

Section	Question	Rubric	Main features considered when scoring
Speaking	3–6	Integrated Speaking	**Delivery** • How clear is your speech? Good responses are fluid and clear, have good pronunciation, a natural pace, and natural-sounding intonation patterns. • Even at the highest level, there may be some minor problems; however, they do not cause difficulty for the listener. **Language use** • How effectively do you use grammar and vocabulary to convey ideas? In a good response, there is control of both basic and more complex language structures, and appropriate vocabulary is used. • Even at the highest level, some minor or systematic errors may be noticeable; however, they do not obscure meaning. **Topic development** • How fully do you answer the question, and how coherently do you present your ideas? Are you able to synthesize and summarize the information that was presented? In a good response, the relationship between ideas is clear and easy to follow, as is the progression from one idea to the next. Good responses generally use all or most of the time allotted. • Even at the highest level, a response may have minor inaccuracies about details or minor omissions of relevant details.
Writing	1	Integrated Writing	**Quality of the writing** • A good response is well organized. Use of grammar and vocabulary is appropriate and precise. **Completeness and accuracy of the content** • In a good response, important information from the lecture has been successfully selected, and it is coherently and accurately presented in relation to relevant information from the reading. • Even at the highest level, a response may have occasional language errors; however, they do not result in inaccurate or imprecise presentation of content or connections.
Writing	2	Independent Writing	**Quality of the writing** • A good response effectively addresses the topic and task; it is well developed. It is also well organized. Use of grammar and vocabulary is appropriate and precise. • Even at the highest level, a response may have minor lexical or grammatical errors; however, they do not interfere with meaning.

TOEFL iBT® Speaking Scoring Rubric—Independent Tasks

Score	General Description	Delivery	Language Use	Topic Development
4	**The response fulfills the demands of the task, with at most minor lapses in completeness. It is highly intelligible and exhibits sustained, coherent discourse. A response at this level is characterized by all of the following:**	Generally well-paced flow (fluid expression). Speech is clear. It may include minor lapses, or minor difficulties with pronunciation or intonation patterns, which do not affect overall intelligibility.	The response demonstrates effective use of grammar and vocabulary. It exhibits a fairly high degree of automaticity with good control of basic and complex structures (as appropriate). Some minor (or systematic) errors are noticeable but do not obscure meaning.	Response is sustained and sufficient to the task. It is generally well developed and coherent; relationships between ideas are clear (or clear progression of ideas).
3	**The response addresses the task appropriately, but may fall short of being fully developed. It is generally intelligible and coherent, with some fluidity of expression though it exhibits some noticeable lapses in the expression of ideas. A response at this level is characterized by at least two of the following:**	Speech is generally clear, with some fluidity of expression, though minor difficulties with pronunciation, intonation, or pacing are noticeable and may require listener effort at times (though overall intelligibility is not significantly affected).	The response demonstrates fairly automatic and effective use of grammar and vocabulary, and fairly coherent expression of relevant ideas. Response may exhibit some imprecise or inaccurate use of vocabulary or grammatical structures or be somewhat limited in the range of structures used. This may affect overall fluency, but it does not seriously interfere with the communication of the message.	Response is mostly coherent and sustained and conveys relevant ideas/information. Overall development is somewhat limited, usually lacks elaboration or specificity. Relationships between ideas may at times not be immediately clear.

TOEFL iBT® Speaking Scoring Rubric—Independent Tasks, *continued*

Score	General Description	Delivery	Language Use	Topic Development
2	The response addresses the task, but development of the topic is limited. It contains intelligible speech, although problems with delivery and/or overall coherence occur; meaning may be obscured in places. A response at this level is characterized by at least two of the following:	Speech is basically intelligible, though listener effort is needed because of unclear articulation, awkward intonation, or choppy rhythm/pace; meaning may be obscured in places.	The response demonstrates limited range and control of grammar and vocabulary. These limitations often prevent full expression of ideas. For the most part, only basic sentence structures are used successfully and spoken with fluidity. Structures and vocabulary may express mainly simple (short) and/or general propositions, with simple or unclear connections made among them (serial listing, conjunction, juxtaposition).	The response is connected to the task, though the number of ideas presented or the development of ideas is limited. Mostly basic ideas are expressed with limited elaboration (details and support). At times relevant substance may be vaguely expressed or repetitious. Connections of ideas may be unclear.
1	The response is very limited in content and/or coherence or is only minimally connected to the task, or speech is largely unintelligible. A response at this level is characterized by at least two of the following:	Consistent pronunciation, stress, and intonation difficulties cause considerable listener effort; delivery is choppy, fragmented, or telegraphic; frequent pauses and hesitations.	Range and control of grammar and vocabulary severely limits (or prevents) expression of ideas and connections among ideas. Some low level responses may rely heavily on practiced or formulaic expressions.	Limited relevant content is expressed. The response generally lacks substance beyond expression of very basic ideas. Speaker may be unable to sustain speech to complete task and may rely heavily on repetition of the prompt.
0	Speaker makes no attempt to respond OR response is unrelated to the topic.			

TOEFL iBT® Speaking Scoring Rubric—Integrated Tasks

Score	General Description	Delivery	Language Use	Topic Development
4	The response fulfills the demands of the task with, at most, minor lapses in completeness. It is highly intelligible and exhibits sustained, coherent discourse. A response at this level is characterized by all of the following:	Speech is generally clear, fluid and sustained. It may include minor lapses or minor difficulties with pronunciation or intonation. Pace may vary at times as speaker attempts to recall information. Overall intelligibility remains high.	The response demonstrates good control of basic and complex grammatical structures that allow for coherent, efficient (automatic) expression of relevant ideas. Contains generally effective word choice. Though some minor (or systematic) errors or imprecise use may be noticeable, they do not require listener effort (or obscure meaning).	The response presents a clear progression of ideas and conveys the relevant information required by the task. It includes appropriate detail, though it may have minor errors or minor omissions.
3	The response addresses the task appropriately, but may fall short of being fully developed. It is generally intelligible and coherent, with some fluidity of expression, though it exhibits some noticeable lapses in the expression of ideas. A response at this level is characterized by at least two of the following:	Speech is generally clear, with some fluidity of expression, but it exhibits minor difficulties with pronunciation, intonation or pacing and may require some listener effort at times. Overall intelligibility remains good, however.	The response demonstrates fairly automatic and effective use of grammar and vocabulary, and fairly coherent expression of relevant ideas. Response may exhibit some imprecise or inaccurate use of vocabulary or grammatical structures or be somewhat limited in the range of structures used. Such limitations do not seriously interfere with the communication of the message.	The response is sustained and conveys relevant information required by the task. However, it exhibits some incompleteness, inaccuracy, lack of specificity with respect to content, or choppiness in the progression of ideas.

TOEFL iBT® Speaking Scoring Rubric—Integrated Tasks, *continued*

Score	General Description	Delivery	Language Use	Topic Development
2	The response is connected to the task, though it may be missing some relevant information or contain inaccuracies. It contains some intelligible speech, but at times problems with intelligibility and/or overall coherence may obscure meaning. A response at this level is characterized by at least two of the following:	Speech is clear at times, though it exhibits problems with pronunciation, intonation or pacing and so may require significant listener effort. Speech may not be sustained at a consistent level throughout. Problems with intelligibility may obscure meaning in places (but not throughout).	The response is limited in the range and control of vocabulary and grammar demonstrated (some complex structures may be used, but typically contain errors). This results in limited or vague expression of relevant ideas and imprecise or inaccurate connections. Automaticity of expression may only be evident at the phrasal level.	The response conveys some relevant information but is clearly incomplete or inaccurate. It is incomplete if it omits key ideas, makes vague reference to key ideas, or demonstrates limited development of important information. An inaccurate response demonstrates misunderstanding of key ideas from the stimulus. Typically, ideas expressed may not be well connected or cohesive so that familiarity with the stimulus is necessary in order to follow what is being discussed.
1	The response is very limited in content or coherence or is only minimally connected to the task. Speech may be largely unintelligible. A response at this level is characterized by at least two of the following:	Consistent pronunciation and intonation problems cause considerable listener effort and frequently obscure meaning. Delivery is choppy, fragmented, or telegraphic. Speech contains frequent pauses and hesitations.	Range and control of grammar and vocabulary severely limits (or prevents) expression of ideas and connections among ideas. Some very low-level responses may rely on isolated words or short utterances to communicate ideas.	The response fails to provide much relevant content. Ideas that are expressed are often inaccurate, limited to vague utterances, or repetitions (including repetition of prompt).
0	Speaker makes no attempt to respond OR response is unrelated to the topic.			

TOEFL iBT® Writing Scoring Rubric—Integrated Tasks

Score	Task Description
5	A response at this level successfully selects the important information from the lecture and coherently and accurately presents this information in relation to the relevant information presented in the reading. The response is well organized, and occasional language errors that are present do not result in inaccurate or imprecise presentation of content or connections.
4	A response at this level is generally good in selecting the important information from the lecture and in coherently and accurately presenting this information in relation to the relevant information in the reading, but it may have minor omission, inaccuracy, vagueness, or imprecision of some content from the lecture or in connection to points made in the reading. A response is also scored at this level if it has more frequent or noticeable minor language errors, as long as such usage and grammatical structures do not result in anything more than an occasional lapse of clarity or in the connection of ideas.
3	A response at this level contains some important information from the lecture and conveys some relevant connection to the reading, but it is marked by one or more of the following: • Although the overall response is definitely oriented to the task, it conveys only vague, global, unclear, or somewhat imprecise connection to the points made in the lecture to points made in the reading. • The response may omit one major key point made in the lecture. • Some key points made in the lecture or the reading, or connections between the two, may be incomplete, inaccurate, or imprecise. • Errors of usage and/or grammar may be more frequent or may result in noticeably vague expressions or obscured meanings in conveying ideas and connections.
2	A response at this level contains some relevant information from the lecture, but is marked by significant language difficulties or by significant omission or inaccuracy of important ideas from the lecture or in the connections between the lecture and the reading; a response at this level is marked by one or more of the following: • The response significantly misrepresents or completely omits the overall connection between the lecture and the reading. • The response significantly omits or significantly misrepresents important points made in the lecture. • The response contains language errors or expressions that largely obscure connections or meaning at key junctures, or that would likely obscure understanding of key ideas for a reader not already familiar with the reading and the lecture.
1	A response at this level is marked by one or more of the following. • The response provides little or no meaningful or relevant coherent content from the lecture. • The language level of the response is so low that is difficult to derive meaning.
0	A response at this level merely copies sentences from the reading, rejects the topic or is otherwise not connected to the topic, is written in a foreign language, consists of keystroke characters, or is blank.

TOEFL iBT® Writing Scoring Rubric—Independent Tasks

Score	Task Description
5	**An essay at this level largely accomplishes all of the following:** • Effectively addresses the topic and task • Is well organized and well developed, using clearly appropriate explanations, exemplifications, and/or details • Displays unity, progression, and coherence • Displays consistent facility in the use of language, demonstrating syntactic variety, appropriate word choice, and idiomaticity, though it may have minor lexical or grammatical errors.
4	**An essay at this level largely accomplishes all of the following:** • Addresses the topic and task well, though some points may not be fully elaborated • Is generally well organized and well developed, using appropriate and sufficient explanations, exemplifications, and/or details • Displays unity, progression, and coherence, though it may contain occasional redundancy, digression, or unclear connections • Displays facility in the use of language, demonstrating syntactic variety and range of vocabulary, though it will probably have occasional noticeable minor errors in structure, word form, or use of idiomatic language that do not interfere with meaning
3	**An essay at this level is marked by one or more of the following:** • Addresses the topic and task using somewhat developed explanations, exemplifications, and/or details • Displays unity, progression, and coherence, though connection of ideas may be occasionally obscured • May demonstrate inconsistent facility in sentence formation and word choice that may result in lack of clarity and occasionally obscure meaning • May display accurate but limited range of syntactic structures and vocabulary
2	**An essay at this level may reveal one or more of the following weaknesses:** • Limited development in response to the topic and task • Inadequate organization or connection of ideas • Inappropriate or insufficient exemplifications, explanations, or details to support or illustrate generalizations in response to the task • A noticeably inappropriate choice of words or word forms • An accumulation of errors in sentence structure and/or usage
1	**An essay at this level is seriously flawed by one or more of the following weaknesses:** • Serious disorganization or underdevelopment • Little or no detail, or irrelevant specifics, or questionable responsiveness to the task • Serious and frequent errors in sentence structure or usage
0	**An essay at this level** merely copies words from the topic, rejects the topic, or is otherwise not connected to the topic, is written in a foreign language, consists of key stroke characters, or is blank.

Appendix B

Audio Track Transcripts

TRACK 1 TRANSCRIPT

Narrator

Listen to a conversation between a student and a librarian.

Librarian

Can I help you?

Student

Yeah, I need to find a review. It's for my English class. We have to find reviews of the play we're reading. But they have to be from when the play was first performed— so I need to know when that was . . . and I suppose I should start with newspaper reviews . . .

Librarian

Contemporary reviews.

Student

Sorry?

Librarian

You want contemporary reviews. What's the name of the play?

Student

It's *Happy Strangers*. It was written in 1962 and we're supposed to write about its influence on American theater—show why it's been so important.

Librarian

Well, that certainly explains why your professor wants you to read some of those old reviews. The critics really tore the play to pieces when it opened. It was just so contro- versial—nobody'd ever seen anything like it on the stage.

Student

Really? It was that big a deal?

Librarian

Oh sure. Of course, the critics' reaction made some people kinda curious about it; they wanted to see what was causing all the fuss. In fact, we were on vacation in New York—I had to be, oh around sixteen or so—and my parents took me to see it. That would've been about 1965.

Student

So that was the year it premiered? Great! But . . . newspapers from back then aren't online, so how do I . . .

Librarian

Well, we have copies of old newspapers in the basement, and all the *major* papers publish reference guides to their articles, reviews, etc. You'll find *them* in the reference stacks in back. But I'd start with 1964. I think the play'd been running for a little while when I saw it.

Student

Oh, how'd you like it? I mean it's just two characters onstage hanging around and basically doing nothing.

Librarian

Well, I was impressed: the actors were famous and, besides, it was my first time in a *real* theater. But you're right—it was definitely different from any plays that we'd read in high school. Of course, in a small town, the assignments are pretty traditional.

Student

I've only read it, but it doesn't seem like it'd be much fun to watch. The story doesn't progress in a, in any sort of logical manner. It doesn't have any real ending either. It just stops. Honestly, y'know, I thought it was kinda slow and boring.

Librarian

Well, I guess you might think that, but when I saw it back then it was anything but boring! Some parts were really funny—but I remember crying, too. But I'm not sure just reading it . . . You know, they've done this play at least once on campus. I'm sure there's a tape of the play in our video library. You might want to borrow it.

Student

That's a good idea. I'll have a better idea of what I *really* think of it—before I read those reviews.

Librarian

I'm sure you'll be surprised that anyone ever found it radical—but you'll see why it's still powerful—dramatically speaking.

Student

Well, there must be *something* about it or the professor wouldn't have assigned it. I'm sure I'll figure it out.

TRACK 2 TRANSCRIPT

Narrator
Listen again to part of the conversation. Then answer the question.

Student
I suppose I should start with newspaper reviews . . .

Librarian
Contemporary reviews.

Student
Sorry?

Librarian
You want contemporary reviews. What's the name of the play?

Narrator
Why does the woman say this:

Librarian
Contemporary reviews.

TRACK 3 TRANSCRIPT

Biology

Narrator
Listen to part of a lecture in a biology class. The class is discussing animal behavior.

Professor

OK, the next kind of animal behavior I want to talk about might be familiar to you. You may have seen, for example, a bird that's in the middle of a mating ritual. And, and suddenly it stops and preens—you know, it takes a few moments to straighten its feathers—and then returns to the mating ritual. This kind of behavior—this doing something that seems completely out of place—is what we call a displacement activity.

Displacement activities are activities that animals engage in when they have conflicting drives—if, if we take our example from a minute ago—if the bird is afraid of its mate, it's conflicted, it wants to mate, but it's also afraid and wants to run away, so instead it starts grooming itself. So the displacement activity, the, the grooming, the straightening of its feathers seems to be an irrelevant behavior.

So what do you think another example of a displacement activity might be?

Male student

How about an animal that, um, instead of fighting its enemy or running away, it attacks a plant or a bush?

Professor

That's a really good suggestion, Carl, but *that's* called redirecting. The animal is *redirecting* its behavior to another object, in this case, the plant or the bush. But that's not an irrelevant or inappropriate behavior—the behavior makes sense—it's appropriate under the circumstances, but what doesn't make sense is the *object* the behavior's directed towards. OK, who else? Carol?

Female student

I think I read in another class about an experiment, um, where an object that the animal was afraid of was put next to its food—next to the animal's food—and the animal, it was conflicted between confronting the object, and eating the food, so instead it just fell asleep. Like that?

Professor

That's *exactly* what I mean. Displacement occurs because the animal's got two conflicting drives, two competing urges, in this case, fear and hunger—and what happens is they *inhibit* each other—they cancel each other out in a way, and a third, seemingly *irrelevant* behavior surfaces . . . through a process that we call disinhibition.

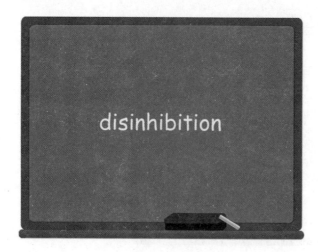

Now, in disinhibition, the basic idea is that two drives that seem to inhibit, to hold back a third drive, well, well, they get in the way of each other in a, in a conflict situation, and somehow lose control, lose their inhibiting effect on that third behavior . . . wh-which means that the third drive surfaces . . . it-it's expressed in the animal's behavior.

Now, these displacement activities can include feeding, drinking, grooming, even sleeping. These are what we call "comfort behaviors." So why do you think displacement activities are so often comfort behaviors, such as grooming?

Male student

Maybe because it's easy for them to do—I mean, grooming is like one of the most accessible things an animal can do—it's something they do all the time, and they have the–the *stimulus* right there, on the outside of their bodies in order to do the grooming—or if food is right in front of them. Basically, they don't have to think very much about those behaviors.

Female student

Professor, isn't it possible that animals groom because they've gotten messed up a little from fighting or mating? I mean, if a bird's feathers get ruffled, or an animal's fur—maybe it's not so strange for them to stop and tidy themselves up at that point.

Professor

That's another possible reason, although it doesn't necessarily explain other behaviors such as eating, drinking, or sleeping. What's interesting is that studies have been done that suggest that the animal's *environment* may play a part in determining what kind of behavior it displays. For example, there's a bird—the wood thrush, anyway when the wood thrush is in an attack-escape conflict—that is, it's caught between the two urges to escape from or to attack an enemy—if it's sitting on a horizontal branch, it'll wipe its beak on its perch. If it's sitting on a vertical branch, it'll groom its breast feathers. The immediate environment of the bird—its immediate, um, its relationship to its immediate environment seems to play a part in which behavior it will display.

TRACK 4 TRANSCRIPT

Narrator

Listen again to part of the lecture. Then answer the question.

Professor

So what do you think another example of a displacement activity might be?

Male student

How about an animal that, uh, instead of fighting its enemy or running away, it attacks a plant or a bush?

Professor

That's a really good suggestion, Carl, but that's called redirecting.

Narrator

What does the professor mean when she says this:

Professor

That's a really good suggestion, Carl, but that's called redirecting.

TRACK 5 TRANSCRIPT

Literature

Narrator

Listen to part of a lecture in a literature class.

Professor

All right, so let me close today's class with some thoughts to keep in mind while you're doing tonight's assignment. You'll be reading one of Ralph Waldo Emerson's best-known essays, "Self-Reliance," and comparing it with his poems and other works. I think this essay has the potential to be quite meaningful for all of you—as young people who probably wonder about things like truth, and where your lives are going . . . all sorts of profound questions.

Knowing something about Emerson's philosophies will help you when you read "Self-Reliance." And basically, one of the main beliefs that he had, was about *truth*. Not that it's something that we can be taught . . . Emerson says it's found within ourselves.

So this truth . . . the idea that it's in each one of us . . . is one of the first points that you'll see Emerson making in this essay. It's a bit abstract, but he's very into, ah, into each person believing his or her own thought. Believing in yourself, the thought or conviction that's true for you.

But actually, he ties that in with a sort of universal truth, something that everyone knows but doesn't realize they know. Most of us aren't in touch with ourselves, in a way, so we just aren't *capable* of recognizing profound truths. It takes geniuses . . . people like, say, Shakespeare, who are unique because when they have a glimpse of this truth—this universal truth—they pay attention to it and express it, and don't just dismiss it like most people do.

So, Emerson is really into each individual believing in, and trusting, him- or herself. You'll see that he writes about . . . well, first, conformity. He *criticizes* the people of his time, for abandoning their own minds and their own wills for the sake of conformity and consistency. They try to fit in with the rest of the world, even though it's at odds with their beliefs and their identities. Therefore, it's best to be a *nonconformist*—to do your own thing, not worrying about what other people think. That's an important point—he really drives this argument home throughout the essay.

When you're reading I want you to think about that, and why that kind of thought would be relevant to the readers of his time. Remember, this is 1838. Self-reliance was a novel idea at the time, and United States citizens were less secure about themselves as individuals and as Americans. The country as a whole was trying to define itself. Emerson wanted to give people something to really think about. Help them find their own way and, ah, what it meant to *be* who they were.

So, that's something that I think is definitely as relevant today as it was then . . . probably, uh . . . especially among young adults like yourselves. You know, uh, college being a time to sort of really think about who you are and where you're going.

Now, we already said that Emerson really emphasized nonconformity, right? As a way to sort of not lose your own self and identity in the world? To have your own truth and not be afraid to listen to it? Well, he takes it a step *further*. Not conforming also means, ah, not conforming with *yourself*, or your past. What does *that* mean? Well, if you've always been a certain way, or done a certain thing, but it's not working for you anymore, or you're not content—Emerson says that it'd be foolish to be consistent even with our own past. Focus on the future, he says: that's what matters more. Inconsistency is good! He talks about a ship's voyage—and this is one of the most famous bits of the essay—how the best voyage is made up of zigzag lines. Up close, it seems a little all over the place, but from farther away the true path shows, and in the end it justifies all the turns along the way.

So, don't worry if you're not sure where you're headed or what your long-term goals are—stay true to yourself and it'll make sense in the end. I mean, *I* can attest to that. Before I was a literature professor, I was an accountant. Before that, I was a newspaper reporter. My life has taken some pretty interesting turns, and here I am, very happy with my experiences and where they've brought me. If you rely on yourself and trust your own talents, your own interests, don't worry. Your path will make sense in the end.

TRACK 6 TRANSCRIPT

Narrator
Listen again to part of the lecture. Then answer the question.

Professor
Remember, this is 1838. Self-reliance was a novel idea at the time, and United States citizens were less secure about themselves as individuals and as Americans.

Narrator
Why does the professor say this:

Professor
Remember, this is 1838.

TRACK 7 TRANSCRIPT

Narrator

Listen to a conversation between a student and a professor.

Professor

Hey Jane. You look like you're in a hurry . . .

Student

Yeah, things're a little crazy.

Professor

Oh, yeah? What's going on?

Student

Oh, it's nothing . . . Well, since it's your class . . . I guess it's OK . . . it's, it's just that I'm having trouble with my group project.

Professor

Ah, yes. Due next week. What's your group doing again?

Student

It's about United States Supreme Court decisions. We're looking at the impact of recent cases on property rights, municipal land use cases, zoning disputes . . .

Professor

Right, OK . . . And it's not going well?

Student

Not really. I'm worried about the other two people in my group. They're just sitting back, not really doing their fair share of the work, and waiting for an A. It's kinda stressing me out, because we're getting close to the deadline and I feel like I'm doing everything for this project . . .

Professor

Ah, the good ole "free-rider" problem.

Student

Free rider?

Professor

Oh, it's just a term that describes this situation: when people in a group seek to get the benefits of being in the group without contributing to the work . . . Anyway, what exactly do you mean when you say they just sit back? I mean, they've been filing their weekly progress reports with me . . .

Student

Yes, but I feel like I'm doing 90 percent of the work. I hate to sound so negative here, but honestly, they're taking credit for things they shouldn't be taking credit for. Like last week in the library, we decided to split up the research into three parts, and then each of us was supposed to find sources in the library for our parts. I went off to the stacks and found some really good material for my part, but when I got back to our table they were just goofing off and talking. So I went and got material for their sections as well.

Professor

Hmm, you know you shouldn't do that.

Student

I know, but I didn't want to risk the project going down the drain.

Professor

I know Theresa and Kevin, I've had both of them in other courses . . . so I'm familiar with their work, and their work habits.

Student

I know, me too, and that's why this has really surprised me.

Professor

Do you . . . does your group like your topic?

Student

Well, I think we'd all rather focus on cases that deal with personal liberties—questions about freedom of speech, things like that—but I chose property rights . . .

Professor

You chose the topic?

Student

Yeah, I thought it would be good for us, all of us, to try something new.

Professor

Maybe that's part of the problem—maybe Theresa and Kevin aren't that excited about the topic—and since you picked it . . . Have you talked. . . to them at all about picking a different topic?

Student

But, we've already got all the sources. And it's due next week. We don't have time to start from scratch.

Professor

OK, well, I'll let you go 'cause I know you're so busy. But you might . . . consider talking to your group about your topic choice . . .

Student

I'll think about it. Gotta run. See you in class.

TRACK 8 TRANSCRIPT

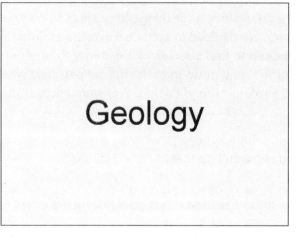

Narrator

Listen to part of a lecture in a geology class.

Professor

Now, we've got a few minutes before we leave for today. So I'll just touch on an interesting subject that I think makes an important point. We've been covering rocks, and different types of rocks, for the last several weeks, but next week we're going to do something a little bit different. And to get started I thought I'd mention something that shows how, uh, as a geologist, you need to know about *more* than just rocks and the structure of solid matter. Moving rocks. You may have heard about them.

It's quite a mystery. Death Valley is this desert plain . . . a dry lakebed in California, surrounded by mountains, and on the desert floor are these huge rocks . . . some of them hundreds of pounds . . . and they move! They leave long trails behind them—tracks you might say—as they move from one point to another. But nobody has been able to figure out *how* they're moving because no one has ever *seen* it happen. Now there are a lot of theories, but all we know for sure is that people aren't moving the rocks. There're no footprints, no tire tracks, and no heavy machinery—like a bulldozer, uh, nothing was ever brought in to move these heavy rocks.

So what's going on? Theory number one: *wind*. Some researchers think powerful, uh, windstorms might move the rocks. *Most* of the rocks move in the same direction as the dominant wind pattern, from southwest to northeast. But some, and this is interesting, move straight west, while some zigzag . . . or even move in large circles. Hmmm . . . how can that be? How 'bout *wind combined with rain*? The ground of this desert is made of clay. It's a desert, so it's dry. But when there is the occasional rain, the clay ground becomes extremely slippery. It's hard for anyone to stand on, walk on.

So, one theory was that perhaps when the ground is slippery, high winds can *then* move the rocks. But five or ten years ago a team of scientists tested that theory. They experimented by flooding an area of the desert with water, and then trying to establish how much wind force would be necessary to move the rocks. They calculated that it would take winds of at least 500 miles an hour to move the rocks. And since winds that strong don't occur anywhere on Earth, they concluded that the wind wasn't the cause, even with slippery ground. Now, more recent research suggests that it would take winds of only *150* miles an hour, not 500, but even winds *that* strong don't occur in Death Valley. So the original experiment's conclusion that wind is not the culprit seems right.

Here's another possibility: *ice*. It's possible that rain on the desert floor could turn to thin sheets of ice when temperatures drop at night. So, if rocks, uh, become embedded in ice, um, OK, could a piece of *ice* with rocks in it be pushed around by the wind? Makes sense, but there's a problem with *this* theory *too*. Rocks *trapped in ice together* would have *moved together* when the ice moved. But that doesn't always happen. The rocks seem to take separate routes. Nevertheless, ice is probably involved, we just don't quite know how yet. And of course there are other theories. Maybe the ground vibrates, or maybe the ground *itself* is shifting, tilting. Maybe the rocks are moved by a magnetic force. Uh, but sadly, all these ideas have been eliminated as possibilities. There's just not enough evidence.

I bet you're saying to yourself, well, why don't scientists just set up video cameras to record what actually happens? Thing is, this is a protected wilderness area, so by law, that type of research isn't allowed. Besides, in powerful windstorms, sensitive camera equipment would be destroyed. So why can't researchers just live there for a while until they observe the rocks moving? Same reason.

So where are we now? Well, despite some recent progress, we still don't have definite answers. So all this leads back to my main point. You need to know about more than just rocks as geologists. The researchers studying moving rocks, well, they combined their knowledge of rocks with knowledge of wind, ice, and such, uh, not successfully, not yet, but y'know . . . they wouldn't even have been able to get started without, uh . . . *earth science* understanding. Knowledge about wind . . . storms . . . you know, *meteorology*. You need to understand *physics*. So for several weeks, like I said, we'll be addressing geology from a *wider* perspective. I guess that's all for today. See you next time.

TRACK 9 TRANSCRIPT

Narrator
Listen again to part of the lecture. Then answer the question.

Professor
Most of the rocks move in the same direction as the dominant wind pattern, from southwest to northeast. But some, and this is interesting, move straight west, while some zigzag . . . or even move in large circles. Hmmm . . . how can that be?

Narrator
What does the professor imply when he says this:

Professor
But some, and this is interesting, move straight west, while some zigzag . . . or even move in large circles. Hmmm . . . how can that be?

TRACK 10 TRANSCRIPT

United States
Government

Narrator
Listen to part of a discussion in a United States government class.

Professor
OK, last time we were talking about government support for the arts. Who can sum up some of the main points? Frank?

Male student
Well, I guess there wasn't *really* any, you know, *official* government support for the arts until the twentieth century. But the first attempt the United States government made to, you know, to support the arts was the Federal Art Project.

Professor
Right. So, what can you say about the project?

Male student
Um, it was started during the Depression, um, in the 1930s, to employ out-of-work artists.

Professor

So was it successful? Janet? What do you say?

Female student

Yeah, sure, it was successful—I mean, for one thing, the project established a lot of, like, community art centers and, uh, galleries in places like rural areas where people hadn't really had access to the arts.

Professor

Right.

Male student

Yeah, but didn't the government end up wasting a lot of money for art that wasn't even very good?

Professor

Uh, some people might say that, but wasn't the primary objective of the Federal Art Project to provide jobs?

Male student

That's true. I mean, it did provide jobs for thousands of unemployed artists.

Professor

Right, but then, when the United States became involved in the Second World War, unemployment was down, and it seemed that these programs weren't really necessary any longer.

So, moving on . . . we don't actually see any govern—er, well, any *real* government involvement in the arts *again* until the early 1960s, when President Kennedy and other politicians started to push for major funding to support and promote the arts. It was felt by a number of politicians that, well, that the government had a *responsibility* to . . . uh, support the arts as sort of, oh what can we say, the soul, or *spirit* of the country. The idea was that there'd be a federal *subsidy*, uh, financial *assistance* to artists and artistic or cultural institutions. And for just those reasons, in 1965, the National Endowment for the Arts was created.

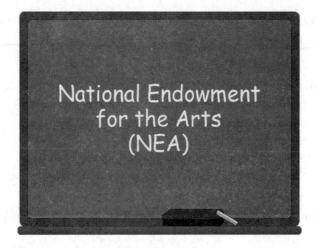

So, it was through the NEA, the National Endowment for the Arts, um, that the arts would develop, would be *promoted* throughout the nation. And then, individual states throughout the country started to establish their *own* state arts councils to help support the arts. There was kind of a cultural explosion—and by the mid-1970s, by 1974, I think, all 50 states had their own arts agencies, their own state arts councils that worked with the federal government, with corporations, artists, performers, you name it.

Male student

Did you just say corporations? How were they involved?

Professor

Well, you see, corporations aren't always altruistic, they might not support the arts unless . . . well, unless the government made it attractive for them to do so, by offering corporations tax incentives to support the arts—that is by letting corporations pay less in taxes if they were patrons of the arts. Uh, the Kennedy Center in Washington, D.C., you may, maybe you've been there, or Lincoln Center in New York. Both of these were built with substantial financial support from corporations. And the Kennedy and Lincoln Centers aren't the only examples—many of your cultural establishments in the United States will have a plaque somewhere acknowledging the support, the money, they've received from whatever corporation. Yes, Janet?

Female student

But aren't there a lot of people who don't think it's the government's role to support the arts?

Professor

Well, as a matter of fact, a lot of politicians who did not believe in government support for the arts, they wanted to do away with the agency entirely for that very reason—to get rid of governmental support—but they only succeeded in taking away about half the annual budget. And as far as the public goes . . . well, there are about as many individuals who disagree with government support as there are those who agree—in fact, with artists in particular, you have lots of artists who support—and who have benefited from—this agency, although it seems that just as many artists oppose a government agency being involved in the arts for many different reasons—reasons like they don't want the government to control what they create. In other words . . . the arguments both for and against government funding of the arts are as many and, and as varied as the individual styles of the artists who hold them.

TRACK 11 TRANSCRIPT

Narrator

Listen again to part of the discussion. Then answer the question.

Male student

Yeah, but didn't the government end up wasting a lot of money for art that wasn't even very good?

Professor

Uh, *some* people might say that, but wasn't the *primary* objective of the Federal Art Project to *provide jobs*?

Narrator

What does the professor imply when she says this:

Professor

Uh, *some* people might say that, but wasn't the *primary* objective of the Federal Art Project to *provide jobs*?

TRACK 12 TRANSCRIPT

Narrator

What do you miss most about your home when you are away? Use specific details in your explanation.

TRACK 13 TRANSCRIPT

Narrator

Many universities now offer academic courses over the Internet. However, some people still prefer learning in traditional classrooms. Which do you think is better? Explain why.

TRACK 14 TRANSCRIPT

Narrator

The computer department is considering making a scheduling change. You will have 45 seconds to read an article in the campus newspaper about the change. Begin reading now.

TRACK 15 TRANSCRIPT

Narrator

Now listen to two students discussing the article.

Male student

I just don't think this will work.

Female student

Why not?

Male student

Because it's not gonna solve the problem. Students are busy at night . . . I mean, we have jobs, families, clubs, social events. Most of us already have something to do every single night of the week.

Female student

I see your point. I sure couldn't fit anything into my schedule during the week—I've got swimming practice most nights.

Male student

Right. And as far as expense goes, I think they're going about it the wrong way. I mean, it costs money to hire more teachers and keep the academic building open later. Which is a lot more expensive than just simply buying more computers.

Female student

More computers?

Male student

That's right. Computer prices have come way down the past few years, so the department won't have to spend as much now as they did in the past. Besides, the computer department classrooms, you know, the rooms themselves, they're actually very big . . . there's plenty of space to add more computers.

Narrator

The man expresses his opinion about the proposal described in the article. Briefly summarize the proposal. Then state his opinion about the proposal and explain the reasons he gives for holding that opinion.

TRACK 16 TRANSCRIPT

Narrator

Now read a passage from a psychology textbook. You have 45 seconds to read the passage. Begin reading now.

TRACK 17 TRANSCRIPT

Narrator

Now listen to part of a lecture on this topic in a psychology course.

Professor

Last month my favorite uncle paid me a surprise visit. I hadn't seen him in many years . . . The doorbell rang, I opened the door, and there was Uncle Pete. Now, I'm sure when I saw him I said something like: "Uncle Pete! What a surprise! How nice to see you!" Anyway, my wife was standing next to me and according to her—I wasn't really aware of this—my eyes got really wide and I broke into a huge big smile. She said I was actually jumping up and down, like a little boy. Well, anyway, later that evening Uncle Pete told me how very, very good he felt when he saw how happy I was to see him.

But compare that with this: my daughter . . . she's six . . . We were building a birdhouse together last week. And I was showing her how to use a hammer and nail. And of course, stupid me, I wasn't being very careful and I smashed my thumb with the hammer. Boy, did it hurt! I almost felt like screaming, but I didn't want to upset my daughter, so I said, "Don't worry, honey. It's nothing." Meanwhile, I was shaking my hand, as if that would stop my thumb from hurting, and my face was contorted in pain. My voice was trembling too. So even though I told my daughter I was OK, I'm sure she didn't believe me. Because she kept asking me if I was OK.

Narrator

Explain how the examples from the professor's lecture illustrate the relationship between verbal and nonverbal communication.

TRACK 18 TRANSCRIPT

Narrator
Now listen to a conversation between two students on campus.

Male student
Hi . . . good morning. Could you help me with something?

Female student
Um. Maybe. What's up?

Male student
Well, I'm a first-year student.

Female student
Everything going OK?

Male student
Actually no. Um, this is a little embarrassing—I think I left my class schedule back at my dorm.

Female student
Hmm. Not a good thing to do on the first day of classes.

Male student
Yeah. So I'm not sure where my class is. I think I remember it was supposed to be here in Smith Hall.

Female student
There's a computer for student use in the student center. You could go over there, look it up and check the room number. But you'd have to hurry.

Male student
Hmmm . . . That's not a bad idea . . . I could check my schedule for the whole rest of the day at the same time . . . I don't know where any of my other classes are either. But I don't want to be late . . . make a bad impression with the professor on the first day. It's actually my very first class—introduction to psychology . . .

Female student

Psychology? Oh, OK. You're definitely in the right building. And if it's introduction to psychology, it's gonna be a big class, in which case it probably meets in a big lecture hall. There are only three lecture halls in the building—one on every floor. Just check each floor till you find yours. There's an elevator, so you should be able to move fast.

Male student

Yeah, but I don't know what the professor looks like or anything. How will I know whether it's my class or not? It'd be sort of embarrassing—sticking my head into each lecture hall asking if I was in the right place.

Female student

Well, you might luck out and find it the first time.

Narrator

Briefly summarize the problem the speakers are discussing. Then state which of the two solutions from the conversation you would recommend. Explain the reasons for your recommendation.

TRACK 19 TRANSCRIPT

Narrator

Listen to part of a talk in an art appreciation class.

Professor

In order for art to communicate—to appeal to the emotions or the intellect—it has to combine various *visual elements* to express meaning . . . or emotion. It's really the visual components of the work—things like color, texture, shape, lines—and how these elements work together that tell *us* something about the work. Artists combine and manipulate these visual elements to express a message or to create a mood.

Think about how a painter might use *color*, for example. You all know from experience that different colors appeal in different ways to the senses and can convey differ-ent meanings. An artist chooses certain colors to evoke a particular mood and make powerful statements. The color red, for example, is a strong color and can conjure up strong emotions . . . such as extreme joy, or excitement . . . or even anger. Blue, on the other hand, is considered a cool color. Blue colors tend to have a calming effect on viewers.

Another visual element important to art is texture. By texture, I mean the surface quality or "feel" of the work . . . its smoothness, or roughness, or softness. . . . Now, of course, in some types of art, the texture is physical—it can actually be touched by the fingers. But in painting, for example, texture can be visual. The way an artist paints certain areas of a painting can create the illusion of texture . . . an object's smoothness, or roughness, or softness. A rough texture can evoke stronger emotions and strength while a smooth texture is more calming and less emotional.

As I said earlier, artists often combine elements to convey a message about the work. Take a painting that, say, uses a lot of strong colors like reds and oranges and . . . and uses brushstrokes that are broad—wide, sweeping brushstrokes that suggest a rough texture. Well, these elements together can convey a wilder, more chaotic emotion in the viewer than, more than in, say . . . a painting with tiny, smooth brushstrokes and soft or pale colors. Artists use these visual effects and the senses they arouse to give meaning to their work.

Narrator

Using points and examples from the lecture, explain the importance of visual elements in painting.

TRACK 20 TRANSCRIPT

Narrator

Now listen to part of a lecture on the topic you just read about.

Professor

Many scientists have problems with the arguments you read in the passage. They don't think those arguments prove that dinosaurs were endotherms.

Take the polar dinosaur argument. When dinosaurs lived, even the polar regions where dinosaur fossils have been found were much warmer than today—warm enough during part of the year for animals that were not endotherms to live. And during the months when the polar regions were cold, the so-called polar dinosaurs could have migrated to warmer areas or hibernated like many modern reptiles do. So the presence of dinosaur fossils in polar regions doesn't prove the dinosaurs were endotherms.

Well, what about the fact that dinosaurs had their legs placed under their bodies, not out to the side, like a crocodile's? That doesn't necessarily mean dinosaurs were high-energy endotherms built for running. There's another explanation for having legs under the body: this body structure supports more weight. So with the legs under their bodies, dinosaurs could grow to a very large size. Being large had advantages for dinosaurs, so we don't need the idea of endothermy and running to explain why dinosaurs evolved to have their legs under their bodies.

OK, so how about bone structure? Many dinosaur bones do have Haversian canals, that's true, but dinosaur bones also have growth rings. Growth rings are a thickening of the bone that indicates periods of time when the dinosaurs weren't rapidly growing. These growth rings are evidence that dinosaurs stopped growing or grew more slowly during cooler periods. This pattern of periodic growth—ya know, rapid growth followed by no growth or slow growth and then rapid growth again—is characteristic of animals that are not endotherms. Animals that maintain a constant body temperature year round, as true endotherms do, grow rapidly even when the environment becomes cool.

TRACK 21 TRANSCRIPT

Narrator
Summarize the points made in the lecture, being sure to explain how they challenge the specific points made in the reading passage.

TRACK 22 TRANSCRIPT

Narrator

Listen to a conversation between a student and a counselor at the university counseling center.

Student

Hi, thanks for seeing me on such short notice.

Counselor

No problem. How can I help?

Student

Well, I think I might've made a mistake coming to this school.

Counselor

What makes you say that?

Student

I'm a little overwhelmed by the size of this place. I come from a small town. There were only 75 of us in my high school graduating class. Everyone knew everyone; we all grew up together.

Counselor

So it's a bit of a culture shock for you, being one of 15,000 students on a big campus in an unfamiliar city.

Student

That's an understatement. I just can't get comfortable in class, or in the dorms, you know, socially.

Counselor

Hmm, well—let's start with your academics. Tell me about your classes.

Student

I'm taking mostly introductory courses, and some are taught in these huge lecture halls.

Counselor

And you're having trouble keeping pace with the material?

Student

No, in fact, I got an A on my first economics paper. It's just that, it's so impersonal. I'm not used to it.

Counselor

Are all your classes impersonal?

Student

Nah . . . It's just that, for example, in sociology yesterday, the professor asked a question. So I raised my hand . . . several of us raised our hands . . . and I kept my hand up because I did the reading and knew the answer. But the professor just answered his own question and continued with the lecture.

Counselor

Well, in a big room, it's possible he didn't notice you. Maybe he was trying to save time. In either case, I wouldn't take it personally.

Student

I suppose. But I just don't know how to, you know, *distinguish* myself.

Counselor

Why not stop by his office during office hours?

Student

That wouldn't seem right, y'know . . . taking time from other students who need help.

Counselor

Don't say that. That's what office hours are for. There's no reason you couldn't pop in to say hi, to, uh, to make yourself known. If you're learning a lot in class, let the professor know. Wouldn't *you* appreciate positive feedback if *you* were a professor?

Student

You're right. That's a good idea.

Counselor

OK, uh, let's turn to your social life. How's it going in the dorms?

Student

I don't have much in common with my roommate or anyone else I've met so far. Everyone's into sports, and I'm more artsy, you know, into music. I play the cello.

Counselor

Ahhh. Have you been playing long?

Student

Since age 10. It's a big part of my life. At home, I was the youngest member of our community orchestra.

Counselor

You're not going to *believe* this! There's a string quartet on campus—all students. And it so happens the cellist graduated last year. They've been searching high and low for a replacement, someone with experience. Would you be interested in auditioning?

Student

Absolutely! I wanted to get my academic work settled before pursuing my music here, but I think this would be a good thing for me. I guess if I really want to fit in here, I should find people who love music as much as I do. Thank you!

Counselor

My pleasure.

TRACK 23 TRANSCRIPT

Sociology

Narrator

Listen to part of a lecture in a sociology class.

Professor

Have you ever heard the one about alligators living in New York sewers? The story goes like this: a family went on vacation in Florida, and bought a couple of baby alligators as presents for their children, then returned from vacation to New York, bringing the alligators home with them as pets. But the alligators would escape and find their way into the New York sewer system where they started reproducing, grew to huge sizes and now strike fear into sewer workers. Have you heard this story? Well, it isn't true and it never happened, but despite that, the story's been around since the 1930s.

Or how about the song "Twinkle, twinkle, little star"? You know "Twinkle, twinkle, little star, how I wonder what you are . . ." Well, we've all heard this song. Where am I going with this? Well, both the song and the story are examples of memes, and that's what we'll talk about, the theory of memes.

A meme is defined as a piece of information copied from person to person. By this definition, most of what you know . . . ideas, skills, stories, songs . . . are memes. All the words you know, all the scientific theories you've learned, the rules your parents taught you to observe . . . all are memes that have been passed on from person to person.

So what? . . . you may say. Passing on ideas from one person to another is nothing new . . . Well, the whole point of defining this familiar process as transmission of memes is so that we can explore its analogy with the transmission of *genes*.

As you know, all living organisms pass on biological information through the genes. What's a gene? A gene is a piece of biological information that gets copied, or replicated, and the copy, or replica, is passed on to the new generation. So genes are defined as replicators . . .

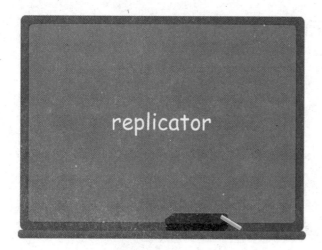

Genes are replicators that pass on information about properties and characteristics of organisms. By analogy, *memes* also get replicated and in the process pass on cultural information from person to person, generation to generation. So memes are also replicators. To be a successful replicator, there are three key characteristics: longevity, fecundity, and fidelity. Let's take a closer look . . .

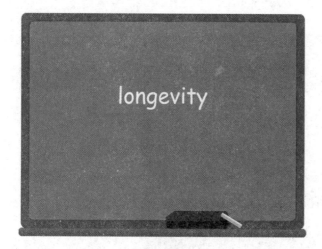

First, longevity. A replicator must exist long enough to be able to get copied and transfer its information. Clearly, the longer a replicator survives, the better its chances of getting its message copied and passed on. So longevity is a key characteristic of a replicator. If you take the alligator story, it can exist for a long time in individual memory—let's say my memory. I can tell you the story now, or ten years from now. The same with the "Twinkle, twinkle" song. So these memes have longevity, because they're memorable, for one reason or another.

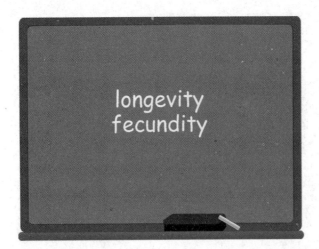

Next, fecundity. Fecundity is the ability to reproduce in large numbers. For example, the common housefly reproduces by laying several thousand eggs. So each fly gene gets copied thousands of times. Memes? Well, they can be reproduced in large numbers as well. How many times have you sung the "Twinkle, twinkle" song to someone? Each time you replicated the song—and maybe passed it along to someone who didn't know it yet, a small child maybe.

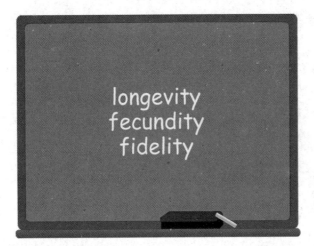

And finally, fidelity. Fidelity means accuracy of the copying process. We know fidelity is an essential principle of genetic transmission. If a copy of a gene is a bit different from the original, that's called a *genetic* mutation, and mutations are usually bad news. An organism often cannot survive with a mutated gene—and so a gene usually cannot be passed on unless it's an exact copy. For *memes*, however, fidelity is not always so important. For example, if you tell someone the alligator story I told you today, it probably won't be word for word exactly as I said it. Still, it will be basically the same story, and the person who hears the story will be able to pass it along. Other memes are replicated with higher fidelity, though—like the "Twinkle, twinkle" song? It had the exact same words twenty years ago as it does now. Well, that's because we see songs as something that has to be performed accurately each time. If you change a word, the others will usually bring you in line. They'll say, "That's not how you sing it," right?

So, you can see how looking at pieces of cultural information as replicators, as memes, and analyzing them in terms of longevity, fecundity, and fidelity, we can gain some insight about how they spread, persist, or change.

TRACK 24 TRANSCRIPT

Narrator
Why does the professor say this:

Professor
If you change a word, the others will usually bring you in line. They'll say, "That's not how you sing it," right?

TRACK 25 TRANSCRIPT

Note: The actual lecture contains color images. The colors from one image are discussed by the professor. You do not need to see the colors to understand the lecture or to answer the questions.

Narrator
Listen to part of a lecture in an astronomy class.

Professor

Last week, we covered some arguments *against* going back to the Moon. But there are compelling reasons *in favor of* another Moon landing, too, um, not the least of which is trying to pinpoint the Moon's age. We could do this, in theory, by studying an enormous impact crater known as the South Pole–Aitken Basin. Ah, it's located in the Moon's south polar region. But, since it's on the *far* side of the Moon, it can only be seen from space. Here's an image of... we'll call it the SPA Basin.

South Pole—Aitken Basin

This color-coded image of the SPA Basin—ahh, those aren't its actual colors, obviously—uh, this image is from the mid-nineties, from an American spacecraft called Clementine. Um, unlike earlier lunar missions, Clementine *didn't* orbit *only* around the Moon's *equator*. Its orbits enabled it to send back data to create *this* topographical map of... well, the gray-and-white area toward the bottom is the *South Pole*. The purples and blues in the middle correspond to low elevations—the SPA Basin itself. Uh, the oranges and reds around it are higher elevations. The Basin measures an amazing 2,500 kilometers in diameter, and its average depth is 12 kilometers. That makes it the biggest known crater in our *solar system*. And it may well be the *oldest*.

Y'know, planetary researchers *love* studying deep craters to learn about the impacts that created them, um, how they redistributed pieces of the planet's crust. And, in *this* case, we especially want to know if any of the mantle, the layer *beneath* the crust, was exposed by the impact. Not everyone agrees, but some experts are *convinced* that whatever created the SPA Basin *did* penetrate the Moon's mantle. And we need to find out, because much more than the crust, the *mantle* contains information about a planet's or moon's *total composition*. And that's *key* to understanding planet formation. Um, Diane?

Female student

So the only way to know the Basin's age is to study its rocks directly?

Professor

Well, from radio survey data, we know that the Basin contains lots of smaller craters. So it must be *really* old—about 4 billion years, give or take a few hundred million years. But that's not very precise. If we had *rock samples* to study, we'd know whether these small craters were formed by impacts during the final stages of *planetary formation*, or if they resulted from *later* meteor showers.

Female student

But if we know *around* how old the Basin is, I'm not sure that's reason enough to go to the Moon again.

Professor

Oh, but such crude estimates . . . mmm, we can do better than that! Besides, there's *other* things worth investigating. Like, is there water ice on the Moon? Clementine's data indicated that the wall of a south polar crater was more *reflective* than expected. So *some* experts think there's probably ice there. Also, data from a later mission indicate significant concentrations of *hydrogen*, and by inference, *water*, less than a meter underground at both poles.

Male student

If there's water, how'd it get there? Underground rivers?

Professor

We think meteors that crashed into the Moon, or tails of passing comets, may have introduced water molecules. Any water molecules that found their way to the floors of craters near the Moon's poles, that water would be perpetually frozen because the floors of those craters are always in shadow. Uh, furthermore, if the water ice was mixed in with rock and dust, it'd be protected from evaporation.

Female student

So, are you saying there might be primitive life on the Moon?

Professor

Uh, that's not my point at all! Um, OK, say there *is* water ice on the Moon. That would be of very *practical* value for a future Moon base for astronauts. Uh, water ice could be melted and purified for *drinking.* It could also be broken down into its component parts—oxygen and hydrogen. Oxygen could be used to breathe. And hydrogen could be turned into *fuel*, rocket fuel. So, water ice could enable the creation of a self-sustaining Moon base someday, a mining camp, perhaps, or, uh, a departure point for further space exploration.

Male student

But hauling tons of equipment to the Moon to make fuel and build a life-support system for a Moon base . . . wouldn't that be too expensive?

Professor

A *permanent* base, uh, may be a ways off, but we shouldn't have to wait for *that*. The dust at the bottom of the SPA Basin really *does* have a fascinating story to tell. What I wouldn't give for a few *samples* of it!

TRACK 26 TRANSCRIPT

Narrator

Listen again to part of the lecture. Then answer the question.

Female student

But if we know *around* how old the Basin is, I'm not sure that's reason enough to go to the Moon again.

Professor

Oh, but such crude estimates . . .

Narrator

What does the professor imply when he says this:

Professor

Oh, but such crude estimates . . .

TRACK 27 TRANSCRIPT

Narrator

Listen to a conversation between a student and a professor.

Student

Hi. I was wondering if I could talk with you about the assignment in the Film Theory class?

Professor

Of course, Jill.

Student

It seems that pretty much everyone else in the class gets what they're supposed to be doing, but *I'm* not so sure.

Professor

Well, the class *is* for students who are really serious about film. You must have taken film courses before?

Student

Yeah, in high school, Film Appreciation.

Professor

Hmm, I wouldn't think that'd be enough. Did you concentrate mainly on form, or content?

Student

Oh, definitely content. We'd watch, say, *Lord of the Flies*, and then discuss it.

Professor

Oh, *that* approach . . . treating film as literature, ignoring what makes it unique . . .

Student

I liked it, though . . .

Professor

Sure, but *that* kind of class . . . well, I'm not surprised you're feeling a little lost. Y'know, we have two introductory courses that are supposed to be taken before you get to *my* course—one in film art, techniques . . . technical stuff . . . and another in film history. So students in the class *you're* in should be pretty far along in film studies. In fact, usually the system blocks anyone trying to sign up for a class they shouldn't be taking, who hasn't taken the courses you're required to do *first*, as *prerequisites*.

Student

Well, I did have a problem with that, but I discussed it with one of your office staff and she gave me permission.

Professor

Of course. No matter how many times I tell them, they just keep on . . . Well, for your own good, I'd really suggest dropping back and starting at the usual place . . .

Student

Yes, but . . . I've already been in this class for four weeks! I'd hate to just drop it now, especially since I find it so different, so interesting.

Professor

I guess *so*—frankly, I can't believe you've lasted this long! These are pretty in-depth theories we've been discussing, and you've been doing OK so far, I guess. But, still, the program's been designed to progress through certain stages. Like any other professional training, we build on previous knowledge.

Student

Then maybe you could recommend some extra reading I can do, to catch up?

Professor

Well, are you intending to study film, as your main concentration?

Student

No. No, I—I'm just interested; I'm actually in marketing, but there seems to be a connection . . .

Professor

Oh, well, in *that* case . . . if you're taking the course just out of *interest* . . . I mean, I'd still highly recommend signing up for the introductory courses at *some* point. But in the *meantime*, there's no harm, I guess, in trying to keep up with *this* class. The interest is clearly there. Uh, instead of any extra reading just now, though, you *could* view some of the *old* introductory lectures—we have 'em on video—*that'd* give you a better handle on the subject. It's still a pretty tall order, and we'll be moving right along, so you'll really need to stay on top of it.

Student

OK, I've been warned. Now, could I tell you about my idea for the assignment . . .?

TRACK 28 TRANSCRIPT

Chemistry

Narrator

Listen to part of a lecture in a chemistry class.

Professor

OK, I know you all have a lot of questions about this lab assignment that's coming up, so I'm gonna take a little time this morning to discuss it.

So you know the assignment has to do with *spectroscopy,* right? And your readings should help you get a good idea of what that's all about. But let's talk about spectroscopy a little now, just to cover the basics.

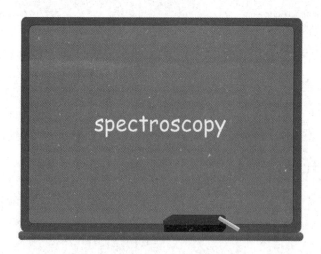

What is spectroscopy? Well, the simplest definition I can give you is that spectroscopy is the study of the interaction between *matter* and *light*. Now visible light consists of different *colors*, or *wavelengths*, which together make up what's called a *spectrum*—a band of colors, like you see in a rainbow. And *all* substances—all forms of matter—can be distinguished according to what wavelengths of light they *absorb* and which ones they *reflect*. It's like—well, every element has what we'd call its own *spectral signature*; if we can *read* that signature, we can identify the element. And that's exactly what spectroscopy does.

Now *laser* spectroscopy, which is the focus of your assignment, works by measuring, very precisely, what parts of the spectrum are *absorbed* by different substances. And it has applications in a lot of different disciplines. And your assignment will be to choose a discipline that interests you and devise an experiment. For example, I'm gonna talk about *art*—I'm *interested* in art. And to me, it's interesting how spectroscopy is used to *analyze* art.

Let's say a museum curator comes to you with a problem. She's come across this painting that appears to be an original—say a Rembrandt—and she wants to acquire it for her museum. But she's got a problem: She's not *absolutely* certain it's an original. So what do you do? How do you determine whether the painting's authentic?

OK, think about the scientific process. You've got a question: Is the painting a Rembrandt? So first, you'd need to make a list of characteristics the painting would have to have to *be* a Rembrandt. *Then* you have to discover whether the painting in question *has* those characteristics.

So first of all, you'll need to know the *techniques* Rembrandt used when he applied paint to canvas—his brushstrokes, how thickly he applied his paint—so you'd need to work with an art historian who has expert knowledge of Rembrandt's style. You'd have to know *when* he created his paintings, um, what *pigments* he used—in other words, what *ingredients* he used to make different colors of paint. 'Cause the ingredients used in paints and binding agents—plus varnishes, finishes, what have you—have changed over time. Since you're trying to verify if it's a Rembrandt, the ingredients in the pigment would need to have been used during Rembrandt's lifetime, in the seventeenth century. And that's where *chemistry* comes in. You've got to find out what's *in* those pigments—learn their composition. And that requires lab work—detective work, really—in a word, *spectroscopy*.

So how do we use spectroscopy? Well, we put an infrared microscope—a spectroscope—on tiny, tiny bits of paint, and using ultraviolet light, we can see the spectral signature of each component part of the pigment. *Then* we compare these signatures with those of particular elements, like zinc or lead, to determine what the pigment was made of.

So you can see why this type of analysis requires a knowledge of the history of pigments, right? How and when they were made. Say we determine a pigment was made with *zinc*, for example. We know the spectral signature of zinc, and it matches that of the paint sample. We *also* know that zinc wasn't discovered until the eighteenth century. And since Rembrandt lived during the *seventeenth* century, we know *he* couldn't've painted it.

Now, spectroscopy has a very distinct advantage over previous methods of analyzing artworks because it's not *invasive*—you don't have to remove *big* chips of paint to do your analysis, which is what other methods require. All you do is train the microscope on tiny *flecks* of paint and analyze them.

Now, a word or two about restoration. Sometimes, original artworks *appear* questionable or inauthentic because they've had so many restorers add touch-up layers to cover up *damage*—damage from the paint having deteriorated over time. Well, spectroscopy can reveal the composition of those touch-up layers too, so we can find out when they were applied. Then, if we want to undo some *bad* restoration attempts, we can determine what kind of process we can use to *remove* them—to dissolve the paint and uncover the original.

TRACK 29 TRANSCRIPT

Narrator
Why does the professor say this:

Professor
Now, a word or two about restoration.

TRACK 30 TRANSCRIPT

Literature

Narrator
Listen to part of a lecture in a literature class.

Professor
Now, we can't really talk about fairy tales without first talking about *folk* tales . . . because there's a strong connection between these two genres, these two types of stories. In fact, many fairy tales started out as folktales.

So, what's a *folk* tale? How would you characterize them? Jeff?

Male student
Well, they're old stories, traditional stories. They were passed down orally within cultures, from generation to generation, so they changed a lot over time; I mean, every storyteller, or maybe every town, might have had a slightly different version of the same folktale.

Professor
That's right, there's *local difference,* and that's why we say folktales are communal.

By "communal," we mean they reflect the traits and the concerns of a particular community at a particular time. So essentially the same tale could be told in different communities, with certain aspects of the tale adapted to fit the specific community. Um, *not* the plot . . . the details of what *happens* in the story would remain constant; that was the thread that held the tale together. But all the other elements, like the location or characters, might be modified for each audience.

OK, so what about *fairy* tales? They also are found in most cultures, but how are they different from folktales? I guess the first question is what is a fairy tale? And don't anyone say, "a story with a fairy in it." Because we all know that very few fairy tales actually have those tiny magical creatures in them. But what else can we say about them? Mary?

Female student

Well, they seem to be less realistic than folktales. Like they have something improbable happening—a frog turning into a prince, say. Oh, that's another common element, royalty . . . a prince or princess. And fairy tales all seem to take place in a location that's nowhere and everywhere at the same time.

Professor

What's the line, ah—how do all those stories start? "Once upon a time, in a faraway land . . ." In the case of *folk* tales, each storyteller would specify a particular location and time, though the time and location would differ for different storytellers. With *fairy* tales, however, the location is generally unspecified, no matter who the storyteller is . . . that "land faraway . . ." We'll come back to this point in a few minutes.

Male student

Um, I thought a fairy tale was just the written version of an oral folktale.

Professor

Well, not exactly, though that is how many fairy tales developed. For example, in the late eighteenth century, the Grimm brothers traveled throughout what's now Germany recording local *folk* tales. These were eventually published—as *fairy* tales—but not before undergoing a process of evolution.

Now, a number of things happen when an oral tale gets written down. First, the language changes, it becomes more formal, more standard—some might say less colorful. It's like the difference in your language depending on whether you're talking to someone or writing them a letter.

Second, when an orally transmitted story is written down, an authoritative version, with a recognized author is created. The communal aspect gets lost; the tale no longer belongs to the community; it belongs to the world, so to speak. Because of this, elements like place and time can no longer be tailored to suit a particular audience, so they become less identifiable, more generalizable to any audience.

On the other hand, descriptions of characters and settings can be developed more completely. In *folk* tales, characters might be identified by a name, but you wouldn't know anything more about them. But in *fairy* tales, people no longer have to remember plots—they're written down, right? So more energy can be put into other elements of the story, like character and setting. So you get more details about the characters, and about where the action takes place, what people's houses were like, whether they're small cabins or grand palaces . . . And it's worth investing that energy because the story, now in book form, isn't in danger of being lost, those details won't be forgotten. If a *folk* tale isn't repeated by each generation, it may be lost for all time. But with a fairy tale, it's always there in a book, waiting to be discovered again and again.

Another interesting difference involves the change in audience—who the stories are meant for. Contrary to what many people believe today, folktales were originally intended for adults, not for children. So why is it that fairy tales seem targeted toward children nowadays?

TRACK 31 TRANSCRIPT

Narrator
Listen again to part of the lecture. Then answer the question.

Female student
And fairy tales all seem to take place in a location that's nowhere and everywhere at the same time.

Professor
What's the line, ah—how do all those stories start? "Once upon a time, in a faraway land . . ."

Narrator
Why does the professor say this:

Professor
What's the line, ah—how do all those stories start? "Once upon a time, in a faraway land . . ."

TRACK 32 TRANSCRIPT

Narrator
Talk about a place you enjoyed going to or visiting when you were a child. Describe the place. Explain why you enjoyed it.

TRACK 33 TRANSCRIPT

Narrator
Do you agree or disagree with the following statement? Why or why not? Use details and examples to explain your answer.

It is more important to study math or science than it is to study art or literature.

TRACK 34 TRANSCRIPT

Narrator

The university has announced a new policy regarding dining services. Read an article about it in the student newspaper. You have 50 seconds to read the article. Begin reading now.

TRACK 35 TRANSCRIPT

Narrator

Now listen to two students discussing the article.

Female student

Did you see that article?

Male student

Yeah—and it sounds like a great idea. It's really good for the students in that program.

Female student

Don't they cook in class anyway?

Male student

Well, yeah, they do . . . but my cousin was in the program a few years ago, and she said that it's very different to cook for a lot of people in that kind of atmosphere than to cook for classmates.

Female student

Why is that?

Male student

Well, in class you can take your time. But, cooking for more people, there's more pressure—I mean, you're in a rush, people are waiting . . . and it might be easy to make a mistake with all that stress . . .

Female student

Then they'll think you're a bad chef, right?

Male student

Absolutely!

Female student

So, OK, it's good practice. But what about the extra cost?

Male student

Well, look at it this way. You've eaten at some of the fancier restaurants in town, right?

Female student

Yeah, there are some great places to eat around here.

Male student

Well, these students . . . they'll be making fantastic meals. And it's gonna be cheaper than going out to one of those restaurants.

Female student

Much cheaper actually . . .

Male student

So, you know, it'll be worth it. The meals will be as good as the ones in those expensive restaurants.

Narrator

The man expresses his opinion about the plan described in the article. Briefly summarize the plan. Then state his opinion about the plan and explain the reasons he gives for holding that opinion.

TRACK 36 TRANSCRIPT

Narrator

Read the passage about target marketing. You will have 45 seconds to read the passage. Begin reading now.

TRACK 37 TRANSCRIPT

Narrator

Now listen to part of a lecture on this topic in a marketing class.

Professor

Nowadays, something you notice more and more is television commercials that are made specifically for certain television programs. So, let's say a company wants to sell a telephone . . . a cell phone. Now, during TV shows that young people watch—you know, shows with pop music or teen serials—they create a commercial that emphasizes how fun the phone is. You know, the phone has bright colors, and they show kids having a good time with their friends. And, well, the company wants the kids watching TV at this time to want to buy this phone—this phone that's made especially for them.

But, the same company will make a different commercial to be shown during, say, a program about business or a business news show. Now, for this group of people, businesspeople, the company will have to show how efficient their phone is, how it can handle all business easily and maybe even save money. And here's the thing—it's basically the same phone; the company has just made two different commercials to appeal to different groups of people.

Narrator

Using the professor's examples, explain the advertising technique of target marketing.

TRACK 38 TRANSCRIPT

Narrator

Listen to a conversation between two students.

Male student

Susan! What happened to your arm?

Female student

It's my wrist, actually—I sprained it last weekend. And I'm kind of upset about it, because I'm supposed to play the violin in my string quartet's big concert next week. We've been practicing for weeks. And we've already sold a bunch of tickets.

Male student

Oh, sorry to hear that. What are you gonna do?

Female student

Well, I was thinking about trying to play anyway. I mean, I really don't want to let the other three group members down. Plus the doctor said my wrist should be feeling better by then.

Male student

OK, so . . . problem solved, right?

Female student

Not exactly—I'm worried that I'm gonna be out of practice. Like, I haven't been able to play the violin since I sprained my wrist. What if I don't play well? I'd make the rest of the group sound bad.

Male student

Why don'tcha get somebody else to take your place?

Female student

Well, there's only one other person I know of who could do it, and that's Jim. He's a great violinist, and I'm sure he'd say yes. . . . The thing is, he's not very reliable. I mean, I'm in the orchestra with him and he's always showing up late for rehearsals.

Male student

Oh . . . so you're not sure you can depend on him.

Female student

Exactly. And we have less than a week left to rehearse for the concert. We'd *really* need him to show up on time for all our rehearsals.

Narrator

Briefly summarize the problem the speakers are discussing. Then state which of the two solutions from the conversation you would recommend. Explain the reasons for your recommendation.

TRACK 39 TRANSCRIPT

Narrator

Now listen to part of a lecture in a psychology class.

Professor

Why do we do the things we do? What drives us to participate in certain activities . . . to buy a certain car . . . or even to choose a certain career? In other words, what motivates us to do what we do?

Well, in studies of motivation, psychologists distinguish between two very different types. Our reasons for doing something, our motivations, can be *extrinsic*—in other words, based on some kind of *external* reward like praise or money . . . or they can be *intrinsic* . . . meaning we engage in the activity because it pleases us *internally*. Both create strong forces that lead us to behave in certain ways; however, intrinsic motivation is generally considered to be more long-lasting than the other.

As I said, extrinsic motivation is . . . *external*. It's the desire to behave in a certain way in order to obtain some kind of external reward. A child, for example, who regularly does small jobs around the house does them not because she enjoys taking out the garbage or doing the dishes but because she knows if she does these things, she'll be given a small amount money for doing them. But how motivated would the child be to continue doing the work if her parents suddenly stopped giving her money for it?

With intrinsic, or internal, motivation we want to do something because we enjoy it, or get a sense of accomplishment from it. Most people who are internally motivated get pleasure from the activity . . . so they just feel good about doing it. For example, I go to the gym several times a week. I don't go because I'm training for a marathon or anything. I just enjoy it. I have more energy after I exercise and I know it's good for my health so it makes me feel good about myself. And that's what's kept me going there for the past five years.

Narrator

Using points and examples from the talk, explain the two types of motivation.

TRACK 40 TRANSCRIPT

Narrator

Now listen to part of a lecture on the topic you just read about.

Professor

Unfortunately, none of the arguments about what the Chaco great houses were used for is convincing.

First—sure, *from the outside* the great houses look like later Native American apartment buildings, but the *inside* of the great houses casts serious doubt on the idea that many people lived there. I'll explain. If hundreds of people were living in the great houses, then there would have to be many *fireplaces* where each family did its daily cooking. But there're very *few* fireplaces. In one of the largest great houses there were fireplaces for only around ten families. Yet there are enough *rooms* in the great house for more than a *hundred* families. So the primary function of the houses couldn't have been residential.

Second, the idea that the great houses were used to store grain maize is unsupported by evidence. It may *sound* plausible that large, empty rooms were used for storage, but excavations of the great houses have *not* uncovered many traces of maize *or* maize containers. If the great houses were used for storage, why isn't there more spilled maize on the floor? Why aren't there more remains of big containers?

Third, the idea that the great houses were ceremonial centers isn't well supported either. Ya know that mound at Pueblo Alto? It contains lots of other materials besides broken pots, stuff you wouldn't expect from ceremonies. For example, there're large quantities of building materials—sand, stone, even construction tools. This suggests that the mound is a just a *trash heap* of construction material, stuff that was thrown away or not used up when the house was being built. The pots in the pile could be regular trash, too, left over from the meals of the construction workers. So the Pueblo Alto mound is *not* good evidence that the great houses were used for special ceremonies.

TRACK 41 TRANSCRIPT

Narrator

Summarize the points made in the lecture, being sure to explain how they cast doubt on the specific theories discussed in the reading passage.

TRACK 42 TRANSCRIPT

Narrator

Listen to a conversation between a student and an employee in the university's career services office.

Student

Hi. Do you have a minute?

Administrator

Sure. How can I help you?

Student

I have a couple of questions about the career fair next week.

Administrator

OK, shoot.

Student

Um, well, are seniors the only ones who can go? I mean, you know, they're finishing school this year and getting their degrees and everything . . . and, well, it seems like businesses would want to talk to them and not first-year students like me . . .

Administrator

No, no. The career fair is open to all our students and we encourage anyone who's interested to go check it out.

Student

Well, that's good to know.

Administrator

You've seen the flyers and the posters around campus, I assume.

Student

Sure! Can't miss 'em. I mean, they all say where and when the fair is . . . just not who should attend.

Administrator

Actually, they do. But it's in the small print. We should probably make that part easier to read, shouldn't we? I'll make a note of that right now. So, do you have any other questions?

Student

Yes, actually I do now. Um, since I'd only be going to familiarize myself with the process—you know, "check it out"—I was wondering if there's anything you'd recommend that I do to prepare.

Administrator

That's actually a very good question. As you know, the career fair is generally an opportunity for local businesses to recruit new employees and for soon-to-be graduates to have interviews with several companies they might be interested in working for. Now, in your case, even though you wouldn't be looking for employment right now, it still wouldn't hurt for you to prepare much like you would if you were looking for a job.

Student

You mean like get my resume together and wear a suit?

Administrator

That's a given. I was thinking more along the lines of doing some research. The flyers and posters list all the businesses that are sending representatives to the career fair. Um, what's your major, or do you have one yet?

Student

Well, I haven't declared a major yet but I'm strongly considering accounting. See, that's part of the reason I want to go to the fair . . . to help me decide if that's what I really want to study . . .

Administrator

That's very wise. Well, I suggest that you get on the computer and learn more about the accounting companies, in particular, that will be attending. You can learn a lot about companies from their Internet Web sites. Then prepare a list of questions.

Student

Questions . . . hmm. So in a way I'll be interviewing them?

Administrator

That's one way of looking at it. Think about it for a second. What do you want to know about working for an accounting firm?

Student

Well, there's the job itself . . . and salary, of course . . . and, um, working conditions . . . I mean, would I have an office or would I work in a big room with a zillion other employees? And . . . um . . . and maybe about opportunities for advancement . . .

Administrator

See? Those are all important things to know. After you do some research you'll be able to tailor your questions to the particular company you're talking to.

Student

Wow, I'm glad I came by here! So, it looks like I've got some work to do.

Administrator

And if you plan on attending future career fairs, I recommend you sign up for one of our interview workshops.

Student

I'll do that.

TRACK 43 TRANSCRIPT

Narrator

Why does the student say this:

Student

So, it looks like I've got some work to do.

TRACK 44 TRANSCRIPT

Economics

Narrator
Listen to part of a lecture in an economics class.

Professor
Now, when I mention the terms "boom" and "bust," what does that bring to mind?

Male student
The dot-com crash of the '90s!

Professor
OK. The *boom* in the late 1990s when all those new Internet companies sprang up and were then sold for huge amounts of money. Then the *bust* around 2000 . . . 2001, when many of those same Internet companies went out of business. Of course, booms aren't *always* followed by busts—we've certainly seen times when local economies expanded rapidly for a while then went back to a normal pace of growth. But, there's a type of rapid expansion, what might be called a "hysterical" or irrational boom that pretty much always leads to a bust. See, people often *create* and *intensify* a boom when they get carried away by some new industry that seems like it'll make 'em lots

of money, fast. You'd think that by the '90s, people would've learned from the past. If they did—well, look at *tulips*.

Male student

Tulips . . .? You mean, like, the flower?

Professor

Exactly. For instance, do you have any idea where tulips are from? Originally, I mean.

Male student

Well, the Netherlands, right?

Professor

That's what *most* people think—but no, they're not native to the Netherlands, or even Europe. Tulips actually hail from an area the Chinese call the "Celestial Mountains" in central Asia—a very *remote* mountainous region.

It was Turkish nomads who first discovered tulips and spread them slowly westward. Now, around the sixteenth century, Europeans were traveling to Istanbul in Turkey as merchants and diplomats. And the Turks often gave the Europeans tulip bulbs as gifts, which they would carry home with them. For the Europeans, tulips were totally unheard of, a great novelty. The first bulbs to show up in the Netherlands, the merchant who received them roasted and ate them—he thought they were a kind of onion.

It turns out that the Netherlands was an ideal country for growing tulips. It had the right kind of sandy soil, for one thing, but also it was a wealthy nation with a growing economy, willing to spend lots of money on new, exotic things—plus the Dutch had a history of gardening. Wealthy people would compete, spending enormous amounts of money to buy the rarest flowers for their gardens.

Soon tulips were beginning to show up in different colors as growers tried to breed them specifically for colors which would make them even more valuable, but they were never completely sure what they would get. Some of the most prized tulips were white with purple streaks or red with yellow streaks on the petals—even a dark purple tulip that was very much prized. What happened then was a craze for these specialized tulips. We call that craze "tulip mania."

So—here we've got all the *conditions* for an-an *irrational* boom: a prospering economy, so more people had more disposable income—money to spend on luxuries—*but* they weren't experienced at *investing* their new wealth. Then along comes a thrilling new commodity—sure, the first specimens were just plain old red tulips, but they could be bred into some extraordinary variations—like that dark purple tulip. And finally, you have an *unregulated* marketplace—no government constraints—where prices could explode. And explode they did, starting in the 1630s.

There was always much more demand for tulips than supply. Tulips didn't bloom frequently like roses; tulips bloomed *once* in the early spring and that was it for the year. Eventually, specially bred, multicolored tulips became so valuable . . . Well, according to records, one tulip bulb was worth 24 tons of wheat or a thousand pounds of cheese. One particular tulip bulb was sold in exchange for a small ship! In other words, tulips were literally worth their weight in gold.

As demand grew, people began selling *promissory* notes guaranteeing the *future* delivery of prized tulip bulbs. The buyers of these pieces of paper would resell the notes at marked-up prices. These promissory notes kept changing hands—from buyer to buyer—until the tulip was ready for delivery. But it was all pure *speculation*, because, as I said, there was no way to know if the bulb was really going to produce the variety, the color, that was promised. But that didn't matter to the owner of the note, the owner only cared about having that piece of paper, so it could be traded later at a profit. And people were *borrowing*—mortgaging their homes, in many cases—to obtain those bits of paper because they were sure they'd found an easy way to make money.

So now you've got all the ingredients for a huge bust—and bust it did, when one cold February morning in 1637, a group of bulb traders got together and discovered that suddenly there were no bidders—nobody wanted to buy. Panic spread like wildfire, and the tulip market collapsed totally.

TRACK 45 TRANSCRIPT

Biology

Narrator
Listen to part of a lecture in a biology class.

Professor

OK, I have an interesting plant species to discuss with you today. Uh, it's a species of a *very* rare tree that grows in Australia—*Eidothea hardeniana*—but it's better known as the Nightcap Oak.

Now, it was discovered only very recently, just a few years ago. Uh, it remained hidden for so long because it's so rare, there're only about, oh, two hundred of 'em in existence. They grow in a rain forest, in a mountain range-range in the north part of New South Wales, which is, uh, a state in Australia. So just two hundred individual trees in all.

Now, another interesting thing about the Nightcap Oak is that it is . . . it represents . . . a-a very old . . . *type*, a kind of a tree that grew . . . a hundred million years ago. Uh, we found fossils that old that bear a remarkable resemblance to the tree. So, it's a *primitive* tree, a living fossil, you might say. It's a relic from earlier times, and it has survived all these years without much change. And . . . it-it's probably a kind of tree from which other trees that grow in Australia today evolved. Just-just to give you an idea of what we're talking about, here's a picture of the leaves of the tree and its flowers.

I dunno how well you can see the flowers; they're those little clusters sitting at the base of the leaves.

OK, what have we tried to find out about the tree since we've discovered it? Hmm, well, how . . . why is . . . is it so rare is one of the first questions. Uh, how is it, uh, how does it reproduce, is another question. Uh, maybe those two questions are actually related? Jim.

Male student

Hmm, I dunno, but I can imagine that . . . for instance . . . uh, seed dispersal might be a factor—I mean, if the, uh, y'know if the seeds cannot really disperse in a wide area then you know the tree may not, uh, *colonize* new areas, it-it can't spread from the area where it's growing.

Professor

Right, that's-that's actually a very good answer. Uh, of course, you might think there might not be many areas where the tree could spread *into*, uh, because, uh, well it's-it's very specialized in terms of the habitat. But that's not really the case here, uh, the-the suitable habitat-habitat that is the actual rain forest is much larger than-than the few hectares where the Nightcap Oak grows. Now, this tree is a flowering tree as I showed you, uh, uh, it-it produces a fruit, much like a plum, on the inside there's a seed with a hard shell. Uh, it-it appears that the shell has to crack open or break down somewhat to allow the seed to soak up water. If the Nightcap Oak remains, if their seeds remain locked inside their shell, they will not germinate. Now actually the seeds, uh, they don't retain the power to germinate for very long, maybe two years, so there's actually quite a short window of opportunity for the seed to germinate. So the shell somehow has to be broken down before this, uh, germination ability expires. And-and then there's a kind of rat that likes to feed on the seeds as well. So, given all these limitations, not many seeds that the tree produces will actually germinate. So this is a possible explanation for why the tree does not spread. It doesn't necessarily explain how it *became* so rare but it explains why it doesn't increase.

OK, so it seems to be the case that this species, uh this Nightcap Oak, is not very good at spreading. However, it seems, though we can't be sure, that it's very good at *persisting* as a population. Uh, uh, we, uh, there-there're some indications to suggest that the population of the Nightcap Oak has not declined over the last, uh, y'know, many hundreds of years. So, it's stayed quite stable; it-it's not a remnant of some huge population that has dwindled in the last few hundred years for some reason. It's not *necessarily* a species in retreat. OK, so it cannot spread very well but it's good at maintaining itself. It's rare but it's not disappearing. OK, the next thing we might wanna ask about a plant like that is what chances does it have to survive into the future. Let's look at that.

TRACK 46 TRANSCRIPT

Narrator
Listen again to part of the lecture. Then answer the question.

Professor
OK, what have we tried to find out about the tree since we've discovered it? Hmm, well, how . . . why is . . . is it so rare is one of the first questions. Uh, how is it, uh, how does it reproduce, is another question. Uh, maybe those two questions are actually related?

Narrator
Why does the professor say this:

Professor
Maybe those two questions are actually related?

TRACK 47 TRANSCRIPT

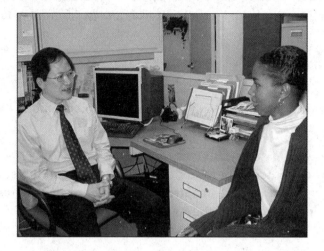

Narrator

Listen to a conversation between a student and a professor.

Student

Professor Martin?

Professor

Hi, Lisa—what can I do for you?

Student

Well, I've been thinking about, you know, what you were saying in class last week? About how we shouldn't wait until the last minute to find an idea and get started working on our term paper?

Professor

Good, good. And have you come up with anything?

Student

Well, yeah, sort of—see, I've never had a linguistics class before, so I was sort of . . . I mean, I was looking over the course description, and a lot of the stuff you've described there, I just don't know what it's talking about, you know? Or what it means. But there was one thing that really did jump out at me . . .

Professor

Yes . . .?

Student

The section on dialects? 'Cause, like, that's the kind of thing that's always sort of intrigued me, you know?

Professor

Well, that's certainly an *interesting* topic, but you may not realize, I mean, the *scope* . . .

Student

Well, especially now, 'cause I've got, like, *one* roommate who's from the South, and *another* one from New York, and we all talk, like, *totally* different, you know?

Professor

Yes, I understand, but . . .

Student

But then I was noticing, like, we don't really get into this till the end of the semester, you know? So I . . .

Professor

So you want some pointers where to go for information on the subject? Well, you could always *start* by reading the chapter in the book on sociolinguistics; that would give you a basic understanding of the key issues involved here.

Student

Yeah, that's what *I* thought! So I started reading the chapter, you know—about how everyone speaks some dialect of their language? And I'm wondering, like, well, how do we even manage to understand each other at all?

Professor

Ah! Yes, an interesting question. You see . . .

Student

So then I read the part about "dialect accommodation"—you know, the idea that people tend to adapt their speaking to make it closer to the speech of whoever they're talking to. And I'm thinking, yeah, *I* do that when I talk with my roommates! And without even thinking about it or anything, you know?

Professor

OK, all right—"dialect accommodation" is a more manageable sort of topic . . .

Student

So I was thinking, like, I wonder just how much other people do the same thing? I mean, there's students here from all over the place; does everyone change the way they talk to some degree, depending on who they're talking to?

Professor

You'd be surprised!

Student

So, anyway, my question is, do you think it'd be OK if I did a project like that for my term paper? You know, find students from different parts of the country, record them talking to each other in different combinations, report on how they accommodate their speech or not, that kind of thing?

Professor

Tell you what, Lisa: Write me up a short proposal for this project—how you're going to carry out the experiment and everything, a-a design plan—and I think this'll work out just fine!

TRACK 48 TRANSCRIPT

Narrator

Listen again to part of the conversation. Then answer the question.

Student

The section on dialects? 'Cause, like, that's the kind of thing that's always sort of intrigued me, you know?

Professor

Well, that's certainly an *interesting* topic, but you may not realize, I mean, the *scope* . . .

Narrator

What can be inferred about the professor when he says this:

Professor

Well, that's certainly an *interesting* topic, but you may not realize, I mean, the *scope* . . .

TRACK 49 TRANSCRIPT

Creative Writing

Narrator

Listen to part of a lecture in a creative writing class.

Professor

All right everybody. The topic for today is, well . . . we're gonna take a look at how to start creating the characters for the stories you're writing. One way of doing that is to come up with what's called a character sketch. I don't mean a sketch like a drawing. I guess that's obvious. It's, um . . . It's . . . a sketch is a way of getting started on defining your characters' personalities.

To begin, how do we create fictional characters? We don't just pull them from thin air, do we? I mean, we don't create them out of nothing. We base them—consciously or unconsciously—we base them on real people. Or, we, um . . . blend several people's traits . . . their attributes . . . into one character.

But when people think fiction, they may assume the characters come from the author's imagination. But the writer's imagination is influenced by . . . by real people. Could be anyone, so pay attention to the people you meet . . . someone in class, at the gym, that guy who's always sitting in the corner at the coffeehouse . . . uh, your cousin who's always getting into dangerous situations. We're pulling from reality . . . gathering bits and pieces of real people. You use these people . . . and the bits of behavior or characteristics as a starting point as you begin to sketch out your characters.

Here's what you should think about doing first. When you begin to formulate a story, make a list of interesting people you know or have observed. Consider *why* they're unique . . . or annoying. Then make notes about their unusual or dominant attributes. As you create fictional characters, you'll almost always combine characteristics from several different people on your list to form the identity and personality of just one character.

Keeping this kind of character sketch can help you solidify your character's personality . . . so that it remains consistent throughout your story. You need to define your characters . . . know their personalities so that you can have them acting in ways that're predictable . . . consistent with their personalities. Get to know them like a friend. You know your friends well enough to know how they'll act in certain situations, right?

Say you have three friends, their car runs out of gas on the highway. John gets upset, Mary remains calm, Teresa takes charge of handling the situation. And, let's say . . . both John and Mary defer to her leadership. They call you to explain what happened. And when John tells you he got mad, you're not surprised because he always gets frustrated when things go wrong. Then he tells you how Teresa took charge, calmed him down, assigned tasks for each person, and got them on their way. Again you're not surprised. It's exactly what you'd expect. Well, you need to know your characters like you know your friends . . . if you know a lot about a person's character, it's easy to predict how they'll behave. So if your characters' personalities are well defined, it'll be easy for you as the writer to portray them realistically . . . believably in any given situation.

While writing character sketches, *do* think about *details*. Ask yourself questions, even if you don't use the details in your story . . . uh, what does each character like to eat, what setting does each prefer . . . the mountains? The city? What about educational background? Their reactions to success . . . or defeat? Write it all down.

But here I need to warn you about a possible pitfall. Don't make your character into a stereotype. Remember, the reader needs to know how your character is different from other people who might fall in the same category. Maybe your character loves the mountains and has lived in a remote area for years. To make sure he's not a stereotype, ask yourself how he sees life differently from other people who live in that kind of setting. Be careful not to make him into the cliché of the rugged mountain dweller.

OK. Now I'll throw out a little terminology . . . it's easy stuff. *Major* characters are sometimes called *round* characters. *Minor* characters are sometimes called . . . well, just the opposite. *Flat*. A round character is fully developed. A flat character isn't— character development is fairly limited. The flat character tends to serve mainly as a, um, a motivating factor. For instance, you introduce a flat character who has experienced some sort of defeat . . . and then your round . . . your main character, who loves success and loves to show off, comes and boasts about succeeding . . . and jokes about the flat character's defeat in front of others . . . humiliates the other guy. The flat character is introduced solely for the purpose of allowing the round character to show off.

TRACK 50 TRANSCRIPT

Narrator
Listen again to part of the lecture. Then answer the question.

Professor
One way of doing that is to come up with what's called a character sketch. I don't mean a sketch like a drawing. I guess that's obvious. It's, um . . . It's, . . . a sketch is a way of getting started on defining your characters' personalities.

Narrator

Why does the professor say this:

Professor

I don't mean a sketch like a drawing.

TRACK 51 TRANSCRIPT

Earth Science

Narrator

Listen to part of a lecture in an earth science class.

Professor

We're really just now beginning to understand how *quickly drastic* climate change can take place. We can see past occurrences of climate change that took place over just a few hundred years. Take, uh, the Sahara desert . . . in Northern Africa.

The Sahara was really different 6,000 years ago. I mean, you wouldn't call it a tropical paradise or anything—ah, or maybe you *would* if you think about how today in some parts of the Sahara it only rains about once a century. Um, but basically, you had greenery and you had water. And what *I* find *particularly* interesting, amazing, really what *really* indicates how *un*-desert-like the Sahara was thousands of years ago, was something painted on a rock: prehistoric art—*hippopotamuses*. As you know, hippos need a lot of water, and hence . . . Hence what?

Female student
They need to live near a large source of water year-round.

Professor
That's right.

Male student
But how's that proof that the Sahara used to be a lot wetter? I mean, the people who painted those hippos . . . well, couldn't they have seen them on their travels?

Professor
OK, in principle they could, Carl. But the rock paintings aren't the only evidence. Beneath the Sahara are huge *aquifers*, basically a sea of fresh water that's perhaps a

million years old, filtered through rock layers. And, ah, and-and then there's fossilized pollen from low shrubs and grasses that once grew in the Sahara. In fact these *plants* still grow, ah, but hundreds of miles away in more vegetated areas. Anyway, it's this fossilized pollen, along with the aquifers, *and* the rock paintings—these three things are all evidence that the Sahara was once much greener than it is today, that there were hippos and probably elephants, and giraffes, and so on.

Male student

So, what happened?

Professor

How did it happen? Well now we're so used to hearing about how human activities are affecting the climate, right; but that takes the focus away from the natural variations in the Earth's climate. Like the Ice Age, right? The planet was practically covered in ice just a few thousand years ago. Now, as far as the Sahara goes, there's some recent literature that points to the migration of the monsoon in that area.

Male/Female student

Huh?

Professor

What do I mean? OK. A monsoon is a seasonal wind that can bring in a large amount of rainfall. Now, if the monsoon *migrates*, well *that* means the rains move to another area, right?

So what *caused* the monsoon to migrate? Well, the answer is the dynamics of Earth's motions—the same thing that caused the Ice Age, by the way. The Earth's *not always* the same distance from the Sun. *And* it's *not always tilting* toward the Sun at the same angle. There're slight variations in these two parameters. They're gradual variations, but their *effects* can be pretty abrupt, and *can* cause the climate to change in *just* a few hundred years.

Female student

That's abrupt?

Professor

Well, yeah, considering that other climate shifts take *thousands* of years, this one's pretty abrupt. So these changes in the planet's motions, they caused the climate to change; but it was also *compounded*. What the Sahara experienced was a sort of *run-away drying* effect.

As I said, the monsoon migrated south—so there was less rain in the Sahara. The *land* started to get *drier*—which in turn caused a huge *decrease* in the amount of *vegetation*, because vegetation doesn't grow as well in dry soil, right? And then, less vegetation means the soil can't hold water as well—the soil *loses* its ability to *retain* water when it *does* rain. So then you have less moisture to help clouds form . . . nothing to evaporate for cloud formation. And then the cycle continues—less rain, drier soil, less vegetation, fewer clouds, less rain, etcetera, etcetera.

Male student

But what about the people who made the rock paintings?

Professor

Good question. No one really knows. But there might be some connection to ancient Egypt. At about the same time that the Sahara was becoming a desert, mmm . . . 5,000 years ago, Egypt *really* began to flourish out in the Nile River Valley. And that's not that far away. So it's only *logical* to hypothesize that a lot of these people migrated to the Nile Valley when they realized that this was more than a temporary drought. And some people take this a step further—and that's OK, that's science—and they hypothesize that this migration actually provided an important impetus in the development of ancient Egypt. Well, we'll stay tuned on that.

TRACK 52 TRANSCRIPT

Narrator

Listen again to part of the lecture. Then answer the question.

Professor

I mean, you wouldn't call it a tropical paradise or anything—ah, or maybe you *would* if you think about how today in some parts of the Sahara it only rains about once a century.

Narrator

Why does the professor say this:

Professor

Or maybe you *would* if you think about how today in some parts of the Sahara it only rains about once a century.

TRACK 53 TRANSCRIPT

Narrator

Talk about a photograph or painting you have seen that was memorable. Explain what you liked or disliked about it.

TRACK 54 TRANSCRIPT

Narrator

Some people have one career throughout their lives. Other people do different kinds of work at different points in their lives. Which do you think is better? Explain why.

TRACK 55 TRANSCRIPT

Narrator

Now read a letter that a student has written to the university newspaper. You have 50 seconds to read the letter. Begin reading now.

TRACK 56 TRANSCRIPT

Narrator

Now listen to two students discussing the letter.

Female student

I totally disagree with Tim's proposal.

Male student

Why?

Female student

Well, look. Tim's my friend, but he's not your typical student. He stays up late partying every night—weeknights too.

Male student

If he parties every night, no wonder he can't pay attention.

Female student

Yes, and most students aren't like that. They come to class prepared and rested, and they can concentrate.

Male student

So you're saying the problem is really Tim.

Female student

Yes. He was in one of my classes last year and whenever I looked at him, he was actually sleeping.

Male student

I guess if he's sleeping, he can't really know what's happening, what other people in class are doing.

Female student

Right. And you want to know what does happen in that last hour of seminar? In a lot of seminars that I've been in, that's when things get interesting.

Male student

Really?

Female student

Yes. That's usually when students get really involved in the discussion and start exchanging important ideas. And if the history department actually did what Tim suggests, well, if they did that, what would happen is you'd lose what might be the most worthwhile part of a seminar.

Narrator

The woman expresses her opinion about the proposal described in the letter. Briefly summarize the proposal. Then state her opinion about the proposal and explain the reasons she gives for holding that opinion.

TRACK 57 TRANSCRIPT

Narrator

You have 45 seconds to read a passage from a psychology textbook. Begin reading now.

TRACK 58 TRANSCRIPT

Narrator

Now listen to part of a lecture on this topic in a psychology class.

Professor

OK, the first kind of memory, we're all very familiar with this, right? You probably remember what you had for dinner last night. You have a conscious memory of last night's dinner, so, um, if I ask you "What did you eat last night?" you could tell me.

But these other kind of memories—implicit memories. They work differently.

Let's take an example from the world of advertising. When you're driving along a highway, you see plenty of billboards—you know, roadside advertisements. You certainly don't remember them all. But they still affect you. Marketing researchers have shown . . . well, to be specific, let's say there's a billboard on the highway advertising a car called "the Panther." The ad shows a big picture of the car. And above the car in huge letters is the name of the car: "Panther." A lot of people drive by the billboard. But . . . ask those drivers later if they saw any advertisements for cars, and, well, they'll think about it, and a lot of them will say no. They honestly don't remember seeing any. They have no conscious memory of the "Panther" billboard. So you ask these same people a different question: You ask, um, OK, ah, you ask them to name an animal starting with the letter P. What do you think they will answer? Do they say "pig"? Pig is the most common animal that starts with the letter P. But they don't say "pig." They say "panther." The billboard had an effect, even though the drivers don't remember ever seeing it.

Narrator

Using the example of the car advertisement, explain what is meant by implicit memory.

TRACK 59 TRANSCRIPT

Narrator

Now listen to a conversation between a professor and a student.

Professor

Hi, Sara. To what do I owe the pleasure of this office visit?

Student

It's my study group, Professor Wilson. We're not getting much studying done, and, you know, none of us did very well on your last quiz.

Professor

Hmm. What's the problem?

Student

Well, we've all become good friends and we joke around a lot instead of studying.

Professor

Hmm . . . Sara, let me ask you this: when do you meet?

Student

Every Friday afternoon.

Professor

Have you thought about changing to another day? By the time Friday afternoon rolls around, all of you are probably exhausted and all you want to do is relax and unwind. It's hard to stay focused at the very end of the week.

Student

Good point, although things have gotten so out of hand, that I'm not sure changing days would help. And we'd lose one or two people if we changed days. Friday afternoon's the only time everyone's available. But it's worth considering.

Professor

OK, but just a second . . . another possibility is . . . Does your group have a leader?

Student

No . . .

Professor

Well, if you had a leader that would help enormously—someone to set an agenda in advance, e-mail it to everyone before the meeting, and then make sure, when you meet, that you stay focused on your goals. And since you seem to be concerned enough about the problem to have come see me, I think that someone might be you.

Student

I guess I could take on that role. But it sounds like work.

Professor

You don't have to do it for the whole semester, Sara. You can start it off, and then perhaps someone else can take over.

Narrator

Briefly summarize the problem the speakers are discussing. Then state which of the two solutions from the conversation you would recommend. Explain the reasons for your recommendation.

TRACK 60 TRANSCRIPT

Narrator

Now listen to part of a talk in an education class.

Professor

One of the hardest parts of teaching is keeping your students' attention. Now, the key to doing this is understanding the *concept* of attention.

Basically, there are two types of attention. The first type is active. Active attention is voluntary—it's when you intentionally make yourself focus on something. And since it requires effort, it's hard to keep up for a long time. OK, so, um, let's say you're teaching a . . . a biology class. And today's topic is frogs. All right, you're standing at the front of the room and lecturing: "A frog is a type of animal known as an amphibian . . ." Well, this isn't necessarily going to keep the students' interest. But most of them will force themselves to pay active attention to your lecture . . . but it's only a matter of time before they get distracted.

Now, the other type of attention is *passive* attention—when it's involuntary. Passive attention requires no effort, because it happens naturally. If something's really interesting, students don't have to *force* themselves to pay attention to it—they do it without even thinking about it. So back to our biology lecture. You start talking about frogs, and then you pull a live frog out of your briefcase. You're describing it while you hold it up . . . show the students how long its legs are and how they're used for jumping, for example. Then maybe you even let the frog jump around a bit on the desk or the floor. In this case, by doing something unexpected . . . something more engaging, you can tap into their passive attention. And it can last much longer than active attention; as long as the frog's still there, your students will be interested.

Narrator

Using points and examples from the talk, explain the difference between active and passive attention.

TRACK 61 TRANSCRIPT

Narrator

Now listen to part of a lecture on the topic you just read about.

Professor

The communal online encyclopedia will probably never be perfect, but that's a small price to pay for what it *does* offer. The criticisms in the reading are largely the result of prejudice against and ignorance about how far online encyclopedias have come.

First, errors: It's hardly a fair criticism that encyclopedias online have errors. Traditional encyclopedias have never been *close* to perfectly accurate. If you're looking for a *really* comprehensive reference work without *any* mistakes, you're not going to find it—on- *or* off-line. The real point is that it's easy for errors in factual material to be corrected in an online encyclopedia—but with the printed and bound encyclopedia, the errors remain for decades.

Second, hacking: online encyclopedias have recognized the importance of protecting their articles from malicious hackers. One strategy they started using is to put the crucial facts in the articles that nobody disputes in a *"read-only"* format, which is a format that no one can make changes to. That way you're making sure that the crucial facts in the articles are reliable. Another strategy that's being used is to have special editors whose job is to monitor all changes made to the articles and eliminate those changes that are clearly malicious.

Third, what's worth knowing about: The problem for traditional encyclopedias is that they have limited space, so they have to decide what's important and what's not. And in practice, the judgments of the group of academics that make these decisions don't reflect the great range of interests that people really have. But space is definitely *not* an issue for online encyclopedias. The academic articles are still represented in online encyclopedias, but there can be a great variety of articles and topics that accurately reflect the great diversity of users' interests. The diversity of views and topics that online encyclopedias offer is one of their strongest advantages.

TRACK 62 TRANSCRIPT

Narrator

Summarize the points made in the lecture, being sure to explain how they oppose the specific points made in the reading passage.

TRACK 63 TRANSCRIPT

Narrator

Listen to a conversation between a student and an employee in the campus computer center.

Computer center employee

Hi, what can I help you with today?

Student

Hi, um, I wanted to—you see, the thing is, I don't know much about computers, so I was wondering if, uh, if there's a class or something . . . so I can learn how to use computers, like to write papers for my classes.

Computer center employee

Oh, I see . . . um, we don't really offer a course for beginners, since most students already have computing experience. But all the computers in our labs have a general tutorial installed on them. You could just go there and run it.

Student

And the tutorial explains everything? I mean, it might sound strange but I've never used a computer.

Computer center employee

Well, all the computer labs on campus are staffed with student assistants, and I'm sure that any one of them would be more than willing to get you started.

Student

Yeah? That sounds good. But is it expensive?

Computer center employee

No, in fact, it won't cost anything; it's one of the services of the computer center.

Student

That's great. How do they—I mean, how do I get in touch with the student assistants? Should I just go to a computer lab and ask whoever's there?

Computer center employee

Sure, you could do that, or I can let you have a list of names of the students who are assistants in the labs. You might know one of them.

Student

Actually, I think I'd prefer someone I don't know, um, so I can ask dumb questions . . . Is there anyone you'd recommend?

Computer center employee

All of our student assistants are really knowledgeable about computers. I mean, they have to be, in order to work in the computer labs . . . It doesn't mean that they're necessarily good at teaching *beginners* . . . but you probably won't be a beginner for very long.

Student

Hope not.

Computer center employee

And I just thought of something else. The bookstore has a lot of books on computers—there might be one for people like you, I mean, people who don't have a lot of experience with computers. I actually bought one for my father so he could learn how to use e-mail, basic word processing, that sort of thing—and it worked pretty well for him.

Student

OK, I'll try that, too. And if the bookstore doesn't have it, they can just order it for me?

Computer center employee

Right. Now is there anything else I can help you with today?

Student

Uh, just the list of names and the times they're working. I'd like to get going on this as soon as possible.

Computer center employee

Right. Good luck.

TRACK 64 TRANSCRIPT

Economics

Narrator

Listen to part of a lecture in an economics class.

Professor

When attempting to understand international trade, some things seem so obvious that they can hardly be controverted, and other points that are important are invisible unless you've thought about the subject carefully.

Consider the following: if there's an increase in imports, let's say, um, let's say imports of furniture, and the domestic producers of furniture find this new competition very difficult and are cutting production and employment, then it seems obvious and easy to understand and many people conclude from this that increasing imports will cause generally greater unemployment at home.

What is not so obvious is that how much we import and how much we export . . . those are interdependent and you can't understand the one without the other. But the exports that are generated are not easily discernable, so most people don't see them. They see only the imports of furniture rising and employment in domestic furniture production falling.

So as a result, many people argue that we ought to protect jobs by limiting imports—either by tariffs, quotas, regulations, or whatever—without realizing that this also has the effect of reducing potential future exports to the rest of the world, things that we can produce very, very . . . cost effectively and therefore profitably.

The fundamental proposition in international economics is that it makes sense to import those things that we . . . that can be produced more economically abroad than at home and export things to the rest of the world that we can produce more cost effectively than produced elsewhere in the world. Therefore, if we limit imports, we put ourselves in danger of not being able to export.

The details of this relationship will take much longer to explain than I can fully go into now but the point of the matter is that gains—the benefits of gains—from international trade result from being able to get things cheaper by buying them abroad than you can make them at home. Now there're some things that we can make at home that are . . . that we can do more economically than they can do abroad.

In the case of the United States, typically high-technology products, uh . . . are things that Americans have innovated in and started firms doing that sort of thing at which they do very well. Whereas goods that produce . . . that use a lot of relatively low skill labor, like furniture production, cotton production, sugar production . . . those are things that are frequently made more inexpensively in places where wage rates are low and the cost of using capital is very high.

However, in Florida they produce a lot of sugar, but the costs are so high, if we didn't have extensive restrictions on imports of sugar, the output of sugar would decline dramatically. But the sugar industry in the U.S. doesn't produce high-paying jobs, it uses resources in ineffective ways and it blocks the import of more cost-effectively produced sugar. It, it's a very bad bargain for the people in the United States to want to protect low-paying jobs thereby halting the growth of world trading and international . . . uh, more international specialization. It would be better to remove restrictions on imports and allow other countries in the world . . . countries that can produce them more cheaply . . . let them specialize in producing those products.

Now, I agree that people who are directly affected by imports, what they focus on . . . is, is that their prospects . . . their job prospects are being reduced, and their economic circumstances are getting worse. And that's a relevant problem and an important problem; what isn't so obvious is . . . that by retraining and relocating people to places and industries where jobs are expanding rather than contracting, we can make the whole economy function more effectively and productively than by trying to block imports.

Um, what is interesting to note is that, even if there were no international trade issues, like imports, any changes that occur in a country's economy—any new technology, change in preferences, change in regulations or whatever—will lead to "adjustments" that lead some sectors of the economy to decline and others to expand.

And that's what we have to figure out, and that's a hard problem to deal with in detail, is how to facilitate people adjusting from sectors where their job prospects are not so good, and in particular where real wages aren't so high, to acquire skills that will permit them to move into higher-paying jobs in other parts of the economy either by retraining or relocating. Helping pay for the relocation of these people would be very helpful, but trying to block the changes is really counterproductive. It makes people in our country poorer, and it makes people elsewhere in the world poorer as well.

TRACK 65 TRANSCRIPT

Marine Biology

Narrator

Listen to part of a lecture in a marine biology class.

Professor

I want to continue our discussion about whales. Specifically, today, um, I want to talk about whale migration—um, why whales head *south* for the winter. Or really why whales in the cold water of the *Northern* Hemisphere head *south* for the winter. Now, not all kinds of whales migrate, but most baleen whales do.

And interestingly enough, we still don't really know why the baleen whales migrate. We do have several theories, however, which I'll discuss today. Uh, can anybody name one reason why baleen whales might migrate south, to the warm tropical water?

Male student

Uh, for food? You know, the whales move to warmer water in order to find a good area to feed.

Professor

Good guess. That should be an obvious reason—after all, most animals that migrate do so for the purpose of finding food. But, uh, that doesn't seem to be the case with baleen whales. To understand why, you need to know something about water temperature. There are a lot of technical reasons that I'm not going to go into right now. But let's just say that nutrients don't rise to the surface of tropical water like they do in other kinds of water. Tropical water simply never gets cold enough. So . . . well, what this means, uh, is that tropical water doesn't have much of the plankton that most whales feed on.

Male student

I don't understand—if there's no plankton, how do the whales survive through the winter?

Professor

Right. How *do* they survive? You see, they don't have to eat anything, because they've stored up so much fat during the summer feeding season that they can just survive off of that. So if they don't need to eat anything, we're back to our original question. Why do baleen whales migrate? Any theories? No?

Well, there's one idea out there that a lot of people believe. In fact, uh, you could say it's the most popular theory we have about whale migration. Basically, the argument is that for baleen whales, migration is a kind of balancing act. Let me explain. On one hand, whales need to take advantage of the summer months by eating as much food as they can. And that's what they can do best in the northern seas. This allows them to build up a lot of fat. But in the winter, food is scarce even in the north, so what the whales need to do is *save* energy. And that's what migrating south can help them do . . . Amanda, you have a question?

Female student

Yes. Um, the balancing-act theory doesn't make sense to me. Maybe whales might need to save energy during the winter, but wouldn't moving ali the way down to tropics make them *lose* energy?

Professor

That's a good point, and it's one reason why this isn't a perfect theory. It *does* cost the whales energy to migrate, but it's easier for whales to save energy in warm water than it is to save energy in cold water, so there might still be, you know, a good reason to move south for the winter. OK?

Now, before moving on to the next chapter, I want to briefly discuss how the baleen whale manages to navigate. It's pretty remarkable, because the whales manage to return to the same places year after year, and have to travel over an enormous area of ocean in order to do it. I mean, it's not like whales can just look at a map, right? So exactly how do they do it?

Well, a lot of experimental work still needs to be done, but we have been able to figure out at least three ways the baleen whale navigates without getting lost. The first is the ability to use Earth's magnetic field like it was a map. That sounds strange, but we know that many birds use that method, use the magnetic field, and it's possible that whales have the biological ability to do the same thing.

Another theory is that if they stay close to the coast, whales might be able to find familiar landmarks and use those as guides. But we don't really know if a whale's eyesight is good enough to be able to do that, so that's not a perfect theory.

And finally, we know that many whales make very loud sounds that can travel literally hundreds of miles underwater. Through a process called echolocation, it's possible that these whales hear the sounds bounce off of islands or other pieces of land and use those echoes as clues to help them find their way.

TRACK 66 TRANSCRIPT

Narrator
Listen again to part of the lecture. Then answer the question.

Professor
To understand why, you need to know something about water temperature. There are a lot of technical reasons that I'm not going to go into right now. But let's just say that nutrients don't rise to the surface of tropical water like they do in other kinds of water.

Narrator
What does the professor mean when she says this:

Professor
There are a lot of technical reasons that I'm not going to go into right now.

TRACK 67 TRANSCRIPT

Narrator
Listen again to part of the lecture. Then answer the question.

Professor
It's pretty remarkable, because the whales manage to return to the same places year after year, and have to travel over an enormous area of ocean in order to do it. I mean, it's not like whales can just look at a map, right?

Narrator
What point does the professor make when she says this:

Professor
I mean, it's not like whales can just look at a map, right?

TRACK 68 TRANSCRIPT

Narrator
Listen to a conversation between a student and a professor.

Student
Hi, uh . . . Professor Anderson . . . wondering if you had a couple minutes . . .

Professor
Of course, Paula . . .

Student
Thanks . . . uh, you sent me a letter recently about doing, uh, an honors project—inviting me to come in and talk about . . .

Professor
Right, right, well, as your academic advisor, it's my job to look out for your academic interests, and based on your grades, and some very positive feedback I've heard from your professors, I wanted to formally invite you to consider doing an honors project . . .

Student

Yeah . . . well, thanks . . . uh, actually I kinda wanted to ask you . . . quite frankly—like how much work it would probably be? I mean, I'm gonna be spending a lot of time applying to law schools next semester and . . .

Professor

Well, let me tell you how it works . . . and then you can decide from there.

Student

OK.

Professor

Basically, the honors project is an opportunity to do . . . some in-depth work on a topic you're interested in before graduating college. You register for the class, but it doesn't work the same way a regular class does—you find a professor who you want to work with—you ask the professor—a sort of mentor who's knowledgeable on the topic you're interested in—the topic you're gonna write your honors thesis on . . .

Student

Writing a *thesis*? That's part of the *project*? Ah, like how many pages are we talking?

Professor

Usually about 50 . . . but it's a valuable experience, writing a thesis paper.

Student

So, basically, after I register for the class, I need to ask a professor who'll sorta help me . . .

Professor

Actually, you need to do that—a professor needs to agree to oversee your honors project—before you register.

Student

Oh, OK . . .

Professor

I mean, I know it sounds kinda daunting, but that's what the professor's there for—to help guide you through the different steps of the process and . . . uh . . . most students are very pleased with the experience . . . they're able to demonstrate advanced research skills, which is important; especially in your case, writing an honors thesis would be a big plus . . .

Student

You think so?

Professor

Absolutely. Especially considering your plans, since you're applying to law schools. It shows initiative, that you've done well as an undergraduate—to be allowed to do the honors project . . . that you're able to work independently and, of course, you would graduate with honors . . .

Student

Yeah, it *does* sound good—it's just, you know, I've never written something like that before, so . . .

Professor

Well, you choose something you're interested in—maybe you can even expand a shorter research paper from another class or . . .

Student

So, like, maybe . . . You know, I took this course from Professor Connelly—his course on Comparative Governments last semester and, uh . . . did pretty well—I wrote a paper actually, on political parties in Venezuela and—and he seemed to like my research. Anyway, he, uh, I got an A in the course.

Professor

Good, so it sounds like you do have a general idea for a topic, and you might know what professor you want to work with . . . and look, it's still a couple weeks before registration, maybe you should talk to Professor Connelly and then get back to me.

Student

Yeah, I will—thanks. I'll come by again sometime next week.

Professor

That's fine. Good luck.

TRACK 69 TRANSCRIPT

Narrator

What does Professor Anderson imply when he says this:

Professor

. . . they're able to demonstrate advanced research skills, which is important; especially in your case, writing an honors thesis would be a big plus . . .

TRACK 70 TRANSCRIPT

Narrator

What does the woman imply when she says this:

Student

Yeah, it does sound good—it's just, you know, I've never written something like that before . . . so . . .

TRACK 71 TRANSCRIPT

Narrator

Listen to part of a lecture in a journalism class. The professor has been discussing newspapers.

Professor

About 40 years ago, half of all Americans felt they'd be lost without a daily newspaper. But today, only one in *ten* Americans say they'd be lost without a paper. In fact, today, half of all Americans say they don't need a newspaper at all. And so people in the newspaper industry are trying to figure out how they can get more people reading the newspaper more often. They're trying to crack journalism's riddle for the ages: what makes people read newspapers? OK, well, let me ask you—as a journalism student, what do *you* think is the answer to this question? Elizabeth?

Female student

Um, I would probably try to improve the content of the newspaper.

Professor

Better content. Hmm. You mean like *well-written* editorials and articles?

Female student

Well, I mean provide more *interesting* content, like, I would first try to find out what readers really want to read . . . and then put *that* into the paper.

Professor

Yes, in fact, not too long ago, there was an extensive study conducted to investigate what draws people to newspapers. Uh, they found out that there's a clear, strong link between satisfaction with *content* and overall readership. Those newspapers that contained what the readers wanted most brought in the most readers. No big surprise there, right? So, what kind of content brings in readers? The study found that *people-centered local news* ranks at the top of the list . . . stories about *ordinary* people. For example, you could write about the experiences of those who were involved in a news story, and their friends and relatives . . . The vantage points would be those of *ordinary* people, not of police or other officials . . . OK? Now the study also showed that people want more stories about movies, TV, and weather, and *fewer* stories and photos about natural disasters and accidents . . . So, to get reader satisfaction, you need to select the right topics, and within those topics, the right news events or stories to cover. Yes, James?

Male student

It seems to me that a lot of what you just mentioned doesn't line up with the principles of good journalism. Catering to readers' tastes may improve overall readership, but what about the social responsibilities that newspapers have? I mean, there are some topics that newspapers *need* to write about in order to serve the public interest. Those topics may not always be fun and interesting for the average reader, but it's still the newspaper's responsibility to make that information available to the public.

Professor

That's a good point. You need a good mix of content. You can't just rush towards an attractive topic and forget about the reporting role of newspapers. There's a danger of going soft—newspapers *do* have to perform their obligations to citizens. So what newspapers sometimes do is to combine serious journalism with a reader-friendly *presentation*. Um, let me give you an example: When the justice department opened an investigation on the local police—some pretty serious stuff that could be boring to some readers—well, one local newspaper ran a lead story on their front page, but they also simplified the format by including small breakout boxes that presented—in a nutshell—the highlights of the story. That way, they could report the serious stories they needed to report, and, and still hold their readers' attention. OK? Uh, going back to the research on readership growth we were talking about . . . Uh, the most vital step of all, the study shows, may be making the paper easier to *use*. How can we make the paper "easier to *use*"? Well, it means stories need to include information, such as phone numbers, times, dates, addresses, Web sites and the like, so that readers can "go and do" things based on what they've read.

Female student

Professor Ellington? Um, when you said we need to make the paper "easier to use," I thought you were gonna say something about use of graphics, colors, and stuff like that.

Professor

Well, I guess those things do help in a way, but it turned out that those contemporary touches, uh, such as more attractive designs, extensive use of color, and informational graphics matter much less than you'd expect. Surprising, isn't it?

Female student

Yeah, it is . . . Um, how about service? Does the study say anything about improving service? I don't think people are gonna subscribe if the paper doesn't arrive, or shows up late . . .

Professor

Or shows up wet, which by the way, happened to me this morning. Oh, absolutely. Service affects readership. In fact, improving your service is much more likely to increase your readership than making changes in your editorial content . . . Not only on-time delivery in good condition, but also things like efficient billing, affordability, um . . . Yes?

Female student

They could also, like, increase the number of sites where they sell single copies.

Professor

Certainly that's one way to improve service.

TRACK 72 TRANSCRIPT

Narrator

What does the student imply when he says this:

Male student

It seems to me that a lot of what you just mentioned doesn't line up with the principles of good journalism. Catering to readers' tastes may improve overall readership, but what about the social responsibilities that newspapers have?

TRACK 73 TRANSCRIPT

Narrator

Listen again to part of the lecture. Then answer the question.

Female student

I don't think people are gonna subscribe if the paper doesn't arrive, or shows up late . . .

Professor

Or shows up wet, which by the way, happened to me this morning. Oh, absolutely. Service affects readership.

Narrator

What does the professor imply when he says this:

Professor

Or shows up wet, which by the way, happened to me this morning. Oh, absolutely.

TRACK 74 TRANSCRIPT

Geology

Narrator

Listen to part of a lecture in a geology class.

Professor

Um, beginning in the late 1960s, geologists began to uncover some evidence of a rather surprising kind when they looked . . . um . . . at various places around the world. What they found out when they examined rocks from about a . . . the period from about 750 million years ago to about 580 million years ago, they found that . . . it seemed that glaciers covered the entire surface of the Earth—from pole to pole, including the tropics.

Um . . . how did they come to this astonishing conclusion? What was the evidence for this? Especially when glaciers today are found only at the poles . . . or in the mountains.

Well, uh . . . basically when glaciers grow and move they leave behind a distinctive deposit consisting of primarily . . . of, at least on the top level, of ground up little bits of rock . . . almost . . . they almost look like rocks that have been deposited by streams, if you've ever seen those. And that's caused because, although the glacier is ice, it is actually flowing very slowly and as it moves it grinds the top layer of rock, it breaks off pieces and carries them away. So when you have glaciation you have a distinctive pattern of these pieces of rock which are called "erratics."

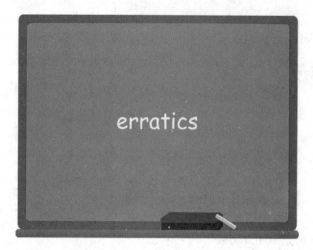

Erratics are rocks . . . they're the stones that are often carried long distances by glaciers.

So, in the 1960s and onward up through the 1990s, we keep finding evidence for glaciation, no matter what the latitude . . . even in tropical latitudes. Now, today there are glaciers in the tropics but only at very high elevations. But 750 million years ago, apparently there were glaciers even at sea level in the tropics.

How could this have happened?

Well, first . . . the growth of glaciers, uh, benefits, if you will, from a kind of a positive feedback loop called the "ice-albedo effect."

With the ice-albedo effect, glaciers—'cause they're white—reflect light and heat more . . . much more than does liquid water . . . or soil and rock, which are dark and absorb heat. So, the more glaciers there are, the more heat is reflected, so the climate gets cooler, and glaciers grow even more.

However . . . normally, on a global scale, there is a major process that functions to curb the growth of glaciers. And, that process involves carbon dioxide.

Now, we're all familiar with the notion that carbon dioxide is what we call a "greenhouse gas." The more carbon dioxide there is in the atmosphere, the more heat the atmosphere retains. That's what a greenhouse gas does. So, the greenhouse-gas effect is kinda the opposite of the albedo effect.

Um . . . now as it happens . . . when silicate rocks, which is a very common class of rock, when they're exposed to the air and to normal weathering, they erode. Carbon dioxide is attracted to these eroding rocks and binds to them, forming calcium carbonate.

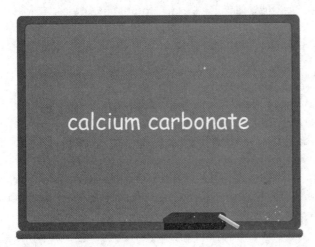

Calcium carbonate is eventually washed into the ocean where it settles to the bottom. This process, this forming of calcium carbonate, has the effect of sucking the carbon dioxide out of the air and storing it at the bottom of the ocean.

Now, follow me here. The process that's sucking carbon dioxide out of the air, keeping the greenhouse gas levels low, cannot happen if the rock is covered with ice.

So, while glaciers reflect light and heat . . . cooling the Earth, they at the same time cover rocks so there's less calcium carbonate formed . . . which leaves more carbon dioxide in the atmosphere. Higher levels of carbon dioxide keep the atmosphere warm . . . which slows the growth of glaciers. So, it's a balance, and the glacier growth remains pretty much under control.

Now, what happened 750 million years ago to upset that balance? It seems a relatively simple explanation actually . . .

750 million years ago . . . all the major continents are rocky, bare, and pretty much lined up along the equator; they hadn't yet moved to where they are today. So, what happened was, perhaps a slight cooling of . . . the very slight and temporary cooling of the Sun—which still happens from time to time—and the Earth starts to cool, the ice starts to spread on the oceans . . . starting at the poles.

Now, by the time the ice reaches about two-thirds of the way to the equator, it's too late.

See . . . because the continents are the last things to be covered by glaciers, they continue weathering . . . the rocks keep eroding and the carbon dioxide levels keep falling . . . So, the ice-albedo effect from the glaciers is increasing in strength while the atmosphere continues to lose its ability to retain heat making glacier growth unstoppable. Now you have what's called a "runaway freeze." And for perhaps as long as 50 million years, possibly with some interludes, the Earth was frozen from pole to pole, like a giant snowball.

TRACK 75 TRANSCRIPT

Narrator
Listen again to part of the lecture. Then answer the question.

Professor

Well, uh . . . basically when glaciers grow and move they leave behind a distinctive deposit consisting of primarily . . . of, at least on the top level, of ground up little bits of rock . . . almost . . . they almost look like rocks that have been deposited by streams, if you've ever seen those.

Narrator

Why does the professor say this:

Professor

. . . they almost look like rocks that have been deposited by streams, if you've ever seen those.

TRACK 76 TRANSCRIPT

Narrator

Sometimes one individual can have a great impact on a group or community. Select one person and explain how you think this person has affected others in the group or community. Give specific details and examples to explain your answer.

TRACK 77 TRANSCRIPT

Narrator

When some people visit a city or country for the first time, they prefer to take an organized tour. Other people prefer to explore new places on their own. Which do you prefer and why?

TRACK 78 TRANSCRIPT

Narrator

A university professor is switching to a new position. Read the article from the university about the professor. You will have 45 seconds to read the article. Begin reading now.

TRACK 79 TRANSCRIPT

Narrator

Now listen to two students discussing the article.

Female student

I don't like this at all.

Male student

Why not? She's done a lot for the philosophy department . . . like, well, hiring some great new teaching assistants . . . and putting together seminars.

Female student

Well, she has trouble organizing schedules.

Male student

Whadda'ya mean?

Female student

Well, she only realized last minute that she didn't have enough teaching assistants in the department, so some classes got cancelled.

Male student

Oh!

Female student

And I wanted to take a special two-week philosophy course in Europe . . . she was supposed to sign all the paperwork, but she didn't do it in time so I missed the whole trip!

Male student

Oh, wow. So organization's not her strong point, I guess.

Female student

Yeah. Besides, she's always critical. A lot of us on the team have complained to the university about her aggressive coaching style.

Male student

Oh, really? I met her . . . I mean, I thought she was nice.

Female student

Humph! Well, my friend . . . she had some serious problems in her family. She went to talk to Professor Fox and . . .

Male student

Yeah? What happened?

Female student

Well, she wanted emotional support from someone she looked up to, but instead Professor Fox made all kinds of critical comments. Maybe she's good at philosophy, but she's not a counselor. When students go to the dean, they go because they need someone to talk to, not so someone can criticize them.

Narrator

The woman expresses her opinion about the change described in the article. Briefly summarize the change. Then state her opinion about the change and explain the reasons she gives for holding that opinion.

TRACK 80 TRANSCRIPT

Narrator

Read the following paragraph from a psychology textbook. You will have 45 seconds to read the passage. Begin reading now.

TRACK 81 TRANSCRIPT

Narrator

Now listen to part of a lecture in a psychology class.

Professor

Let's start with a physical attribute, say, uh, in kittens. Adult cats have extremely good vision, especially at night. But in order for a kitten's eyesight to develop normally, the kitten must be exposed to light during the first four months of its life. Without that, its eyesight will not develop correctly, it will never be able to see as well as it should. Even if the kitten is exposed to plenty of light *after* those four months of darkness, it won't matter, its vision will *never* develop normally.

As far as behavior's concerned, well, have you ever seen how little baby geese line up and then, single-file, they follow their parent goose around? Well, what would happen if they didn't see a parent goose within the first two days of their lives?

Actually, for normal behavior to develop, they must see what to follow within these first two days. What happens is, whatever large moving object they first see during those two days, they'll adopt that object as their parent . . . forever. It can never be changed. For example, suppose after the baby geese were hatched, the only other animal around was, I don't know, say a dog. OK? So the baby geese see a dog, but no other geese. Even though the dog is a totally different species, the geese will adopt it as their parent—they'll follow it around. And even if the parent geese reappear later, it won't matter to the babies—they'll follow the dog. After two days the behavior is fixed and they'll never exhibit the normal behavior of following their real parent—a goose.

Narrator

Using the examples of kittens and geese, explain the idea of a critical period.

TRACK 82 TRANSCRIPT

Narrator

Now listen to a conversation between two students talking about a problem at the dormitory.

Male student

Carrie, how come I always see you eating in the cafeteria lately? Didn't you tell me you had a kitchen in your dorm and you were gonna start to . . .

Female student

Uh-huh . . . and I was gonna start cooking my own meals there.

Male student

So you changed your mind?

Female student

It's not that. The kitchen's just always a mess. It's filthy—dirty dishes everywhere, the trash is overflowing. Nobody ever cleans up so it's gotten really disgusting.

Male student

We had that problem in my dorm last year. We ended up making a schedule. Maybe you should try something like that.

Female student

What do you mean a schedule?

Male student

Well, people had to sign up to use the kitchen. Then whoever used it that day was responsible for cleaning it up.

Female student

So you mean if the kitchen's a mess on Tuesday, you just check and see who used it on Monday? Track 'em down and make 'em clean up the mess?

Male student

Uh-huh. It kinda works . . . as long as people sign up like they're supposed to.

Female student

Well, I was wondering if we could just pay to have someone clean the place, maybe once a week or something. If everybody chipped in a few dollars, we could hire someone to clean the whole kitchen area.

Male student

Wow. That'd be great if you could find someone. You mean like a student or something?

Female student

Yeah. As long as it's not too expensive.

Male student

You should check out the bulletin board in the student center. I've seen notes from students looking for different jobs—even cleaning jobs.

Female student

Good idea. And I'll see what the other people in my dorm wanna do.

Male student

Well, good luck. I hope it works out.

Narrator

Briefly summarize the problem the speakers are discussing. Then state which of the two solutions from the conversation you would recommend. Explain the reasons for your recommendation.

TRACK 83 TRANSCRIPT

Narrator

Now listen to part of a lecture in a business ethics class. The professor is discussing advertising.

Professor

Advertisers often try to sell you things by exaggerating about the quality of their products. It helps them get your attention. And exaggeration in advertising is usually considered acceptable, but not always. In the United States, there are laws to help determine what advertisers can say about their products. Basically, the law says advertisers can exaggerate as long as no one's gonna actually believe the exaggeration and take it literally. So, the exaggeration has to be very extreme. If it's not extreme enough and someone would actually buy the product because they believed the exaggeration, that advertisement may be illegal.

Take this example: a vacuum cleaner manufacturer made a vacuum cleaner that didn't weigh very much, and they wanted to get the point across about how light it was. So they made a TV commercial showing the vacuum cleaner floating in the air while cleaning the house. Well, that was a visual exaggeration. It got people's attention. And because a floating vacuum cleaner is obviously impossible, the commercial was legal because no one would actually believe the visual exaggeration and buy the vacuum cleaner because they thought it floated in the air.

But what if the company wanted to show that the vacuum cleaner was very powerful? What if it made a television commercial where a person uses the vacuum cleaner to perfectly clean this really big and really dirty carpet in, uh, just a few seconds. Well that would really grab your attention. But the thing is, even though that commercial is an exaggeration, you can imagine someone actually believing it and buying the vacuum cleaner and then being very disappointed because the vacuum cleaner couldn't do that. So advertisers can't use an exaggeration like that because it's actually not extreme enough and someone might believe it.

Narrator

Using the example of the vacuum cleaner, explain when it is legally acceptable to use exaggeration in advertising and when it is not.

TRACK 84 TRANSCRIPT

Narrator

Now listen to part of a lecture on the topic you just read about.

Professor

Many people think that if you want to go into business for yourself, it's best to buy a franchise. But recently a study looked closely at franchises, and some of the findings call that idea into question.

One interesting point was that many franchise contracts force franchise owners to . . . to buy very specific goods and services, and those goods and services tend to be overpriced. In other words, even though there are equivalent goods and services available on the market, uh, that are considerably cheaper, the owners aren't *allowed* to buy them.

Another point was about advertising. When you buy a franchise, you agree to pay up to *six percent* of your sum total in sales—that's quite a lot of money. One thing you're supposed to get in return for this money is that the company does the advertising for you. But the company doesn't advertise your business. What gets advertised is the *company's* brand, the *company's* products, which are sold by many other businesses in many other places. It turns out, individual franchise owners mostly get very little benefit—*much* less than they would get by spending even half that money to advertise their own business directly.

Finally, the biggest issue: security. Starting a franchise is not the most secure option out there. True, it's less risky than starting an independent business. But there's a *third* option that the passage didn't talk about. You can buy an *already existing independent* business from a previous owner. And the study showed that independent businesses bought from previous owners have *twice* as much chance of success during the first four years as franchises.

TRACK 85 TRANSCRIPT

Narrator
Summarize the points made in the lecture, being sure to explain how they challenge specific points made in the reading passage.

TRACK 86 TRANSCRIPT

Narrator
Listen to a conversation between a student and an admissions officer at City College.

Student
Hi. Can I ask you a few questions about starting classes during your summer session?

Admissions officer
Sure. Ask away! It starts next week, you know.

Student
Yeah, and I want to get some required courses out of the way so I can . . . maybe I can graduate one term earlier and get out into the job market sooner.

Admissions officer
That sounds like a good idea. Let me pull up the summer school database on my computer here . . .

Student
OK.

Admissions officer
OK, there it is. What's your student ID number?

Student
Oh, well, the thing is . . . I'm not actually admitted *here*. I'll be starting school upstate at Hooper University in the fall. But I'm down here for the summer, staying with my grandparents, 'cause I have a summer job near here.

Admissions officer

Oh, I see, well . . .

Student

So I'm outta luck?

Admissions officer

Well, you would be if you were starting anywhere but Hooper. But City College has a sort of special relationship with Hooper . . . a full exchange agreement . . . so our students can take classes at Hooper and vice versa. So if you can show me proof . . . um, your admissions letter from Hooper, then I can get you into our system here and give you an ID number.

Student

Oh, cool. So . . . um . . . I wanna take a math course and a science course—preferably biology. And I was also hoping to get my English composition course out of the way, too.

Admissions officer

Well all three of those courses are offered in the summer, but you've gotta understand that summer courses are condensed—you meet longer hours and all the assignments are doubled up because . . . it's the same amount of information presented and tested as in a regular term, but it's only six weeks long. Two courses are considered full time in summer term. Even if you weren't working, I couldn't let you register for more than that.

Student

Yeah, I was half expecting that. What about the schedule? Are classes only offered during the day?

Admissions officer

Well, during the week, we have some classes in the daytime and some at night, and on the weekends, we have some classes all day Saturday or all day Sunday for the six weeks.

Student

My job is pretty flexible, so one on a weekday and one on a weekend shouldn't be any problem. OK, so after I bring you my admissions letter, how do I sign up for the classes?

Admissions officer

Well, as soon as your student ID number is assigned and your information is in our admissions system, you can register by phone almost immediately.

Student

What about financial aid? Is it possible to get it for the summer?

Admissions officer

Sorry, but that's something you would've had to work out long before now. But the good news is that the tuition for our courses is about half of what you're going to be paying at Hooper.

Student

Oh, well that helps! Thank you so much for answering all my questions. I'll be back tomorrow with my letter.

Admissions officer

I won't be here then, but do you see that lady sitting at that desk over there? That's Ms. Brinker. I'll leave her a note about what we discussed, and she'll get you started.

Student

Cool.

TRACK 87 TRANSCRIPT

Narrator

Listen again to part of the conversation. Then answer the question.

Student

So I'm outta luck?

Admissions officer

Well, you would be if you were starting anywhere but Hooper.

Narrator

What does the woman mean when she says this:

Admissions officer

Well, you would be if you were starting anywhere but Hooper.

TRACK 88 TRANSCRIPT

World History

Narrator

Listen to part of a lecture in a world history class.

Professor

In any introductory course, I think it's always a good idea to step back and ask ourselves "What are we studying in this class, and why are we studying it?"

So, for example, when you looked at the title of this course in the catalog— "Introduction to World History"—what did you think you were getting into . . . what made you sign up for it—besides filling the social-science requirement?

Anyone . . .?

Male student

Well . . . just the—the history—of everything . . . you know, starting at the beginning . . . with . . . I guess, the Greeks and Romans . . . the Middle Ages, the Renaissance . . . you know, that kinda stuff . . . like what we did in high school.

Professor

OK . . . Now, what you're describing is *one* approach to world history.

In fact, there are several approaches—basic "models" or "conceptual frameworks" of what we study when we "do" history. And what you studied in high school—what I call the "Western-Heritage Model," this used to be the most common approach in U.S. high schools and colleges . . . in fact, it's the model I learned with, when I was growing up back—oh, about a hundred years ago . . .

Uh . . . at Middletown High School, up in Maine . . . I guess it made sense to *my* teachers back then—since, well, the history of western Europe *was* the cultural heritage of everyone in my class . . . and this remained the dominant approach in most U.S. schools till . . . oh, maybe . . . 30, 40 years ago . . . But it doesn't take more than a quick look around campus—even just this classroom today—to see that the student body in the U.S. is much more diverse than my little class in Middletown High . . . and this Western-Heritage Model was eventually replaced by—or sometimes combined with—one or more of the newer approaches . . . and I wanna take a minute to describe these to you today, so you can see where *this* course fits in.

OK . . . so . . . up until the mid-twentieth century, the basic purpose of most world-history courses was to learn about a set of values . . . institutions . . . ideas . . . which were considered the "heritage" of the people of Europe—things like . . . democracy . . . legal systems . . . types of social organization . . . artistic achievements . . .

Now, as I said, this model gives us a rather *limited* view of history. So, in the 1960s and '70s it was combined with—or replaced by—what I call the "Different-Cultures Model." The '60s were a period in which people were demanding more relevance in the curriculum, and there was criticism of the *European* focus that you were likely to find in all the academic disciplines. For the most part, the Different-Cultures Model didn't challenge the basic assumptions of the Western-Heritage Model. What it did was insist on representing *other* civilizations and cultural categories, *in addition* to those of western Europe . . .

In other words, the heritage of *all* people: not just what goes back to the Greeks and Romans, but also the origins of African . . . Asian . . . Native American civilizations. Though more inclusive, it's still, basically, a "heritage model" . . . which brings us to a *third* approach, what I call the "Patterns-of-Change Model."

Like the Different-Cultures Model, this model presents a wide cultural perspective. But, with this model, we're no longer *limited* by notions of fixed cultural or geographical boundaries. So, then, studying world history is not so much a question of how a particular nation or ethnic group developed, but rather it's a look at common themes—conflicts . . . trends—that cut across modern-day borders of nations or ethnic groups. In my opinion, this is the best way of studying history, to better understand current-day trends and conflicts.

For example, let's take the study of the Islamic world. Well, when I first learned about Islamic civilization, it was from the perspective of Europeans. Now, with the Patterns-of-Change Model, we're looking at the past through a wider lens. So *we* would be more interested, say, in how interactions with Islamic civilization—the religion . . . art . . . literature—affected cultures in Africa . . . India . . . Spain . . . and so on.

Or . . . let's take another example. Instead of looking at each cultural group as having a separate, *linear* development from some ancient origin, in *this* course we'll be looking for the common themes that go beyond cultural or regional distinctions. So . . . instead of studying . . . a particular succession of British kings . . . or a dynasty of Chinese emperors . . . in *this* course, we'll be looking at the broader concepts of monarchy, imperialism . . . and political transformation.

TRACK 89 TRANSCRIPT

Narrator
Listen again to part of the lecture. Then answer the question.

Professor
So, for example, when you looked at the title of this course in the catalog—"Introduction to World History"—what did you think you were getting into . . . what made you sign up for it—besides filling the social-science requirement?

Narrator
What is the professor's attitude?

TRACK 90 TRANSCRIPT

Environmental Science

Narrator
Listen to part of a lecture in an environmental science class.

Professor
OK, now let's talk about another environmental concern—soil erosion. It's a major problem, all around the world. Sometimes erosion damages soil so severely that the land can no longer be cultivated and it's just abandoned. That happened in a big way right here in the United States. Some of you have probably read the novel *The Grapes of Wrath*. And maybe you remember that the story took place in the 1930s, during the time of what was called the Dust Bowl.

Dust Bowl is a term we use to describe an ecological and human disaster that took place in the southern Great Plains region. For nearly eight years, dust and sand blew across the area and covered everything. It was so bad it even made breathing and eating difficult . . . and farmers could only look on helplessly as their crops were destroyed and the land . . . and their lives . . . ruined.

Now, there'd always been droughts and strong winds in that region. But that was OK because the native grasses had deep roots in the ground that were able to hold the soil in place. So the wind wasn't able to, you know, erode the soil too badly. This changed, though, between 1900 and 1930. Agriculture was expanding rapidly then, and lots of farmers in the southern Great Plains wanted to grow wheat and other crops they could sell for cash—uh, crops that would be profitable. So they ripped up much of the grassland to plant these crops like wheat, which *don't* hold the soil down nearly as well. At the same time, livestock—uh, cattle, too many of them—were feeding on grasses in the area and damaging a lot of the grassland. So these animals caused even more erosion of the soil.

It didn't help that many of the actual owners of the land were not living anywhere near the area—a lot of the landowners lived way back east, and rented out the land to local people who lived on the land and worked on it, but, um, didn't have much reason to take really good care of it. I mean, it wasn't their land, right? The tenant farmers weren't really interested in conserving someone *else's* soil—not for the long term, anyway.

Also, some thought the land couldn't really be damaged—you know, that the soil was so rich and deep that . . . it didn't matter if the topsoil, the soil on the surface, blew away. They thought they could just plow up more. But they were wrong. Good topsoil takes a long time to form—it can literally take *thousands* of years to create good topsoil that will grow vegetation—and a very short time to ruin it. So after only a few years of excessive plowing, the land pretty much couldn't be farmed anymore. And people moved on to other places and let the old areas just sit there. And when they didn't plant anything on that land, that made it vulnerable to even more erosion. So it was kind of a vicious cycle, you could say.

Another problem, ironically, was that advances in technology were actually *destroying* the land, instead of improving it. A lot of farmers were using huge new tractors that dug deep into the ground and tore up a lot of the soil.

And then, of course, there was the weather. You know, when people look back on the Dust Bowl era, they tend to blame the drought—the lack of rain between 1934 and

1937. We can't ignore the drought—I mean, it was the worst on record at the time and did help bring on this disaster. But—without the soil destruction—the drought alone wouldn't have resulted in the devastation we call the Dust Bowl. It was poor farming techniques that made that happen.

Since then, though, we've paid more attention to trying to *prevent* a future Dust Bowl. One thing Congress did was enact a massive government effort to improve soil conservation, called the Soil Erosion Act. Under this law, large stretches of land in the southern Great Plains were identified as being at risk for erosion and were taken out of production and turned into permanent grassland. What that did—by protecting the land from excessive farming—was to stabilize the soil. Also, the Soil Erosion Act helped educate farmers to practice better soil conservation techniques, like reducing how often they plowed and using better equipment that would, you know, minimize damage to the soil structure.

TRACK 91 TRANSCRIPT

Narrator
Listen again to part of the lecture. Then answer the question.

Professor
A lot of the landowners lived way back east, and rented out the land to local people who lived on the land and worked on it, but, um, didn't have much reason to take really good care of it. I mean, it wasn't their land, right?

Narrator
Why does the professor say this:

Professor
I mean, it wasn't their land, right?

TRACK 92 TRANSCRIPT

Narrator

Listen to a conversation between a student and his academic advisor.

Student

Excuse me, Ms. Chambers? Um, I don't have an appointment, but I was kinda wondering if you had a minute to help me with something.

Academic advisor

Oh, sure. Have a seat.

What's on your mind?

Student

Well, uh . . . I guess I really don't know where to start . . . It's not just one class. It's . . . I'm not doing all that great. Like on my homework assignments. And in class. And I don't know why. I mean, I just don't get it! I-I read the assignments and I do the homework and I'm still not doing too well . . .

Academic advisor

Um, which classes? You mean, like Spanish . . . you're taking Spanish, right?

Student

Oh, no, not Spanish . . . if it weren't for Spanish I'd really be in trouble . . . no, but it's really all the others, psychology and sociology especially.

Academic advisor

Is it the material, what you read in the textbooks? You don't understand it?

Student

No, that's just it—I think I understand stuff when I read it . . .

Academic advisor

You don't re . . .

Student

Remember? Well, I remember names and definitions, but . . . like, in class, when the professor asks us about the theories, what they're all about, I never have the answer.

Academic advisor

Sounds like you're trying to learn by memorizing details, instead of picking out the main points of the reading. So, tell me, how do you study?

Student

Well, I—I . . . I mean, I read the assigned chapters, and I try to underline everything . . . like all of the words I don't know, and I always memorize the definitions. But, I dunno, when I get back in class, it always seems like the other students've gotten a better handle on what was in the reading. So, maybe it's just me . . .

Academic advisor

Oh, it's not. Believe me. Lots of students . . . You know, my first year as a college student . . . I really had a hard time. I spent hours reading in the library . . . but I was just wasting time, 'cause I wasn't really studying the right things. I did the same sort of thing it sounds like you're doing, not focusing on what's really important in the reading, but on the smaller details.

Student

Yeah, maybe. But I spend so much time studying, it seems like I should be doing better.

Academic advisor

The first year of college can be a little overwhelming, I know. Point is, lots of students have trouble adjusting at first, you know, figuring out how to study, how to use their time, you know, to your best advantage. It's good that you do the assigned readings . . . but, you've . . . well, I think you're unnecessarily underlining and memorizing. That takes a lot of time, and, well, it's not the best use of your time. Here's something you can do: when you read, just read the assigned sections, and then . . . and without looking back at the text—write a summary of the key points, the main ideas in the chapter. And after you do that, it-it's good to go back and reread the text. And you look for any examples you can find to support those key points. Let me show you an example of what I mean.

TRACK 93 TRANSCRIPT

Astronomy

Narrator

Listen to part of a lecture in an astronomy class.

Professor

I'll tell you a story about how one astronomy problem was solved. It happened many years ago, but you'll see that it's interesting and still relevant. Two, three hundred years ago, astronomers already had telescopes, but they were not as powerful as those we have now. Let's say . . . they were at the level of telescopes amateur astronomers use today. Tell me, what do you see in the night sky when you use a telescope like that? Quick, tell me.

Female student

Planets . . .

Professor

Right . . .

Male student

Even . . . like . . . the moons of Jupiter?

Professor

Right . . .

Female student

Stars.

Professor

OK . . . what else? . . . You think that's all? . . . Ever heard of nebulae? . . . I bet you have . . . Well, let's just, um, put it up anyway . . .

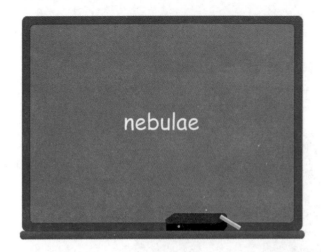

Nebulae are small fuzzy patches you see in the sky, they look like little clouds. Many of them have a spiral shape, and that's why we called them *spiral* nebulae . . . So astronomers in the eighteenth century . . . *eighteenth* century . . . when they looked through the telescope, they could see planets—and they knew those were planets . . . the moons of Jupiter—and they knew they were the moons of Jupiter . . . and then they saw spiral nebulae and they didn't have a clue.

What could those be? So, some of them thought—"these things are cloudy and fuzzy, so they're probably small clouds of cosmic dust, and they don't have to be very far away from us." But there were others who thought, "OK, the things *look* small and fuzzy, but *maybe* they're actually distant galaxies of stars, but we can't see the stars, because they're *so* far away and they seem so tiny that they *look* like dust, and even the whole galaxy looks like a tiny little cloud."

Which of the two theories do you think was more . . . uh, surprising?

Male student
The galaxy one.

Professor
And why?

Male student

Well, I mean it assumed that the nebulae are not what they look like at first sight. The first theory assumed that, right?

Professor

OK. And now tell me this . . . which one would have seemed more likely at the time?

Male student

Uh . . . They couldn't tell.

Professor

Right. Two morals here: first, there can be different explanations for the same observation. And second, "obvious" doesn't necessarily mean "right" . . . What happened next was . . . for a long time nothing. More than 150 years. No one could decide . . . Both hypotheses seemed plausible . . . And a lot was at stake—because if the *galaxy* theory was right, it would be proof that the universe is enormous . . . and if the *dust* theory was right . . . maybe *not* so enormous. So the size of the universe was at stake . . . Finally in the 1920s we came up with a telescope that was strong enough to tell us something new here. When we used it to look at the spiral nebulae, we saw . . . well, we were not absolutely sure . . . but it really looked like there were stars in those nebulae. So not dust after all, but stars . . .

But how far away were they, really? How would you measure that? Any ideas? Laura?

Female student

Well, how about measuring how strong those stars shine? Because, if the star is far away, then its light would be weak, right?

Professor

Yes . . . but there's a problem here. You need to know how bright the star is in the first place, because some stars are naturally much brighter than others. So, if you see a star that's weak . . . it can mean one of two things . . .

Female student

Oh . . . it's either far away or it's just a weak star.

Professor

And you can't really always tell which. But you're on the right track. There is a kind of star where you can *calculate* its natural brightness . . . and—you guessed it—we found some in the nebulae. It's called a *variable* star—or a "variable" for short—because its brightness *varies* in regular intervals. I won't go into detail here, but . . . basically . . . the longer the interval, the brighter the star, so from the *length* of those intervals we were able to calculate their natural brightness. This told us how distant they were—and many turned out to be very, very far away. So we can be sure that the spiral nebulae really *are* very distant galaxies—which is what some eighteenth-century astronomers *guessed* but didn't have the instruments to prove . . .

Now, one reason I told you this story is that *today* there are still plenty of situations when we see something out there, but we really aren't sure *what* it is. An example of one such mysterious observation would be gamma-ray bursters.

We've known about these gamma-ray bursters for a long time now, but we can't all agree on what they are.

TRACK 94 TRANSCRIPT

Narrator

Listen again to part of the lecture. Then answer the question.

Professor

But how far away were they, really? How would you measure that? Any ideas? Laura?

Female student

Well, how about measuring how strong those stars shine? Because, if the star is far away, then its light would be weak, right?

Professor

Yes . . . but there's a problem here. You need to know how bright the star is in the first place, because some stars are naturally much brighter than others. So, if you see a star that's weak . . . it can mean one of two things . . .

Female student

Oh . . . it's either far away or it's just a weak star.

Narrator

What can be inferred about the student when she says this:

Female student

Oh . . . it's either far away or it's just a weak star.

TRACK 95 TRANSCRIPT

Art History

Narrator

Listen to part of a lecture in an art history class.

Professor

Today we're going to talk about how to look at a piece of art, how to "*read*" it—what you should look for . . . what aspects of it you should evaluate. A lot of people think that if you stand in front of a work of art and gaze at it for a couple of minutes, you're evaluating it. But truly *reading* a piece of art, evaluating it *properly*, is a complex process, a process that takes *time*.

When we're confronted with a piece of art, there're several things we have to keep in mind, for example, its beauty . . . that's where aesthetics comes in.

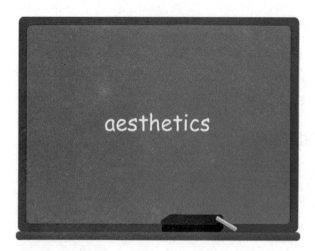

Aesthetics is the philosophy that deals with the definition of beauty, which goes all the way back to ancient Greece. They, um, the early Greek philosophers said that beauty and art are based on imitation. Their feeling about art was that it's beautiful when it imitates life; they thought that the *truthfulness* of an image, how truthful it is to life, determines its value as art. Today we have a broader definition of aesthetics.

Now *don't* identify aesthetics as personal taste. Taste is bound by time; taste is tied to a society, a given set of moral values, usually. You may not like a piece of art from a different culture—it may not be your taste—but you appreciate its beauty 'cause you recognize certain aesthetic principles. Art generally adheres to certain aesthetic principles like balance, uh, balanced proportions, contrast, movement, or rhythm.

We'll discuss aesthetics more in detail when we look at some pieces of art together. Another thing to keep in mind in evaluating art is that art has a *purpose*, generally determined by the artist. You may not know what it is, and you don't need to know what it is to appreciate a piece of art, but it helps. For example, if you know what the artist's purpose is . . . if you know that a piece of art expresses the artist's feeling about a political or social situation, you'll probably look at it differently.

Now, besides beauty and purpose, what are the other aspects of a piece of art that need to be evaluated? Very simple—you examine a piece of art following these four formal steps. The first step is *description* . . . describe physical characteristics of the piece—like this painting is large, it's oil on canvas. Describe the subject—it's a person, it's a landscape—or predominant colors like, um, earth colors . . . that's a description.

OK? So, you've described the piece. The next step is *analysis*. You're looking at the piece for any universal symbols, characters, or themes it might contain. Certain symbols are universal, and the artist counts on your understanding of symbols. Even colors have symbolic significance, as you may know. And also *objects* depicted in a piece of art are often used to represent an abstract idea. Like wheels or spheres—they look like circles, right?—so wheels and spheres represent wholeness and continuity. I have a handout, a list of these symbols and images and their interpretations, that I'll give you later. But for now, the point is that after you describe the piece of art, you *analyze* its content . . . you determine whether it contains elements that the artist is using to try to convey a certain meaning.

If it does, the next step is *interpretation*. Interpretation follows analysis very closely. You try to interpret the meaning of the symbols you identified in the piece. Almost all art has an obvious and an implied meaning. The implied meaning is hidden in the symbolic system expressed in the piece of art. What we see depicted is *one* scene, but there can be several levels of meaning. Your interpretation of these symbols makes clear what the artist is trying to tell us.

The last step is *judgment or opinion*—what do you think of the piece, is it powerful or boring?— but I give that hardly any weight. If the four steps were to be divided up into a chart, then description, analysis, and interpretation would take up 99 percent. Your opinion is not important in understanding a piece of art. It's nice to say: I like it . . . I wouldn't mind hanging it over my couch, but to evaluate a piece of art, it's not critical.

OK. Now you know what I mean by "reading" a piece of art, and what it entails. Try to keep all that in mind next time you go to an art museum. I can tell you right now that you probably won't be able to look at more than 12 pieces of art during that visit.

OK, now let's look at a slide of a piece of art and try to "read" it together.

TRACK 96 TRANSCRIPT

Narrator
What does the professor imply when he says this:

Professor
Try to keep all that in mind next time you go to an art museum. I can tell you right now that you probably won't be able to look at more than 12 pieces of art during that visit.

TRACK 97 TRANSCRIPT

Narrator

Talk about a city or town you have visited in the past. Explain what you liked most about the city and why. Include specific reasons and examples in your response.

TRACK 98 TRANSCRIPT

Narrator

Some people enjoy watching movies or television in their spare time. Others prefer reading books or magazines. State which you prefer and explain why.

TRACK 99 TRANSCRIPT

Narrator

Read the announcement about City University's plans for the campus gym. You will have 45 seconds to read. Begin reading now.

TRACK 100 TRANSCRIPT

Narrator

Listen to two students discussing the plan.

Male student

Hey, have you read about this . . . the plans for the gym?

Female student

Yeah, but I could sure think of better things to do with the money.

Male student

You're kidding. I thought you'd be all for it. You go to the gym all the time.

Female student

Yeah, but I never have any problem. Sure there're a lot of people there but I never have to wait to use the exercise bikes, or even the weight machines. Do you?

Male student

Not really. It's not *that* busy.

Female student

The other thing is . . . well, we have all sorts of exercise programs, a terrific swimming pool that's always open, great running paths, all kinds of sports teams. I'm just saying that a bunch of new machines in the gym aren't gonna make any difference. People like to get their exercise in different ways . . . and on this campus there're already plenty of choices.

Male student

You may be right . . .

Narrator

The woman expresses her opinion about the plan described in the announcement. Briefly summarize the plan. Then state her opinion about the plan and explain the reasons she gives for holding that opinion.

TRACK 101 TRANSCRIPT

Narrator

Now read the passage about keystone species. You will have 50 seconds to read the passage. Begin reading now.

TRACK 102 TRANSCRIPT

Narrator

Now listen to part of a lecture on this topic in a biology class.

Professor

Let's take the elephant, for example. Elephants are an important species in the African grasslands. Without them, the grasslands actually stop being grasslands at all if you can believe it—they change to forests. What happens is that in the grasslands some types of seeds other than grasses can sprout and begin to grow, which . . . if they're left alone . . . they could eventually grow into shrubs or trees. But what happens is that elephants come along and eat the sprouting plants . . . or the plants get crushed under the elephants' feet. And even if a plant or two manage to survive, it won't last long because sooner or later the elephant will knock it over or pull it out of the ground.

So what if the elephants weren't there and these plants were allowed to grow to maturity? Well, pretty soon there'd be whole clusters of trees. Their branches and leaves would shade the grasses . . . and without the sunlight, the grasses won't survive. So pretty soon the grass disappears, trees grow in its place and eventually the whole grassland changes to forest.

And as you can imagine the elephant has an impact on other animal species in the habitat as well. A lot of animals in this habitat rely on the grasses for food, for example. When the grasses disappear—when their food source disappears—these animals are eventually forced to leave. Gradually, some new species come into the habitat—species that are better suited to life in the forest. These new species replace the ones that left. So you can see the influence of the elephant on the environment is significant.

Narrator

The professor gives examples of the effects of elephants on the African grasslands habitat. Using the examples from the talk, explain why elephants are considered a keystone species.

TRACK 103 TRANSCRIPT

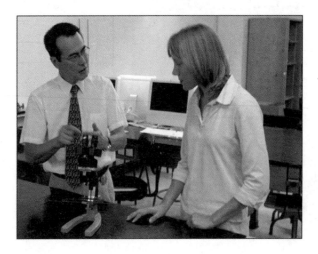

Narrator

Listen to a conversation between two biology instructors.

Female instructor

Good morning, Paul.

Male instructor

Morning. Hey, I just heard something about a problem with registration for one of the biology classes? Do you know anything about that?

Female instructor

Yeah. It looks like the Developmental Biology class is already full. Some of the students are complaining—it's a required course for them and they're pretty upset that they can't get it in this semester . . . and it's not offered next semester.

Male instructor

I can see that. They have to take that class before they can take some of the upper-level courses. So how many students are we talking about?

Female instructor

Well, so far, it looks like there are about 10 students who couldn't get in but need to take the course this semester.

Male instructor

Well, we should open a new section. I'm sure we can hire another teaching assistant to teach the class. Or maybe one of the TAs would be willing to teach two classes—they always want the extra money.

Female instructor

A new section's a great idea but are all 10 students really gonna be available at the same time?

Male instructor

Maybe not, but if they really need the course, they'll have to revise their schedules . . . it *is* a requirement.

Female instructor

Hmm. Another option is to get some of the students who don't need the class this semester . . . get them to drop the class. We should probably focus on the first-year students since they don't really need the class yet.

Male instructor

We could send out a letter explaining the situation . . . and let them know that they'll get top priority if they want to register for the class next year.

Female instructor

We might have to deal with some angry students.

Male instructor

Well, what can we do?

Narrator

Briefly summarize the problem the speakers are discussing. Then state which of the two solutions from the conversation you would recommend. Explain the reasons for your recommendation.

TRACK 104 TRANSCRIPT

Narrator

Now listen to part of a lecture in a creative writing class.

Professor

As writers, you want the dialogue in your story to have impact. Well, there are many ways to do that, and I'm gonna talk about two of them—exaggeration and understatement. Now, understatement is the opposite of exaggeration, but you can actually use them both to do the same thing—to create emphasis or impact. Let's compare them and see how they do that.

OK, exaggeration. When you want your characters to emphasize a point, you can have them describe things or their feelings as bigger or more extreme than they really are. For example, your main character comes back from a very long walk and she's very tired. Well, you can have her say "Boy, I'm tired." *Or* you can have her say, "I can't take another step." Well, *of course* she can take another step, but you see, if she exaggerates, she'll make her point in a more forceful and interesting way.

But you can also create emphasis with *understatement*, and like I said it's the opposite of exaggeration, but it does the same thing. With understatement you emphasize by saying, by saying *less*, by saying less than you mean. That sounds paradoxical, so I'll give you an example. From real life.

My friend Ed is a very talented cook. So last week he cooked me a delicious meal. Now, I could've said to him, "This food is really great, Ed," but that's kinda boring. Plus, Ed *knew* I thought the food was delicious. I'd eaten three servings. So instead I said, "This food's not bad, Ed." Now clearly the food was a lot *better* than *not bad*. But by understating, by describing the food as—as *less* good than it really was, I actually made a stronger statement. The characters in your stories can do this too.

Narrator

Using the examples mentioned by the professor, describe two ways that writers create emphasis when writing dialogue.

TRACK 105 TRANSCRIPT

Narrator

Now listen to part of a lecture on the topic you just read about.

Professor

Even if computerized smart cars meet all the technological expectations set for them, it's not clear that they'd produce the benefits some have predicted.

Smart cars will still get into some accidents. After all, even the most technologically advanced devices fail occasionally. And since the smart car technology will allow cars to be more tightly packed together on the roads, these accidents will be pileups that involve many more cars and so be much worse than accidents that occur today. Overall, there is little reason to believe that smart cars will save lives or reduce the number of injuries in automobile accidents.

Second, let's talk about the potential to increase highway speeds and therefore decrease commuting time. Well, history has consistently shown that when some driving convenience is introduced, more and more people decide to drive because they expect an easier driving experience. But then the increased number of drivers in the case of smart cars of the future would not decrease commuting time. This is because the traffic congestion caused by the additional cars on the road would not allow the drivers to take advantage of the smart cars' potential for higher speeds.

And finally, it's not reasonable to expect that smart cars will save drivers money. The global positioning technology required to direct smart cars to their desired destinations is very expensive, and smart cars will need other costly technologies too, such as sensors that control how far a smart car stays behind the car in front of it. Moreover, the advanced technology of smart cars will make repairs to them more expensive than repairs on conventional automobiles. These new expenses will more than offset the expected savings on the repair and replacement of traditional mechanical car parts.

TRACK 106 TRANSCRIPT

Narrator

Summarize the points made in the lecture, being sure to explain how they challenge specific points made in the reading passage.

TOEFL® Test Prep
PLANNER

Contents

Foreword

Congratulations! You've made the right decision to take the TOEFL® test—the test that gives you the unmatched advantage over other English-language tests.

There's no question that the TOEFL test is the most widely accepted English-language test in the world—that's why we say the TOEFL test can help you "go anywhere." More than 8,500 colleges, universities and agencies in 130 countries accept TOEFL scores, including the U.S. and Canada as well as the U.K. and Australia. This gives you the flexibility of sending your test scores to any of these destinations. It's no wonder more than 27 million people have taken the TOEFL test since it was introduced in 1964.

The TOEFL test is also the most highly respected English-language test in the world. In fact, it's the only test that simulates university classroom and campus life and was developed with the help of leading universities. By doing well on the TOEFL iBT® test, you will prove you have the reading, listening, speaking and writing skills that universities are looking for—and show that you can effectively combine these skills to communicate your ideas in and out of the classroom. Preparing for the test will help you build the English skills you need to succeed in an academic setting and beyond.

TOEFL® Test Prep Planner

That's the purpose of this *TOEFL Test Prep Planner*—to help you understand how to prepare for the test effectively and to help you build the English skills you need to succeed. Chapter 1 provides you with a test preparation plan to use in the eight weeks leading up to your test date. Chapter 2 gives you general information about the test and scoring. Chapters 3 through 6 provide more information about the four sections of the test as well as activities you can do to build your skills. Chapter 7 tells you what to do on and after test day.

PLAN

We've also created a special website with useful links to accompany the *Planner* at **www.ets.org/toefl/planner**.

ePLAN

Sample Questions

We know that working with sample questions is essential to preparing for the test, so the *Planner* includes examples of question types from each of the four skills sections. See Appendix 1.

Test takers have told us that simulations of the test are also important, so the chart below shows you where to find sample questions that can simulate the test to varying degrees. Some of these samples are included on the *Planner* website, while others are available for purchase in order to enhance your preparation experience.

Source of Authentic Sample Questions

Source	Number of Questions	Format	Simulation of the TOEFL iBT® Testing Experience	Where Available
Free Sample Questions	At least one of each question type: 14 Reading 11 Listening 6 Speaking 2 Writing	Download (with audio and sample Speaking responses)	Medium	**ePLAN** www.ets.org/toefl/planner
		Print	Low	**PLAN** Appendix 1: Sample questions
TOEFL iBT® Test Online Sampler®	13 Reading 11 Listening 3 Speaking 1 Writing	Online	High	**SAMP** Link to it from your online test registration profile
The Official Guide to the TOEFL® Test	Hundreds of practice questions and essay topics, including full practice tests	eBook or paper book with DVD	Medium	**OG** www.ets.org/toefl/guide
TOEFL® Practice Online	4 complete tests available, with same-day scoring and feedback	Online	High	**TPO** www.ets.org/toeflpractice

Other free resources that you may find helpful on the path to your destination:

- TOEFL website at ***www.ets.org/toefl***
- TOEFL *Go Anywhere* website at ***www.toeflgoanywhere.org***
- TOEFL® TV Channel at ***www.youtube.com/TOEFLtv***

The Path to Your TOEFL® Destination

You need to complete many steps to get to the college or university of your choice. We hope you've been progressing on the path to your TOEFL® Destination by completing Steps 1 through 4 below. If not, please work on completing these four steps now. Then move on to Step 5 to use this Planner to prepare and practice for the test.

Choose your destinations

If you don't know where to apply, choose from the 8,500 institutions in 130 countries in the **TOEFL® Destinations Directory** at **www.toeflgoanywhere.org**.

Know your destination deadlines and requirements

Research application deadlines and score requirements for each of your university or college destinations. You can start your score requirement research with the **TOEFL Destinations Directory** and then contact the institution for more specific requirements. If you're applying for postgraduate studies, find out if your institution requires the *GRE®* or other tests. You can go to the GRE website at **www.ets.org/gre** for more information.

Decide when and where to take the test

Choose an available test date from among 4,500 testing locations in over 165 countries. Plan to take the test at least two to three months before your institution's application deadline.

Register for the TOEFL iBT® Test three to four months before your test date

Register at your **TOEFL® Test Resource Centre**, if you have one in your area. You can also register by phone, online or by mail. Go to **www.toeflgoanywhere.org** for more information on how to register.

Prepare and practice

Use this *TOEFL Test Prep Planner* and follow the test preparation plan during the eight weeks leading up to your test date.

CHAPTER 1 Using the *Planner*

You've been studying English for some time now, so you've developed a level of proficiency in your reading, listening, speaking and writing skills. Now you'll want to make sure you're familiar with the test format and that you're ready to do your best. This *Planner* gives you test information, sample questions and activities to build your skills, and much more.

> To supplement the *Planner* materials, we encourage you to purchase these additional resources:
>
> Two complete tests on **TOEFL® Practice Online** at **www.ets.org/toeflpractice**. TOEFL Practice Online allows you to experience the real test and get instant scores and feedback.
>
> ***The Official Guide to the TOEFL® Test*** at **www.ets.org/toefl/guide**. This book provides practice with hundreds of real TOEFL questions and has a CD-ROM with full-length, authentic practice tests. It is available in both eBook and print formats.

Getting Started

It's important that you surround yourself with English and use it as much as possible between now and test day. Be sure to keep in mind that memorizing and cramming aren't good ways to prepare for the TOEFL test.

We've provided you with a plan to help you thoroughly prepare for the test in the eight weeks leading up to test day. The chart on the following pages indicates each week's objective, tasks to complete and resources to help you complete them, as well as a checklist so you can check off each task as you complete it.

Following is the actual order of the test sections: Reading, Listening, Speaking and Writing. The *Planner* leads the chapters with Speaking (with Reading, Listening and Writing following) because Speaking is often the skill students are least familiar and comfortable with; however, you may wish to change this order to work on improving your weakest skills first.

WEEK 1		
OBJECTIVES	**TASKS AND RESOURCES**	**COMPLETED**
Determine your target scores	• Determine your total score (and section scores if available) by researching the score requirements of your TOEFL® Destination institution at **www.toeflgoanywhere.org**.	Target scores: Reading _____ Listening _____ Speaking _____ Writing _____ **Total** _____
Familiarize yourself with the test	• Read *Planner* Chapter 2: About the TOEFL iBT® Test. • **ePLAN** Review the Test Overview section on the *Planner* website **www.ets.org/toefl/planner**.	☐ ☐
Learn from others' test experiences	• Join online chat rooms, blogs or social networking sites. • Network with students who have taken the test.	☐ ☐
View and experience the *TOEFL iBT® Test Online Sampler®*	• **SAMP** Access the Sampler from the "View Order" link on your profile when you register online.	☐
Take a complete TOEFL practice test to establish your starting point	• **TPO** Go to **www.ets.org/toeflpractice** to purchase tests. • Take one complete practice test now to establish your starting point. • Chart your scores in the checklist column. Add all of your section scores to calculate your total score. Convert your ratings on the Speaking and Writing sections to scaled scores by using the conversion chart in Appendix 6.	☐ ☐ My scores: Reading _____ Listening _____ Speaking _____ Writing _____ **Total** _____
Purchase *The Official Guide to the TOEFL® Test*	• **OG** *The Official Guide to the TOEFL® Test* includes hundreds of TOEFL passages, questions and topics from previous tests. It includes a CD-ROM with complete practice tests. • Purchase the book online at **www.ets.org/toefl/guide** or from your local bookstore in eBook or print format.	☐ ☐

WEEK 2		
OBJECTIVES	**TASKS AND RESOURCES**	**COMPLETED**
Learn about the Speaking section	• Read *Planner* Chapter 3: Speaking.	☐
View and experience sample Speaking questions	• See sample Speaking questions in *Planner* Appendix 1.	☐
	• Review Speaking Scoring Guides in *Planner* Appendix 3 to understand what score levels mean.	☐
	• **ePLAN** Listen to sample responses and view raters' comments on the *Planner* website **www.ets.org/toefl/planner** to help you identify your current level and understand what a response at your desired level is like. Refer to the Scoring Guides as you listen.	☐
Practice your Speaking skills	• Pick three general activities and three targeted activities from Chapter 3 (pages 17–20) to work on your Speaking skills. • **OG** Use the Speaking chapter in *The Official Guide to the TOEFL® Test* (Chapter 4) for more practice.	Activity 1 _____ Activity 2 _____ Activity 3 _____ Activity 4 _____ Activity 5 _____ Activity 6 _____
WEEK 3		
OBJECTIVES	**TASKS AND RESOURCES**	**COMPLETED**
Learn about the Reading section	• Read *Planner* Chapter 4: Reading.	☐
View and experience sample Reading questions	• **ePLAN** Review sample Reading questions in *Planner* Appendix 1 and experience them on the *Planner* website **www.ets.org/toefl/planner**.	☐
Practice your Reading skills	• Pick three general activities and three targeted activities from Chapter 4 (pages 23–25) to work on your Reading skills. • **OG** Use the Reading chapter in *The Official Guide to the TOEFL® Test* (Chapter 2) for more practice.	Activity 1 _____ Activity 2 _____ Activity 3 _____ Activity 4 _____ Activity 5 _____ Activity 6 _____

Reading as much as possible in English is an essential part of building your reading skills.

Go to www.lexile.com/toefl for a list of books that are associated with TOEFL iBT® skill levels.

WEEK 4		
OBJECTIVES	TASKS AND RESOURCES	COMPLETED
Learn about the Listening section	• Read *Planner* Chapter 5: Listening.	☐
View and experience sample Listening questions	• **ePLAN** Review sample Listening questions in *Planner* Appendix 1 and experience them on the *Planner* website **www.ets.org/toefl/planner**.	☐
Practice your Listening skills	• Pick three general activities and three targeted activities from Chapter 5 (pages 28–30) to work on your Listening skills. • **OG** Use the Listening chapter in *The Official Guide to the TOEFL® Test* (Chapter 3) for more practice.	Activity 1 _____ Activity 2 _____ Activity 3 _____ Activity 4 _____ Activity 5 _____ Activity 6 _____
WEEK 5		
OBJECTIVES	TASKS AND RESOURCES	COMPLETED
Learn about the Writing section	• Read *Planner* Chapter 6: Writing.	☐
View and experience sample Writing questions	• See sample Writing questions in *Planner* Appendix 1.	☐
	• Review Writing Scoring Guides in *Planner* Appendix 4 to understand what score levels mean.	☐
	• **ePLAN** Read sample responses and raters' comments in Appendix 1 to help you identify your current level and understand what a response at your desired level is like. Refer to the Scoring Guides as you read.	☐
Practice your Writing skills	• Pick three general activities and three targeted activities from Chapter 6 (pages 34–37) to work on your Writing skills. • **OG** Use the Writing chapter in *The Official Guide to the TOEFL® Test* (Chapter 5) for more practice.	Activity 1 _____ Activity 2 _____ Activity 3 _____ Activity 4 _____ Activity 5 _____ Activity 6 _____

WEEK 6		
OBJECTIVES	**TASKS AND RESOURCES**	**COMPLETED**
Planning for test day	• Read *Planner* Chapter 7: Test Day and Beyond and gather the documents you will need to take with you.	
Take a complete TOEFL practice test to measure your progress	• **OG** Take a complete practice test in *The Official Guide to the TOEFL® Test*. Use the instructions in the *Guide* to calculate your Reading and Listening scaled scores. • Time yourself for each section and try to simulate the test setting.	My scores: Reading _____ Listening _____
Get evaluations for Speaking and Writing	• Ask a teacher or tutor to evaluate your Speaking responses to the practice test using the Scoring Guides in Appendix 3 of the *Planner*. Use the conversion charts in Appendix 6 to convert the ratings to a scaled score. • Ask a teacher or tutor to evaluate your Writing responses to the practice test using the Scoring Guides in Appendix 4 of the *Planner*. Use the conversion charts in Appendix 6 to convert the ratings to a scaled score.	My scores: Speaking _____ Writing _____
Practice more on your weakest skills	• Compare your scores to your first test in Week 1. Decide which skills to focus on. • Review the *Planner* chapters that correspond to your weakest skills. • Complete three additional activities for each of your weakest skills. • **OG** Use Chapters 2 through 5 of *The Official Guide to the TOEFL® Test* for more practice.	☐ ☐ Activity 1 _____ Activity 2 _____ Activity 3 _____

WEEK 7		
OBJECTIVES	**TASKS AND RESOURCES**	**COMPLETED**
Take a second complete TOEFL practice test to establish your readiness for test day	• **TPO** Take a second complete practice test online at **www.ets.org/toeflpractice**. Add all of your section scores to calculate your total score. Convert your ratings on the Speaking and Writing sections to scaled scores by using the conversion chart in Appendix 6. • Stay in Timed Mode as much as possible to simulate the test setting. • Review the directions for each section as you go through the practice test. • Compare these scores to the scores on your online practice test from Week 2 to Week 7. Decide which of the four skills to focus on.	My scores: Reading _____ Listening _____ Speaking _____ Writing _____ **Total** _____ ☐ ☐ ☐

Continue preparing	• Focus on improving your weakest skills using the *Planner* and *The Official Guide to the TOEFL® Test*.	☐

WEEK 8		
OBJECTIVES	**TASKS AND RESOURCES**	**COMPLETED**
Continue preparing	• Focus on improving your weakest skills using the *Planner* and *The Official Guide to the TOEFL® Test*.	☐
Take another practice test	• **OG** Take another complete practice test in *The Official Guide to the TOEFL® Test*. Use the instructions in the *Guide* to calculate your Reading and Listening scaled scores.	My scores: Reading _____ Listening _____
	• Time yourself for each section and try to simulate the test setting.	☐
Get evaluations for Speaking and Writing	• Ask a teacher or tutor to evaluate your Speaking responses to the practice test using the Scoring Guides in Appendix 3 of the *Planner*. Use the conversion charts in Appendix 6 to convert the ratings to a scaled score. • Ask a teacher or tutor to evaluate your Writing responses to the practice test using the Scoring Guides in Appendix 4 of the *Planner*. Use the conversion charts in Appendix 6 to convert the ratings to a scaled score.	My scores: Speaking _____ Writing _____
Gather your documents	• Review *Planner* Chapter 7: Test Day and Beyond.	☐
	• You'll need a photo ID and your Registration Confirmation. Check with your TOEFL Test Resource Centre or **www.ets.org/toefl/id** for ID requirements in your country.	☐
	• Return to your online registration profile and print out your confirmation. Check for any changes in your testing details.	☐
	• Get directions to your testing site and make transportation plans.	☐

CHAPTER 2

About the TOEFL iBT® Test

The TOEFL iBT® test measures the English language skills important for effective communication in an academic setting. It consists of four sections: Reading, Listening, Speaking and Writing. The entire test is about four hours long, and all sections are taken on the same day.

The TOEFL iBT test uses integrated tasks that require test takers to combine skills just as they would in a real academic setting. The integrated questions ask test takers to:

- read, listen and then speak in response to a question

- listen and then speak in response to a question

- read, listen and then write in response to a question

Test Format

The following chart shows the possible number of questions and the timing for each section of the test. The time limit for each section varies according to the number of questions. Every test contains either a longer Reading section or a longer Listening section.

Test Section	Number of Questions	Timing
Reading	3–4 passages, 12–14 questions each	60–80 minutes
Listening	4–6 lectures, 6 questions each 2–3 conversations, 5 questions each	60–90 minutes
BREAK		10 minutes
Speaking	6 tasks: 2 independent and 4 integrated	20 minutes
Writing	1 integrated task 1 independent task	20 minutes 30 minutes

Test Administration

- The TOEFL iBT® test is administered via computer from a secure Internet-based network.

- Instructions for answering questions are given with each section. Test takers can take notes throughout the entire test. At the end of testing, all notes are collected and destroyed to ensure test security.

- For the Speaking section, test takers wear headphones and speak into a microphone. Responses are digitally recorded and sent to the ETS Online Scoring Network where three to six human raters score the responses.

- For the Writing section, test takers type their responses. Responses are sent to the ETS Online Scoring Network, where they are rated by four raters—two human raters for the integrated task, one human rater and one *e-rater®* for the independent task. (With *e-rater*, your responses are scored by the computer.)

- All human raters are trained and certified by ETS and are continuously monitored throughout the day each time they rate.

- Scores are reported both online and by mail.

About Test Scores

Score Scales

The TOEFL iBT test provides scores in four skill areas:

Reading	0–30
Listening	0–30
Speaking	0–30
Writing	0–30
Total Score	**0–120** (The total score is the sum of the four section scores.)

Score Reports

The score reports provide information about your readiness to participate and succeed in academic studies in an English-speaking setting. Score reports include:

- four skill scores

- total score

Scores are reported online approximately ten days after the test. You can view your scores online free of charge. Paper copies are mailed shortly after the scores are posted online if you opted to receive a hard copy. Please see Appendix 2 for a sample examinee score report.

Colleges, universities and agencies also can view your scores online and/or receive paper score reports when you have selected them as score recipients. You can do this free of charge for up to four score recipients when you register, or you can do it after the test for a small fee. See Chapter 7 for more information.

Score Requirements

Each institution sets its own requirements for TOEFL iBT® scores. These minimums depend on factors such as the applicant's field of study, the level of study (undergraduate or graduate), whether the applicant will be a teaching assistant and whether the institution offers English as a Second Language support for its students.

ETS has collected the score requirements of many TOEFL® Destination institutions. For your convenience, these are included in the **TOEFL Destinations Directory** at **www.toeflgoanywhere.org**. However, we advise you to check with your particular program or department at your target destination to find out if they have any special score requirements.

Speaking

Academic Speaking Skills

The Speaking section measures your ability to speak English effectively in academic settings, during class as well as outside the classroom. The tasks in this section resemble the real-life situations that students encounter:

- **During a class**, students are expected to respond to questions, participate in academic discussions, summarize what they read and hear, and express their views on topics under discussion.

- **Outside the classroom**, students participate in casual conversations, express their opinions and communicate with people in such places as the bookstore, the library, the cafeteria and the housing office.

Speaking Section Description

In the Speaking section, you will be asked to speak on a variety of topics that draw on personal experience, campus-based situations and academic content. The Speaking section is approximately 20 minutes long and includes six questions.

The first two questions are called Independent Speaking Tasks because they require you to draw entirely on your own ideas, opinions and experiences when you respond.

The other four questions are called Integrated Speaking Tasks because they require you to integrate your English-language skills—listening and speaking, or listening, reading and speaking—just as you must during class and outside the classroom.

Speaking Task Types

TASK TYPE	TASK DESCRIPTION	TIMING
Independent Tasks		
1. Personal Preference	This question asks you to express and defend a personal choice from a given category—for example, important people, places, events or activities that you enjoy.	Preparation time: 15 seconds Response time: 45 seconds
2. Choice	This question asks you to make and defend a personal choice between two contrasting behaviors or courses of action.	Preparation time: 15 seconds Response time: 45 seconds
Integrated Tasks		
	Read/Listen/Speak	
3. Campus Situation Topic: Fit and Explain	• A reading passage (75–100 words) presents a campus-related issue. • A listening passage (60–80 seconds; 150–180 words) comments on the issue in the reading passage. • The question asks you to summarize the speaker's opinion within the context of the reading passage.	Preparation time: 30 seconds Response time: 60 seconds
4. Academic Course Topic: General/Specific	• A reading passage (75–100 words) broadly defines a term, process or idea from an academic subject. • An excerpt from a lecture (60–90 seconds; 150–220 words) provides examples and specific information to illustrate the term, process or idea from the reading passage. • The question asks you to combine and convey important information from the reading passage and the lecture excerpt.	Preparation time: 30 seconds Response time: 60 seconds
	Listen/Speak	
5. Campus Situation Topic: Problem/Solution	• The listening passage (60–90 seconds; 180–220 words) is a conversation about a student-related problem and two possible solutions. • The question asks you to demonstrate an understanding of the problem and to express an opinion about solving the problem.	Preparation time: 20 seconds Response time: 60 seconds
6. Academic Course Topic: Summary	• The listening passage (90–120 seconds; 230–280 words) is an excerpt from a lecture that explains a term or concept and gives concrete examples to illustrate that term or concept. • The question asks you to summarize the lecture and demonstrate an understanding of the relationship between the examples and the overall topic.	Preparation time: 20 seconds Response time: 60 seconds
TOTAL		**20 minutes**

Speaking Responses

Like all the other sections of the TOEFL iBT® test, the Speaking section is delivered via computer. For all Speaking tasks, you'll use a headset with a microphone.

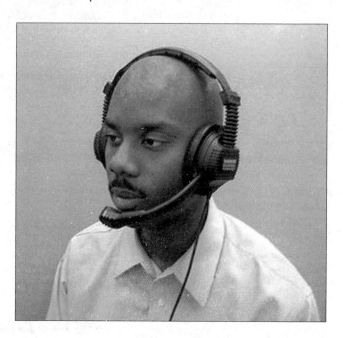

For Speaking questions that involve listening, you'll hear short spoken passages or conversations. For Speaking questions that involve reading, you'll read short written passages on your computer screen. You can take notes throughout the Speaking section and use your notes when you respond to the questions.

Your responses will be recorded and sent to the ETS Online Scoring Network where they will be scored by experienced raters.

How Speaking Responses Are Scored

Your responses will be scored holistically. This means that raters listen for various features in your response and assign a single score based on the overall skill you display in your answer. Although scoring criteria vary somewhat depending on the question, the raters generally will be listening for the following features in your answer:

- **Delivery:** How clear and fluid your speech is, including good pronunciation, natural pacing and natural-sounding intonation patterns.

- **Language Use:** How effectively you use grammar and vocabulary to convey your ideas.

- **Topic Development:** How fully you answer the question and how coherently you present your ideas. Good responses generally use all or most of the time allotted, and the relationship between ideas and the progression from one idea to the next is clear and easy to follow.

For more detailed criteria, see the Speaking Scoring Guides in Appendix 3. These will help you better understand how responses are evaluated.

It's important to note that raters don't expect your response to be perfect, and high-scoring responses may contain occasional errors and minor lapses in any of the three areas described above.

Speaking Skills Practice

The best way to practice speaking is with native speakers of English. In some countries, you can find English-speaking tutors or assistants to help you with conversation skills and overall communication skills. If you can't do that, find a friend to practice speaking with every day.

Targeted Activities

Independent Speaking

Try the following activities to build the skills you'll need for the Independent Speaking tasks:

- Make a list of topics that are familiar to you and practice speaking about them. The topics can be academic or non-academic (sports, hobbies, travel, etc.).

- Think for 20 seconds about what you did yesterday, then recount your experiences in one minute. Remember to use the past tense of verbs and use connecting words and phrases, such as "first," "then" and "while I was."

- Think for 20 seconds about what you plan to do tomorrow, then talk about it for one minute.

- Think of a story with which you are familiar. Tell the story to several different people. Try to tell the story faster each time.

- Collect a number of pictures from magazines and newspapers. Look at each picture, then describe it in one minute. Describe the same thing more than once, using different adjectives and adding details.

Complete these Week 2 tasks and update the checklist on page 9.

- See sample Speaking questions in *Planner* Appendix 1 and experience them on the *Planner* website at **www.ets.org/toefl/planner**.

- Review Speaking Scoring Guides in *Planner* Appendix 3 to understand what score levels mean.

- **ePLAN** Listen to sample responses and view raters' comments on the *Planner* website to help you identify your current level and your desired level.

General Speaking Practice

- Practice using language for giving opinions, language for describing problems and solutions, and language to compare and contrast.

- Learn to use idiomatic and informal speech naturally and appropriately by listening to native English speakers and trying to mimic their expressions.

- Practice using contractions, such as *it's*, *there's*, *I'm* and so on, in order to sound more natural when speaking.

- Work on pronunciation, including word stress, intonation patterns and pauses. There are a number of products and websites that can help you develop pronunciation skills, including *Pronunciation in English* from AmEnglish.com® and ETS.

- State an opinion or a preference for something familiar and present clear, detailed reasons for your choices. Use connecting words or phrases to help explain your opinion (for example, "the reason I prefer" or "this is important to me because").

- Make a recommendation about a topic of concern or interest to you and explain why your idea is the best way to proceed.

- Think about topics related to student life (for example, the types of classes you enjoy taking or the best place to study). For each topic, write down two reasons to explain your preference and speak on this topic for one minute.

- Write down topics on slips of paper. Each day, choose one randomly and practice giving a one-minute response. Repeat your responses to each topic two or three times to build fluency.

Targeted Activities

Integrated Speaking

These activities can help build the skills you'll need for the Integrated Speaking tasks:

- Listen to a talk on the National Geographic website at **www.nationalgeographic.com/** and take notes. Then use your notes to give a summary of the talk to a friend and eventually record a one-minute oral summary.

- Read an article or listen to a talk on an issue that interests you (for example, the environment). Prepare an outline for a one-minute opinion speech about the article or talk. Your outline should include your opinion, two points to support your opinion and one detail/reason to support each point.

- Find campus newspaper articles on the Internet. After reading the articles, express your opinions about them to a friend.

- Read a short article from a newspaper or a textbook. Write down two or three questions and then answer them orally. Eventually, record your answers to the questions.

- Find a textbook in English that includes study questions at the end of each chapter. Practice answering the questions orally. Start by reading about subjects with which you're familiar and later move on to less familiar subjects.

- Find listening and reading material on the <u>same</u> topic. The material can contain similar or different views. The listening material can be a news report on a current topic on TV or radio, and the reading material can be a newspaper or Internet report.

  - Take notes or create lists of important points on the listening and reading material.

  - Do separate oral summaries of the information in the listening and reading material. Practice paraphrasing using different words and grammatical structures.

  - Combine the information from the reading and listening material and explain in writing how they relate. Later, practice explaining it orally using only your notes for reference.

  - State an opinion about the ideas and information presented in the reading and listening material and explain how they relate.

  - If the reading and/or listening material describes a problem, suggest and explain your own solution to the problem.

Practice Tips for the Speaking Section

- When you practice for the TOEFL iBT® Speaking section, take 15 seconds to think about what you're going to say before you speak. Write down a few key words and ideas and plan how you will organize your response. Don't attempt to write down exactly what you're going to say. It's a waste of your time, and raters will be able to detect responses that are read and will give them a lower rating.

- Record your responses and replay them. Evaluate your effort by asking yourself these questions:
  - Did I complete the task?
  - Did I speak clearly?
  - Did I make grammatical errors?
  - Did I use words correctly?
  - Did I organize my ideas clearly and appropriately?
  - Did I use the time effectively?
  - Did I speak too quickly or too slowly?
  - Did I pause too often?

- Record your response another time a few days later. Compare these responses with your earlier responses.

- Ask an English teacher or tutor to evaluate your recordings using the appropriate TOEFL iBT Speaking Scoring Guides from Appendix 3.

Complete these Week 2 tasks and update the checklist on page 9.

- Pick three general activities and three targeted activities from pages 19–21 to work on your Speaking skills.

- **OG** Use the Speaking chapter in *The Official Guide to the TOEFL® Test* (Chapter 4) for more practice.

Group Speaking Activities

Have fun trying these activities to practice your speaking skills with friends or a study group:

- Make "note cards" with description prompts. For example, describe your favorite restaurant, your best friend or an ideal house. Put the cards face down, choose one and respond in 45 seconds.

- Join a club whose members meet to converse in English about movies, music and travel. If a club doesn't exist in your area, start one. Invite native English speakers to join you.

- With a group, list opinion topics and write these on cards. Topics might include research papers vs. oral presentations, laptops vs. desktops, school uniforms vs. wearing regular clothes to school, and so on. Each person chooses a card, prepares a one-minute presentation and then presents to the group. The speaker must support his or her opinion with reasons. The group then can debate each topic.

- Divide group members into pairs. Have each pair of partners choose a common problem college students face and brainstorm two solutions to the problem. They should prepare role-plays in which one person describes the problem and the other provides the solutions and indicates which solution he or she prefers and why.

- Practice using transition words and phrases such as *however, first, on the other hand* and *in contrast* to help listeners follow your speech. With a group, write as many transitions as you can think of on cards. Each person must randomly choose one card and then create two sentences connected by the transition word on the card. You can use a timer and allow each person 30 seconds to respond.

- Set up a discussion club with a group of friends. Each week, one member chooses a talk or a speech (available online or in audio or video form) and everyone in the group listens to it. When the group gets together, the leader for that week summarizes the talk/speech and leads a discussion on the topic.

Reading

Academic Reading Skills

The Reading section measures your ability to understand university-level academic texts and passages. In many academic settings around the world, students are expected to read and understand information from textbooks and other academic materials written in English. The following are three purposes for academic reading:

Reading to Find Information

- Effectively scanning text for key facts and important information

- Increasing reading fluency and rate

Basic Comprehension

- Understanding the general topic or main idea, major points, important facts and details, vocabulary in context, and pronoun usage

- Making inferences about what is implied in a passage

Reading to Learn

- Recognizing the organization and purpose of a passage

- Understanding relationships between ideas

- Organizing information into a category chart or a summary in order to recall major points and important details

- Inferring how ideas connect throughout the passage

Reading Section Description

The TOEFL iBT® Reading section includes three to four reading passages. There are 12 to 14 questions per passage. You have 60 to 80 minutes to answer all the questions in the section.

Complete these Week 3 tasks and update the checklist on page 9.

- **ePLAN** Review sample Reading questions in Planner Appendix 1 and experience them on the *Planner* website at www.ets.org/toefl/planner.

Reading Passages

TOEFL iBT® Reading passages are excerpts from university-level textbooks that would be used in introductions to a discipline or topic. The excerpts are changed as little as possible because the goal is to assess how well you can read the kind of writing that is used in an academic environment.

The passages will cover a variety of different subjects. You don't need to be familiar with the topic of a passage. All the information you need to answer the questions will be in the passage itself.

Often passages present information about the topic from more than one perspective or point of view. This is something you should note as you read because you'll usually be asked at least one question that allows you to show that you have understood the general organization of the passage.

You must read through or scroll to the end of each passage before receiving questions on that passage. Once the questions appear, the passage appears on the right side of the computer screen. The questions are on the left. (To see how they appear on screen, download the sample questions on the *Planner* website.)

Reading Question Formats

There are three question formats in the Reading section:

- Questions with four choices and a single answer in traditional multiple-choice format

- Questions with four choices and a single answer that ask you to "insert a sentence" where it fits best in a passage

- "Reading to learn" questions with more than four choices that ask you to select more than one answer

Each passage is accompanied by a "reading to learn" question. These questions test your ability to recognize how the passage is organized and to understand the relationships among facts and ideas in different parts of the passage.

For these questions, you're asked to sort information and place the text options provided into a **category chart** or **summary**. The summary questions are worth up to two points each. The chart questions are worth up to three points if there are five options presented, and up to four points if there are seven options presented.

Reading Skills Practice

You can improve your reading skills in English by reading regularly, especially university textbooks or other materials that cover a variety of subject areas—such as sciences, social sciences, arts, business—and are written in an academic style.

The Internet is one of the best resources for reading material, but books, magazines or journals of any kind are very helpful as well. It's best to include material that is more academic in style, the kind that would be found in university courses.

> Reading as much as possible in English is an essential part of building your reading skills. Go to **www.lexile.com/toefl** for a list of books that are associated with TOEFL iBT® skill levels.

General Reading Activities

You might try these general activities to practice your reading skills:

- Increase your vocabulary by keeping a journal of new words:

    - Group word lists by academic subject areas—such as biology, geology, psychology—and create flash cards to review the words frequently.

    - Learn to recognize the meanings of prefixes, suffixes and common roots of words.

- Study the organization of academic texts:

    - Look for the main ideas and the supporting details and pay attention to the relationship between them. Notice how the end of one sentence relates to the beginning of the next sentence.

    - Make a list of the important points of the passage and then write a summary of it. If the text is a comparison, be sure your summary reflects that. If the text argues two points of view, be sure both are reflected in your summary.

- Work with a friend to improve your reading skills. You read an article from a journal or magazine and your friend reads a different article. Each person makes up five basic information questions (who, what, where, when, how and why). Exchange articles, read the new article and answer each other's questions.

- Read a Reading passage from *The Official Guide to the TOEFL® Test* or from any academic text. Think about the main idea of each paragraph and then write a "headline" for each paragraph. The "headline" should be short (five to eight words) and it should capture the main idea of the paragraph. Then write a five- to six-sentence summary of the entire passage.

- Make a copy of an article from a newspaper or from an academic text. Cut the text into paragraphs and then try to put the text back together. Look for words that give you clues about the ordering of the paragraphs to help you put the text back together.

- Work on increasing your reading speed. This can be done by timing yourself as you read. Read a short text (article or short reading from a text) once and record the time it takes you to read it. Then read it again and try to improve your reading speed.

- Set up a book club with your classmates or friends. Have each person choose something for everyone to read. Set up a schedule and discuss one reading at each meeting.

- Keep a reading log in which you write summaries or responses to texts you read.

> The TOEFL iBT® Reading section does not measure summarizing skills, but learning to summarize reading passages will help you on the Speaking and Writing sections.

Targeted Activities

Reading to Find Information

Try these activities to practice for "Reading to Find Information" questions:

- Scan passages to find and highlight key facts (dates, numbers, terms) and information. Look for capital letters, numbers and symbols, and special formatting (such as italics) as you scan.

- Look for words in a passage that have the same meaning. Highlight each one with the same color marker. Then look at the way the writer used these words with similar meanings.

Targeted Activities

Reading for Basic Comprehension

Try these activities to practice for "Reading for Basic Comprehension" questions:

- Practice skimming a passage quickly to get a general impression of the main idea instead of carefully reading each word and each sentence. Practice reading the introductory paragraph, the first sentences of paragraphs and the concluding paragraph to get the gist of a passage.

- Develop the ability to skim quickly and identify major points. After skimming a passage, read it again more carefully and write down the main idea, major points and important facts.

- Choose some unfamiliar words in a passage and guess the meaning from the context (surrounding sentences). Then look the words up to confirm their meaning.

- Underline all pronouns (for example: he, him, they, them, etc.) and identify the nouns to which they refer in the passage.

- Paraphrase individual sentences in a passage. Then paraphrase entire paragraphs.

Targeted Activities

Reading to Learn

- Whenever you read, identify the passage type (cause/effect, compare/contrast, classification, problem/solution, description, narration).

- Organize the information in the passage:

  - Make a list of the major points of the passage and the minor points that support them.

  - If the passage categorizes information, create a chart and place the information in appropriate categories.

  - Create an oral or written summary of the passage using the charts, lists and outlines.

About charts and the TOEFL iBT® Reading section: You won't be asked to create charts on the test. Instead, a chart with possible answer choices will be provided and you'll be asked to fill in the chart with the correct choices. By creating practice charts, however, you can practice categorizing information, and soon will be able to do so with ease.

Complete these Week 3 tasks and update the checklist on page 9.

- Pick three general activities and three targeted activities from pages 25–27 to work on your Reading skills.

- **OG** Use the Reading chapter in *The Official Guide to the TOEFL® Test* (Chapter 2) for more practice.

Listening

Academic Listening Skills

The Listening section measures your ability to understand spoken English. In academic settings, you must be able to listen to lectures and conversations. Academic listening is typically done for one of the three following purposes:

Listening for Basic Comprehension

- Comprehend the main idea, major points and important details related to the main idea

Listening for Pragmatic Understanding[1]

- Recognize a speaker's attitude and degree of certainty
- Recognize a speaker's function or purpose

Connecting and Synthesizing[2] Information

- Recognize the organization of information presented
- Understand the relationships between ideas presented (for example: compare/contrast, cause/effect or steps in a process)
- Make inferences and draw conclusions based on what is implied in the material
- Make connections among pieces of information in a conversation or lecture
- Recognize topic changes in lectures and conversations, and recognize introductions and conclusions in lectures

Listening Section Description

Listening material in the test includes academic lectures and conversations in which the speech sounds very natural. You can take notes on any listening material throughout the entire test.

---

[1]Pragmatic understanding: To understand a speaker's purpose, attitude, degree of certainty, etc.
[2]Synthesize: To combine information from two or more sources

Most of the questions that follow the lectures and conversations are traditional multiple-choice questions with four answer choices and a single correct answer. There are, however, some other types of questions:

- Multiple-choice questions with more than one answer (for example: two answers out of four or more choices)

- Questions that require you to put in order events or steps in a process

- Questions that require you to match objects or text to categories in a table

Listening Material	Number of Questions	Timing
4–6 lectures, 3–5 minutes long	6 questions per lecture	60–90 minutes
2–3 conversations, about 3 minutes long	5 questions per conversation	

Academic Lectures

The lectures in the TOEFL iBT® test reflect the kind of listening and speaking that occurs in the classroom. In some of the lectures, the professor does all or almost all of the talking, with an occasional comment by a student. In other lectures, the professor may engage the students in discussion by asking questions that are answered by the students. The photos that accompany the lectures indicate whether one person or several people will be speaking.

Conversations in an Academic Setting

The conversations in the TOEFL iBT test may take place during an office meeting with a professor or teaching assistant, or during a service encounter with university staff. The contents of the office conversations are generally academic in nature or related to course requirements. Service encounters could involve conversations about a housing payment, registering for a class or requesting information at the library. The photos that accompany the conversations help you imagine the setting and the roles of the speakers.

Listening Skills Practice

Listening to the English language frequently and reading a wide variety of academic materials is the best way to increase vocabulary and improve listening skills.

Watching movies and television shows and listening to the radio provide excellent opportunities to build listening skills. You are typically more engaged when you listen to entertaining material. Movies, television shows and live interviews are especially useful because they also provide visual reinforcement and cues.

Complete these Week 4 tasks and update the checklist on page 10.

- **ePLAN** Review sample Listening questions in *Planner* Appendix 1 and experience them on the *Planner* website at **www.ets.org/toefl/planner**

Audiotapes and CDs of books, lectures and presentations are equally valuable and are available at libraries and bookstores. Also, many public libraries and most universities have their public lectures available online. Lectures with transcripts are particularly helpful. The Internet is a great resource for listening material—visit websites such as **www.npr.org**, **www.cnn.com/services/podcasting**, **www.audiobooksforfree.com**, **www.youthradio.org**, **www.bbc.co.uk/radio** and **www.bbc.co.uk/worldservice/learningenglish**.

General Listening Activities

You might try these general activities to build your listening skills:

- Listen to different kinds of material on a variety of topics, of increasing length and difficulty.

  - Start with recordings on familiar topics and gradually progress to topics that are new to you.

  - First, listen to conversations, television shows and movies, and then listen to programs with academic content, such as NPR and BBC broadcasts. Start with short segments and progress to longer segments.

  - Listen several times to each recording:

    o For beginners, listen first with English subtitles, if they are available. Then, without subtitles, listen for the main ideas and key details.

    o Listen again to understand the connections between ideas, the structure of the talk and/or the speakers' attitudes and to distinguish fact from opinion.

  - Listen actively:

    o Take notes as you listen for main ideas and important details. Write down key words only, not every word.

    o Keep a log of the new words and expressions you hear. Check the spelling and meaning in a dictionary.

    o Ask yourself about the basic information presented in the recording (Who? What? When? Where? Why? How?).

    o Make predictions about what you will hear next.

    o Use your notes to summarize what you've heard.

  - Copy a script from an online news story, lecture or talk, movie or podcast. Delete or cover every fifth word on the script. Listen to the recording, and try to write in the missing words.

> The Listening section does not measure summarizing skills, but practicing summarizing is useful for the integrated tasks in the Speaking and Writing sections.

- Listen to the news or a lecture online and read the script at the same time. Listen closely and highlight the stressed words in the script. Try to identify **why** the speaker stresses specific words.

- Listen to a portion of a lecture or talk and create a list of important points. Use the list to write a brief summary. Gradually listen to the entire lecture and combine the summaries for each part into a summary of the whole lecture.

Targeted Activities

Listening for Pragmatic Understanding

- As you listen to movies, television shows and lectures:

  - Think about what each speaker hopes to accomplish. What is the purpose of the lecture or conversation? For example, is the speaker apologizing, complaining, inviting or making suggestions?

  - Notice each speaker's style. Is the language formal or casual? How certain does each speaker sound? Is the speaker's voice calm or emotional? What does the speaker's tone of voice tell you?

  - Notice the speaker's degree of certainty. How sure is the speaker about the information? Does the speaker's tone of voice indicate something about his/her degree of certainty?

  - Pay attention to the way stress and intonation patterns are used to convey meaning. Replay segments multiple times, listening for shades of meaning. This will help you understand a speaker's point of view.

  - Listen for changes in topic. What transitions are used?

  - Listen for repetitions of ideas and paraphrases. How do speakers reinforce their points?

Vocabulary tip: Don't memorize low-frequency technical vocabulary. These words are usually defined within a text or listening passage. Focus on learning high-frequency language that crosses all disciplines.

Targeted Activities

Listening to Connect and Synthesize Ideas

- As you are listening to recorded lectures or talks:

    - Think about how what you're hearing is organized. Listen for the signal words that indicate the introduction, major steps or ideas, examples and the conclusion or summary.

    - Identify the relationships between ideas. Possible relationships include cause/effect, compare/contrast and steps in a process.

    - Listen for transitions that show connections and relationships between ideas. How do speakers introduce and organize their points?

    - Predict what information or idea will be expressed next.

    - Stop the recording at various points. Summarize what you just heard or what you've heard up to that point.

    - Practice listening for and comparing two speakers' viewpoints. Which speaker supports the idea and which is against it? What words do speakers use to support their ideas? Are the words mainly positive or negative?

Vocabulary tip: Understanding phrasal verbs and common idioms will help you with the Listening section of the TOEFL iBT® test because phrasal verbs and idioms are often used in informal conversations.

Complete these Week 4 tasks and update the checklist on page 10.

- Pick three general activities and three targeted activities from pages 30–32 to work on your Listening skills.

- **OG** Use the Listening chapter in *The Official Guide to the TOEFL® Test* (Chapter 3) for more practice.

Writing

Academic Writing Skills

The Writing section measures your ability to write in English in an academic setting. In all academic situations where writing in English is required, you must be able to present your ideas in a clear, well-organized manner.

Often you'll need to write a paper or an essay response on an exam about what you've been learning in class. This requires combining information you've heard in lectures with what you've read in textbooks or other materials. For this type of writing—often referred to as **integrated writing**—you must be able to:

- Take notes on what you hear and read, and use your notes to organize information before writing

- Summarize, paraphrase and cite information accurately from source material

- Write about the ways the information you heard relates to the information you read

You also must be able to write essays that express and support your opinions. In this type of writing—known as **independent writing**—you express an opinion and support it based on your own knowledge and experience.

For example, you may be asked to write an essay about a controversial issue. You would use past personal experience to support your position.

> Planning before you write is an important skill to develop. In your university or college, you will have to write papers and essay exams that will require such skills.

Writing Section Description

The total time for the Writing section is 50 minutes. You'll write responses to two writing tasks: an Integrated Writing Task and an Independent Writing Task.

The Integrated Writing Task comes first because it requires some listening and you'll be wearing headphones. When you finish the Integrated Writing Task, which takes about 20 minutes, you may take the headphones off to work on the Independent Writing Task. You'll then have 30 minutes to complete the Independent Writing Task.

You'll type your responses on the computer keyboard, and then your responses will be sent to the ETS Online Scoring Network.

Task Type	Description
Task 1	
Integrated Writing Task Read/Listen/Write	• You read a short text of about 230–300 words (reading time: three minutes) on an academic topic. • You may take notes on the reading passage. • The reading passage disappears from the screen during the lecture that follows. It reappears when you begin writing so you can refer to it as you work. • You listen to a speaker discuss the same topic from a different perspective. The listening passage is about 230–300 words long (listening time: two minutes). • The listening passage provides additional information that relates to points made in the reading passage. You may take notes on the listening passage. • You write a summary in connected English prose of important points made in the listening passage and explain how these relate to the key points of the reading passage. Suggested response length is 150–225 words; however, there is no penalty for writing more as long as it is in response to the task presented.
Task 2	

Independent Writing
 	
Writing from Experience and Knowledge
	• You write an essay that states, explains and supports your opinion on an issue. An effective essay will usually contain a minimum of 300 words; however, you may write more if you wish.
	• You must support your opinions or choices rather than simply list personal preferences or choices.
	• Typical essay questions begin with statements such as:
	  – Do you agree or disagree with the following statement? Use reasons and specific details to support your answer.
	  – Some people believe [X]. Other people believe [Y]. Which of these two positions do you prefer/agree with? Give reasons and specific details.

How Writing Responses Are Scored

Your responses to all writing tasks are sent to the ETS Online Scoring Network. The responses are rated by four raters—two human raters for the integrated task and by one human rater and one *e-rater*® for the independent task. (With *e-rater*, your responses are scored by the computer.)

Your responses are rated on a scale of zero to five according to the Writing Scoring Guides in Appendix 4. Your average score on the two writing tasks is converted to a scaled score of 0 to 30. (See Appendix 6 for a chart that helps you convert the average score on your responses to a scaled score.)

- Your response to the Integrated Writing Task is scored on the quality of your writing (organization, appropriate and precise use of grammar, and vocabulary) and the completeness and accuracy of the content.

- The independent writing essay is scored on the overall quality of your writing: development, organization, and appropriate and precise use of grammar and vocabulary. It doesn't matter whether you agree or disagree with the topic—the raters are trained to accept all varieties of opinions.

For both of the writing tasks, the raters recognize that your response is a first draft. You're not expected to produce a comprehensive essay about a specialized topic. You can receive a high score with an essay that contains some errors.

Writing Skills Practice

General Writing Activities

Be sure you have developed fundamental writing skills before you progress to more targeted practice. Check to see if you can do the following:

- Learn the conventions of spelling, punctuation and paragraph creation.

- Study the organization of good paragraphs and essays. A good paragraph discusses ONE main idea. This idea is usually written in the first sentence, which is called the topic sentence. In essay writing, each paragraph should discuss one aspect of the main idea of the essay.

- Before you write, think about verb tenses that logically fit your topic. Are you writing about something in the past? Then you might use the simple past, present and past perfect, past continuous—tenses that naturally fit together.

- Read your writing three or four times; each time, check for a different thing. Make a checklist of errors you commonly make (for example: verb tenses, run-on sentences, subject-verb agreement).

- Reread your writing and circle common, uninteresting expressions (for example: *get, nice, things, stuff*). In your second draft, replace these with stronger words and phrases (for example: *obtain, pleasant, objects, possessions*). See how many alternate words you can come up with.

- Practice using transitions to show the relationship between ideas. Use words and phrases such as "on the one hand" or "in conclusion" to create a clear structure for your response.

- Practice typing on a QWERTY keyboard, the type of computer keyboard used in English-speaking countries. The name comes from the first six letters in the top row of the keyboard.

Complete these Week 5 tasks and update the checklist on page 10.

- See sample Writing questions in *Planner* Appendix 1.

- Review Writing Scoring Guides in *Planner* Appendix 4 to understand what score levels mean.

- **ePLAN** Read sample responses and raters' comments in Appendix 1 to help you identify your current level and understand what a response at your desired level is like. Refer to the Scoring Guides as you read.

> **Vocabulary tip:** Expand your vocabulary by doing crossword puzzles and other word games. These are available on sites like http://www.yourdictionary.com. This website also has a "Word of the Day."

Targeted Activities

Independent Writing

Try the following activities to build the skills you'll need for the Independent Writing tasks:

- Make a list of familiar topics and write essays about them. Practice taking 30 minutes to plan, write and revise each essay.

  - Think about and list all ideas related to a topic or task before writing. This is also called "prewriting."

  - Identify one main idea and create a list of some major points to support that idea. Develop the essay by using appropriate explanations and details.

  - When your essay is complete, reread what you have written. Make sure your supporting ideas are clearly related to your main point and are developed in detail.

- Read a sample essay response from Appendix 1 or in *The Official Guide to the TOEFL® Test* and make an outline of the essay. Include the main idea and supporting points for each paragraph. Paraphrase the key points in your own words and summarize the essay you read.

- Read articles and essays written by professional writers that express opinions about an issue, such as a social, environmental or educational issue. Identify the writer's opinion(s). Notice how the writer addresses possible objections to the opinion(s).

Practice Tips for the Writing Section

- Use the sample Independent Writing topics in Appendix 5 of the *Planner* and Chapter 5 of *The Official Guide to the TOEFL® Test* to practice writing for the TOEFL iBT® test. Time yourself, taking 30 minutes to read the question, plan your work and write your essay. Review your essay and ask yourself these questions:

    - Did I complete the task?

    - Did I write clearly?

    - Did I make grammatical errors?

    - Did I use words correctly?

    - Did I organize my ideas clearly and coherently?

    - Did I use the time effectively?

- When practicing the Integrated Writing response:

    - Plan your time carefully (for example, two to three minutes to plan, 15 minutes to write, two to three minutes to edit).

    - Start your response with a strong topic statement that clearly shows the main point of the lecture.

    - Show how the points made in the lecture relate to specific points made in the reading. Do not simply summarize the reading and the writing.

- Ask an English teacher or tutor to evaluate your essay using the appropriate Writing Scoring Guides from Appendix 4 and to give you feedback.

Targeted Writing Activities

Paraphrasing

In your academic classes, you must be careful never to plagiarize (copy another writer's words without acknowledging the source). Paraphrasing is an important skill because you are expressing ideas about something from source material in your own words. Practice paraphrasing words, phrases, sentences and entire paragraphs frequently using the following activities:

- Learn to find synonyms. Pick 10–15 words or phrases in a passage and quickly think of synonyms without looking them up in a dictionary or thesaurus.

- Practice writing a sentence using the noun form of a word and then convey the same meaning using the verb form.

- Try paraphrasing two or three sentences. Later, move on to paraphrasing paragraphs and longer passages.

- Write a paraphrase of a reading passage using only your notes. If you haven't taken notes, write the paraphrase without looking at the original text. Check your paraphrase to make sure it's factually accurate and that you've used different words and grammatical structures.

> **Vocabulary tip:** Randomly choose a word from your vocabulary log. Define the word, use it in a sentence, and see how many words with similar meanings you can list.

Targeted Activities

Integrated Writing

You can do these activities to build the skills you'll need for the Integrated Writing tasks:

- Find a textbook in English that includes questions about the material at the end of a chapter and practice writing answers to the questions.

- Read academic articles and listen to related lectures.

  - Take notes in your own language and then take notes in English.

  - Make a list of the major points and important details.

  - Use your list to write a summary of the major points and important details. Be sure to paraphrase using different words and grammatical structures.

  - Ask your teacher to review your writing and help you correct your errors.

  - Gradually decrease the time it takes you to read the material and write these summaries.

- Practice finding main points by listening to recorded lectures or talks online. Stop the recording about every 30 seconds to write out a short summary of what you heard. Replay the recording to check your summary.

- Read two articles on the same topic. Write a summary of each, and then explain the ways in which they are similar and the ways in which they are different.

- Listen to a recorded news story online. In a newspaper or online, read another story on the same news item. The material can provide similar or different views.

  - Take notes on the material.

  - Summarize both the written and spoken portions. Clearly identify which source you are referring to throughout your summary.

  - Combine the information and discuss how the materials relate. Explain how the ideas are similar, how one idea expands upon another, or how the ideas differ or contradict each other.

- Watch a movie with a friend or go to a restaurant together. Ask your friend's opinion of the movie or restaurant; take some notes. Read an online review of the same movie or restaurant. Write a response comparing your friend's opinions with the online review.

- Read an opinion or editorial piece from a newspaper. Interview a friend, classmate, family member or teacher on the same topic. Write a response comparing your interview with the written response.

> Be sure to paraphrase! On the TOEFL iBT® test, you will receive a score of zero if you copy words from the reading passage.

- Practice integrating all four language skills.

  - Listen to an online lecture and take notes. Then prepare both an oral and a written summary. Find and read a text on the same topic. Take notes. Then prepare both an oral and a written summary of the lecture and reading. Later, discuss the reading and lecture with a friend. Prepare a vocabulary list of the important words on the topic.

  - Read an essay from an academic text or from *The Official Guide to the TOEFL® Test*. Take notes on the main and supporting details. Use your notes to summarize the essay orally. Record your summary. Then listen to your summary to make sure you have included all the main points of the essay. Finally, write your own essay on the same topic.

> **Complete these Week 5 tasks and update the checklist on page 10.**
>
> - Pick three general activities and three targeted activities from pages 35–39 to work on your Writing skills.
>
> - **OG** Use the Writing chapter in *The Official Guide to the TOEFL® Test* (Chapter 5) for more practice.

CHAPTER 7 Test Day and Beyond

You've registered and practiced, and now you're ready to take the TOEFL iBT® test. Here are some tips that will help make your test day go smoothly:

- **Set your alarm early.** Give yourself plenty of time to get ready. If you have trouble getting up, ask a friend to give you a call.

- **Get plenty of rest.** Don't stay up late, and avoid caffeine the night before the test. Try to stay relaxed.

- **Eat a good meal.** Don't skip a meal on test day. Eat something with protein and a piece of fruit to help your mind stay alert.

TOEFL® Test Day Tips

You've practiced hard and now you are ready for your big day.

Here is some information to prepare you for the testing experience itself.

1 Plan Your Trip

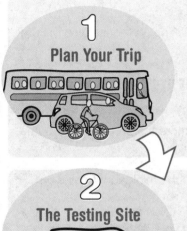

Plan your trip to the testing site:
Check the identification (ID) requirements for your testing location at **www.ets.org/toefl/id**.

Determine the best way to travel and how long it takes to get to the testing site. You need to arrive 30 minutes before your scheduled start time.

The day before your test, check your online profile for any details that may have changed, such as testing room or start time.

Make sure to bring your photo ID and registration confirmation with you.

2 The Testing Site

Arriving at the testing site:
You will need to present acceptable ID and your registration confirmation to enter the testing site.

A photo opportunity:
Your picture will be taken and displayed at your test station and on your official score report.

3 Your Testing Station

Your testing station:
You will be assigned a seat a few minutes before your start time.

No electronic devices or food are allowed in the testing room. For other restrictions, check the website at **www.ets.org/toefl**.

You can use the restroom at any time, but remember — the clock does not stop for your test.

4 The TOEFL Test

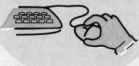

Total length of the test:
4 hours

Reading	Listening	Break	Speaking	Writing
60 – 80 minutes, 36 – 56 questions. Read passages, then respond to questions.	60 – 90 minutes, 34 – 51 questions. Listen to lectures or a classroom discussion, then respond to questions.	Mandatory 10-minute break for all test takers.	20 minutes, 6 tasks. Using a microphone, speak about familiar topics, and discuss material you read about and listen to.	50 minutes, 2 tasks. Read a passage, listen to a recording and then write your response (keyboard typing).

For more information, visit **www.ets.org/toefl**

What To Expect on Test Day

General Test-Taking Tips

Here are some test-taking strategies to follow during the test:

- **Know the directions** in each section before the test by taking a practice test. This will help you avoid wasting time during the test.

- **Click Help** to review the directions **only when absolutely necessary**—the test clock doesn't stop when Help is used.

- **Carefully read each question.** Some questions ask for more than one answer. Some questions have "not," so they ask about a negative situation.

- **Don't panic.** Concentrate on the current question only. Don't think about how you answered or should have answered other questions.

- **Avoid spending too much time on any one question.** If you've thought about a question and you still don't know the answer, eliminate as many answer choices as possible. Then select the best remaining choice.

- **Pace yourself** so you have enough time to answer every question. Be aware of the time limit for every section/task and budget enough time for each. You can hide the time clock, but check the clock periodically to monitor your progress. The clock will automatically alert you when five minutes remain in Listening and Reading as well as in Writing.

- **The toolbar** tells you how many questions you've answered and how many remain. Use this information to decide whether you need to go faster or slower.

- **Review in Reading.** You can go back to review and change your responses in the Reading section by clicking **Review**. It's best to do this only after you've answered all the questions.

After the Test

After you take the test and receive your scores, you can determine whether you need to take the test again. If you do, we recommend that you prepare with additional activities in the *Planner*, reviewing the practice tests in *The Official Guide* and taking additional practice tests on TOEFL® Practice Online (**www.ets.org/toeflpractice**).

Score Reports

Scores are reported online approximately ten days after the test. You can view your scores online free of charge. Paper score reports are mailed shortly after the scores are posted online. Please see Appendix 2 for a sample examinee score report.

Sending Your Scores

You can select up to four TOEFL® Destinations as score recipients for free when you register.

In addition to the destinations you select with your registration, you can send your scores to as many other institutions as you choose for a small fee. You can order by logging into your online profile, by mail or by fax. Go to **www.ets.org/toefl** for more information.

Performance Feedback

Score reports also include feedback that indicates whether your performance was high, medium or low and describes what test takers in these score ranges typically know and can do with the English language.

Lexile® Measures

You can build your English-language reading skills by matching your TOEFL iBT® Reading score with a Lexile® measure. Your Lexile measure allows you to find books that reflect your reading ability and interests and are challenging enough to help strengthen your reading skills. MetaMetrics®, Inc. and ETS offer this free service to take the guesswork out of choosing the right materials for you to read. Go to **www.lexile.com/toefl** for more information.

APPENDIX 1

Sample Questions

Following are print versions of sample questions from each of the four skills sections. You can access these questions on the *Planner* website (**www.ets.org/toefl/planner**) along with sample responses for the Speaking and Writing sample questions. These sample questions are in addition to the free TOEFL iBT® Online Sampler that you receive with online test registration. See page 3 for a list of all the Sources for Authentic TOEFL® Questions.

Reading Section

Meteorite Impact and Dinosaur Extinction

There is increasing evidence that the impacts of meteorites have had important effects on Earth, particularly in the field of biological evolution. Such impacts continue to pose a natural hazard to life on Earth. Twice in the twentieth century, large meteorite objects are known to have collided with Earth.

5

If an impact is large enough, it can disturb the environment of the entire Earth and cause an ecological catastrophe. The best-documented such impact took place 65 million years ago at the end of the Cretaceous period of geological history. This break in Earth's history is marked by a mass extinction, when as many as half the species on the planet

10   became extinct. While there are a dozen or more mass extinctions in the geological record, the Cretaceous mass extinction has always intrigued paleontologists because it marks the end of the age of the dinosaurs. For tens of millions of years, those great creatures had flourished. Then, suddenly, they disappeared.

15   The body that impacted Earth at the end of the Cretaceous period was a meteorite with a mass of more than a trillion tons and a diameter of at least 10 kilometers. Scientists first identified this impact in 1980 from the worldwide layer of sediment deposited from the dust cloud that enveloped the planet after the impact. This sediment layer is enriched in the rare metal iridium and other elements that are relatively abundant in a meteorite but

20   very rare in the crust of Earth. Even diluted by the terrestrial material excavated from the crater, this component of meteorites is easily identified. By 1990 geologists had located the impact site itself in the Yucatán region of Mexico. The crater, now deeply buried in sediment, was originally about 200 kilometers in diameter.

25   This impact released an enormous amount of energy, excavating a crater about twice as large as the lunar crater Tycho. The explosion lifted about 100 trillion tons of dust into the atmosphere, as can be determined by measuring the thickness of the sediment layer formed when this dust settled to the surface. Such a quantity of material would have blocked the sunlight completely from reaching the surface, plunging Earth into a period

30   of cold and darkness that lasted at least several months. The explosion is also calculated to have produced vast quantities of nitric acid and melted rock that sprayed out over much of Earth, starting widespread fires that must have consumed most terrestrial forests and grassland. Presumably, those environmental disasters could have been responsible for the mass extinction, including the death of the dinosaurs.

35

40 Several other mass extinctions in the geological record have been tentatively identified with large impacts, but none is so dramatic as the Cretaceous event. But even without such specific documentation, it is clear that impacts of this size do occur and that their results can be catastrophic. What is a catastrophe for one group of living things, however, may create opportunities for another group. Following each mass extinction, there is a sudden evolutionary burst as new species develop to fill the ecological niches opened by the event.

45 Impacts by meteorites represent one mechanism that could cause global catastrophes and seriously influence the evolution of life all over the planet. According to some estimates, the majority of all extinctions of species may be due to such impacts. Such a perspective fundamentally changes our view of biological evolution. The standard criterion for the survival of a species is its success in competing with other species and adapting to slowly changing environments. Yet an equally important criterion is the ability of a species to

50 survive random global ecological catastrophes due to impacts.

Earth is a target in a cosmic shooting gallery, subject to random violent events that were unsuspected a few decades ago. In 1991 the United States Congress asked NASA to investigate the hazard posed today by large impacts on Earth. The group conducting the

55 study concluded from a detailed analysis that impacts from meteorites can indeed be hazardous. Although there is always some risk that a large impact could occur, careful study shows that this risk is quite small.

1. The word "pose" on line 2 is closest in meaning to

   a. claim

   b. model

   c. assume

   d. present

2. In paragraph 2, why does the author include the information that dinosaurs had flourished for tens of millions of years and then suddenly disappeared?

    a. To support the claim that the mass extinction at the end of the Cretaceous is the best-documented of the dozen or so mass extinctions in the geological record

    b. To explain why as many as half of the species on Earth at the time are believed to have become extinct at the end of the Cretaceous

    c. To explain why paleontologists have always been intrigued by the mass extinction at the end of the Cretaceous

    d. To provide evidence that an impact can be large enough to disturb the environment of the entire planet and cause an ecological disaster

3. Which of the following can be inferred from paragraph 3 about the location of the meteorite impact in Mexico?

    a. The location of the impact site in Mexico was kept secret by geologists from 1980 to 1990.

    b. It was a well-known fact that the impact had occurred in the Yucatán region.

    c. Geologists knew that there had been an impact before they knew where it had occurred.

    d. The Yucatán region was chosen by geologists as the most probable impact site because of its climate.

4. According to paragraph 3, how did scientists determine that a large meteorite had impacted Earth?

    a. They discovered a large crater in the Yucatán region of Mexico.

    b. They found a unique layer of sediment worldwide.

    c. They were alerted by archaeologists who had been excavating in the Yucatán region.

    d. They located a meteorite with a mass of over a trillion tons.

5. The word "excavating" on line 25 is closest in meaning to

    a. digging out

    b. extending

    c. destroying

    d. covering up

6. The word "consumed" on line 32 is closest in meaning to

    a. changed

    b. exposed

    c. destroyed

    d. covered

7. According to paragraph 4, all of the following statements are true of the impact at the end of the Cretaceous period EXCEPT:

    a. A large amount of dust blocked sunlight from Earth.

    b. Earth became cold and dark for several months.

    c. New elements were formed in Earth's crust.

    d. Large quantities of nitric acid were produced.

8. The phrase "tentatively identified" on line 36 is closest in meaning to

    a. identified after careful study

    b. identified without certainty

    c. occasionally identified

    d. easily identified

9. The word "perspective" on line 46 is closest in meaning to

    a. sense of values

    b. point of view

    c. calculation

    d. complication

10. Paragraph 6 supports which of the following statements about the factors that are essential for the survival of a species?

    a. The most important factor for the survival of a species is its ability to compete and adapt to gradual changes in its environment.

    b. The ability of a species to compete and adapt to a gradually changing environment is not the only ability that is essential for survival.

    c. Since most extinctions of species are due to major meteorite impacts, the ability to survive such impacts is the most important factor for the survival of a species.

    d. The factors that are most important for the survival of a species vary significantly from one species to another.

11. Which of the sentences below best expresses the essential information in the following sentence?

    Earth is a target in a cosmic shooting gallery, subject to random violent events that were unsuspected a few decades ago.

    Incorrect choices change the meaning in important ways or leave out essential information.

    a. Until recently, nobody realized that Earth is exposed to unpredictable violent impacts from space.

    b. In the last few decades, the risk of a random violent impact from space has increased.

    c. Since most violent events on Earth occur randomly, nobody can predict when or where they will happen.

    d. A few decades ago, Earth became the target of random violent events originating in outer space.

12. According to the passage, who conducted investigations about the current dangers posed by large meteorite impacts on Earth?

    a. Paleontologists

    b. Geologists

    c. The United States Congress

    d. NASA

13. Look at the four letters (**A**, **B**, **C**, and **D**) that indicate where the following sentence could be added to the passage in paragraph 6.

    This is the criterion emphasized by Darwin's theory of evolution by natural selection.

    Where would the sentence best fit?

    Impacts by meteorites represent one mechanism that could cause global catastrophes and seriously influence the evolution of life all over the planet. **(A)** According to some estimates, the majority of all extinctions of species may be due to such impacts. **(B)** Such a perspective fundamentally changes our view of biological evolution. **(C)** The standard criterion for the survival of a species is its success in competing with other species and adapting to slowly changing environments. **(D)** Yet an equally important criterion is the ability of a species to survive random global ecological catastrophes due to impacts.

    Choose the place where the sentence fits best.

    a. Option A

    b. Option B

    c. Option C

    d. Option D

14. An introductory sentence for a brief summary of the passage is provided below. Complete the summary by selecting the THREE answer choices that express the most important ideas in the passage. Some sentences do not belong in the summary because they express ideas that are not presented in the passage or are minor ideas in the passage. **This question is worth 2 points.**

Write your answer choices in the spaces where they belong. You can write in the number of the answer choice or the whole sentence.

Scientists have linked the mass extinction at the end of the Cretaceous with a meteorite impact on Earth.
•
•
•

Answer choices

(1) Scientists had believed for centuries that meteorite activity influenced evolution on Earth.

(2) The site of the large meteorite impact at the end of the Cretaceous period was identified in 1990.

(3) There have also been large meteorite impacts on the surface of the Moon, leaving craters like Tycho.

(4) An iridium-enriched sediment layer and a large impact crater in the Yucatán provide evidence that a large meteorite struck Earth about 65 million years ago.

(5) Large meteorite impacts, such as one at the end of the Cretaceous period, can seriously affect climate, ecological niches, plants, and animals.

(6) Meteorite impacts can be advantageous for some species, which thrive, and disastrous for other species, which become extinct.

Key to Reading Section:

1. d
2. c
3. c
4. b
5. a
6. c
7. c
8. b
9. b
10. b
11. a
12. d
13. d
14. 4, 5, 6

Listening Section

Directions: The Listening section measures your ability to understand conversations and lectures in English. In this sample, you will read one conversation and one lecture and answer questions after each conversation or lecture. The questions typically ask about the main idea and supporting details. Some questions ask about a speaker's purpose or attitude. Answer the questions based on what is stated or implied by the speakers. Most questions are worth one point. If a question is worth more than one point, it will have special directions that indicate how many points you can receive.

- In an actual test, you will be able to take notes while you listen and use your notes to help you answer the questions. Your notes will not be scored.

CONVERSATION TRANSCRIPT

(Narrator) Listen to a conversation between a student and her basketball coach and then answer the questions.

(Male coach) Hi, Elizabeth.

(Female student) Hey, Coach. I just thought I'd stop by to see what I missed while I was gone.

(Male coach) Well, we've been working real hard on our plan for the next game . . . I've asked Susan to go over it with you before practice this afternoon, so you'll know what we're doing.

(Female student) Okay.

(Male coach) By the way, how did your brother's wedding go?

(Female student) Oh, it was beautiful. And the whole family was there. I saw aunts and uncles and cousins I hadn't seen in years.

(Male coach) So it was worth the trip.

(Female student) Oh definitely. I'm sorry I had to miss practice, though. I feel bad about that.

(Male coach) Family's very important.

(Female student) Yep. Okay, I guess I'll see you this afternoon at practice, then.

(Male coach) Just a minute. There are a couple of other things I need to tell you.

(Female student) Oh, okay.

(Male coach) Uh . . . First, everybody's getting a new team jacket.

(Female student) Wow. How did that happen?

(Male coach) A woman who played here about 20, 25 years ago came through town a few weeks ago and saw a game, and said she wanted to do something for the team, so . . .

(Female student) So she's buying us new jackets?

(Male coach) Yep.

(Female student) Wow, that's really nice of her.

(Male coach) Yes, it is. It's great that former players still care so much about our school and our basketball program . . . Anyway you need to fill out an order form. I'll give it to you now, and you can bring it back this afternoon. I've got the forms from the other players, so as soon as I get yours we can order. Maybe we'll have the jackets by the next game.

(Female student) OK.

(Male coach) Great. And the next thing is, you know Mary's transferring to another college next week, so we'll need someone to take over her role as captain for the second half of the season. And the other players unanimously picked you to take over as captain when Mary leaves.

(Female student) Wow. I saw everybody this morning, and nobody said a word.

(Male coach) They wanted me to tell you. So, do you accept?

(Female student) Of course! But Susan's a much better player than I am. I'm really surprised they didn't pick her.

(Male coach) They think you're the right one. You'll have to ask them their thoughts.

(Female student) Okay . . . I guess one of the first things I'll have to do as captain is make sure we get a thank-you card out to the lady who's buying us the jackets.

(Male coach) Good idea. I have her address here somewhere.

(Female student) And I'll make sure the whole team signs it.

(Male coach) Good. That's all the news there is. I think that's it for now. Oh, let me get you that order form.

1.   What are the speakers mainly discussing?

     a. How the woman should prepare for the next game

     b. The woman's responsibilities as team captain

     c. Things that happened while the woman was away

     d. The style of the new team uniforms

2.   Who is buying new jackets for the team?

     a. The coach

     b. The captain of the team

     c. A former player

     d. A group of basketball fans

3.   There are two answers for the next question. Mark two answers.

     Why is the woman surprised to learn that she has been chosen as the new team captain?

     a. She is not the best player on the team.

     b. Her teammates did not tell her about the decision.

     c. She does not have many friends on the team.

     d. She has missed a lot of practices.

4. Read part of the conversation again. Then answer the question.

   (Female student) I'm sorry I had to miss practice, though. I feel bad about that.

   (Male coach) Family's very important.

   What does the man mean when he says: "Family's very important."

      a. He hopes the woman's family is doing well.

      b. He would like to meet the woman's family.

      c. The woman should spend more time with her family.

      d. The woman had a good reason for missing practice.

5. Why does the coach say: "Good. That's all the news there is. I think that's it for now."

      a. He wants to know if the woman understood his point.

      b. He wants the woman to act immediately.

      c. He is preparing to change the topic.

      d. He is ready to end the conversation.

LECTURE TRANSCRIPT

(**Narrator**) Listen to part of a lecture in a literature class.

(**Male professor**) Today I'd like to introduce you to a novel that some critics consider the finest detective novel ever written. It was also the first. We're talking about *The Moonstone* by Wilkie Collins. Now, there are other detective stories that preceded *The Moonstone* historically—Um, notably the work of Poe . . . Edgar Allen Poe's stories, such as "The Murders in the Rue Morgue" and . . . "The Purloined Letter." Now these were short stories that featured a detective . . . uh, probably the first to do that. But *The Moonstone*, which follows them by about twenty years—it was published in 1868—this is the first full-length detective novel ever written.

Now, in *The Moonstone*—if you read it as . . . uh, come to it as a contemporary reader— what's interesting is that most of the features you find in almost any detective novel are in fact already present. Uh, it's hard at this juncture to read this novel and realize that no one had ever done that before, because it all seems so strikingly familiar. It's, it's really a wonderful novel and I recommend it, even just as a fun book to read, if you've never read it. Um, so in *The Moonstone*, as I said, Collins did much to establish the conventions of the detective genre. I'm not gonna go into the plot at length, but, you know, the basic set-up is . . . there's this diamond of great . . . of great value, a country house, the diamond mysteriously disappears in the middle of the night, uh, the local police are brought in, in an attempt to solve the crime, and they mess it up completely, and then the true hero of the book arrives. That's Sergeant Cuff.

Now, Cuff, this extraordinarily important character . . . well, let me try to give you a sense of who Sergeant Cuff is, by first describing the regular police. And this is the dynamic that you're going to see throughout the history of the detective novel, where you have the regular cops—who are well-meaning, but officious and bumblingly inept—and they are countered by a figure who's eccentric, analytical, brilliant, and . . . and able to solve the crime. So, first the regular police get called in to solve the mystery—Um, in this case, detective, uh, Superintendent Seegrave. When Superintendent Seegrave comes in, he orders his minions around, they bumble, and they actually make a mess of the investigation, which you'll see repeated—um, you'll see this pattern repeated, particularly in the Sherlock Holmes stories of a few years later where, uh, Inspector Lestrade, this well-meaning idiot, is always countered, uh, by Sherlock Holmes, who's a genius.

So, now Cuff arrives. Cuff is the man who's coming to solve the mystery, and again he has a lot of the characteristics that future detectives throughout the history of this genre will have. He's eccentric. He has a hobby that he's obsessive about—in this . . . in his case, it's the love of roses. He's a fanatic about the breeding of roses; and here think of Nero Wolfe and his orchids, Sherlock Holmes and his violin, a lot of those later classic detective heroes have this kind of outside interest that they . . . they go to as a kind of antidote to the evil and misery they encounter in their daily lives. At one point, Cuff says

he likes his roses because they offer solace, uh, an escape, from the world of crime he typically operates in.

Now, these detective heroes . . . they have this characteristic of being smart, incredibly smart, but of not appearing to be smart. And most importantly, from a kind of existential point of view, these detectives see things that other people do not see. And that's why the detective is such an important figure, I think, in our modern imagination. In the case of *The Moonstone*—I don't want to say too much here and spoil it for you—but the clue that's key to . . . the solving of the crime is a smeared bit of paint in a doorway. Of course, the regular police have missed this paint smear or made some sort of unwarranted assumption about it. Cuff sees this smear of paint—this paint, the place where the paint is smeared—and realizes that from this one smear of paint you can actually deduce the whole situation . . . the whole world. And that's what the hero in a detective novel like this . . . brings to it that the other characters don't—it's this ability to, uh, see meaning where others see no meaning and to bring order . . . to where it seems there is no order.

6. What is the lecture mainly about?

    a. A comparison of two types of detective novels

    b. Ways in which detective novels have changed over time

    c. *The Moonstone* as a model for later detective novels

    d. Flaws that can be found in the plot of *The Moonstone*

7. In what way is *The Moonstone* different from earlier works featuring a detective?

    a. In its unusual ending

    b. In its unique characters

    c. In its focus on a serious crime

    d. In its greater length

8. According to the professor, what do roses in *The Moonstone* represent?

   a. A key clue that leads to the solving of the mystery

   b. A relief and comfort to the detective

   c. Romance between the main characters

   d. Brilliant ideas that occur to the detective

9. Why does the professor mention a smeared bit of paint in a doorway in *The Moonstone*?

   a. To describe a mistake that Sergeant Cuff has made

   b. To show how realistically the author describes the crime scene

   c. To exemplify a pattern repeated in many other detective stories

   d. To illustrate the superior techniques used by the police

10. What can be inferred about the professor when he says this: "Uh, it's hard at this juncture to read this novel and realize that no one had ever done that before, because it all seems so strikingly familiar."

    a. He is impressed by the novel's originality.

    b. He is concerned that students may find the novel difficult to read.

    c. He is bored by the novel's descriptions of ordinary events.

    d. He is eager to write a book about a less familiar subject.

11. What does the professor imply when he says this: ". . . well, let me try to give you a sense of who Sergeant Cuff is, by first describing the regular police."

    a. Sergeant Cuff is unlike other characters in *The Moonstone*.

    b. The author's description of Sergeant Cuff is very realistic.

    c. Sergeant Cuff learned to solve crimes by observing the regular police.

    d. Differences between Sergeant Cuff and Sherlock Holmes are hard to describe.

Key to Listening section:

1. c
2. c
3. a, b
4. d
5. d
6. c
7. d
8. b
9. c
10. a
11. a

Speaking Section

Directions: The Speaking section in the test measures your ability to speak about a variety of topics.

- In questions 1 and 2, in an actual test, your response will be scored on your ability to speak clearly and coherently about familiar topics.

- In questions 3 and 4, in an actual test, you will first read a short text and then listen to a talk on the same topic. You will have to combine appropriate information from the text and the talk to provide a complete answer. Your response will be scored on your ability to accurately convey information, and to speak clearly and coherently. In this sampler, you will **read** both the text and the talk.

- In questions 5 and 6, in an actual test, you will listen to part of a conversation or lecture. Then, you will be asked a question about what you have heard. Your response will be scored on your ability to accurately convey information, and to speak clearly and coherently. In this sampler, you will **read** the conversation.

- In an actual test, you will be able to take notes while you read and while you listen to the conversations and talks. You may use your notes to help prepare your responses.

- Preparation and response times for an actual test are noted in this text. Candidates with disabilities may request time extensions.

- Sample candidate responses and score explanations can be found in the online version of the sampler. The scoring rubric used to score actual responses can be found on the TOEFL® website's "Download Library" page.

1. Talk about a pleasant and memorable event that happened while you were in school. Explain why this event brings back fond memories.

   Preparation Time: 15 seconds
   Response Time: 45 seconds

2. Some people think it is more fun to spend time with friends in restaurants or cafés. Others think it is more fun to spend time with friends at home. Which do you think is better? Explain why.

   Preparation Time: 15 seconds
   Response Time: 45 seconds

3. Read the following text and the conversation that follows it. Then, answer the question.

The Northfield College Student Association recently decided to make a new purchase. Read the following announcement in the college newspaper about the decision. (Reading time in an actual test would be 45-50 seconds.)

Good News for Movie Fans

The Student Association has just purchased a new sound system for the Old Lincoln Hall auditorium, the place where movies on campus are currently shown. By installing the new sound system, the Student Association hopes to attract more students to the movies and increase ticket sales. Before making the purchase of the new equipment, the Student Association conducted a survey on campus to see what kind of entertainment students liked best. Going to the movies ranked number one. "Students at Northfield College love going to the movies" said the president of the Student Association, "so we decided to make what they already love even better. We're confident that the investment into the sound system will translate into increased ticket sales."

(Male student) I really think the Student Association made a bad decision.

(Female student) Really? Why? Don't you like going to the movies?

(Male student) Sure I do. But this new purchase is just a waste of money.

(Female student) What do you mean? It's supposed to sound really good.

(Male student) Yeah, well, I'm sure it does, but, in Old Lincoln Hall? I mean that building must be 200 years old! It used to be the college gym! The acoustics are terrible.

(Female student) So you're saying there'll be no improvement?

(Male student) That's right. And also, I seriously doubt that going to the movies is the number one social activity for most students.

(Female student) Yeah, but that's what students said.

(Male student) Well, of course that's what they said. What else is there to do on campus?

(Female student) What do you mean?

Appendix 1: Sample Questions

(Male student) I mean, there isn't much to do on campus besides go to the movies. If there were other forms of, uh recreation, or other social activities, you know, I don't think most students would have said that going to the movies was their first choice.

Question: The man expresses his opinion of the Student Association's recent purchase. State his opinion and explain the reasons he gives for holding that opinion.

Preparation Time: 30 seconds
Response Time: 60 seconds

4. Read a passage from a psychology textbook and the lecture that follows it. Then answer the question. (Reading time in an actual test would be 45-50 seconds.)

Flow

In psychology, the feeling of complete and energized focus in an activity is called flow. People who enter a state of flow lose their sense of time and have a feeling of great satisfaction. They become completely involved in an activity for its own sake rather than for what may result from the activity, such as money or prestige. Contrary to expectation, flow usually happens not during relaxing moments of leisure and entertainment, but when we are actively involved in a difficult enterprise, in a task that stretches our mental or physical abilities.

(Male professor) I think this will help you get a picture of what your textbook is describing. I had a friend who taught in the physics department, Professor Jones, he retired last year. . . . Anyway, I remember . . . this was a few years ago . . . I remember passing by a classroom early one morning just as he was leaving, and he looked terrible: his clothes were all rumpled, and he looked like he hadn't slept all night. And I asked if he was OK. I was surprised when he said that he never felt better, that he was totally happy. He had spent the entire night in the classroom working on a mathematics puzzle. He didn't stop to eat dinner; he didn't stop to sleep . . . or even rest. He was that involved in solving the puzzle. And it didn't even have anything to do with his teaching or research; he had just come across this puzzle accidentally, I think in a mathematics journal, and it just really interested him, so he worked furiously all night and covered the blackboards in the classroom with equations and numbers and never realized that time was passing by.

Question: Explain *flow* and how the example used by the professor illustrates the concept.

Preparation Time: 30 seconds
Response Time: 60 seconds

5. Read the following conversation between two students and then answer the question.

(Female student) How's the calculus class going? You're doing better?

(Male student) Not really. I just can't get the hang of it. There're so many functions and formulas to memorize, you know? And the final . . . It's only a few weeks away. I'm really worried about doing well.

(Female student) Oh . . . You know, you should go to the tutoring program and ask for help.

(Male student) You mean, in the Mathematics building?

(Female student) Ya. Get a tutor there. Most tutors are doctoral students in the math program. They know what they're talking about, and for the final test, you know, they'd tell you what to study, how to prepare, all of that.

(Male student) I know about that program . . . but doesn't it cost money?

(Female student) Of course. You have to register and pay by the hour . . . But they've got all the answers.

(Male student) Hmm . . .

(Female student) Another option, I guess, is to form a study group with other students. That won't cost you any money.

(Male student) That's a thought . . . although once I was in a study group, and it was a big waste of time. We usually ended up talking about other stuff like what we did over the weekend.

(Female student) But that was for a different class, right? I've actually had some pretty good experiences with study groups. Usually students in the same class have different strengths and weaknesses with the material . . . if they're serious about studying, they can really help each other out. Think about it.

Question: Briefly summarize the problem the speakers are discussing. Then state which solution you would recommend. Explain the reasons for your recommendation.

Preparation Time: 20 seconds
Response Time: 60 seconds

6.　Read part of a lecture in a biology course and then answer the question.

(Female professor) Human beings aren't the only animals that use tools. It's generally recognized that other animals use tools as well . . . use them naturally, in the wild, without any human instruction. But when can we say that an object is a tool? Well, it depends on your definition of a tool. And in fact, there are two competing definitions—a narrow definition and a broad one. The narrow definition says that a tool is an object that's used to perform a specific task . . . but <u>not just any</u> object. To be a tool, according to the narrow definition, the object's gotta be <u>purposefully changed</u> or <u>shaped</u> by the animal, or human, so that it can be used that way. It's an object that's <u>made</u>. Wild chimpanzees use sticks to dig insects out of their nests . . . but most sticks lying around won't do the job . . . they might be too thick, for example. So the sticks have to be sharpened so they'll fit into the hole in an ant hill or the insect nest. The chimp pulls off the leaves and chews the stick and trims it down that way until it's the right size. The chimp doesn't just find the stick . . . it . . . you could say it <u>makes</u> it in a way.

But the <u>broad</u> definition says an object doesn't have to be modified to be considered a tool. The broad definition says a tool is <u>any</u> object that's used to perform a specific task. For example, an elephant will sometimes use a stick to scratch its back . . . it just picks up a stick from the ground and scratches its back with it . . . It doesn't modify the stick, it uses it just as it's found. And it's a tool, under the broad definition, but under the narrow definition it's not because, well, the elephant doesn't change it in any way.

Question: Using points and examples from the talk, describe the two different definitions of tools given by the professor.

Preparation Time: 20 seconds
Response Time: 60 seconds

Writing Section

Directions: These sample tasks in the Writing section measure your ability to write in English in an academic environment. There will be 2 writing tasks.

- For the first task in this sampler, you will read a passage and part of a lecture about an academic topic. Then you will write a response to a question that asks you about the relationship between the lecture and the reading passage. Try to answer the question as completely as possible using information from the reading passage and the lecture. The question does not ask you to express your personal opinion. Your response will be judged on the quality of your writing and on how well your response presents the points in the lecture and their relationship to the reading passage.

- For the second task, you will demonstrate your ability to write an essay in response to a question that asks you to express and support your opinion about a topic or issue. Your essay will be scored on the quality of your writing. This includes the development of your ideas, the organization of your essay, and the quality and accuracy of the language you use to express your ideas.

- At the end of the writing section, in this sampler you will find two sample essays for each question, the score they received, and an explanation of how they were scored.

- In an actual test, you will be able to take notes while you listen and use your notes to help you answer the questions.

1. Read the following passage and the lecture which follows. In an actual test, you will have 3 minutes to read the passage. Then, answer the question. In the test, you will have 20 minutes to plan and write your response. Typically, an effective response will be 150 to 225 words.

READING PASSAGE

Critics say that current voting systems used in the United States are inefficient and often lead to the inaccurate counting of votes. Miscounts can be especially damaging if an election is closely contested. Those critics would like the traditional systems to be replaced with far more efficient and trustworthy computerized voting systems.

In traditional voting, one major source of inaccuracy is that people accidentally vote for the wrong candidate. Voters usually have to find the name of their candidate on a large sheet of paper containing many names—the ballot—and make a small mark next to that name. People with poor eyesight can easily mark the wrong name. The computerized voting machines have an easy-to-use touch-screen technology: to cast a vote, a voter needs only to touch the candidate's name on the screen to record a vote for that candidate; voters can even have the computer magnify the name for easier viewing.

Another major problem with old voting systems is that they rely heavily on people to count the votes. Officials must often count up the votes one by one, going through every ballot and recording the vote. Since they have to deal with thousands of ballots, it is almost inevitable that they will make mistakes. If an error is detected, a long and expensive recount has to take place. In contrast, computerized systems remove the possibility of human error, since all the vote counting is done quickly and automatically by the computers.

Finally some people say it is too risky to implement complicated voting technology nationwide. But without giving it a thought, governments and individuals alike trust other complex computer technology every day to be perfectly accurate in banking transactions as well as in the communication of highly sensitive information.

LECTURE TRANSCRIPT

(Narrator) Now listen to part of a lecture on the topic you just read about.

(Female professor) While traditional voting systems have some problems, it's doubtful that computerized voting will make the situation any better. Computerized voting may seem easy for people who are used to computers. But what about people who aren't? People who can't afford computers, people who don't use them on a regular basis—these people will have trouble using computerized voting machines. These voters can easily cast the wrong vote or be discouraged from voting altogether because of fear of technology. Furthermore, it's true that humans make mistakes when they count up ballots by hand. But are we sure that computers will do a better job? After all, computers are

programmed by humans, so "human error" can show up in mistakes in their programs. And the errors caused by these defective programs may be far more serious. The worst a human official can do is missing a few ballots. But an error in a computer program can result in thousands of votes being miscounted or even permanently removed from the record. And in many voting systems, there is no physical record of the votes, so a computer recount in the case of a suspected error is impossible! As for our trust of computer technology for banking and communications, remember one thing: these systems are used daily and they are used heavily. They didn't work flawlessly when they were first introduced. They had to be improved on and improved on until they got as reliable as they are today. But voting happens only once every two years nationally in the United States and not much more than twice a year in many local areas. This is hardly sufficient for us to develop confidence that computerized voting can be fully trusted.

Question: Summarize the points made in the lecture, being sure to explain how they oppose specific points made in the reading passage.

2. Read the question below. In a real test, you will have 30 minutes to plan, write, and revise your essay. Candidates with disabilities may request a time extension. Typically, an effective response will contain a minimum of 300 words.

Question: Do you agree or disagree with the following statement?

A teacher's ability to relate well with students is more important than excellent knowledge of the subject being taught.

Use specific reasons and examples to support your answer.

Sample responses

Below are candidates' responses exemplifying scores of 5 and 4 for both Writing tasks. The scoring guides used to score actual responses can be found in Appendix 3 and 4.

QUESTION 1, RESPONSE A, SCORE OF 5

The lecture explained why the computerized voting system can not replace the traditional voting system. There are the following three reasons.

First of all, not everyoen one can use computers correctly. Some people do not have access to computers, some people are not used of computers, and some people are even scared of this new technology. If the voters do not know how to use a computer, how do you expect them to finish the voting process through computers? This directly refutes the reading passage which states that computerized voting is easier by just touching the screen.

Secondly, computers may make mistakes as the people do. As computers are programmed by the human beings, thus erros are inevitable in the computer system. Problems caused by computer voting systems may be more serious than those caused by people. A larger number of votes might be miss counted or even removed from the system. Furthermore, it would take more energy to recount the votes. Again this contradicts what is stated in the reading which stated that only people will make mistakes in counting.

Thirdly, computerized voting system is not reliable because it has not reached a stable status. People trust computers to conduct banking transactions because the computerized banking system is being used daily and frecuently and has been stable. How ever, the voting does not happen as often as banking thus the computerized voting system has not been proved to be totally reliable.

All in all, not everyone can use a computer properly, computer cause mistakes and computerized voting system is not reliable are the main reasons why computerized voting system can not replace the traditional voting system.

Score explanation

This response is well organized, selects the important information from all three points made in the lecture, and explains its relationship to the claims made in the reading passage about the advantages of computerized voting over traditional voting methods.

First, it counters the argument that computerized voting is more user-friendly and prevents distortion of the vote by saying that many voters find computers unfamiliar and some voters may end up not voting at all.

Second, it challenges the argument that computerized voting will result in fewer miscounts by pointing out that programming errors may result in large-scale miscounts and that some errors may result in the loss of voting records.

Third, it rejects the comparison of computerized voting with computerized banking by pointing out that the reliability of computerized banking ("reached a stable status") has been achieved though frequent use, which does not apply to voting.

There are occasional minor language errors: for example, "people not used of computers"; "miss counted"; "computer cause mistakes"; and the poor syntax of the last sentence ("All in all . . . "). Some spelling errors are obviously typos: "everyoen." The errors, however, are not at all frequent and do not result in unclear or inaccurate representation of the content.

The response meets all the criteria for the score of 5.

QUESTION 1, RESPONSE B, SCORE OF 4

The leture disgreed with the article's opinions. It's not a better solution to use the computerized voting systems.

Firstly, it might be hard for the voters who don't use the computer so often, or the users who is fear of the technology, even some of voters can not aford a computer. Touch screen may also be hard to use for people who is not familiar with computers. Secondly, computer is programmed by human beings, which means it can also have errors. Instead of human being's counting error, which only results one or two counting error in number, an errror in the program code could cause tramendous error in number. In case of the computer crash or disaster, it may lost all the voting information. We can not even to make a re-count. Lastly, our daily banking or other highly sensitive infomation system, is actually improved as time goes by. They were also problematic at the beginning. As we use them so often, we have more chances to find problems, and furturemore, to fix and improve them. However, for the voting system, we only use them every 2 years nationally and some other rare events. We just don't use it often enough to find a bug or test it thoroughly.

Score explanation

The response selects most of the important information from the lecture and indicates that it challenges the main argument in the reading passage about the advantages of computerized voting systems ("it's not a better solution").

First, the response explains that some people will not find computers to be user-friendly; however, it fails to relate this clearly to the point made in the passage that computerized voting will prevent distortion of the vote. That is clearly an omission, but it is minor.

Second, the response does a good job of pointing out how programming and errors can cause greater problems than miscounts cause in the traditional voting system.

Third, the response provides a nice explanation of how the frequent use of systems like the banking system has contributed to such systems' reliability, and then it contrasts that with the computerized voting system.

There are more frequent language errors throughout the response—for example, "users who is fear"; "some of voters can not aford"; "people who is not familiar"; "it may lost"; and "can not even to make." Expressions chosen by the writer occasionally affect the clarity of the content that is being conveyed: "results one or two counting error in number . . . an errror in the program code could cause tramendous error in number" and "use them every 2 years nationally and some other rare events." However, it should be noted that in these cases, a reader can derive the intended meaning from the context.

Due to the more frequent language errors that on occasion result in minor lapses of clarity and due to minor content omission, especially in the coverage of the first lecture point, the response cannot earn the score of 5. At the same time, since the language errors are generally minor and mostly do not interfere with the clarity of the content and since most of the important information from the lecture is covered by the writer, the response deserves a higher score than 3. It meets the criteria for the score of 4.

QUESTION 2, RESPONSE A, SCORE OF 5

I remember every teacher that has taught me since I was in Kindergarten. If a friend wants to know who our first grade teacher was in elementary school, all they have to do is ask me. The teachers all looked very kind and understanding in my eyes as a child. They had special relationships with nearly each and every one of the students and were very nice to everyone. That's the reason I remember all of them.

A teacher's primary goal is to teach students the best they can about the things that are in our textbooks and more important, how to show respect for one another. They teach us how to live a better life by getting along with everyone. In order to do that, the teachers themselves have to be able to relate well with students.

My parents are teachers too. One teaches Plant Biology and one teaches English, but that's not the reason I'm calling them "teachers." They are teachers beacuse they teach me how to act in special situations and how to cooperate with others. I have a brother, and my parents use different aproaches when teaching us. They might scold my brother for surfing the internet too long because he doesn't have much self-control and they need to restrain him. He almost never studies on his own and is always either drawing, playing computer games, or reading. On the other hand, they never tell me off for using the computer too long. I do my own work when I want and need to because that brings me the best results and my parents understand that. They know that I need leisure time of my own and that I'll only play until needed. My parents' ability to relate well with my brother and I allows them to teach, not just the subject they teach but also their excellent knowledge on life.

Knowlegde of the subject being taught is something taken for granted, but at the same time, secondary. One must go through and pass a series of courses and tests in order to become a teacher. Any teacher is able to have excellent knowledge of their subject but not all teachers can have the ability to relate well with students.

A teacher's primary goal is to teach students the best they can about how to show respect for one another, so teachers use different approaches when teaching, and knowledge of the subjet being taught is secondary. For these reasons, I claim with confidence that excellent knowledge of the subject being taught is secondary to the teacher's ability to relate well with their students.

Score explanation

This essay conveys the idea that as important as teaching knowledge is, it is as important if not more important for teachers to possess other qualities, all of which the writer classifies as necessary for being able to relate well with students. Those other qualities include having "special relationships" with students; the teaching of respect (in the first two paragraphs); and taking different approaches for different individuals. The writer develops the last idea primarily by using a clearly appropriate extended and complex example of the writer's own parents, who are teachers but whose special qualities in raising the writer and the writer's brother had to do more with taking varied approaches. The writer then goes on to convey that knowledge is a given—"something

taken for granted"—because all teachers take course work and pass tests to gain their jobs but not all have the qualities the writer considers more important.

This response very effectively addresses the topic and the task. It is true that this response is different from most essays: the overall idea is stated explicitly but only at the end of the essay. However, because of very good language structure and good conceptual transitions between ideas, the reader is able to follow the writer's development of ideas without becoming confused. The response is thus seen to be well organized. Errors in language are almost nonexistent here. This response meets all of the 5-level criteria from the Scoring Guide.

QUESTION 2, RESPONSE B, SCORE OF 4

I disagree with the idea that the possessing the ability to relate well with student is more important than excellent knowledge of the subject being taught for a teacher. There are several reasons why I disagree with that idea.

First, teachers' job is to educate their student with their knowledge. The ability to relate well with their student is something a counselor should possess, not a teacher. That's why the board of education gives an award to a teacher with an excellent knowledge of the subject they teach. Teachers who can get along with their students but have no knowledge can be popular and be liked by his or her students, however I don't consider a teacher with no knowledge a good teacher.

Second, Students go to schools because they want to learn knowledge from their teachers not to get along with their teachers. I knew a math teacher who was well known among other mathematics teachers. Some students always complained how he never entertains his students which made many of his students to fall asleep. Nevertheless, all of his classes were all full even before the semester began because many students who were eager to learn already booked in. He won the Apples prize (it's given to a noticed teacher annually) a couple of times and that enabled students to firmly believe in his way of teaching.

Thirdly, teachers are responsible for conceding their knowledge to their next generation. Teachers already had an experience of getting advantaged education from college. Teachers should not let that previlege become useless and workless. We all learn because we want to become the better person that this world needs. Students will also eventually grow up to be influencing other people and teachers should volunteerily be their students' role models.

For conclusion, I think the most important quality a teacher must have is an excellent knowledge of the subject they teach, not an ability to relate well with their students.

Score explanation

This is a more traditional-looking essay that is organized with a point of view in the first paragraph stating the writer's disagreement with the writing prompt, followed by three pieces of supporting reasons and examples.

The second paragraph makes the point that counselors are the ones who are supposed to relate to students and that teachers with no knowledge are not worthwhile as teachers.

In the third paragraph the writer tries to describe the fact that knowledge is important by stating that students wanted to take courses from a teacher who was known to possess special knowledge even though they knew the teacher was not entertaining.

The fourth paragraph contains the very interesting idea that teachers have the obligation to pass on what they have had the privilege of learning, but this paragraph in particular has a few problems with somewhat unclear expression of concepts: (1) errors of word choice in the word "conceding" (not clear exactly what word is intended here) and in the term "'advantaged' education" (advanced education or advantages of

education?) and (2) a problem with unclear connection of ideas (why is it said that "We all learn because we want to become the better person that this world needs?").

Overall, this essay is well organized, but the slightly unclear connection of ideas and the language chosen, especially in the final paragraph, prevent this response from rising above the 4 level.

Sample Score Report

Here's a sample score report. It includes scaled scores for all four sections. The reports also provide performance feedback on all four skills. Note: This sample shows only the performance feedback for Reading and Listening.

TOEFL.
Internet-based Test Examinee Score Report
for the Test of English as a Foreign Language

Test Date:	**22 Oct 2005**
Sponsor Code:	**6283**
Inst. Code: Dept. Code:	

Registration Number: **4234 5678 9123 4567**

Name: **Tanaka, Miki**

Gender: **Female** Native Country: **Japan**

Date of Birth: **19 May 1987** Native Language: **Japanese**

0802
9993
2229
7766

TANAKA, MIKI
1A 23-4 BCD567 EF891
FGHIJ RD
MNLOPQ 234 JAPAN

SAMPLE ONLY

TOEFL SCALED SCORES	
Reading	17
Listening	17
Speaking	14
Writing	17
Total Score	**65**

The face of this document has a multicolored background -- not a white background.

00

Reading Skills	Level	Your Performance
Reading	Intermediate (15–21)	Test takers who receive a score at the **INTERMEDIATE** level, as you did, typically understand academic texts in English that require a wide range of reading abilities, although their understanding of certain parts of the texts is limited. Test takers who receive a score at the **INTERMEDIATE** level typically • have a good command of common academic vocabulary but still have some difficulty with high-level vocabulary; • have a very good understanding of grammatical structure; • can understand and connect information, make appropriate inferences, and synthesize information in a range of texts but have more difficulty when the vocabulary is high level and the text is conceptually dense; • can recognize the expository organization of a text and the role that specific information serves within a larger text but have some difficulty when these are not explicit or easy to infer from the text; and • can abstract major ideas from a text but have more difficulty doing so when the text is conceptually dense.

Listening Skills	Level	Your Performance
Listening	Intermediate (14–21)	Test takers who receive a score at the **INTERMEDIATE** level, as you did, typically understand conversations and lectures in English that present a wide range of listening demands. These demands can include difficult vocabulary (uncommon terms or colloquial or figurative language), complex grammatical structures, and/or abstract or complex ideas. However, lectures and conversations that require the listener to make sense of unexpected or seemingly contradictory information may present some difficulty. When listening to conversations and lectures like these, test takers at the **INTERMEDIATE** level typically can • understand explicitly stated main ideas and important details, especially if they are reinforced, but may have difficulty understanding main ideas that must be inferred or important details that are not reinforced; • understand how information is being used (for example, to provide support or describe a step in a complex process); • recognize how pieces of information are connected (for example, in a cause-and-effect relationship); • understand, though perhaps not consistently, ways that speakers use language for purposes other than to give information (for example, to emphasize a point, express agreement or disagreement, or convey intentions indirectly); and • synthesize information from adjacent parts of a lecture or conversation and make correct inferences on the basis of that information, but may have difficulty synthesizing information from separate parts of a lecture or conversation.

Speaking Skills	Level	Your Performance
Speaking about Familiar Topics	Limited (1.5–2.0)	Your responses indicate some difficulty speaking in English about everyday experiences and opinions. Listeners sometimes have trouble understanding you because of noticeable problems with pronunciation, grammar, and vocabulary. While you are able to respond partially to the questions, you are not able to fully develop your ideas, possibly due to limited vocabulary and grammar.
Speaking about Campus Situations	Fair (2.5–3.0)	Your responses demonstrate an ability to speak in English about reading material and experiences typically encountered by university students. You are able to convey relevant information about conversations, newspaper articles, and campus bulletins; however, some details are missing or inaccurate. Limitations of grammar, vocabulary, and pronunciation at times cause difficulty for the listener. However, they do not seriously interfere with overall communication.
Speaking about Academic Course Content	Limited (1.5–2.0)	In your responses, you are able to use English to talk about the basic ideas from academic reading or lecture materials, but, in general, you include few relevant or accurate details. It is sometimes difficult for listeners to understand your responses because of problems with grammar, vocabulary, and pronunciation. Overall, you are able to respond in a general way to the questions, but the amount of information in your responses is limited and the expression of ideas is often vague and unclear.

Writing Skills	Level	Your Performance
Writing based on Reading and Listening	Fair (2.5–3.5)	You responded to the task, relating the lecture to the reading, but your response indicates weaknesses such as • an important idea or ideas may be missing, unclear, or inaccurate; • there may be unclarity in how the lecture and the reading passage are related; and/or • grammatical mistakes or vague/incorrect uses of words may make the writing difficult to understand.
Writing based on Knowledge and Experience	Fair (2.5–3.5)	You expressed ideas with reasons, examples, and details, but your response indicated weaknesses such as • you may not provide enough specific support and development for your main points; • your ideas may be difficult to follow because of how you organize your essay or because of the language you use to connect your ideas; and/or • grammatical mistakes or vague/incorrect uses of words may make the writing difficult to understand.

THIS IS THE ONLY PERSONAL RECORD YOU WILL RECEIVE. PLEASE RETAIN FOR YOUR RECORDS.

This score report provides both section scores and a total score. An analysis of your strengths and weaknesses in English is included. The level pertaining to each skill should not be generalized beyond the performance on this test. Skill levels and their associated descriptions are not intended for use by colleges as part of their admission criteria and will not be shared unless you have granted permission.

Information About Scores: The following scaled scores are reported for TOEFL iBT. A total score is not reported when one or more sections have not been administered. These scores have the following ranges:

Sections	Scaled Scores
Reading	0 – 30
Listening	0 – 30
Speaking	0 – 30
Writing	0 – 30
Total Score	0 – 120

Institution Code Numbers: The code numbers on this score report are the ones you selected at the time you registered. If any of the numbers you indicated are not shown, they were incorrect and the TOEFL office was unable to send those score reports. To have official score reports sent, follow the directions on the attached Score Report Request Form.

DEPT.	WHERE THE REPORT WAS SENT
02	Admissions office of a graduate school of management (business)
03	Admissions office of a graduate school of law
01, 04-99	Admissions office for graduate study in a field other than management (business) or law according to the codes marked on your answer sheet
00	Admissions office for undergraduate study or an institution or agency that is not a college or university

Score Legends:

Reading Skills	
Level	Scaled Score Range
High	22 – 30
Intermediate	15 – 21
Low	0 – 14

Speaking Skills		
Level	Task Rating	Scaled Score Range
Good	3.5 – 4.0	26 – 30
Fair	2.5 – 3.0	18 – 25
Limited	1.5 – 2.0	10 – 17
Weak	0 – 1.0	0 – 9

Listening Skills	
Level	Scaled Score Range
High	22 – 30
Intermediate	14 – 21
Low	0 – 13

Writing Skills		
Level	Task Rating	Scaled Score Range
Good	4.0 – 5.0	24 – 30
Fair	2.5 – 3.5	17 – 23
Limited	1.0 – 2.0	1 – 16
Score of Zero	0	0

Further information about TOEFL iBT scoring is in the Learners and Test Takers section of the TOEFL Web site at **www.ets.org/toefl**.

Scoring Guides– Speaking

These are the Scoring Guides for the Speaking section. Go to the *Planner* website **www.ets.org/toefl/planner** for sample Speaking questions and responses. As you view and listen, refer to the Scoring Guides to better understand the score levels.

Scoring Guide for Independent Speaking

(Questions 1 & 2)

Score	General Description	Delivery	Language Use	Topic Development
4	The response fulfills the demands of the task, with at most minor lapses in completeness. It is highly intelligible and exhibits sustained, coherent discourse. A response at this level is characterized by all of the following:	Generally well-paced flow (fluid expression). Speech is clear. It may include minor lapses or minor difficulties with pronunciation or intonation patterns, which do not affect intelligibility.	The response demonstrates effective use of grammar and vocabulary. It exhibits a fairly high degree of automaticity with good control of basic and complex structures (as appropriate). Some minor (or systemic) errors are noticeable, but do not obscure meaning.	Response is sustained and sufficient to the task. It is generally well developed and coherent; relationships between ideas are clear (or clear progression of ideas).
3	The response addresses the task appropriately, but may fall short of being fully developed. It is generally intelligible and coherent, with some fluidity of expression, though it exhibits some noticeable lapses in the expression of ideas. A response at this level is characterized by at least two of the following:	Speech is generally clear, with some fluidity of expression, though minor difficulties with pronunciation, intonation, or pacing are noticeable and may require listener effort at times (though overall intelligibility is not significantly affected).	The response demonstrates fairly automatic and effective use of grammar and vocabulary and fairly coherent expression of relevant ideas. Response may exhibit some imprecise or inaccurate use of vocabulary or grammatical structures used. This may affect overall fluency, but it does not seriously interfere with the communication of the message.	Response is mostly coherent and sustained and conveys relevant ideas/information. Overall development is somewhat limited; usually lacks elaboration or specificity. Relationships between ideas may at times not be immediately clear.
2	The response addresses the task, but development of the topic is limited. It contains intelligible speech, although problems with delivery and/or overall coherence occur; meaning may be obscured in places. A response at this level is characterized by at least two of the following:	Speech is basically intelligible, though listener effort is needed because of unclear articulation, awkward intonation or choppy rhythm/pace; meaning may be obscured in places.	The response demonstrates limited range and control of grammar and vocabulary. These limitations often prevent full expression of ideas. For the most part, only basic sentence structures are used successfully and spoken with fluidity. Structures and vocabulary may express mainly simple (short) and/or general propositions, with simple or unclear connections made among them (serial listing, conjunction, juxtaposition).	The response is connected to the task, though the number of ideas presented or the development of ideas is limited. Mostly basic ideas are expressed with limited elaboration (details and support). At times, relevant substance may be vaguely expressed or repetitious. Connections of ideas may be unclear.

Score	General Description	Delivery	Language Use	Topic Development
1	The response is very limited in content and/or coherence or is only minimally connected to the task, or speech is largely unintelligible. A response at this level is characterized by at least two of the following:	Consistent pronunciation, stress and intonation difficulties cause considerable listener effort; delivery is choppy, fragmented or telegraphic; frequent pauses and hesitations.	Range and control of grammar and vocabulary severely limit (or prevent expression of) ideas and connections among ideas. Some low-level responses may rely heavily on practiced or formulaic expressions.	Limited relevant content expressed. The response generally lacks substance beyond expression of very basic ideas. Speaker may be unable to sustain speech to complete task and may rely heavily on repetition of the prompt.
0	Speaker makes no attempt to respond OR response is unrelated to the topic.			

Scoring Guide for Integrated Speaking

(Questions 3, 4, 5 and 6)

Score	General Description	Delivery	Language Use	Topic Development
4	The response fulfills the demands of the task, with at most minor lapses in completeness. It is highly intelligible and exhibits sustained, coherent discourse. A response at this level is characterized by all of the following:	Speech is generally clear, fluid and sustained. It may include minor lapses or minor difficulties with pronunciation or intonation. Pace may vary at times as speaker attempts to recall information. Overall intelligibility remains high.	The response demonstrates good control of basic and complex grammatical structures that allow for coherent, efficient (automatic) expression of relevant ideas. Contains generally effective word choice. Though some minor (or systematic) errors or imprecise use may be noticeable, they do not require listener effort (or obscure meaning).	The response presents a clear progression of ideas and conveys the relevant information required by the task. It includes appropriate detail, though it may have minor errors or minor omissions.
3	The response addresses the task appropriately, but may fall short of being fully developed. It is generally intelligible and coherent, with some fluidity of expression, though it exhibits some noticeable lapses in the expression of ideas. A response at this level is characterized by at least two of the following:	Speech is generally clear, with some fluidity of expression, but it exhibits minor difficulties with pronunciation, intonation or pacing, and may require some listener effort at times. Overall intelligibility remains good, however.	The response demonstrates fairly automatic and effective use of grammar and vocabulary, and fairly coherent expression of relevant ideas. Response may exhibit some imprecise or inaccurate use of vocabulary or grammatical structures or be somewhat limited in the range of structures used. Such limitations do not seriously interfere with the communication of the message.	The response is sustained and conveys relevant information required by the task. However, it exhibits some incompleteness, inaccuracy, lack of specificity with respect to content or choppiness in the progression of ideas.

Score	General Description	Delivery	Language Use	Topic Development
2	The response is connected to the task, though it may be missing some relevant information or contain inaccuracies. It contains some intelligible speech, but at times problems with intelligibility and/or overall coherence may obscure meaning. A response at this level is characterized by at least two of the following:	Speech is clear at times, though it exhibits problems with pronunciation, intonation or pacing, and so may require significant listener effort. Speech may not be sustained at a consistent level throughout. Problems with intelligibility may obscure meaning in places (but not throughout).	The response is limited in the range and control of vocabulary and grammar demonstrated (some complex structures may be used, but typically contain errors). This results in limited or inaccurate connections. Automaticity of expression may be evident only at the phrasal level.	The response conveys some relevant information but is clearly incomplete or inaccurate. It is incomplete if it omits key ideas, makes vague reference to key ideas, or demonstrates limited development of important information. An inaccurate response demonstrates misunderstanding of key ideas from the stimulus. Typically, ideas expressed may not be well connected or cohesive so that familiarity with the stimulus is necessary in order to follow what is being discussed.
1	The response is very limited in content or coherence or is only minimally connected to the task. Speech may be largely unintelligible. A response at this level is characterized by at least two of the following:	Consistent pronunciation and intonation problems cause considerable listener effort and frequently obscure meaning. Delivery is choppy, fragmented or telegraphic. Speech contains frequent pauses and hesitations.	Range and control of grammar and vocabulary severely limits (or prevents) expression of ideas and connections among ideas. Some very low-level responses may rely on isolated words or short utterances to communicate ideas.	The response fails to provide much relevant content. Ideas that are expressed are often inaccurate or limited to vague utterances or repetitions (including repetition of prompt).
0	Speaker makes no attempt to respond OR response is unrelated to the topic.			

APPENDIX 4 — Scoring Guides–Writing

These are the Scoring Guides for the Writing section. Go to the *Planner* website **www.ets.org/toefl/planner** for sample Writing questions and responses. As you view and listen, refer to the Scoring Guides to better understand the score levels.

Scoring Guide for Integrated Writing

Here is the official Scoring Guide used by raters when they read the Integrated Writing Task.

Score	Task Description
5	A response at this level successfully selects the important information from the lecture and coherently and accurately presents this information in relation to the relevant information presented in the reading. The response is well organized, and occasional language errors that are present do not result in inaccurate or imprecise presentation of content or connections.
4	A response at this level is generally good in selecting the important information from the lecture and in coherently and accurately presenting this information in relation to the relevant information in the reading, but it may have minor omission, inaccuracy, vagueness or imprecision of some content from the lecture or in connection to points made in the reading. A response is also scored at this level if it has more frequent or noticeable minor language errors, as long as such usage and grammatical structures do not result in anything more than an occasional lapse of clarity or in the connection of ideas.
3	A response at this level contains some important information from the lecture and conveys some relevant connection to the reading, but it is marked by one or more of the following: <ul><li>Although the overall response is definitely oriented to the task, it conveys only vague, global, unclear or somewhat imprecise connection of the points made in the lecture to points made in the reading.</li><li>The response may omit one major key point made in the lecture.</li><li>Some key points made in the lecture or the reading, or connections between the two, may be incomplete, inaccurate or imprecise.</li><li>Errors of usage and/or grammar may be more frequent or may result in noticeably vague expressions or obscured meanings in conveying ideas and connections.</li></ul>
2	A response at this level contains some relevant information from the lecture, but is marked by significant language difficulties or by significant omission or inaccuracy of important ideas from the lecture or in the connections between the lecture and the reading. A response at this level is marked by one or more of the following: <ul><li>The response significantly misrepresents or completely omits the overall connection between the lecture and the reading.</li><li>The response significantly omits or significantly misrepresents important points made in the lecture.</li><li>The response contains language errors or expressions that largely obscure connections or meaning at key junctures, or that would likely obscure understanding of key ideas for a reader not already familiar with the reading and the lecture.</li></ul>

Score	Task Description
1	A response at this level is marked by one or more of the following: • The response provides little or no meaningful or relevant coherent content from the lecture. • The language level of the response is so low that it is difficult to derive meaning.
0	A response at this level merely copies sentences from the reading, rejects the topic or is otherwise not connected to the topic, is written in a foreign language, consists of keystroke characters or is blank.

Scoring Guide for Independent Writing

Score	Task Description
5	An essay at this level largely accomplishes all of the following: • Effectively addresses the topic and task • Is well organized and well developed, using clearly appropriate explanations, exemplifications and/or details • Displays unity, progression and coherence • Displays consistent facility in the use of language, demonstrating syntactic variety, appropriate word choice and idiomaticity, though it may have minor lexical or grammatical errors
4	An essay at this level largely accomplishes all of the following: • Addresses the topic and task well, though some points may not be fully elaborated • Is generally well organized and well developed, using appropriate and sufficient explanations, exemplifications and/or details • Displays unity, progression and coherence, though it may contain occasional redundancy, digression or unclear connections • Displays facility in the use of language, demonstrating syntactic variety and range of vocabulary, though it will probably have occasional noticeable minor errors in structure, word form or use of idiomatic language that do not interfere with meaning
3	An essay at this level is marked by one or more of the following: • Addresses the topic and task using somewhat developed explanations, exemplifications and/or details • Displays unity, progression and coherence, though connection of ideas may be occasionally obscured • May demonstrate inconsistent facility in sentence formation and word choice that may result in lack of clarity and occasionally obscure meaning • May display accurate but limited range of syntactic structures and vocabulary
2	An essay at this level may reveal one or more of the following weaknesses: • Limited development in response to the topic and task • Inadequate organization or connection of ideas • Inappropriate or insufficient exemplifications, explanations or details to support or illustrate generalizations in response to the task • A noticeably inappropriate choice of words or word forms • An accumulation of errors in sentence structure and/or usage
1	An essay at this level is seriously flawed by one or more of the following weaknesses: • Serious disorganization or underdevelopment • Little or no detail, irrelevant specifics or questionable responsiveness to the task • Serious and frequent errors in sentence structure or usage
0	An essay at this level merely copies words from the topic, rejects the topic or is otherwise not connected to the topic, is written in a foreign language, consists of keystroke characters or is blank.

Sample Independent Writing Topics

The following is a list of some of the actual Independent Writing topics on former versions of the TOEFL® test. You'll see topics very similar to these on the test. None of the topics requires specialized knowledge. Most topics are general and are based on the common experience of people in general and students in particular. Whatever the topic, you'll be asked to give your opinion and to support your opinion with specific reasons and examples.

Sample Writing Topic List

- It has been said, "Not everything that is learned is contained in books." Compare and contrast knowledge gained from experience with knowledge gained from books. In your opinion, which source is more important? Why? Use specific reasons and examples to support your answer.

- Choose **one** of the following transportation vehicles and explain why you think it has changed people's lives:

  - automobile

  - bicycle

  - airplane

  Use specific reasons and examples to support your answer.

- Some people prefer to work for a large company. Others prefer to work for a small company. Which would you prefer? Use specific reasons and details to support your choice.

- Should a city try to preserve its old, historic buildings or destroy them and replace them with modern buildings? Use specific reasons and examples to support your opinion.

- If you were an employer, which kind of worker would you prefer to hire: an inexperienced worker at a lower salary or an experienced worker at a higher salary? Use specific reasons and details to support your answer.

- Do you agree or disagree with the following statement? Technology has made the world a better place to live. Use specific reasons and examples to support your opinion.

- If you could go back to some time and place in the past, when and where would you go? Why? Use specific reasons and details to support your choice.

- In your opinion, what is the most important characteristic (for example, honesty, intelligence, a sense of humor) that a person can have to be successful in life? Use specific reasons and examples from your experience to explain your answer.

- The government has announced that it plans to build a new university. Some people think that your community would be a good place to locate the university. Compare the advantages and disadvantages of establishing a new university in your community. Use specific details in your discussion.

- Imagine that you have received some land to use as you wish. How would you use this land? Use specific details to explain your answer.

APPENDIX 6

Speaking and Writing Score Conversion Charts

The responses on both the Speaking and Writing sections are sent to the ETS Online Scoring Network.

Speaking

Responses for each of the six tasks in Speaking are rated by three to six raters on a scale from 0 to 4 according to the Scoring Guides on pages 79–81. The mean (average) of all six tasks is then converted to a scaled score of 0 to 30.

Writing

Responses for the two tasks in Writing are rated on a scale from 0 to 5 according to the Scoring Guides on pages 82–83. The mean (average) of the scores on the two tasks is then converted to a scaled score of 0 to 30.

Following are the conversion charts for Speaking and Writing. When you have a teacher or tutor, evaluate your responses to questions from *The Official Guide*. You can use these charts to convert your average scores on all the tasks to a scaled score.

Converting Rating Averages to Scaled Scores for the Writing and Speaking Sections of the TOEFL iBT® Test

WRITING RATING AVERAGE	SCALED SCORE
5.00	30
4.75	29
4.50	28
4.25	27
4.00	25
3.75	24
3.50	22
3.25	21
3.00	20
2.75	18
2.50	17
2.25	15
2.00	14
1.75	12
1.50	11
1.25	10
1.00	8
	7
	5
	4
	0

SPEAKING RATING AVERAGE	SCALED SCORE
4.00	30
3.83	29
3.66	28
3.50	27
3.33	26
3.16	24
3.00	23
2.83	22
2.66	20
2.50	19
2.33	18
2.16	17
2.00	15
1.83	14
1.66	13
1.50	11
1.33	10
1.16	9
1.00	8
	6
	5
	4
	3
	2
	1
	0

Note: Performance on the Speaking and Writing sections of the TOEFL iBT® test is evaluated based on ratings of 0 to 5 for each of the two Writing tasks and 0 to 4 for each of the six Speaking tasks. The tables above show how the mean scores of the two Writing tasks and the average ratings of six Speaking tasks are converted to a scaled score of 0 to 30.

 Notes

Notes

Notes

Notes